HANDBOOKS

ARIZONA

TIM HULL

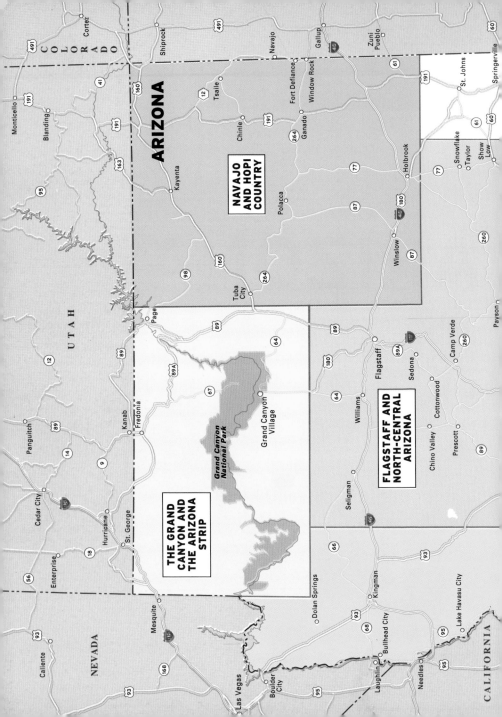

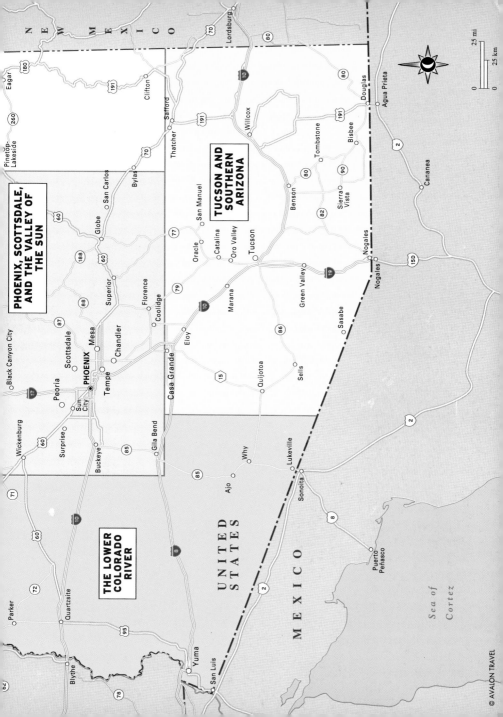

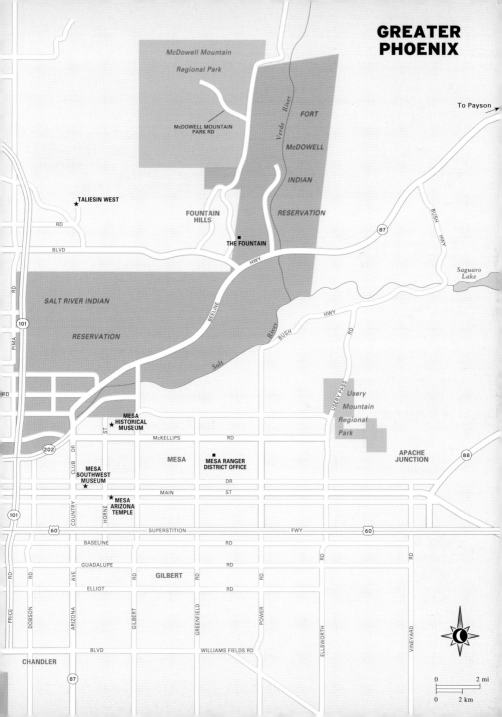

Contents

▶ **Discover Arizona** **8**
Planning Your Trip 10
Explore Arizona 14
 • A Grand Road Trip 14
 • Feel the Heat:
   A Hot Summer Weekend 17
 • Sky Island Hopping 18
 • The Ruins of Lost Cultures 20
 • A Grand Canyon
   Family Adventure 21
 • Back to the Old West 24

▶ **Phoenix, Scottsdale, and
the Valley of the Sun** **25**
Sights 31
Sports and Recreation 41
Entertainment and Events 46
Shopping 49
Accommodations 50
Food 52
Scottsdale and the North Valley . . 57
Around the Valley of the Sun 64

Information and Services 73
Getting There and Around 73

▶ **Tucson and
Southern Arizona** **75**
Tucson and Vicinity 78
The Santa Cruz Valley 107
The Cochise Trail 119

▶ **Flagstaff and
North-Central Arizona** **131**
Flagstaff and Vicinity 135
Prescott and the Verde Valley . . . 149
Sedona and Red Rock Country . . . 167
Rim Country and the
   White Mountains 175

▶ **Navajo and Hopi Country** . . . **182**
The Navajo Nation 186
Hopiland 197
The High Desert 200

▶ **The Grand Canyon and the Arizona Strip** **205**
Gateways to the Canyon 209
The Grand Canyon 212
The Arizona Strip 241

▶ **The Lower Colorado River** .. **254**
Lake Mead
  National Recreation Area 258
Kingman and Vicinity 262
Lake Havasu City and Vicinity ... 269
Yuma and Vicinity 277

▶ **Background** **284**
The Land 284
Flora and Fauna 291
History 295
Economy and Government 299
People 301

▶ **Essentials** **305**
Getting There and Around 305
Accommodations 307
Food 308
Tips for Travelers 309
Health and Safety 310
Information and Services 312

▶ **Resources** **314**
Suggested Reading 314
Internet Resources 318

▶ **Index** **319**

▶ **Map Index** **337**

Discover Arizona

Arizona is authentic. It's too hot to fake it, too rugged to tell tall tales, too beautiful to commit to the hard sell. All of its institutions, its attractions, and even its mythologies were forged through hard experience, trial, and error.

This is even true of the land, built by the movement and explosion of the earth – canyons ripped open and mountains kicked up over millennia of shaking and oozing. This roiling has provided a wonderland of diversity, building – all at once – hot and verdant desert scrublands, cool evergreen mountain forests, dry sweeping grasslands, and red-rock, river-carved, fairy-tale canyons, all of which merge with a horizon lit most evenings with postcard-ready sunsets. It remains one of the most exotic destinations in North America, with endless variety, iconic scenery, and a dark history of which the world has never tired.

You will be surprised and changed by Arizona. Here you can easily happen upon an old pioneer graveyard, forgotten and ignored, on a strip of undeveloped desert right next to a gathering of just-built dream homes. This may be the perfect image for the dichotomies of this landscape. Everything here is either ancient or five minutes old.

There's a reason all those road movies feature scenes in the Grand Canyon State. There's no better way to see all the state has to offer than to

pile in a car and hit the open road. Less than a day's drive from anywhere, you can discover something unexpected, whether it be the calm and sunny ease of life along the lower Colorado River, where houseboats and water-skiers pass by great monuments to engineering, or a chance meeting with a rare tropical bird hiding out in the riparian mist of a sky island.

In many a traveler's imagination, this place is the home to rattle-snakes, tumbleweeds, and vast tracts of arid wilderness. Luckily, Arizona still has all of these; there are still trackless spaces to explore. But the face Arizona shows to most of the world belies the leaps this once isolated territory has made. The youngest state in the lower 48 is one of the fastest-growing regions in the nation, and while near constant growth makes for sometimes rancorous debates about land use and natural resources, it serves to create in Arizona a dynamism – a flux that perpetuates itself. It is never boring here, and it is always beautiful and unknowable. There is always something, or someone, being created anew . . . changing . . . blooming.

Planning Your Trip

▶ WHERE TO GO

Phoenix, Scottsdale, and the Valley of the Sun

Arizona's largest metro area holds 10 cities linked together to create a sprawling megalopolis of glass high-rises and labyrinthine, stacked freeways spreading out over a hot Sonoran Desert valley. Visitors and residents alike tend to refer to the whole area as the Valley of the Sun, or simply Phoenix, after the valley's largest city. There are pockets of urbanity out in the sprawl, like Scottsdale with its art galleries, high-style eateries and resorts and golf courses, and Tempe with its college-town nightlife, shopping and museums. This area has the state's best resorts and restaurants, nightlife, museums, and Arizona's largest airport. The city's rural desert rings are home to old mining towns, river canyons, and saguaro forests.

Tucson and Southern Arizona

Tucson, the state's second-largest city and the one with the most character and history, anchors this region of saguaro forests, sweeping grasslands, and quirky desert outposts. Towering Sky Island mountain ranges shoot up from the long desert seas, and the nearby Mexican border looms equally large in this region's culture and history. Even better, they say a few of those myths and legends of the Old West actually happened here.

Flagstaff and North-Central Arizona

Arizona's sap-scented high country begins around mile-high Prescott and rises to a great ponderosa pine forest stretching east and north. Even higher is snowy Flagstaff and the bald-rock tip of the San Francisco Peaks, their slopes variegated by white-and-yellow aspens among the evergreens. The pinelands continue across the Mogollon Rim, and on to the conifer-ringed meadows and the clear

Phoenix seen through the feature known as Hole-in-the-Rock at Papago Park.

horses at Pipe Springs National Monument

barren red cliffs, sagebrush plains, and the water-and-red-rock mazes of Lake Powell.

The Lower Colorado River

The Lower Colorado River flows the length of far western Arizona to Mexico, creating a river-border through this barren hot zone of jagged rock mountains populated by big-horn sheep. The views are long and empty save for the toughest cactus, scrub, and wildflower. The river is a blue-and-green band of rustling, splashing life, and all living things here are drawn to it, whether they be rare birds or water-skiers.

streams of the White Mountains. Along the way, Sedona offers fine dining, self-healing, red-rock buttes and shady streambeds.

Navajo and Hopi Country

The high desert grasslands in Arizona's northeastern plateau country are dotted with a few old cattle and railroad towns, trading posts, and an empty, pastel-painted desert strewn with broken swirling-stone trees. The Vast Navajo Nation is cut deep with red-sandstone canyons in which abandoned cliff-face cities and the tracks of dinosaurs create a timeless atmosphere that can be entrancing. On the edge of Black Mesa, the Hopi live atop high cold cliffs occupied for more than a thousand years.

The Grand Canyon and the Arizona Strip

The Kaibab Plateau rises in the Four Corners tablelands in northwestern Arizona; river-cut more than a mile deep into the plateau is Arizona's signature attraction and one of the world's most sought-after landscapes—the only canyon on earth deserving of the grand title. Between the canyon's forested rims is the lonely Arizona Strip, empty save for high

IF YOU HAVE...

- **ONE WEEK:** Visit Tucson and Southern Arizona and Grand Canyon.

- **TWO WEEKS:** Add North-Central Arizona, Rim Country and the White Mountains, and Phoenix, Scottsdale, and the Valley of the Sun.

- **THREE WEEKS:** Add the Navajo Nation, Hopiland, and the High Desert.

- **FOUR WEEKS:** Add the Lower Colorado and Arizona's West Coast.

Mules still do much of the heavy lifting in and out of the Grand Canyon.

▶ WHEN TO GO

Spring is the best time to be on Arizona's lowland deserts. From late February through until May, the weather is gorgeous on the deserts, often in the high 70s and 80s from the Lower Colorado River region across the desert belt to the New Mexico border. Spring is also bloom-time on the desert, when all the dormant wildflowers come to life, and all the spiny cacti burst with vivid color. If you visit the lowlands during this time of year you are likely to come away with a vastly altered opinion of aridity. The desert-country tourist season is at its high point during these months, so make reservations in advance.

In summer, head for the high country. It is warm, tending often toward hot during the day, and cool, clear, and star-filled at night. In late summer the rains come, late-afternoon downpours that clean the air and get the creeks rising. Summer is the busy tourist season in this region, as it is at Grand Canyon and in Indian Country. You are bound to encounter crowds at most of the major attractions, and you'll need to make reservations.

the Mogollon Rim in North-Central Arizona

▶ BEFORE YOU GO

A trip to Arizona requires a certain amount of advance planning, especially if you're going to be hiking the Grand Canyon, riding the Colorado's rapids, or renting a houseboat. A permit to spend even one night inside the canyon requires a reservation at least six months in advance, more if you want to stay in the gorge's only lodge, Phantom Ranch. If you're hoping to float down the Colorado, start planning at least a year in advance. Bring your passport or birth certificate along if you're planning to cross the U.S.-Mexico border.

You need to be prepared for a lot of car time. The towns, sights, and attractions are scattered throughout the state, and most of them are far from the two main urban centers of Phoenix and Tucson. You must have a car and you can't really avoid spending a good deal of time in it.

What to Take

Your Arizona-bound knapsack should include a few essential items no matter what the season. These include, first and foremost, a good pair of hiking or walking shoes. Don't get a big, bulky, arctic-expedition pair, but day-hikers or at least a pair of tough running shoes or trainers are a necessity. At nearly every National Park or National Monument that you'll visit, there's some kind of short hike you have to take in order to *really* appreciate what you're seeing. A water bottle is always nice to have around, and you'll probably want to include a small pack for carrying snacks and water on day hikes or sightseeing excursions. Sunscreen is a necessity in any season; if you're not in a hot harsh-sun desert you're in mountain country where the sun shines hard and dangerous. A hat is a must, and one with a brim wide enough to cast a shadow on your neck is recommended. Think about bringing along a pair of binoculars; they are always handy when spotting bighorn sheep, petroglyphs, and rare birds.

Even if you're going to be in the desert in the summer, bring along a light jacket. In some of the outer regions away from the city the air cools a bit, and if you rise in elevation, which is easy to do, the nights will be much cooler. In the high country, layers will serve you best. It is often warm in the day and cold at night, even in summer.

As for style, think casual and utilitarian—everybody else does. If you're going to be staying or dining at any of the top resorts, a few fancy outfits might be in order. Otherwise, jeans and T-shirts, shorts and tank tops, flip-flops, rock sandals, and general outdoor style are the norm.

along the road leading to Lee's Ferry on the Colorado River

forgotten political mural in Oatman

Explore Arizona

► A GRAND ROAD TRIP

The best way to see Arizona is from behind the wheel of your own car. A road-trip through the heart of the American Southwest provides a unique opportunity to see this exotic region from the ground up.

Day 1

Arrive at Sky Harbor Airport in Phoenix, head to a hotel in downtown Phoenix, Scottsdale, or Tempe. Introduce yourself to the desert by taking a scenic drive out to Cave Creek and Carefree. Have dinner at El Encanto in Cave Creek.

Day 2

Get an early start and spend the morning touring Taliesin West, the Heard Museum, or the Phoenix Art Museum. Leave the city via I-17 north to Prescott. Stop for a late lunch and a slice of pie midway at the Rock Springs Café. Spend the night at one of downtown Prescott's historic hotels or bed-and-breakfasts. Have dinner at The Palace and hit up a few Whiskey Row watering holes.

Day 3

Get up early and eat breakfast at the Dinner Bell. Walk around downtown Prescott and tour the museums, shops, and galleries. Be sure to visit the Sharlot Hall Museum. Head north on scenic Highway 89A to Jerome. Stay at the Jerome Grand Hotel and have dinner at Asylum.

Day 4

Have breakfast at the Mile High Grill and take a walk around Jerome. Head down 89A to Sedona. Check into your hotel, and then head out to explore the red rocks, galleries, and shops of Sedona. Eat dinner at Oaxaca in uptown.

Cacti's spines discourage hurtful munching.

Chapel of the Holy Cross in Sedona

Petrified Forest

Canyon de Chelly

Day 5

Spend the day shopping, hiking, sightseeing, and exploring Sedona and the Verde Valley. Check out Montezuma's Castle, hike into red-rock country, or take a jeep tour through the redlands.

Day 6

Eat breakfast at the Coffee Pot in Sedona, then head north on Highway 89A through Oak Creek Canyon. Stop for a hike or to splash around in the water at Slide Rock State Park. Continue north to Flagstaff and check into one of the historic hotels downtown. Stroll and shop downtown, then have dinner and beers at Beaver Street Brewery.

Day 7

Wake up and head out to visit the Museum of Northern Arizona in Flagstaff, then go north and east for a tour of Wupatki, Sunset Crater, and Walnut Canyon. In the late afternoon, drive east to Winslow and check into La Posada. Have dinner in the Turquoise Room. Order a box lunch from the restaurant for the next day.

Day 8

Spend the morning touring the Painted Desert and the Petrified Forest near Holbrook. Then take I-40 to Highway 191

north to Chinle on the Navajo Reservation. Stay at the Thunderbird Lodge near Canyon de Chelly or at one of the chains in Chinle.

Day 9

Spend the morning hiking into Canyon de Chelly to the White House Ruins and driving the scenic rim roads, or hire a Navajo guide and go deeper into the canyon. After

statue at La Posada Hotel

Grand Canyon's South Rim

lunch head north on Highway 191, west on Highway 160, then north on Highway 163 to Kayenta and Monument Valley. Get a hotel room in Kayenta and then drive through Monument Valley late in the afternoon and watch the sun set.

Day 10

Eat breakfast in Kayenta and then head west on Highway 160 past Tuba City to Cameron. Take Highway 64 west to Grand Canyon National Park and make your way to the east entrance. Check out the Desert View sights, then drive on into Grand Canyon Village and have dinner at El Tovar. Spend the night at El Tovar or The Bright Angel Lodge. Get up early and hike down one of the South Rim trails for as far as you feel like going. If you're not a hiker, take a mule ride to the river and back. Spend the remainder

of the day looking around the rim and staring into the gorge.

Day 11

This day will be spent mostly in the car driving from the high country down to Tucson and Southern Arizona. Leave the Grand Canyon early through the south entrance and take I-40 east to I-17 south. In Phoenix, follow the signs to I-10 south to Tucson. You'll probably arrive in the late afternoon. Check into the Hotel Congress, the Arizona Inn, or one of the area's bed-and-breakfasts, and then head to Mi Nidito for a Mexican-food dinner.

Day 12

Get up early and spend the morning walking around Saguaro National Park (west) and visiting the nearby Arizona-Sonora

FEEL THE HEAT: A HOT SUMMER WEEKEND

When the mercury rises above 100°F in the Sonoran Desert (usually around late May), the resorts in Phoenix and Scottsdale lower their prices to levels most of us can actually afford. Not only does this offer a chance to have a romantic getaway on a budget, it gives the neophyte an opportunity to experience the heat of the desert in all its glory.

You haven't truly experienced the Arizona desert until you've "felt the heat," and a romantic weekend at one of the valley's resorts offers a comfortable way of doing so. Example: The historic, Frank Lloyd Wright-inspired **Arizona Biltmore Resort and Spa,** still the state's most romantic and stylish resort, offers inclusive "romance" packages with spa treatments, chocolate-covered strawberries, a gourmet dinner and more, which are discounted by about $300 per night late May-mid-September. Individually, the same room that goes for $685 in April costs about $189 in July.

Other sumptuous resorts that lower their prices or offer affordable getaway packages in the summer include the magnificent **Boulders Resort** in Scottsdale, with summer prices starting at $129 per night, and the **Fairmont Scottsdale Princess Resort,** with rooms starting at $179 per night. In March, when the weather in the Valley is usually perfect, similar accommodations will cost you at least $600 per night.

When you're not lolling poolside in a shady cabana or getting a pedicure, consider spending part of one day touring the (air-conditioned) **Phoenix Art Museum** or the **Heard Museum,** or even **Taliesin West** – though this option won't be as comfortable as the others. Since you're saving all that money at the resort, summer is a perfect time to do some shopping at one of the high-end (and climate controlled) shopping centers in Scottsdale and Phoenix, like **Scottsdale Fashion Square** and **Biltmore Fashion Park.** The golf prices go down considerably during the summer as well, and you might just be able to survive a round or two if you start early in the morning. But you won't want to spend too much time out on the course. First of all, it's dangerous – literally. Plus, this is a couple's getaway, and there's no place cooler (or hotter for that matter) than your affordable room at one of the world's top resorts.

Wright's winter quarters in Scottsdale, Taliesin West

Desert Museum. Have lunch at the museum's café and then drive south on I-19 to see San Xavier del Bac. After visiting the church, keep heading south to Tubac and Tumacacori. Stroll through the shops and galleries at Tubac or check out the Mission Tumacacori. Have dinner at Wisdom's in Tumacacori or continue south on I-19 and walk across the U.S.-Mexico border at Nogales and eat at one of the restaurants in the tourist district. Drive back to your hotel in Tucson and relax.

Day 13

This day is a kind of Southern Arizona grab-bag. Drive through the San Pedro Valley or the Mountain Empire. Do some wine-tasting in Elgin, shop in Bisbee, or drive the dirt roads into the Huachuca Mountains and up to the Coronado National Memorial. Visit Chiricahua National Monument, Cochise Stronghold, Patagonia, Madera Canyon, Kartchner Caverns, or Tombstone. A full, busy day will allow you to make, say, three or four major stops, depending on your personal interests and the amount of time you spend at any one place. You'll likely arrive back at your hotel in Tucson late.

Day 14

Wake up early and take a stroll through one of Tucson's downtown neighborhoods or 4th Avenue and the University District. On your way north on I-10 to the airport in Phoenix, stop off at Picacho Peak State Park for a last hike, or detour to Casa Grande National Monument for a last look at native Arizona.

► SKY ISLAND HOPPING

There are few places in the world quite like Southern Arizona's Sky Island region, where high, forested mountains rise above the hot rustling desert. Hikers, bird-watchers, and nature-lovers will enjoy spending a busy week in this rare basin-and-range landscape, and in the middle of it all is Tucson, the state's second largest city and a metropolis with plenty of unique dining, entertainment, and culture. The best time to go is in the spring when the sun is not yet angry and beating incessantly on the land. Temperatures will be in the 70s and 80s, and there might even be a slight cool breeze most days. The wild flowers will be in bloom and the whole desert will be alive with new life.

Day 1

Fly into Tucson International Airport and drive south on I-19 for about half an hour to Madera Canyon in the Santa Rita Mountains. Stay at one of the three lodges in the canyon. Spend the afternoon bird-watching and hiking.

Madera Canyon

The closest you are likely to get to an elusive mountain lion is at the Arizona-Sonora Desert Museum.

Day 2

Hike to the top of Mount Wrightson early in the morning or hire a birding guide for a dawn expedition. Transfer to the Hotel Congress, The Arizona Inn, or the Lodge on the Desert in Tucson. After lunch, head west and tour the Arizona-Sonora Desert Museum and Saguaro National Park (west). Eat dinner at Mi Nidito or El Charro.

Day 3

Get an early start and drive the Sky Island Scenic Highway into the Santa Catalina Mountains. Check out Winterhaven and maybe ride the ski lift to the top of the peak. Go for a hike or have a picnic in the mountains. Head back to Tucson in the afternoon and head to the Fourth Avenue District to shop and have dinner and a few drinks.

Day 4

Get up early and head east to visit Kartchner Caverns. Then, head into the Huachuca Mountains near Sierra Vista. Drive up to the Ramsey Canyon Preserve and to the Coronado National Memorial and hike around, look for birds, or just take in the sweeping views. Drive to Bisbee and spend the night in one of the old mining town's historic hotels.

Day 5

Spend the morning looking around Bisbee and shopping, then take Highway 191 north to the Cochise Stronghold. Spend some time looking around the Dragoon Mountains and reading the displays about the Apache Indians. Find a hotel room in Wilcox and check out the old buildings and museums on historic Railway Avenue.

THE RUINS OF LOST CULTURES

Arizona and the Southwest are home to many native cultures that are no longer around to tell their stories, legends, and mythologies. Luckily, the ruins of the Hohokam, the Anasazi, the Salado, the Sinagua and others are protected throughout the state by federal law. You could make a whole trip out of visiting these mysterious structures, discovering the lost cultures that once scraped much more than subsistence out of the uncaring land.

HOHOKAM AND SALADO TRIBES

Use Phoenix and the Valley of the Sun as your base as you discover ruins left behind by the Hohokam and Salado tribes.

- **Pueblo Grande Museum and Archeological Park:** Discover how the Hohokam coaxed an empire out of the delicately balanced Salt River Valley here at the ruin and museum in the middle of the bustling metropolis, near the ruins of the canals the Hohokam built to irrigate the desert.

- **Tonto National Monument:** Take the back-country route called the **Apache Trail** past Roosevelt Dam, east of the city, and witness a well-preserved cliff dwelling once inhabited by the Salado tribe that rises above slopes crowded with Saguaros.

- **Casa Grande Ruins National Monument:** Located between Phoenix and Tucson, this monument is the largest example of Hohokam architecture left, the huge molded-dirt apartment building called Casa Grande.

SINAGUA TRIBE

Use Sedona or Flagstaff as your base for visiting the awesome ruins of North-Central Arizona's vanished Sinagua tribe.

- **Montezuma's Castle National Monument:** Located in the Verde Valley, this is one of the best-preserved cliff-dwellings in the southwest.

- **Walnut Canyon National Monument:** East of Flagstaff, it seems like a lost world where a long-gone culture once built a busy village on the rim and along the walls of a hidden canyon.

- **Wupatki National Monument:** Just north of Flagstaff, this monument preserves the ruins of several awesome red-sandstone great houses.

ANASAZI TRIBE

- **Navajo Nation:** The abandoned cliff-cities of the Anasazi are on display here in northeastern Arizona.

- **Navajo National Monument:** While visiting the monument at Tsegi Canyon, you can spot the ruin called **Betatakin** from the rim, nestled in a natural rock alcove above a bottomland forest.

- **Keet Seel:** Sign up for a 16-mile round-trip hike below the rim to spend the night near the spectacularly preserved ruin hidden deep in the canyon.

- **Canyon de Chelly National Monument:** Also on Navajoland, don't miss this area where you can hike down a slick-rock trail and stand in awe before the **White House Ruin.**

Montezuma's Castle National Monument

Day 6

Get an early start and head to Chiricahua National Monument. Spend the day exploring the Chiricahuas. Late in the afternoon, drive south on Highway 181 to Highway 191, then on to Douglas to spend the night at the historic Gadsden Hotel.

Day 7

Leave Douglas early and take Highway 90 and Highway 82 through the Mountain Empire to the Santa Cruz Valley. Stop for a stroll though the lush Patagonia-Sonoita Creek Preserve. Go through Nogales, then head north on I-19 toward Tucson, stopping to check out Tubac, Tumacacori and San Xavier del Bac. Catch a late flight home out of Tucson.

lichen-covered hoodoos at Chiricahua National Monument

▶ A GRAND CANYON FAMILY ADVENTURE

The Grand Canyon, while a backcountry-lover's paradise, is also a fun place for families—just ask TV's Brady Bunch. This itinerary does include one night below the rim and so requires you to secure reservations and permits far in advance. The best time to go is spring or October.

Day 1

Take an early morning flight into Phoenix's Sky Harbor Airport, rent a car, and drive north to Williams (170 miles). Park your car and catch the Grand Canyon Railway to Grand Canyon National Park's South Rim. Check into your family-sized cabin at Bright Angel Lodge and then explore and go sightseeing around Grand Canyon Village, getting acclimated to the huge gorge in front of you. Eat dinner at El Tovar.

Grand Canyon's Hopi House, by architect Mary Colter

Day 2

Tour the South Rim, visiting all the historic buildings and the lookouts. If your kids are around the ages of 4–12, before you start your sightseeing, take them to the Visitor Center at Canyon View Information Plaza and get them in the Junior Rangers program. The ranger will give them age-appropriate booklets and throughout the day they'll earn a Junior Ranger badge and patch by fulfilling the fun and educational requirements, which include attending one of the ranger-led programs offered throughout the day. Have dinner at one of the casual eateries on the South Rim and get a good night's sleep—you'll need it.

Day 3

If you are hiking, get a very early start down either the Bright Angel Trail or the South Kaibab Trail. Don't carry your own bags. Spend a few extra bills to have the mules do it, so you and the family can enjoy the hike and really see the scenery. If you're riding with a mule-train to the bottom, show up at the appointed time and place and saddle up. You'll arrive at Phantom Ranch near the Colorado River late in the day. (You have to reserve a cabin and meals at the cantina up to a year beforehand. A mule trip will be all-inclusive, but if you're hiking you'll need to make separate reservations.) Take a shower, explore Phantom Ranch, dip your feet in Bright Angel Creek, walk to the river, and relax in the inner gorge. Eat a hearty meal at the cantina and attend a ranger-led program before collapsing into bed.

Day 4

Get up early, eat breakfast at the cantina, and spend the day exploring the inner gorge, the river, and Phantom Ranch. The rangers can tell you the best day hikes and sights in the inner canyon and suggest all kinds of fun activities for the kids.

The remote Kaibab Plateau on the Grand Canyon's North Rim is often cloaked in winter snow.

An early-morning mule train crosses a bridge over the Colorado River in Grand Canyon's inner gorge.

Day 5

Wake up early, eat breakfast, and head out, either on a mule or on foot. It'll take you most of the day to get out of the canyon. If you're hiking and you came down the Bright Angel Trail, head up the South Kaibab for a different view. If you came down the South Kaibab, hike out using the Bright Angel so you can see lush Indian Gardens. When and if you make it out of the canyon, treat yourselves to a nice dinner and relax and recover for the rest of the day.

Day 6

Spend the morning seeing the canyon for the last time and shopping for souvenirs. Catch the train back to Williams and check into the Grand Canyon Railway Hotel. Have dinner at Rod's Steakhouse in Williams, then head back to the hotel to swim or soak in the hot tub.

Day 7

Head south to Phoenix after breakfast at the Pine Country Restaurant in Williams. Make the long drive south to Phoenix, stopping for a late lunch just outside of the city at Rock Springs Café. Catch your flight at Sky Harbor, and head home.

Rod's Steakhouse in Williams

BACK TO THE OLD WEST

The conquistadores, miners, cowboys, outlaws, and myth-makers of the Old West all left an imprint on Arizona, and their descendants do what they can to keep those imprints from fading back into the deserts and the canyons. Listed below are some of the fascinating historical sights you can visit in Arizona.

SOUTHERN ARIZONA

Southern Arizona represents the northern extreme of the Spanish crown's great New World empire, while southwestern Arizona is full of the legends and kitsch of the Old West. Here you will find the following:

- **Tubac State Historic Park:** Visit this historic park which preserves the memories and artifacts of the Spanish's New World empire.

- **Coronado National Monument:** Tour the remote monument in the Huachuca Mountains which marks the trail used by Coronado as he trudged north toward the Seven Cities of Cibola.

- **Bisbee:** Visit an example of an old west mining town rich with antique stores and artisan boutiques.

- **Tombstone:** Examine several forensic exhibits on that world-famous seconds-long gunfight that took place in the town's still-dusty streets.

- **Yuma Prison State Historic Park:** See what awaited those outlaws and bandits who ran afoul of territorial law.

NORTH-CENTRAL ARIZONA

- **Zane Grey Cabin:** Pay your respects to one of the Old West's greatest myth-makers. Here you can see an exact replica of Grey's hunting cabin (the real one burned down in 1990), complete with period decorations and furniture, and learn all about the prolific author's passion for Arizona's Mogollon Rim region.

- **Jerome:** See the history of hard-rock mining in this preserved mountainside town.

- **Riordan Ranch State Park:** Peek into the private lives of two 19th century Flagstaff lumber barons featured at this state park.

- **Pipe Spring National Monument:** Discover what it was like to live on a lonely fortified ranch in the late 1800s at this Arizona's Strip sight.

a cowboy carving in Williams

PHOENIX, SCOTTSDALE, AND THE VALLEY OF THE SUN

If you spend enough time in the desert basin known locally, and somewhat obviously, as the Valley of the Sun (often just "the Valley"), there will undoubtedly come a time when you will ask yourself, "Why would they build a megalopolis *here?*"

This question will likely come up during the month of July or thereabout, when it's 110°F in the shade and you're slogging to your car through a heat-storing parking lot somewhere. Don't lose heart, though. There is much in this mostly urbanized valley to do and see, eat and watch, find and buy.

A loose affiliation of cities and suburbs anchored by Phoenix, and spreading to the wild northern Sonoran Desert that waits along its edges, the Valley of the Sun is one of the largest metro areas in the nation and as such can boast world-class hotels, restaurants, museums, theaters, sports, and shopping.

It's the logical place to begin an Arizona adventure; it's the transportation, government, and cultural hub of the state. Here you will see the hubris and shortsightedness that oftentimes have typified the settling of the urban West. But here also you will see novel attempts to live with the desert and its strange beauty, like Frank Lloyd Wright's Taliesin West and the ruins of the ancient canal-building Hohokam.

And if you're here during one of the two or three "springs" that soothe the long summer's violent tendencies, and you're playing golf in December, or hiking around the rugged Superstition Mountains in January in shorts, you might end up forgetting that you ever questioned

© TIM HULL

HIGHLIGHTS

(**Heard Museum:** Discover the histories and ways of life of Arizona's many Native American communities at this renowned institution, filled with artistic, ceremonial, and daily-life artifacts from both ancient history and more modern times (page 34).

(**Phoenix Art Museum:** Spend hours browsing through one of the Southwest's top cultural depositories, where you'll see a spectacular array of the art of the American West and of the Western world (page 35).

(**Taliesin West:** Tour architect Frank Lloyd Wright's desert masterpiece, a rare ex-

ample of how humans can settle on the wild desert without marring or destroying it in the process (page 57).

(**The Apache Trail:** Take a daylong back-road adventure on the city's rugged desert edges, passing by three glassy blue lakes ringed by sagauro, and through a few sleepy and forgotten mining towns (page 66).

(**Casa Grande Ruins National Monument:** Explore the mysterious remains of a crumbling Hohokam great house (page 70).

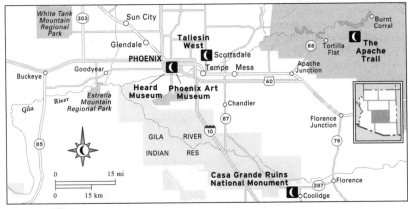

LOOK FOR (TO FIND RECOMMENDED SIGHTS, ACTIVITIES, DINING, AND LODGING.

the wisdom of the Valley's founders and instead ask yourself, "Why don't I live here?"

HISTORY

Phoenix wasn't really discovered so much as it was rediscovered, as its name suggests. The Salt River Valley, once home to prehistoric canal-crossed, mud-mound cities and thousands of Hohokam, was largely depopulated and ignored from about 1500 until the 1860s, when a few farmers moved in to supply hay and sundries to the troops at Fort McDowell, a nearby

outpost in the Indian Wars. Soon a group of moneymen from Wickenburg, a mining community just to the northwest, looked out over the arid valley, still crisscrossed by the husks of the well-built ancient canals, and envisioned an agricultural empire. An educated British speculator among them got drunk and proclaimed the valley would henceforth be called Phoenix, as it would rise, like the mythical bird, from the Hohokam ashes to become a great American city. Or so the story goes.

The first lots went on sale in 1870, and

THE HOHOKAM

The Sonoran Desert is not a wasteland of shifting dunes, nor a place to make it through at all costs but never to stop and settle. While such may be the popular conception of a desert, first-time visitors to central and southern Arizona are often surprised to see so much vegetation, so much diversity, and so much evidence of eons of human habitation.

That's not to say it has always been easy to live here; prior to the damming of the Southwest's rivers, a drought or a flood could wipe out a lifetime's worth of progress, and you never really knew with any confidence if the annual rains would come too heavy or too light or not at all. There are usually two rainy seasons in the Sonoran Desert: In mid-summer the Mexican Monsoon sends moisture north every late afternoon, and in winter the rains come again, hopefully. The twice-a-year rains, though scant compared to nearly every other place (the whole 100,000-square-mile desert gets less than 15 inches per year), allow for myriad dry-land-adapted plants and animals to thrive here.

People too have thrived here for thousands of years, taking advantage of the once-perennial desert rivers like the Gila, the Salt, the Santa Cruz, and the San Pedro. Because of damming, overuse, and other factors, none of these rivers is much of a river anymore, but each of them long ago provided a healthy, if unpredictable, lifeline for the complex culture of the Hohokam, desert farmers who lived in the Sonoran river valleys from the beginning of the common era (A.D. 1) to about 1450. They disappeared from the valleys about 100 years before the Spanish arrived, leaving behind great mud ruins and more than 1,000 miles of irrigation canals built with stone and wooden tools.

The Hohokam culture went through several stages before reaching its golden age from around 1150 to 1450, also called the classic period. During this time, the tribe's irrigation farming of the Salt River Valley produced a surplus of maize, beans, squash, and cotton, and the culture grew more complex, the buildings bigger, and the population denser. Ball courts like those found in Mesoamerica were built in Hohokam villages, and pottery became more beautiful and less strictly utilitarian. At the culture's high point, there were as many as 40,000 Hohokam living in the valley, irrigating some 100,000 acres of farmland using canals that were still intact and useable when Anglo-Americans arrived in the 19th century. Evidence of this golden age can be seen at ruins like Pueblo Grande in Phoenix and Casa Grande between Phoenix and Tucson.

Then, around 1450, it all fell apart. This is roughly the same time when the Anasazi cultures of the Four Corners region were also coming to an abrupt end, and the theories behind both collapses are similar, though by no means universally accepted. The culprits include soil salinization, disease, warfare, flood, drought, climate change, internal unrest, overpopulation, and various combinations thereof. The O'odham cultures, formerly called the Pima and Papago Indians, tell stories about how their ancestors overthrew the Hohokam cities along the Salt River because they had grown arrogant. Many archeologists believe that the Hohokam were the ancient forbears of today's Sonoran Desert tribes, and oral tradition among the Hopi of northeastern Arizona links that culture to the Hohokam as well.

the Sonoran Desert

© TIM HULL

many of them sold to residents of Prescott, the territorial capital 100 miles to the north. By the 1880s the railroad had arrived and farmers had rebuilt the Hohokam canals, tapping the wild Salt River, a major tributary of the Gila, to great effect. Victorian homes soon replaced adobe shacks, and the Anglos went about turning the desert into a pretty typical, if a bit stifling, American city—and a steadily growing one at that. From its very beginnings Phoenix has been a largely Anglo town, and it has less of the historic Hispanic cultural influence one sees in Tucson.

Before long the territorial capital was moved from Prescott to Phoenix, which would become the center of power and influence in the new state as well. Energetic community boosters would brand the Salt River Valley, for the sake of gathering tourism and health-seeker money to the desert, the Valley of the Sun. But the Salt, like many arid-land rivers, was fickle and wild, flooding one day and trickling the next, making large-scale agriculture a risky endeavor. Valley farmers wanted it controlled, and the federal government, under the auspices of the Reclamation Act of 1902, put up the money to build Roosevelt Dam, then the largest of its kind in the world, to hold back and mediate the river. The dam transformed the valley and led to an agriculture boom concentrated largely on cotton and citrus. The two World Wars increased demand for the valley's agriculture products and brought in military installations and military industry to spur an already steady growth rate. After World War II, and especially after 1951, when air-conditioning became affordable, growth became torrential, and it hasn't really let up yet. The city keeps sprawling, and now relies on its own growth, rather than agriculture, as an economic engine. Where once there were cotton fields and citrus groves, now single-family tract housing and chain-store strip malls predominate. Phoenix is today the largest city in the Southwest and the fifth largest city in the nation. Forecasters have been saying for years that, one day not long in the future, the sprawl will reach unbroken all the way through Tucson and on to the

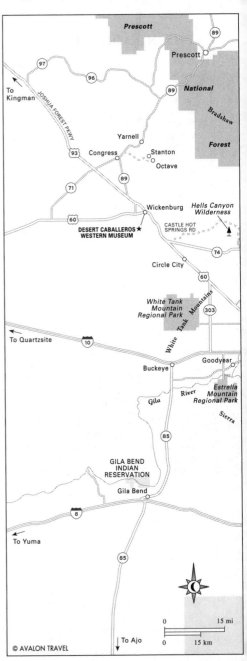

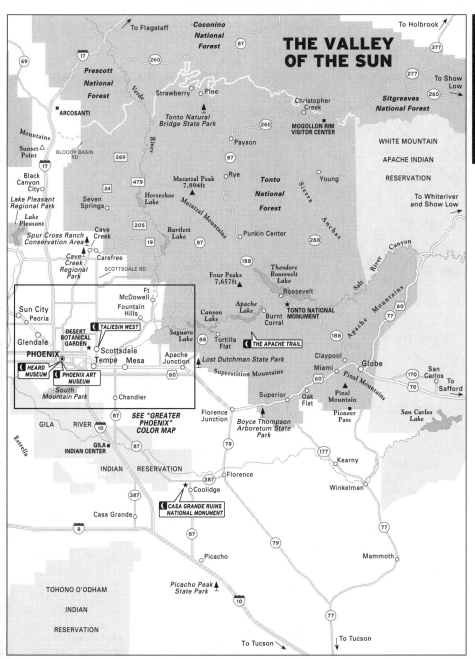

© TIM HULL

a rare cloudy day in the Valley of the Sun seen through Hole-in-the-Rock in Papago Park, near Tempe

especially the Phoenix Art Museum, the Heard Museum, the Arizona Museum of Natural History, the contemporary art museums in Mesa and Scottsdale, and the art and natural history museums at Arizona State University. You could spend a full day or two checking out the excellent Phoenix Zoo, the Phoenix Botanical Garden, the Mormon Temple in Mesa, the Deer Valley Rock Art Center, and the Pueblo Grande Archeological site. A full day could be easily given over to downtown Scottsdale, shopping and eating, or to downtown Phoenix, looking at the historic buildings, shopping, and lunching; an afternoon spent strolling, shopping, and eating on Tempe's Mill Avenue or in Glendale's historic downtown is never a waste of time. Another full day or more could be spent driving the rugged Apache Trail and exploring the dusty old mining towns on the Valley's outer edges.

From May until the end of October, a full half of the year, a visit to Phoenix includes the risk of extreme heat. Risk becomes ridiculous folly June through September, when temperatures can and do reach 110°F and higher, as the heat-island effect created by all that concrete and asphalt turns the Valley into a monstrous oven that doesn't really cool down even when the moon replaces the angry sun. It is, yes, a dry heat—but does the man cooked alive in an oven scream less than one boiled alive in a pot? Seriously though, it does make a difference—90°F with high humidity is much worse than 110 with none at all. Still, experiencing Phoenix in the summer is likely to be a bit uncomfortable, though these days it's possible to feel the heat only on rare occasions; say, walking from your car through a parking lot and into a store—a brief burn of reality between air-conditioned sanctuaries. It is best to avoid daytime outdoor activities during the worst days of summer, but summer is also a good time to find a deal. If you can take the heat, you'll find prices at the high-class resorts in town drastically reduced, offering a chance for those of us who aren't movie stars and millionaires to experience a little pampering and stylish lounging. The best days to be in the Valley are from October through November

Mexican border, and to the west and north in similar proportions.

PLANNING YOUR TIME

The Valley of the Sun comprises 10 incorporated cities and some 2,000 square miles, but most of the uniform sprawl deserves only pinpointed attention from the visitor. To see the highlights deeply and to taste the desert-city thrills, you'll need a week at least, but a long weekend suffices for a memorable once-over. An extra day could be spent touring the outer desert rings. If you're planning on spending time in other parts of Arizona during your trip, don't spend more than two or three days in Phoenix, depending on how much time you have. It is best used as a transportation hub and jumping-off station—the best place to begin but not the main focus of an Arizona journey.

That being said, going deep into the Valley's offerings has its rewards. You could spend a full day or more touring the area's museums,

and March through May. These are the "spring" months, when all is right and perfect in the desert. December through February isn't too bad either, though one should expect to be wearing sweaters and light jackets, especially at night.

ORIENTATION

Phoenix proper sits in the center of a large basin surrounded by rugged ranges: the McDowell Mountains to the northeast; the White Tank Mountains to the west; the Sierra Estrella to the southwest; the Superstition Mountains to the east; and the South Mountains to the south. In the northeasterly portion of the metro area the Phoenix Mountains provide a convenient landmark in an otherwise rather flat and repetitive urban landscape. The mountains surrounding the Salt River Valley are rocky and dry, topped by cactus and creosote, much shorter and hotter than the 9,000-foot and higher sky islands of the southern Sonoran region. The whole basin used to be run through by the Salt River, but the Roosevelt Dam and other factors long ago dried up the riverbed scar.

While there are many incorporated towns across the basin, for the purposes of the traveler and tourist, the Valley can be conveniently sliced into a few general regions that make the megalopolis easier to digest. These include: **Downtown and Central Phoenix,** wherein you'll find many of the Valley's sights and stops, bounded, roughly, by 7th Street on the east and 7th Avenue on the west, and by I-17 on the south and Camelback Road on the north. Central Avenue is a main north–south corridor road that runs across the Valley from the Phoenix Mountains to the South Mountains; the **East Valley,** which includes **Tempe, Arizona State University, and Mesa; Scottsdale and the North Valley,** which includes Scottsdale, just to the northeast of central Phoenix, and the small resort towns of Carefree and Cave Creek; and the **West Valley,** which includes Glendale. Even longtime residents rarely distinguish between the towns when they're deciding at which restaurant to eat or which shopping center to patronize, though it is true that if you live in Tempe or Scottsdale you're not likely to be found too often in Glendale. Unless you're paying close attention, you likely won't notice right away that you've left one city and entered another. The area's many freeways makes getting around somewhat easy, though you should expect traffic jams everywhere during the rush hours, roughly 6–10 A.M. and 4–7 P.M. on weekdays.

I-10 runs east–west through the center of the Valley, and then turns south along the eastern flank of central Phoenix, skirting Sky Harbor Airport and heading southeast to Tucson and beyond. I-17 runs east–west from its interchange with I-10 near 7th Street on the east and then, around 7th Avenue on the west, it moves north through the northwest valley all the way to Flagstaff. The Loop 202 freeway runs mostly east–west through the East Valley, continuing east from where the I-10 turns south; and the Loop 101 runs north–south and east–west in a loop around the northern, western, and eastern outer edges of the city.

Sights

DOWNTOWN AND CENTRAL

Over the last decade or more, downtown Phoenix has been going through a kind of renaissance, an effort that has dubbed it **Copper Square.** The area roughly bounded by 7th Street on the east, 7th Avenue on the west, Fillmore Street on the north, and Jackson Street on the south is the historic heart of the city and should be visited to get an idea of where the metropolis has been and where it hopes to go in the future. The **Downtown Phoenix Partnership** (541 E. Van Buren St., Suite B-1, 602/254-8696, www.copper square.com) watches over the 90-block area, where you'll find museums, restaurants, theaters, sports arenas, shops, hotels, and parks, and the partnership's orange-shirted ambassadors (hotline: 602/495-1500) can help you with any questions or concerns you have while in the area.

Heritage Square

Phoenix was re-founded by Anglos, most of whom were Victorians through and through despite their isolation out here in adobeland. With the coming of the railroad in the 1880s, building materials other than mud and rocks became available, and the homes in the Valley began to reflect this; suddenly the adobe huts of the early years were replaced by red-brick and lumber homes, some of them as big and ornate as anything in the East. The remains of Phoenix's Victorian past can be seen at this downtown collection of museums and restaurants (115 N. 6th St., 602/262-5071, www.phoenix.gov/parks/heritage.html), especially through a tour of the **Rosson House** (602/262-5029, www.rossonhousemuseum.org,

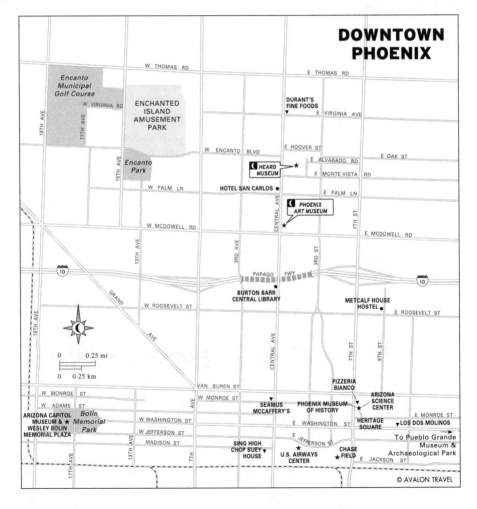

© AVALON TRAVEL

© TIM HULL

Rosson House at downtown's Heritage Square

10 A.M.–4 P.M. Wed.–Sat., noon–4 P.M. Sun., $5 adults, $2 kids under 12), a refurbished Victorian showcase built in 1895 at a cost of about $8,000. The tour takes about 45 minutes and will likely disabuse one of any lingering notions that what passed for the good life in late 19th century America didn't find its way out to the frontier as well. Nearby the **Teeter House** (602/252-4682), a little Midwestern bungalow built in 1899, is now a Victorian tearoom. The **Stevens House,** a red-brick Midwestern bungalow built in 1901, now houses the **Arizona Doll and Toy Museum** (602/253-9337, 10 A.M.–4 P.M. Tues.–Sat., noon–4 P.M. Sun., $3 adults, $1 kids under 12), of interest only to kids and other toy enthusiasts.

ARIZONA SCIENCE CENTER
The kids will also enjoy this popular science museum (602/716-2000, www.azscience.org, 10 A.M.–5 P.M. daily, $9, kids under 12 $7), which has more than 300 hands-on exhibits, a planetarium (undergoing remodeling, which started in late 2007), and an IMAX theater. There are displays on water and how we use it, and on all the disparate parts and technologies that go into the typical single-family home. There are also really good exhibits on the human body and the brain; and hands-on displays about gravity and other natural forces, geology, and other earth sciences. There's a unique and eye-opening exhibit on various kinds of networks, and an interactive display about music and how it works. There are a few exhibits that are somewhat Arizona-specific, but most of the museum is general and geared toward kids. On a weekday during school hours you're liable to run into a rowdy school tour group. The science center hosts several traveling shows each year, which are typically the most interesting and worthwhile exhibits to see. Check the website before traveling to see what's in town; recent popular traveling exhibitions featured artifacts from the *Titanic* and the bones of dinosaurs that once roamed the desert, back when it wasn't a desert at all.

PHOENIX MUSEUM OF HISTORY

For a relatively comprehensive tour of the history of human life in the Valley, with a concentration on the histories of the Anglos that built Phoenix, check out this small museum next to the science center (602/253-2734, www.pmoh .org, 10 A.M.–5 P.M. Tues.–Sat., $6, kids under 12 $3). There are some really cool artifacts here from the pioneer days, a lot of saved ephemera and old sepia photos of the somewhat sleepy farming valley before it went all megalopolis. It's quite a striking contrast to peruse this museum and then step out into the hot, crowded sprawl—it's difficult to see how one became the other, and so quickly.

◖ Heard Museum

It is possible for the observant visitor to this essential Arizona museum (2301 N. Central Ave., 602/252-8848, www.heard.org, 9:30 A.M.–5 P.M. daily, $10, kids under 12 $5) to come away with a rather deep knowledge of the cultures, religions, and histories of the state's indigenous peoples. If you're planning on

spending any time in Arizona's other regions, a stop here first will enhance your trip tenfold.

The museum was the 1929 brainchild of one of the Valley's most influential couples, Dwight and Maie Heard. Dwight Heard was the onetime publisher of the *Arizona Republican,* now the *Arizona Republic,* the state's largest newspaper both then and now. There was hardly a civic improvement in Phoenix's early 20th century history that didn't have Dwight's hand in it, including the Roosevelt Dam. It was primarily Maie who developed the museum, however, as Dwight died just before its official opening.

Today the museum has 10 galleries featuring the art, artifacts, and historical narratives of each of the state's tribes. The large display on the Hopi is particularly comprehensive and includes Barry Goldwater's Katsina Collection. It's not all static history though; several galleries feature the best in contemporary art by Native Americans and others. Sculptures dot the grounds while artists demonstrate their methods to onlookers. There are also galleries

NORA NARANJO-MORSE, SANTA CLARA PUEBLO, B. 1953; "KHWEE-SENG" (WOMAN-MAN), 1994; BRONZE, 48.5" X 58" X 11"; THE HEARD MUSEUM, PHOENIX, ARIZONA; GIFT OF THE DIAL CORPORATION

bronze sculpture by Nora Naranjo-Morse at the Heard Museum

specifically geared toward kids, with hands-on displays about Native American culture, many of them featuring the various ingenious methods native people have developed over the eons allowing them to live well in an arid country.

After you've spent time in the galleries you can grab a bite or a drink at the museum's **Arcadia Farms Café** (602/251-0204, www .arcadiafarmscafe.com/heard/, 9:30 A.M.–3 P.M. daily, $6–12), which serves Southwestern-inspired dishes like posole and tamales, as well as sandwiches, salads, beer, wine, and cocktails. If you're in the market for Native American art (or if you just like looking at it), especially that produced by Hopi and Navajo artists, don't miss the museum's store, which has a good selection of books as well.

There's also a **Heard Museum North** (32633 N. Scottsdale Rd., 480/488-9817) in north Scottsdale, and a **Heard Museum West** (16126 N. Civic Center Plaza, 623/344-2200 in Surprise, in the far West Valley, both showing items from the main museum's permanent collection.

Phoenix Art Museum

The state's largest and best art museum and one of the better collections in the Southwest, the Phoenix Art Museum (1625 N. Central Avenue, 602/257-1222, www.phxart.org, 10 A.M.–9 P.M. Tues., free after 3 P.M.; 10 A.M.–5 P.M. Wed.–Sun, $10 adult, $4 kids under 17) is the high-water mark of the Valley's sometimes rather shallow cultural stream. Here you will find exactly what you'd expect from an art museum in the West as well as much that will likely surprise you.

What you'd expect is an excellent collection of Western-American art; the museum has that very definitely and is home to the Cowboy Artists of America annual show and sale. There are important and representative works by Eanger Irving Couse—whose arresting "The Captive" should not be missed—Fredric Remington, and other well-known Western artists. One particular highlight is an otherworldly Arizona landscape by the fantasist illustrator Maxfield Parrish, who manages to capture

that strange, fantastical vibe the desert sometimes gives off. There's also a worthy collection of Latin American art, featuring paintings by Frieda Kahlo, Rufina Tamayo, and others, along with Spanish-era art and religious items. The eclectic modern and contemporary galleries manage to be challenging without becoming ridiculous, and there are interesting displays on fashion and Asian art. The miniatures gallery should not be overlooked, with its little model-room displays on interior design through the ages. Plan on spending several hours or even half a day here. A café (10 A.M.–3 P.M. Tues.–Sun., drinks and dessert until 5 P.M.) serves good soups and sandwiches and desserts, and the gift shop sells a wide selection of prints, books, and the usual museum store fare. Art lovers would do well to check the museum's website before traveling, as several large special exhibitions are put on every year.

Arizona Capitol Museum and Wesley Bolin Memorial Plaza

A neoclassical, copper-domed monument to power on the western edge of downtown, the Arizona Capitol building, built in 1901, is no longer the center of day-to-day legislative work here at the bustling state capitol complex. It's now a museum (1700 W. Washington St., 602/926-3620, 8 A.M.–5 P.M. Mon.–Fri., 11 A.M.–4 P.M. Sat., www.lib.az.us/museum/, free) with displays on the state's political history, its flora and fauna, and its symbols and industries. Definitely worth seeing are the large paintings in the fourth-floor galleries with heroic and mythical depictions of Arizona's past, and a few exhibits of historic furniture and other items from the territorial days. Just east of the capitol is a large plaza crowded with monuments to various heroes of Arizona and American history, including a large equestrian statue of Padre Kino and a black-wall memorial to the state's Vietnam veterans. This is a good place for a springtime walk, but it isn't worth visiting in the summer unless you have a particular interest in Arizona history. If you do, neither of these sights should be missed.

Pueblo Grande Museum and Archaeological Park

The Valley's ubiquitous construction cranes can usually be seen bending and rising at work from the smooth-dirt moundtops of this ancient Hohokam ruin (4619 E. Washington St., 602/495-0901, www.phoenix.gov/pueblo, 9 A.M.–4:45 P.M. Mon.–Sat., noon–4:45 P.M. Sun., $2, kids under 17 $1), a canal-side city that reached the peak of its power and population just before it was abandoned around 1450. Here you'll also see the remains of one of the hundreds of canals the Hohokam dug through the Valley to harness the Salt River—canals that formed the basis for more modern agricultural pursuits as well. There's a short trail that takes you to various points around the main ruin, which looks like a well-worked mound of dirt. Particularly interesting is the collection of Hohokam model-homes along the trail, built according to what archeologists think domestic structures may have looked liked in the Valley's ancient past. The contrast with today's tract homes and McMansions is striking to say

the least. Though not as large as the spectacular Casa Grande to the east, Pueblo Grande, a rare city-center ruin, is recommended to anyone interested in the Hohokam and to those who want to learn how past cultures have tried to live with the desert rather than against it. A small, informative museum has displays on the Hohokam—who they were, how they developed, and where they went.

Encanto Park

This lush, duck-pond park east of the city center (2605 North 15th Ave., 602/261-8991, 5:30 A.M.–11 P.M. daily) was once the place to go on a hot Phoenix afternoon, and it's still a really peaceful, green, trickling-water oasis within the heat-island sprawlscape. It borders one of the Valley's most tourable residential neighborhoods, the **Encanto-Palmcroft Historic District.** This district, with its winding, manicured streets, each home more elegant and each lawn better landscaped than the next, was Phoenix's first and best garden-style suburb, planned and built in the 1920s by Dwight

the Chinese Cultural Center

Heard. It's fun to drive slowly through the neighborhood and see the style and grace that upper-middle-class merchants and city leaders once brought to Valley living. The Spanish Colonial Revival and Monterrey Revival homes and the tall palms lining many of the streets—nonnative to Arizona except in a small pocket canyon near Yuma—gives the whole neighborhood a dreamy pre-war California feel. Over at the park, kids will enjoy the old-school county fair–style rides at **Enchanted Island Amusement Park** (602/254-1200, www.enchantedisland.com, $1 for single ride, $12.50 all-day pass).

Chinese Cultural Center

This gathering of Chinese-style buildings housing restaurants, stores, and gardens near Sky Harbor Airport is the closest thing to Chinatown this side of California (668 North 44th St., 602/273-7268, www.phxchinatown .com). There are several good restaurants here, serving seafood, Szechuan, Cantonese, and Shanghai-style Chinese cuisine in sleek Asian-modern interiors. There are also stores selling authentic Chinese gifts, furniture, household items, clothing, and herbs. The beautiful Chinese gardens re-create the architecture and landmarks of ancient Chinese cities. This is a great place to go for lunch and a stroll around the gardens and the shops, where you may find something unique that you had no idea you'd see in Phoenix.

EAST VALLEY

The East Valley can be said to begin around the twisted red-rock humps of **Papago Park,** east on Van Buren from downtown and just north of Tempe. The region includes Mesa, a crowded, seemingly unending band of sprawl east of Tempe that is the third-largest city in Arizona and the part-time home to thousands of snowbirds and RV parks. Mesa was founded in the late 19th century by Mormon pioneers from Utah and is still a largely Mormon-dominated town with the state's biggest Latter-day Saints temple. Tempe, along the banks of the once-mighty Salt River, is home to Arizona State University, the state's largest

university and one of the largest public land-grant schools in the Southwest. Chandler and Gilbert are also nearby, both of them former agricultural burgs that have grown and spread mightily during the housing booms of the last few decades.

Phoenix Zoo

This excellent zoo (455 N. Galvin Pkwy., 602/273-1341, www.phoenixzoo.org, 7 A.M.–2 P.M. weekdays, 7 A.M.–4 P.M. Sat.–Sun. in summer, 9 A.M.–5 P.M. daily in spring, 9 A.M.–4 P.M. daily in winter, $14 adults, $6 kids under 12) in Papago Park was called the "Maytag Zoo" when it first opened in 1962 in honor of its main booster, Robert Maytag, a scion of the appliance family. Today it's the nation's largest privately owned, nonprofit zoo, hosting more visitors every year than any other Valley attraction. You'll see all the usual suspects here, from the mountain lions and big horn sheep that stalk Arizona's wildlands to the rare Arabian oryx, which the zoo is credited with saving from near extinction. Along the way, as you walk along three paved trails through the zoo's clean, lush grounds, you'll commune with lions, elephants, camels, giraffes, and too many birds to name. You can catch a ride on a camel, walk through the frenetic Monkey Village, and stare for as long as you want to at the invariably sleepy big cats. A newer exhibit lets you get up close and personal (sort of) with stingrays and even sharks. Don't miss the Baboon Kingdom, where you can watch those exceedingly humanlike crea tures interact (often hilariously), and be su to walk the Arizona Trail, where you'll w ness what you're missing out there in the d ert. Plan on spending at least half of the here, and happily so.

Desert Botanical Garden

This 50-acre garden in Papago Park (1 Galvin Pkwy., 480/941-1225, www.d 7 A.M.–8 P.M. summer, 8 A.M.–8 P.M the year, $10 adults, $4 kids under ! very best place to go to learn abou ert's unique flora, other than the itself, of course. Actually, the garden might be even better than the raw desert—you aren't risking your life by coming here in the summer, and there are signs everywhere explaining what each stickery bush and thorn-heavy succulent is called and why. There are several special exhibitions each year, including art installations by visiting artists. You can eat here at the small, delicious Patio Café and purchase a strange alien cactus for yourself. If you have any interest in the desert Southwest's unique and always-threatened plantlife, consider spending a few hours strolling the garden's easy pathways. In the summer it can be a bit trying, but it's not completely out of the question, as all that plantlife growing close together gives off a cooling vibe and a shady feeling, even when the sun is beating incessantly.

Tempe Town Lake

Tempe Town Lake (620 N. Mill Ave.,

480/350-8625, www.tempe.gov/lake/, free), a large, city-center waterway just off Tempe's main street, represents an ambitious, long-term attempt to bring back a bit of the Salt River, at least for the sake of pedal-boating and waterside jogging, to the Salt River Valley. It's a pleasant place to stroll, jog, and bike, or you can even lounge around on the grass at **Tempe Beach Park** (www.tempe.gov/lake/recreation/), where there's always something going on. You can rent a pedal boat or a kayak, or take a electric-boat cruise on the lake. Kids will love to put on their swimsuits and dash around the cool water features at **Splash Playground** (open Apr.–Sept., free), where they'll also learn about water and why it's so important here in the desert. At the western edge of the park, near the inflatable dam that holds the lake together, check out the gleaming new **Tempe Center for the Arts** (700 W. Rio Salado Pkwy., 480/350-2829,

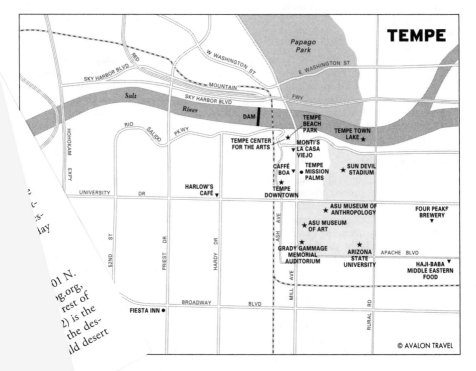

© AVALON TRAVEL

© TIM HULL

A floating dam keeps imported water in the Salt River channel passing through central Tempe, creating a waterside park and walkway.

www.tempe.gov), which hosts Broadway-style shows, local theater, music, and dance performances; it also has a small gallery.

Arizona State University

If you walk around the sprawling, palm tree–lined ASU campus (University Dr. and Mill Ave., 480/965-9011, www.asu.edu) at any time during the spring or early fall months, you might wonder whether school is actually in session. You'll probably see co-eds lounging around the grass in bikinis and several Frisbee and football games going on. It's not that ASU students aren't serious—most of them are, and the university is among the top state schools in the nation in several categories—but it's truly difficult to take life too seriously when the weather is so perfect, and it usually is while school is in session.

Along with prime people-watching, there are two museums that may entice the visitor to campus. The **ASU Art Museum** (480/965-2787, www.asuartmuseum.asu.edu, 11 A.M.–9 P.M. Tues., 11 A.M.–5 P.M. Wed.–Sat., 1 P.M.–5 P.M. Sun., free) has some excellent contemporary art pieces, and the Americas Gallery has an extremely varied display of paintings and

drawings from across the New World, arranged in a kind of living room wall–style that is very effective. Don't miss Luis Jimenez's lithograph, *Southwest Pieta*—an indigenous take on the classic Christian art pose. The **ASU Museum of Anthropology** (480/965-6224, www.asu .edu/clas/shesc/asuma/, 11 A.M.–3 P.M. Mon.–Fri. during school year, by appointment in summer, free) puts on several interesting exhibits throughout the year relating to human cultures in the Southwest and around the world. Every year from November through January, a Dias de Los Muertos (Day of the Dead) exhibition interprets and celebrates this most mysterious and fascinating of New World traditions.

DEER VALLEY ROCK ART CENTER

This rock art site (3711 W. Deer Valley Rd., 623/582-8007, www.asu.edu/clas/shesc/dvrac/, 9 A.M.–5 P.M. Tues.–Sat. and noon–5 P.M. Sun. Oct.–Apr., 8 A.M.–2 P.M. Tues.–Sun. May–Sept., $7, $3 kids under 12) in the far North Valley is protected by ASU, and scholars are involved in ongoing research here into the forms and meanings of the petroglyphs that cover the Southwest. The more than 1,500 petroglyphs on

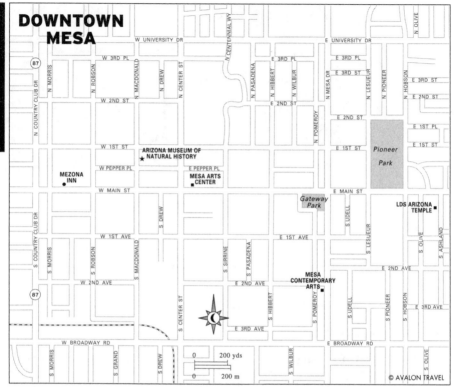

this 46-acre preserve were scraped and scratched by the Hohokam and other tribes that inhabited the valley until about 1450. There's a small museum and a quarter-mile trail that you can walk along and view some of the state's finest examples of the ancient rock art. Make sure to take binoculars, as some of the best work is off the trail. Not recommended in the summer.

Mesa Contemporary Arts

One wouldn't expect to find this excellent contemporary art museum (1 E. Main St., 480/644-6500, www.mesaartscenter.com, 10 A.M.–5 P.M. Tues.–Wed., 10 A.M.–8 P.M. Thurs.–Sat., 12 P.M.–5 P.M. Sun., $3.50) in staid Main Street Mesa, but here it is, and it is highly recommended to anyone who wants to witness the most current moment in painting, sculpture,

and other mediums. Three galleries in this cool, spare space inside the **Mesa Arts Center** show revolving exhibitions featuring primarily artists from the Southwest, California, and Mexico, but not necessarily—in fact rarely—what most would think of as Southwestern-style art. The shows are typically provocative and singular—a recent exhibition featured works by Latino artists from the collection of Cheech Marin, of Cheech and Chong fame. This museum, along with a similar contemporary space in nearby Scottsdale, is must-see proof that the Valley isn't exactly the cultural graveyard it can sometimes appear to be.

Arizona Museum of Natural History

The Valley's only natural history museum (53 N. MacDonald, 480/644-2230, www.azmnh.org,

10 A.M.–5 P.M. Tues.–Fri., 11 A.M.–5 P.M. Sat., 1–5 P.M. Sun., $8 adults, $4 kids under 12) has quite a few hulking dinosaur skeletons in its Dinosaur Hall, and its three-story Dinosaur Mountain is definitely something to see, but the most interesting exhibits here are related to the history of the Southwest, including models of a Spanish-era mission and a territorial jail. The exhibition about Arizona in the movies is fascinating, and the newer exhibit on the Hohokam is one of the best around. This is a great place to stop prior to traveling to other parts of the state, a kind of one-stop lesson on the nature and people of Arizona and the southwest through the ages—especially recommended to parents who are hoping to sneak a little education into a Southwestern vacation.

Arizona Temple Visitor's Center

Non-Mormons can't go inside this beautiful temple (525 East Main St., Mesa, 480/964-7164, 9 A.M.–9 P.M. daily, free) on 20 green acres near the original Mesa townsite, but those interested in the mysterious and fascinating world of the Latter-day Saints church can stop by and see the outside (which some say resembles the biblical Temple of Herod). Construction on the LDS temple, the first built in Arizona—a state that has welcomed Mormon settlers for generations—began in 1922, and the building was dedicated in 1927. The beautiful grounds include a cactus garden and reflecting pools, and the visitors center has some displays and a film about the LDS church.

Sports and Recreation

Phoenicians love to get outdoors—with more than 300 sunny days a year, they really don't have a choice in the matter. They keep their parks and recreation areas immaculate. There are well-trod desert hiking trails a short drive from just about anywhere in town. But Phoenix's official sport is golf, and there are many courses to choose from and play on year-round.

HIKING, BIKING, AND HORSEBACK RIDING

The Valley's hiking trails sometimes seem more like running tracks with all the Lycra and MP3-players strapped to tan sweaty arms one is apt to see in any of the urban-area desert preserves, so close to the bustle and yet almost secluded if it weren't for all those people. Still, if you're staying in Phoenix for more than a few days, any one of these easily accessible desert parks makes for a pleasant outing. If you want a real desert hike, though, save your energy for a trek into the Superstition Mountains on the Valley's eastern edge (see *Around the Valley of the Sun* in this chapter).

Phoenix Mountains

Here you will find the Valley's favorite hiking trail (2701 E. Squaw Peak Ln., www.phoenix .gov/parks/phxmtns.html, 5 A.M.–11 P.M. daily), a 1.2-mile one-way hunched-over climb up to what was, prior to the Iraq War, one of the more politically incorrect landmarks in the state—Squaw Peak. The term squaw has long had negative connotations for Native Americans, so in 2003 the peak was renamed Piestewa Peak, after Lori Piestewa, a Navajo soldier who was killed in Iraq. You are sure to run into a crowd on the trail on any given day, but if any of those days are clear you can see all of the Valley and beyond spread out before you. The **Piestewa Peak Summit Trail** is a really easy, if vertical, hike, and kids won't have a problem with it.

A little bit tougher is the hike up **Camelback Mountain,** just a touch higher than its nearby sister at 2,704 feet. Within the **Echo Canyon Recreation Area** (E. McDonald Dr., www .phoenix.gov/parks/hikcmgud.html, sunrise to sunset) the mile-long one-way **Summit Trail** is a popular hike, and you may have to wait for a parking spot on weekends. You gain more than 1,000 feet on the way up, so it's not to

© TIM HULL

The Summit Trail to the top of Piestewa Peak in the Phoenix Mountains is one of the most popular walks in the valley.

be taken lightly. There are parts of the trail that are hewn out of slick rock with handrails alongside for help. From the top you can see everything, whether you want to or not.

South Mountain Park and Preserve

Forming the Valley's southern border, the obviously named South Mountains can't be missed—they are the ones with all the communication towers and antennae shooting up from their peaks like pins in a hard-rock cushion. The 16,000-acre desert preserve (10919 S. Central Ave., www.phoenix.gov/parks/southmnt.html, 5 A.M.–11 P.M. daily) is popular with Valley residents as an exercise field; bicyclists in particular enjoy climbing the high, twisting paved road to the lookout peak and then shooting rocket-like back down to the desert floor. One feels a little bad cruising slowly behind them on the curvy way up to Dobbins Point, the park's highest accessible point at 2,300 feet, which is a favorite pastime of less active Phoenicians and their visitors. There are several dry, rocky trails through the rugged, cactus-and-creosote desert, most of them accessed off the main road up to the top and most of them up-and-down routes that aren't too difficult. Right after the main entrance, there's a trail-map station across from the Civilian Conservation Corps-built rock house, in which you'll find public bathrooms. The trails, nearly 58 miles of them, are open to hikers, mountain bikers, and horses. Mountain bikers will find some fun, moderately tough single tracks here. For an easy and representative loop hike or bike ride, try a 3.5-mile round-trip jaunt on the **National Trail** to Hidden Valley. The trail is rough and rocky, and slick from wear in some places, but the views are spectacular and the saguaros plentiful. You pick up the trail at the top of the Summit Road at the Buena Vista Lookout. The National Trail crosses the entire park, if you're really feeling ambitious.

A trail-ride through the desert atop a friendly horse could possibly take one back to the days of the conquistadores who first traversed this blasted land looking for treasure. If you want to try it, check out **Ponderosa Stables** (10215 S. Central Ave., 602/268-1261, www.arizona-horses.com, $28 for 1 hour), just before the park's main entrance.

Papago Park

Even closer to the action is this twisting red-rock desert park just east of central Phoenix (Van Buren St. and Galvin Pkwy., 602/256-3220, www.phoenix.gov/parks/papago.html), a fun place to tear around on a mountain bike for a while or scramble up to Hole-in-the-Rock, a, well, a big hole in a jutting-rock hill through which the valley opens up beautifully. It's an easy climb up a very short trail, and then you can sit in the little smooth notch—which, the archeologists will tell you, lines up perfectly with a building at Pueblo Grande a few miles to the southwest—and look out over the land. Facing west, this is a particularly good spot for sunset viewing. Walking trails crisscross the park, and there are dozens of picnic tables and even a lagoon for fishing.

GOLF

Seen from the air, the Valley of the Sun appears to be stamped illogically with wide swaths of short green grass, all dotted with man-made duck ponds and sandy beach interruptions. The 300-plus days of sunshine enjoyed here allow for year-round golf—the waking dream of your average Rust Belt duffer. As such, an inordinate amount of desert has been rolled over with grass, creating a golfer's paradise and a fairly questionable use of resources. The golf-lover will likely disagree, however, especially during a bright morning round in November, the raw, dry desert mountains framing beauti-fully the impossibly green fairways. There are dozens of courses throughout the Valley, many of them linked to famous resorts. For the best resort-style courses in the area, see *The Valley's Top Five Resorts* sidebar. The Valley also has some of the most popular municipal courses in the nation, each of them a bargain com-pared to the fancier places and competing just fine when it comes to lushness and creative

design. Many of the municipal courses host more 100,000 rounds of golf per year, so it's a good idea to make tee times in advance. You might want to book a tee time at a course be-fore traveling—the city's golf course web pages allow for easy online reservations up to eight days in advance.

Perhaps the Valley's most environmen-tally thoughtful course is the municipal **Cave Creek Golf Course** (15202 N. 19th Ave., 602/866-8076, www.ci.phoenix.az.us/sports/golf.html, $15–21 for residents, $25–31 nonresidents), a par 72 built on a reclaimed landfill; but you won't notice—it's green and tree-lined and is the Valley's most popular public course. One of the oldest courses in the state, built in 1935 near Encanto Park, the city center's lush and attractive oasis, **Encanto Golf Course** (2755 N. 15th Ave., 602/253-3963, www.ci.phoenix.az.us/sports/golf.html, $21–30 for residents, $25–44 for nonresidents) is a par 70 municipal course lined, like its titular park, with tall shaggy palm trees. At Papago Park in the East Valley, the green of the links at **Papago Golf Course** (5595 E. Moreland St., 602/275-8428, www.ci.phoenisx.az.us/sports/golf.html, $35 resi-dents, $46 nonresidents) contrasts perfectly with red rock hills all around. The Par 72 mu-nicipal course is very popular and hosts the Phoenix Open qualifying rounds. Just south in Tempe, the **ASU Karsten Golf Course** (1125 E. Rio Salado Pkwy., 480/921-8070, www.asukarsten.com, $32–108) stretches out near the Salt River bed, catching the shadow of Sun Devil Stadium—a rolling and twisting course that is particularly difficult.

SALT RIVER TUBING

A leisurely, convivial float down the Salt is a desert-living tradition, especially during the un-relenting shine of summer. **Salt River Tubing and Recreation** (480/984-3305, www.saltriv-ertubing.com, 9 A.M.–7 P.M. daily May–Sept., last tube rented at 3:30 P.M., $14 per person, per tube, includes shuttle to launch) rents out tubes all summer, shuttling seekers of cool water to a launch on the Salt River just below Saguaro

Lake, east of the city in the Tonto National Forest. You can rent an extra inner tube to hold your ice chest, and stock it with cans of beer and soda (no glass allowed) and sandwiches—and make sure to include some water, too. The party can get a bit drunken and adult on some days, especially the weekends. Kids must be at least eight years old and four feet tall to go along. There are some fun rapids and a quick current in places, depending on the water release schedule at the lake, but mostly it's a slow and sunny float along a thin band of shallow, cool, green-blue water, flanked by rock- and saguaro-lined canyon walls and thick riparian greenbelts. There are several beach landings along the way where floaters stop and picnic. Don't expect to be alone, and don't count on quiet or the sounds of nature all the time; a few waterborne revelers along the way will typically blast music and hoot and yell, depending on how much beer is left. You can choose from two-, three-, and five-hour trips weekdays, and a six-hour trip is offered on weekends. To get to the rental office, head north for 15 miles from U.S. 60 on the Power Road in Mesa. Always call before going out there, though; the trips are subject to weather and water flow.

SPECTATOR SPORTS

Everybody in the Valley is from somewhere else, or so the conventional wisdom says. The metropolis is indeed a transient city in a transient state; people are always moving in and out and the new replaces the barely old at a whirlwind clip. This reality is both good and bad for the city's several major league sports clubs. There's always a built-in crowd of local devotees, and casual fans will usually turn out in droves when one of the big midwestern or Eastern teams is in town. When the Chicago Cubs come to visit every summer, it's sometimes difficult to see the Diamondbacks fans among all those blue shirts. That being said, most of the local teams have been able to ingratiate themselves with the natives, the longtime residents, and the new arrivals alike simply by doing what a sports team is supposed to do: winning.

The Arizona Diamondbacks

One of the more successful of Arizona's teams in recent times has been Major League Baseball's Arizona Diamondbacks (602/514-8400 or 888/777-4664, www.arizona.diamondbacks.mlb.com), with barely 10 years as a big league team and a World Series trophy in the clubhouse. With one of the best scouting programs in the game, lately the D-Backs have skewed younger, introducing future superstars to big-time playoff baseball and beginning a new tradition of smart, fast, and fundamental National League ball that has locals filling the seats at **Chase Field** (401 E. Jefferson St., 602/462-6799 or 800/821-7160, tours offered 9:30 A.M., 11 A.M., and 12:30 P.M. Mon.–Sat. year round, $6, kids under 12 $4) downtown, one of the few ballparks in the world with a retractable roof. The roof is closed during most of the season with the air conditioners blasting—the only way baseball can be played in the desert without killing players. Individual game tickets range in price from $5 for nosebleed seats to $215 for a clubhouse box. A decent seat will cost you between $15–40. Though the team is very popular in the valley, most of the time tickets can be purchased the day of the game at the ballpark. If one of the big Midwestern or Eastern teams are in town, like the Chicago Cubs or, during interleague play, the Detroit Tigers, you will need to plan far ahead.

The Phoenix Suns

The quick play of the Phoenix Suns (602/379-7900, www.nba.com/suns/), led by superstar guard Steve Nash and center Shaquille O'Neil, has made the NBA team a constant threat to win it all these last several years. The Suns also have a long and storied history, with the likes of Charles Barkley, Dan Majerle—who still has a restaurant in town—Danny Ainge, and Dennis Johnson once wearing the purple and orange. The Suns often battle the LA Lakers for supremacy in the Western Conference's Pacific League, and the stands at the huge **U.S. Airways Center** (201 E. Jefferson St.) downtown are always packed with fans.

The Phoenix Coyotes

Coached by professional hockey's all-time leading scorer, "The Great One," Wayne Gretzky, the Phoenix Coyotes (480/563-7825, www .coyotes.nhl.com) regularly make a strong run for the playoffs in the NHL's Western Conference. Their new stadium, **Jobing.com Arena** (6751 N. White Out Way, Glendale), opened in 2006.

The Arizona Cardinals

The most consistently disappointing of Phoenix's sports teams, the Arizona Cardinals (602/379-0102, www.azcardinals .com) haven't had much in the way of wins since they moved to the Valley of the Sun from St. Louis in 1987—they failed to make the NFL playoffs for the 10th straight season in 2008. There are a few good reasons for future hope, however. In 2006 the team opened **University of Phoenix Stadium** (1 Cardinals Dr., Glendale), a gleaming new headquarters that has fans more excited about the team than they have been in years. Despite a slow start and some injuries, the team and their fans are hoping that former University of Southern California star quarterback Matt Leinert will be their savior in the near future.

ASU Sports

The various teams that play under the name **ASU Sun Devils** (480/965-2381, www .thesundevils.cstv.com, box office open

DESERT HARDBALL: SPRING TRAINING AND CACTUS LEAGUE BASEBALL

In many parts of the country, March is a month for scraping ice off windshields, digging out of snow drifts, and hoping that global warming hurries up just a bit with all that melting. Spring may be just around the corner, but that corner seems way up ahead.

In the Valley of the Sun, however, March is perfect: a little brisk in the morning, warm in the afternoon, and light-jacket cool at night. Oh, and every single day of the month there are several Major League Baseball games played at intimate ballparks all over town.

Nine teams, including the beloved Chicago Cubs, spend Spring Training in the Valley, and three others play in Tucson, though that may change soon. In 2009, the Los Angeles Dodgers (now in Florida) and the Chicago White Sox (now in Tucson) should be set up in Glendale in the West Valley, and several other teams are rumored to be leaving Florida and heading to the Valley of the Sun in the coming years. If it isn't already, the valley is poised to be the major Spring Training site in the nation by decade's end.

The teams play at various stadiums around the valley, and ticket prices range $7-22 for most games. A great place to start planning your Spring Training vacation is at www.cactusleague.com, which has all the information and schedules; or you can call the individual stadiums for ticket information.

The **Chicago Cubs** play at **Hohokam Park** (1235 N Center St., Mesa, 480/964-4467 or 800/905-3315) and, with so many Midwest refugees in the valley, always draw a big crowd. The **San Francisco Giants** play at **Scottsdale Stadium** (7408 E. Osborn Rd., Scottsdale, 480/312-2856 or 800/225-2277). The **Milwaukee Brewers** play at **Maryvale Baseball Park** (3600 N. 51st Ave., Phoenix, 800/933-7890), and the **San Diego Padres** and the **Seattle Mariners** play at **Peoria Sports Complex** (16101 N. 83rd Ave., Peoria, 623/773-8270). The **Oakland Athletics** play at **Phoenix Municipal Stadium** (5999 E. Van Buren St., Phoenix, 602/392-0074), and the **Kansas City Royals** and the **Texas Rangers** play at **Surprise Recreation Campus** (15960 N. Bullard Ave., Surprise, 623/222-2222). The **Los Angeles Angels of Anaheim** play at **Tempe Diablo Stadium** (2200 W. Alameda Dr., Tempe, 480/350-5205).

beginning Aug. 16 and throughout school year, 9 A.M.–5 P.M. Mon.–Fri., 9 A.M.–noon Sat.) are typically pretty good, and often, especially in baseball and football, very good. The students and the many ASU alumni who stuck around the Valley really get into it, and tickets for the bigger games aren't easy to come by. Barry Bonds played his college baseball here, as did many other big leaguers. Jake "The Snake" Plummer, formerly quarterback for the Arizona Cardinals and then the Denver Broncos, was a college star on the Sun Devil football field.

Entertainment and Events

LIVE MUSIC

The excellent **Phoenix Symphony** (602/495-1999, www.phoenixsymphony.org) puts on dozens of pops and classics concerts throughout the year at downtown's beautiful **Symphony Hall** (75 N. 2nd St.). The hall is also home to the **Arizona Opera Company** (602/266-7464), which presents mostly classic, well-known operas with creative set designs and top-notch performers. A few blocks away, the spectacular **Dodge Theatre** (400 West Washington, 602/379-2888, www.dodge theatre.com) welcomes a constant stream of headlining national acts, including an impressive array and big-name comedians and rock bands. But perhaps the best seat in the Valley is at the intimate **Celebrity Theatre** (440 N. 32nd St., 602/267-1600, www.celebrity theatre.com). The theater's round stage makes every seat in the house a perfect one, and a wide variety of performers appear every year—jazz bands, crooners, rappers, classic rock, and nearly everything else. The acts here aren't usually as big as the ones that play at the Dodge or at the huge outdoor **Cricket Pavilion** (2121 N. 83rd Ave., 602/254-7599, www .cricket-pavilion.com), but you'll want to check the website; if any band or performer you like is playing at Celebrity Theatre, you should definitely think about going.

Clubs

The **Rhythm Room** (1019 E. Indian School Rd., 602/265-4842, www.rhythmroom.com) is an excellent venue to catch local and national touring acts playing blues, rock, and country, and on any given night of the week there's likely to be some roots-heavy band you've never heard (but one you'll be happy you did hear) tearing up the stage. For mostly blues jams and concerts, check out **Char's House of Blues** (4631 N. Seventh Ave., 602/230-0205, www .charshastheblues.com), where you can also watch all the Valley's sports teams on big TVs. A younger crowd hangs out at the East Valley's **The Clubhouse Music Venue** (1320 E. Broadway Rd., 480/968-3238, www.club housemusicvenue.com), voted best local music venue by the *Phoenix New Times.* Here you'll see local, regional, and national bands of the rock, punk, reggae, and alternative persuasions, and there's food and a rowdy bar as well. Many of the shows are all ages, meaning that music-lovers 18 and over are allowed in; drinkers, however, won't be disappointed, as there is a separate bar open during all-ages shows.

THEATER

The Valley's premier live theater venue is the **Herberger Theater Center** (222 E. Monroe St., 602/254-7399, www.herbergertheater.org) downtown—you'll know you've found it when you see the fascinating dancing nude sculptures out front. Here you can see original productions by the **Arizona Theatre Company** (502 W. Roosevelt, 602/256-6995, www .aztheatreco.org), one of the nation's finest regional theater companies, and one that is never daunted by difficult, unique work. The smaller **Actor's Theatre of Phoenix** (911 N. 4th, 602/253-6701, www.actorstheatrephx.org) also puts on plays at the Herberger, offering theatergoers a chance to catch some cutting-edge productions as well as entertaining favorites. Even

CITY OF PHOENIX

The Herberger Theater Center houses three theaters and four performance companies.

if you don't have tickets to see one of the many theater, music, and live performance shows put on at the classic **Orpheum Theatre** (203 West Adams Street, 602/262-6225, www.ci.phoenix.az.us/stages/orpheum.html), you might want to step into the gorgeous old venue for a look around. The theater, one of the Valley's oldest, recently went through a multimillion-dollar reformation and has been restored to its 1927 glory. If style and beauty and design are the ultimate criteria, this is probably the best venue in the Valley.

CINEMA

For art-house and independent films, Tempe's **Harkin's Valley Art** (509 S. Mill Ave., 480/446-7272) is the best venue in the Valley, showing the films you won't see at the multiplex in a cool, if a bit rickety, old building on Mill Avenue.

COMEDY

The **Tempe Improv Comedy Theater** (930 E. University, 480/921-9877, www.tempeimprov

.com) is where *Saturday Night Live* alum and Tempe favorite son David Spade cut his stand-up teeth. The Improv hosts mostly mid-level stand-ups, though often a big name like Dana Carvey or Richard Lewis will take the stage. The kitchen serves pretty good dinners—hamburgers, chicken dishes, and even prime rib ($8.95–16.95). The comedy here is usually very funny, and a night spent before the stage gives you an opportunity to see some rising stars and to laugh until your drink comes out your nose.

NIGHTLIFE

There are a lot of young people in Phoenix—it's in many ways a very young city. There are also a lot of retirees, and even a few people in between somewhere. They all manage to come together when the sun goes down. Like so many desert creatures, they love the nightlife. There's upscale and dive-scale, there are sports bars and ultra cool lounges, rock bars, honky-tonks, and hookahs. Hidden somewhere out in that hot sprawl there's a place that offers what you want. The best place to identify both the new and the classic is the *Phoenix New Times,* an alternative weekly you'll find free everywhere. Also look for *GetOut,* a free guide to entertainment and dining in the East Valley; and *Nightlife! Magazine,* a free guide to all of the Valley's nocturnal activities.

Downtown and Central

The sports and rock-and-roll memorabilia on the walls and the classic rock cover-bands on the stage make Phoenix native Alice Cooper's combo "rock-'n'-jock" restaurant and bar **Alice Cooperstown** (101 E. Jackson St., 602/253-7337, www.alicecooperstown.com) a fun place to spend an evening in downtown Phoenix, especially after a D-Backs or Suns game, when the place is usually packed. Ready-made Irish and English "pubs" are starting to pop up all over the country these days, but central Phoenix's **George & Dragon Pub** (4240 N. Central Ave., 602/241-0018) is the real deal, and it has been around forever. A great selection of beers of tap—heavy on the delicious brews of the British Isles—a well-stocked jukebox, billiards, and good eats (the bangers and mash are particularly good) make this authentic pub a perfect place to spend an hour or ten. **The Blooze Bar** (12014 N. 32nd St., 602/788-4574, www.thebloozebar.com) has rockabilly and alternative rock bands on a regular basis and a younger crowd, while **Durant's** (2611 N. Central Ave., 602/264-5967, www .durantsaz.com) is a bit more upscale, a Phoenix classic with the best martini in town.

East Valley

Head over to **Mill Avenue** in Tempe and party with the ASU crowd; there are several clubs and bars along Mill, and there's bound to be a fashionable and beautiful crowd anywhere you stop. In the same general area, **Casey Moore's** (850 S. Ash Ave., 480/968-9935, www.myspace.com/caseymoore) is a favorite among ASU students, faculty, and still-partying alumni, with a mist-cooled patio, good beers, and huge plates of oysters. For one of the best handcrafted beers in the Valley, try **Four**

Peaks Brewing Company (1340 E. 8th St., 480/303-9967, www.fourpeaks.com) near campus, and if you're looking to dance the night away you can't go wrong with Valley institution **Graham Central Station** (7850 S. Priest Dr., Tempe, 480/496-4336 grahamcentralstation.com), with four nightclubs under one roof, including a country and western dance floor, a Karaoke bar, a Top 40 dance club, and all kinds of crazily debauched contests and activities. If you're looking for an authentic desert honky-tonk, drive way out east to Apache Junction and hit **Arizona Joe's** (417 S. Winchester Rd., Apache Junction, 480/983-6115). You can't get much more authentic, and there's usually an unheard-of but good country band playing.

West Valley

In Glendale and the West Valley **Barwinkles** (5930 W. Greenway Rd. #27, Glendale, 602/938-9330, www.barwinkles .com) is the place to be, with good food and drinks, a friendly local crowd, and TVs with the game on. The **Stardust Lounge** (4346 West Olive Ave., 623/937-1877) is a cool honky-tonk with a regular lineup and great country bands.

FESTIVALS AND EVENTS

At the end of December and into the first days of January, the Valley celebrates college football with the Fiesta Bowl Parade, Fiesta Bowl Block Party, and, of course, the **Fiesta Bowl** (www.fiestabowl.org) at University of Phoenix Stadium in Glendale. In February the popular **VNS Book Sale** (602/265-6805, www .vnsabooksale.org) has more than 600,000 used books for sale at the fair grounds.

In March, the **Heard Museum Guild Indian Fair & Market** (602/253-8848, www .heardguild.org) includes more than 600 artists, and Spring Training and Cactus League (www.cactusleague.com) brings MLB teams to the Valley for a game every day of the month. In April, **NASCAR Subway Fresh Fit 500** (www.nascar.com) roars into town, bringing the popular sport's top drivers with it.

In October the **Arizona State Fair** and

the **Heard Museum Spanish Market** keep locals and visitors busy, and in November the cars return for the **NASCAR Checker Auto** **Parts 500.** In December, don't miss the popular **Pueblo Grande Museum Indian Market** (602/495-0901, www.phoenix.gov/pueblo).

Shopping

DOWNTOWN AND CENTRAL
Even if you don't feel like shopping, take a walk around the gardens and ponds at downtown's **Arizona Center** (400 E. Van Buren St., 602/271-4000, www.arizonacenter.com), a big open-air mall with an eclectic assortment of shops, boutiques, restaurants, and a movie theater. This is a great place to shop for Arizona-style gifts, especially if what you're looking for is a bit on the kitschy side. If you can't find anything to buy, you won't regret the stroll through one of the Valley's greenest attractions. The upscale **Biltmore Fashion Park** (24th St. and Camelback Rd., 602/955-8400, www.shopbiltmore.com) along Camelback Road is the Valley's finest shopping mall, with Saks 5th Avenue, Ralph Lauren, and dozens of other high-end shops. You'll want to spend the whole day here if you're a shopping enthusiast with money to burn, and there are several restaurants to choose from for a memorable lunch or dinner. If you're looking for recycled treasures and secret missing links check out the **Historic District Antique Mall** (539 W. McDowell Rd., 602/253-3778, www.historicdistrict antiquemall.com), a great place to get lost in the knickknacks of history and all the variations in the American style. On 7th Avenue between Camelback and Indian School roads, in the **Melrose District,** you'll find a host of retro boutiques, thrift stores, and hip home-decor shops.

EAST VALLEY
If the clothes at the Biltmore's Saks are too expensive, drive over to Tempe and the **Arizona Mills** (5000 Arizona Mills Cir., 480/491-7300, www.arizonamills.com, 10 A.M.–9:30 P.M. Mon.–Sat., 11 A.M.–7 P.M. Sun.), an outlet mall that has a Saks outlet (called Off 5th) and dozens of other outlet shops, including Ann Taylor, Kenneth Cole, and many more. This mall is huge and clean and has a fun gaming center for the kids and several restaurants. Also in Tempe, take a stroll along Mill Avenue, where you'll find all kinds of hip shops and boutiques; while Mill used to be quite a bit funkier than it is today, the bigger corporate stores that overtook it about a decade ago still have a lot of good shopping to offer.

WEST VALLEY
Shopping Districts
Historic Downtown Glendale (59th and Glendale aves.) and the nearby **Catlin Court Historic District** in the northwest Valley offer the Valley's quaintest shopping; the streets of downtown Glendale are lined with gaslamps and crowded antique stores, while Catlin Court is an historic residential neighborhood whose white picket fence–fronted bungalows have been turned into boutiques and restaurants. This area is a must-visit for those who enjoy walking in picturesque small-town settings and finding unique and unknown items to take home.

Book Stores
The Valley isn't exactly a book-hunter's paradise, but there are a few stores worth checking out. The best bookstore in town is the legendary **Changing Hands Bookstore** (6428 S. McClintock Dr., 480/730-0205, www .changinghands.com, 10 A.M.–9 P.M. Mon.–Fri., 9 A.M.–9 P.M. Sat., 10 A.M.–7 P.M. Sun.) in Tempe, which sells an excellent mixture of new and used books. The statewide chain **Bookmans,** selling all manner of used media, including books, CDS, DVDs, games, and

much more, has two well-stocked locations in the Valley, one in the North Valley (8034 N. 19th Ave., 602/433-0255,www.bookmans .com, 9 A.M.–10 P.M. daily), and one in Mesa, in the East Valley (1056 S. Country Club Dr., 480/835-0505, www.bookmans.com, 9 A.M.–10 P.M. daily). All Bookmans locations offer free wireless Internet.

Accommodations

The accommodations scene in the Valley is ruled by the big chains and resorts. If you're hoping to find something a bit more distinctive and independent, expect to pay for it accordingly. The best time to find bargains is in summer, when nearly every big hotel and resort slashes its prices to attract business to the infernal desert. Year-round deals can be found in Tempe, in the East Valley, where there are a few independent hotels that offer a nice room for a fair price.

DOWNTOWN AND CENTRAL
$50-100
The best deal in town is the **Metcalf House Hostel** (1026 North 9th Street, 602/254-9803, http://home.earthlink.net/~phxhostel/, $18–25 dorm room, $30–45 private room), but you really have to be a hostel kind of person to enjoy it. You can stay in a dorm room or pay extra for a private room, but you share the bathrooms and kitchen area. There's a shady courtyard, coin-operated laundry, and a common area with a piano; the staff is friendly and laid-back, and the house is centrally located downtown. The hostel has no air-conditioning, and as a result is closed during July and August. You may find it too hot to sleep there in June and September as well.

The **Budget Lodge Motel** (402 W. Van Buren, 602/254-7247, $45–89 d) is inexpensive and basic, though the neighborhood is a bit on the dodgy side.

$100-250
Downtown's big, beautiful **Hyatt Regency Phoenix** (122 N. 2nd St., 602/252-1234, www.hyatt.com, $139–289 d) is right in the beating heart of the city center, close to all the action. The towering hotel has three restaurants, an outdoor wading pool and hot tub,

and comfortable, high-style rooms. The most distinctive accommodation in the Valley is the historic **(Hotel San Carlos** (202 N. Central Ave., 602/253-4121, www.hotelsancarlos.com, $98–240 d), located right downtown with a facade that brings back the golden-age of big city hotels. As it was with other historic Arizona hotels, the San Carlos, opened in 1928, was a favorite stop of Hollywood stars during the first half of the 20th century, and was one of the first high-rise hotels in the Southwest with full air-conditioning and electric elevators. The hotel now celebrates its glory days with themed rooms and memorabilia. The rooms are comfortable and chic, and the whole place has a kind of over-stuffed retro-cool ambiance that you'll get nowhere else.

Families should consider the **Embassy Suites Phoenix-Biltmore** (2630 E. Camelback Rd., 602/955-3992, www.embassysuites.com, $89–199 d), conveniently located along the central Camelback corridor and offering affordable suites with refrigerators, TVs, and a lot of space; amenities include a pool and hot tub, free made-to-order breakfast, and a complimentary cocktail hour every night.

Over $250
The **Wyndham Phoenix Hotel** (50 E. Adams St., 602/333-0000, www.wyndham.com, $280–449) is downtown's biggest and nicest high-rise, right in the middle of everything and offering spacious, tasteful rooms—style, elegance, and haute comfort galore.

The **Ritz-Carlton** (2401 E. Camelback Rd., 602/468-0700, www.ritzcarlton.com, $349–429 d) along the Camelback Corridor is a gorgeous hotel with large, comfortable rooms and great views of the mountains and valley. It

© TIM HULL

Downtown's historic Hotel San Carlos opened in 1928.

has all the amenities one would expect for the price, including a truly spectacular pool area.

EAST VALLEY
$50-100

The **Twin Palms** (225 E. Apache Blvd., Tempe, 480/967-9431, www.twinpalmshotel.com, $79–159) right near Arizona State University is a good bargain; it has a pool, free high-speed Internet, complimentary breakfast, and access to ASU's huge fitness and recreation center. It's close to everything in Tempe and the East Valley and isn't too far from central Phoenix. The rooms are basic and comfortable, and each one has a refrigerator and a microwave. Another good bargain is the **Mezona Inn** (250 W. Main St., Mesa, 480/834-9233, www.mezonainn .com, $69–169 d), located in downtown Mesa, with a pool and clean, basic rooms.

$150-250

The 【 **Fiesta Inn** (2100 S. Priest Dr., Tempe, 480/967-1441, www.fiestaresrot.com, $149–189) in Tempe, a favorite among visiting ASU parents, isn't the only Valley hotel to call itself Frank Lloyd Wright–inspired, but it is certainly the most affordable. This sumptuous but not-

too-pricey resort has tasteful Old Southwest–style rooms and common areas, acres of saltillo tile, and sharp, rustic-looking decor all around. It has a big glistening blue pool, heated in the winter, a great restaurant and lounge with complimentary finger foods at happy hour, and service that rivals much pricier places.

Over $250

The **Tempe Mission Palms** (60 E. 5th St., Tempe, 480/894-1400, www.missionpalms.com, $259 d) in downtown Tempe is a beautiful property, with a huge pool and tennis courts on the roof overlooking the entire valley. It has its own cozy bar and restaurant, and is within walking distance to the shops and restaurants on Mill; the rooms have a Southwest style and the courtyards are lush and watered. This is the most luxurious place to stay in Tempe, and a bit less pricey than similarly appointed places in Phoenix.

WEST VALLEY

In Historic downtown Glendale the **Glendale Gaslight Inn** (5747 W. Glendale Ave., 623/934-9119, www.glendalegaslightinn.com, $99–349 d) is a charming, upscale place right in the middle of the increasingly popular West

THE VALLEY'S TOP FIVE RESORTS

The **Arizona Biltmore** (2400 E. Missouri Ave., Phoenix, 602/955-6600, www.arizonabiltmore.com), covering 39 acres at the base of the Phoenix Mountains, is the Valley's most famous, and still in most ways its best resort. Other places may come and go, but this Frank Lloyd Wright-inspired (and, many contend, designed – Wright received a consulting fee on the project) "Jewel of the Desert" just keeps getting better with age. There are 738 guest rooms, including one- and two-bedroom villas, eight swimming pools, seven tennis courts, two 18-hole golf courses at the country club next door, a spa, an enormous outdoor chess set, and four restaurants, including **Wright's at the Biltmore** (6 A.M.-10 P.M. daily). The Arizona Biltmore History Package ($238-437) is a great way to discover the resort; it includes a tour of the grounds, dinner, a night in one of the historic rooms, plus two tickets to Wright's Taliesin West.

The **Boulders Resort and Golden Door Spa** (34631 N. Tom Darlington Dr., Carefree, 480/488-9009, $119-749 d), out in the wild desert of Carefree, has been named America's top spa 14 years in a row, offering gorgeous suites, casitas, villas, and haciendas in a secluded setting outside of the city. It provides far and above the norm in comfort, style, and recreation. **The Phoenician** (6000 E. Camelback Rd., 480/941-8200, www.thephoenician.com, $365-775) along the Camelback corridor has an excellent golf course, high-end style, and a Center for Well-being. The **Royal Palms** (5200 E. Camelback Rd, 602/840-3610, www.royalpalmshotel.com), right by the Phoenician at the base of Camelback Mountain, is a lush hideout with all the amenities and then some. **The Fairmont Scottsdale Princess** (7575 E. Princess Dr., 480/585-4848, www.fairmont.com/scottsdale, $129-819 d) is a five-diamond resort in downtown Scottsdale with unbelievably comfortable and richly decorated rooms, suites, and casitas, as well as golf courses, three restaurants, and one of the top spas in the nation.

Valley shopping and dining district, offering several individually decorated rooms of various sizes, including some with kitchens. The inn offers wireless Internet throughout and serves up excellent pastries and coffee in your room every morning. There's a well-stocked and romantic wine bar on the premises with live jazz on the weekends.

At Glendale's huge new **Westgate** complex just a few miles west of historic downtown Glendale on Glendale Avenue, you'll find several big new chain hotels right next to two new stadiums—home of the NFL's Arizona Cardinals and the NHL's Phoenix Coyotes. The Westgate center also has a host of mid-range and upscale shopping and eating options, all conveniently located right next to the stadiums.

Food

In many ways, Phoenix and the Valley of the Sun began as clean slates, uncluttered by too much history and tradition, available for residents and visitors to scrawl on at will, creating amalgams and collages by cross-pollinating everything they've seen or heard or tasted before arriving in the desert. The new always finds a foothold here, right up until it is replaced by something else. This is especially true of the area's dining life. But while the details may be changing all the time, the lifestyle remains constant: creative and eclectic, with a particular dedication, like the Valley's residents now and throughout history, to fusion.

If none of the recommendations below appeal, the daily *Arizona Republic* keeps an excellent, up-to-the-second guide to the Valley's constantly changing dining scene on its website, www.azcentral.com/ent/dining/; and the alternative weekly *Phoenix New Times* (www.phoenixnewtimes.com) publishes entertaining and knowledgeable reviews and listings on Valley eateries.

It's always a good idea to call ahead and attempt to make a reservation, even though for most places you probably won't need one; this is especially smart in the Valley, where you may have to drive a ways through busy traffic to get anywhere. At most of the area's fancier places, reservations are recommended, if not required. Only the highest-end restaurants are going to have anything approaching a dress code, and that is usually business casual for the most part, but with a jacket. The vast majority of Valley hosts and hostesses won't bat an eye at your jeans or even your flip-flops, especially during summer.

DOWNTOWN AND CENTRAL
Fine Dining

Even if the New American creations at **Wright's at the Biltmore** (2400 East Missouri Ave., 602/381-7632, www.arizonabiltmore.com/dining/wrights.asp, 6–10 P.M. daily, 11 A.M.–2 P.M. Sun. brunch, $20–40), the famous resort's signature restaurant, weren't consistently memorable, the interior, stamped with the etched-concrete block soul of Frank Lloyd Wright, would still require a visit from restaurant connoisseurs. The five-course tasting menu ($76 per person), while pricey, provides the best opportunity to dig deep into the restaurant's charms. The best main courses are usually fresh river fish with some sort of fabulous, native materials–built sauce. Reservations are a good idea.

For well-prepared and inspired French-style food try James Beard Award–winning Chef Christopher Gross's **Christopher's Fermier Brasserie** (2584 E. Camelback Rd., 602/522-2344, www.fermier.com, lunch and

dinner daily, $6.95–13 lunch, $16–32 dinner), at Biltmore Fashion park along the Camelback Corridor. The truffle-infused filet mignon ($32) makes one weak at the knees. The tasting menu ($60 per person) is relatively affordable and comes with appetizers, main course, cheese, and dessert. Christopher's is more affordable as a lunch destination, and the food is simpler but just as good—mostly sandwiches, soups, pasta dishes, and wood-fired pizzas, which you can also get at **Paolo's Wine Bar** inside the restaurant, a stylish place to try a wide variety of wines while nibbling on all kinds of different cheeses and sliding down fresh oysters.

Steaks and Chops

Durant's Fine Foods (Central and Virginia, 602/264-5967 www.durantsfinefoods.com, 11 A.M.–10 P.M. Mon.–Thurs., 11 A.M.–11 P.M. Fri., 5–11 P.M. Sat., 4:30–10 P.M. Sun., $9–20 lunch, $21–67 dinner) downtown is the archetypal retro-haute steak house and lounge, where you can get a juicy slice of prime rib, a perfectly cooked steak, and an expert martini served by a professional, tuxedoed wait staff. Durant's has been serving the same food in the same location for more than 50 years and has a loyal following, so you'll probably want to get reservations.

Mexican

Aunt Chilada's Squaw Peak (7330 N. Dreamy Draw Dr., 602/944-1286, www.auntchiladas.com, lunch, dinner, and bar daily, $5.50–11.95) serves delicious Mexican food in an historic building in the shadow of the Phoenix Mountains. **Los Dos Molinos** (1010 E. Washington St., 602/528-3535, 11 A.M.–2:30 P.M. and 5–9 P.M. Tues.–Fri., 11 A.M.–9 P.M. Sat., closed Sun.–Mon.) downtown has a fun, cluttered atmosphere and basic Northern Mexico favorites.

The **Barrio Café** (2814 N. 16th St., 602/636-0240, www.barriocafe.com, 11 A.M.–10 P.M. Tues.–Thurs., 11 A.M.–10:30 P.M. Fri., 5–10:30 P.M. Sat., 11 A.M.–9 P.M.

Sun., brunch 11 A.M.–3 P.M., closed Mon., $8–14) gets quite a bit more creative, serving a rare (for Arizona) modern Mexican cuisine from many different regions. This is not the place for chimichangas and chicken enchiladas. Try the slow roasted pork, and somebody at the table should order Oaxacan black mole, one of Mexico's famous sauces created by nun-chefs in the 19th century. The bar has over 200 different varieties of tequila.

Irish Pub

Downtown's **Seamus McCaffery's** (18 W. Monroe, 602/253-6081, www.seamus mccaffreys.com, lunch and dinner daily, $5–12), right below the San Carlos Hotel, has excellent fish and chips and pours a perfect pint of Guinness. This is a friendly, laid-back place for lunch, dinner, or drinking.

Italian and Pizza

Another Valley winner of the prestigious James Beard Award, Chris Bianco operates **Pizzeria Bianco** (623 E. Adams St. at Heritage Square, 602/258-8300, www.pizzeriabianco.com, 5–10 P.M. Tues.–Sat., $6–14) out of a historic brick building at downtown's Heritage Square. The pizza is the best in the Valley, and, according to many critics, the best in the nation as well. This is a small, romantic and very hip place, and it takes a while to get a table and an equal while to get your pizza. It is all without a doubt worth it. Go here if you love pizza; you'll be sorry to miss it. Next door **Bar Bianco** (602/528-3699, 4–11 P.M. Tues.–Sat.) has a wide selection of wine and a warm atmosphere, with picnic tables on a grassy, candlelit patio; and over on Central **Pane Bianco** (4404 N. Central Ave., 602/234-2100, 11 A.M.–3 P.M. Tues.–Sat., $2–8) has outdoor tables and takeout sandwiches, like the house-made mozzarella with tomato and basil, and tuna and red onions.

In the Arcadia neighborhood along the

© TIM HULL

Another Valley of the Sun winner of the prestigious James Beard Award, Chris Bianco operates Pizzeria Bianco out of a historic brick building at downtown's Heritage Square.

Camelback Corridor some of the best Italian food in the Valley is served at **Daniel's Italian Cuisine** (4225 E. Camelback Rd., 602/952-1522, 5–10 P.M. Mon.–Sat., $8.95–13.95), which has a romantic courtyard and delicious, rather unexpected entrées.

Asian

Sing High Chop Suey House (27 W. Madison St., 602/253-7848, lunch and dinner daily, $8–13), holding on to its romantic Old West name, is the oldest Chinese place in the Valley, operated by the same family for more than 70 years in what used to be Phoenix's Chinatown long ago. The dishes here are consistently good, all the basics and some surprises, too. The **Silver Dragon Chinese Restaurant** (8946 N. 19th Ave., 602/674-0151, 11 A.M.–9:30 P.M. Mon., Tues., and Thurs., 11 A.M.–10 P.M. Fri. and Sun., 4:30–10 P.M. Sat., closed Wed., $8–13) has a familiar Americanized menu that's pretty tasty, but also serves an alternative selection of more traditional and authentic Chinese fare (ask the waitstaff).

Vegetarian

◖ **Supreme Master Ching Hai Vegetarian House** (3239 E. Indian School Rd., 602/264-3480, www.veggiehouse.com, 11 A.M.–2:30 P.M. and 5–9 P.M. Tues.–Sat., closed Sun.–Mon., $5.50–10) is 100 percent vegan but you wouldn't know it unless they told you so. The delicious and spicy Asian-style dishes are prepared with all kinds of faux-meat protein that really adds flavor and zest to the dishes. Vegetarians, especially vegans, will be in ecstasy here.

EAST VALLEY
Fine Dining

The strange New Native American cuisine at **Kai** (5594 West Wild Horse Pass Blvd., 602/385-5726, www.wildhorsepassresort.com, dinner Tues.–Sat., $20–53), one of the most unusual five-star restaurants in the West, seems at first completely foreign, but one soon realizes that most of the foreign-sounding ingredients are actually as native as can be. Indeed, the chefs at Kai, which means "seed" in the local O'odham language, are so dedicated to the local food revolution that they serve baby lettuce hand-picked by children from the Gila River Indian Reservation. The menu is fascinating, and the interior is proof that Native American motifs can be made new and surprising again.

Cafés

You'll likely see a few hung-over A.S.U. students trying to quell their head-fire in bacon grease at **Harlow's Café** (1021 W. University Dr., 480/829-9444, 7 A.M.–2 P.M. daily, $5–8), a favorite and filling greasy spoon in Tempe. Head here for no-frills, short-order comfort food for breakfast or lunch. Special fans of the genre should definitely visit.

Burgers and Steaks

Monti's La Casa Vieja (100 South Mill Ave., 480/967-7594, www.montis.com, 11 A.M.–10 P.M. Sun.–Thurs., 11 A.M.–11 P.M. Fri.–Sat., $11.95–25) occupies the oldest standing building in Tempe, across from the now-closed flower mill and ferry stop that gave the riverside suburb its life in the early days. Monti's has atmosphere to spare; good steaks, burgers, and prime rib; and a crowded, fun cantina. Another Valley favorite is **Rustler's Rooste** (8383 S. 48th St., 602/431-6474, www.rustlers rooste.com, 5–10 P.M. daily, $14.95–29.95), a cowboy-style steakhouse that seeks to re-create a rough-hewn ranch mess-hall near South Mountain. Here you'll get pots of cowboy beans and steaming ears of corn, thick steaks, as well as an always-celebratory atmosphere and expansive views of the desert and city. This place is great for families and has a relatively inexpensive kids' menu offering small steaks and ribs. If you're just visiting Arizona, this may be your one chance to try fried rattlesnake.

You won't find many handcrafted

microbrews better than the varieties served at **Four Peaks Brewing Company** (1340 E. 8th St., 480/303-9967, www.fourpeaks.com, 11 A.M.–2 A.M. Mon.–Sat., 10 A.M. Sunday brunch, happy hour 3–7 P.M. and 10 P.M.–close daily, $7.50–17), near campus in Tempe, and the pub eats and entrées—burgers, sandwiches, pizzas, and some really excellent starters—are equally good. The happy hour features cheap appetizers and drinks and is always a fun time.

Middle Eastern

☾ Haji-Baba Middle Eastern Food (1513 E. Apache Blvd., 480/894-1905, 11 A.M.–8 P.M. Mon.–Sat., noon–5 P.M. Sun. takeout only, $5–8), a storefront in a strip mall just south of the ASU campus in Tempe, serves without a doubt the best Middle Eastern food in Arizona. The baba ghanoush is amazing, as are the hummus, gyros, kabobs, and falafel. The place is laid-back and casual, with a bustling grocery store operating behind a thin partition; it's often packed, and the service can be a bit lackadaisical, but the food is perfect and cheap.

Italian

Caffe Boa (398 S. Mill Ave., 480/968-9112, www.cafeboa.com, 11 A.M.–10 P.M. Sun.–Wed., 11 A.M.–11 P.M. Thurs.–Sat. $7.95–30) serves the East Valley's best Italian and Mediterranean food in an intimate setting in the busy Mill Avenue District. The panini here are particularly good for lunch, and there's a new dinner menu every month, always featuring delectable and creative pasta dishes grounded in tradition.

Indian and Vegetarian

Perhaps the best Indian food in the state is served out of the **Delhi Palace** (933 E. University Dr. #103, 480/921-2200, www .indiandelhipalace.com, 5–10 P.M. daily, 11:30 A.M.–2:30 P.M. lunch buffet Mon.–Fri., 11:30 A.M.–4:30 P.M. Sat.–Sun., $5–15) near A.S.U., offering the well-known dishes prepared well; the service can be patchy, but you will never leave unsatisfied, especially after partaking in the buffet.

The **Udupi Café** (1636 N. Scottsdale Rd., 480/994-8787, www.udupicafeaz.com, 11 A.M.–3 P.M. and 5–9:30 P.M. Sun., Mon., Wed., Thurs., $5–15) serves rather different Indian fare, dishes that may be unfamiliar to haunters of American-style Indian joints exclusively. If you're feeling a bit experimental, though, this is the place to go. Some 80 percent of the food here is vegan, so those brave souls will want to go crazy.

Mexican

The food at **Casa Reynoso** (3138 S. Mill Ave., 480/966-0776, 11 A.M.–8:30 P.M., Tues.–Thurs., 11 A.M.–9:30 P.M., Fri.–Sat., 11 A.M.–8 P.M. Sun., closed Mon., $20–40) is prepared from old family recipes passed down from an older place in the Central Arizona mining region of Globe-Miami. The Mexican food here is a bit more authentic than your average chimichanga hut, and the hacienda-style building gives the place an Old Mexico aura that makes for a fun night out just slightly north of the border.

WEST VALLEY

If you're in the northwest Valley around breakfast time don't miss **Kiss the Cook Restaurant** (4915 W. Glendale Ave., 623/939-4663, 6 A.M.–3 P.M. Mon.–Fri., 7 A.M.–3 P.M. Sat., 7 A.M.–1 P.M. Sun., $5–8), which serves the old American favorites in an antique-shop interior.

Try the authentic and tasty German food (and don't miss the beer garden) at Valley favorite **Haus Murphys** (5739 W. Glendale Ave., 623/939-2480, www.hausmurphys .com, 11 A.M.–2 P.M. and 5–9 P.M. Tues.–Fri., 11 A.M.–4 P.M. and 5–9 P.M. Sat., 3–8 P.M. Sun., $9–17).

Scottsdale and the North Valley

Scottsdale suffers somewhat from its reputation as being high-toned, high-dollar, and maybe even a little pretentious. This isn't the case, however, in most corners of the always-growing city, which has won numerous national awards for being generally livable, clean, and attractive. It's true that you see more Hummers and Beemers within Scottsdale's city limits than in other parts of the Valley (save Paradise Valley just to the north, a mostly residential community that is one of the richest in the nation), but a day's visit here will likely reveal that there is much more to Scottsdale than beautiful rich people and their high-walled resorts.

SIGHTS
Downtown

Visitors to Scottsdale, a citrus-growing suburb turned international resort destination and art center, primarily come to stroll, shop, and eat in the city's bustling downtown area, which includes Old Town, Fifth Avenue, and the Arts District (www.downtownscottsdale.com), among others. There are dozens of Native American and Western Art galleries and trading posts, boutiques selling Southwestern-style items both authentic and touristy, contemporary art galleries with a flair for the most current styles, restaurants from hamburger huts to highbrow gourmet, and lots of coffeehouses and cool watering holes.

The downtown is roughly defined by Chaparral Road on the north, Osborn Road on the south, Miller Road to the east and 68th Street on the west. Within these general boundaries there are several distinct districts, though they all kind of meld into one another. The attractions here are art-searching, shopping and window-peering, eating and drinking, and general strolling and people-watching. In the Arts District, between Goldwater Boulevard and Scottsdale Road, you'll find a collection of art galleries to rival any other

artsy block in the Southwest, home to a popular Art Walk every Thursday night. On scenic Fifth Avenue you'll find more than 80 boutiques and shops selling mostly Southwestern and Native American items. Here you'll also find **Bob Parks' Horse Fountain,** a collection of dramatic equestrian statues jumping out of a huge fountain. The nearby Arizona Canal has been the site recently of a revitalization, with several new shopping centers bustling with credit-card carriers. Between Indian School Road and 2nd Street, just east of Scottsdale Road and west of Brown Avenue is Old Town Scottsdale, where you'll find some of the older buildings in downtown. Like all of the other districts in downtown Scottsdale, however, unless you are searching for art, shopping, eating, drinking, or just watching other people do so, there's not much else to do.

Scottsdale Museum of Contemporary Art

It's fitting that the only art museum in Arizona dedicated strictly to the new and the now is in Scottsdale, one of the magnetic centers of art in the Southwest. You won't find any howling coyotes or Kokopelli here; the works are edgy, sometimes confusingly avant-garde, and always interesting. **SmoCA** (7374 East 2nd Street, 480/994-2787, www.smoca.org, 10 A.M.–5 P.M. Tues.–Wed., 10 A.M.–8 P.M. Thurs., 10 A.M.–5 P.M., Fri.–Sat., noon–5 P.M. Sun., $7 adults, $5 students, kids under 15 free, admission free Thurs.) is located just across the street from the Center for the Arts and has five galleries in a spare, modern space that used to be a movie theater. Special shows and exhibitions rotate often and there's always at least one gallery showing work from the museum's permanent collection.

◖ Taliesin West

Architect Frank Lloyd Wright spent the money

© TIM HULL

Architect Frank Lloyd Wright spent many years constructing his winter quarters (Taliesin West) in the desert north of Scottsdale.

he made from his masterpiece **Falling Water** on a large swath of desert northeast of Scottsdale, and from about 1937 onward he spent a portion of each year living in the desert with his apprentices and building what would become **Taliesin West** (12621 Frank Lloyd Wright Blvd., 480/860-2700, recorded tour info 480/860-8810, www.franklloydwright.org, 8:30 A.M.–5:30 P.M.). If every house built in the desert used the natural landscape in the same way as this wondrous complex does, the Valley would be a very different, better place today. Familiar Wright motifs, like his ubiquitous compression-and-release entranceways, Oriental touches, and native-rock-and-mortar aesthetic, are on display at this truly unique and important attraction.

You can only see Taliesin by tour, but the guides are knowledgeable and very enthusiastic about Wright's work and legacy. Since the complex is still used and lived in today by fellows of Taliesin Associated Architects, a group carrying on the spirit of Wright's work, some buildings may be off limits during a tour. There are several tours to choose from, including an in-depth, three-hour, behind-the-scenes look around ($45). The most popular tour is the 90-minute **Insights Tour** (9 A.M.–4 P.M. daily, every half-hour Nov. –Apr., every hour

May.–Oct., $32) which includes a look at the beautiful Garden Room and the living quarters as well as all of the sights included in the one-hour **Panorama Tour** (10:15 A.M., 12:15 P.M., and 2:15 P.M. daily, $27). They change the tour schedules sometimes, so it's a good idea to call before you go. Arrive a little early so you can check out the excellent bookstore and gift shop, which sells Frank Lloyd Wright–inspired knickknacks and just about every book ever published by or on the master.

Carefree and Cave Creek

Drive north on Scottsdale Road (about 15 miles from Phoenix) through a beautiful, if disappearing, stretch of desert to these tiny resort-style towns full of galleries, antique stores, restaurants, and artisan shops—a perfect daylong escapade to the Valley's northeastern outer reaches. Along the way, watch for the large signs on the side of the road pointing out various representative Sonoran Desert flora. In late February, the **Carefree Fine Art & Wine Festival** attracts artists, artisans, and wine-lovers from across the nation. This drive is very popular with motorcycle groups, and on any given weekend (though not so much in the summer) the area is likely to be somewhat crowded.

FOOD AND ACCOMMODATIONS

Don't leave this area without stopping for lunch or dinner at **⟨** **El Encanto** (6248 E. Cave Creek Rd., 480/488-1752, lunch and dinner daily, $5–16), serving what is perhaps the Valley's best Mexican food from comfortable booths that look out on a Spanish-style enclosed courtyard with a pond, atop which elegant swans lazily float. Try the prickly-pear margarita—sweet and delicious with a perfect kick.

Not surprisingly, this mid- to high-end burg has not a few bed-and-breakfasts. If you feel like spending a few nights out in the semi-wild desert, where it's at least five degrees cooler than the citified valley and the sky is dark and starry at night, try **Sleepy Hollow Bed & Breakfast** (5522 E. Tapekim Rd., Cave Creek, 480/488-9402), offering two rooms and a suite in a beautiful desert setting, with a patio area with an outdoor fireplace. The **Spur Cross Bed & Breakfast** (38555 N. School House Rd., Cave Creek, 480/473-1038, www.spurcrossbnb.com, $139–400) rents four nice rooms with outside entrances and has a hot tub and wireless Internet.

Recreation

Scottsdale is a bit greener than many desert cities, and there are quite a few parks and open spaces within the relatively small area of the town. One of the best of these is the long multi-use trail that winds through the center of the mostly residential neighborhoods along Hayden Road from Indian Bend Road south to Tempe—about 13 miles of greenspace for bikers, joggers, walkers, and skaters called the **Indian Bend Wash Greenbelt** (Scottsdale Parks and Recreation, 7340 Scottsdale Mall, 480/312-7957, www.scottsdaleaz.gov). Along this unique flood-control system, which channels intermittent desertland floods—mostly in the late summer monsoon season—into Indian Bend Wash while at the same time creating a fine exercise and recreation belt through the length of the town, you'll see a steady stream of bikers, in-line skaters, and joggers, especially in the mornings. The path passes through several city parks and golf courses as it makes its way south all the way to Tempe Town Lake. There's not really a set-aside, signed starting block for the Greenbelt, but a good place to pick it up is at **Chaparral Park** (5401 N. Hayden Rd., 480/312-2353).

If you'd like to get out of the city a bit and into the desert, head out to the **McDowell Mountain Regional Park** (16300 McDowell Mountain Park Dr., 480/471-0173, www.maricopa.gov/parks/mcdowell), a 21,000-acre desert preserve northeast of Scottsdale proper with miles of desert hiking, biking, and equestrian trails. This is an excellent setting for getting to know the Sonoran Desert. To get to the park from Scottsdale, take Shea Boulevard east to Fountain Hills Boulevard, which heads north and turns into McDowell Mountain Road leading into the park. If you've got some extra time think about stopping in the retirement haven of Fountain Hills and seeing the world's biggest fountain; continue on Shea past Fountain Hills Boulevard and then turn north on Saguaro Boulevard, which will take you right past **Fountain Park** and **The Fountain,** and then meets with Fountain Hills Boulevard, which leads to the preserve.

Inside the park, there are various trails for hiking and biking and horseback riding; one of the more popular short hikes is the three-mile North Trail. The 15-mile Pemberton Trail is the toughest and longest hike in the park.

GOLF

There are about 200 golf courses in the Valley of the Sun, and about 50 of them are in Scottsdale, a town as famous for its golf as for its galleries and resorts. You'll likely find the golf courses in Scottsdale to be a bit more challenging and considerably more beautiful and dramatic than those in surrounding communities, but they are also considerably more expensive. But for a true golf lover, this is where you'll want to splurge.

Kierland Golf Club (15636 N. Clubgate Dr., 480/922-9283, www.kierlandgolf.com) is a gorgeous 27-hole, par-36 desert course along Scottsdale Road just south of Frank Lloyd Wright Boulevard. It's part of the Weston

Kierland Resort and Spa but is open to the public. The greens are shocking against the hard desert scenery, which has been left to itself along the edges of the greenery, making for a uniquely Arizona golfing experience. It's not cheap. It'll cost you about $210 per person in the high season, and about $85 per person during the hottest days the summer. The course offers some twilight hour prices that are significantly cheaper, however. You can book a tee time online, and it's recommended that you do so before traveling if you want to play any of Scottsdale's courses.

The fabulous **Troon North Golf Club** (10320 E. Dynamite Blvd., 480/585-5300, www.troonnorthgolf.com) in the far northeast Valley is a much-sought-after golfing experience for duffers the world over. It's probably the most beautiful public course in the Valley, though one could say that about many fairways here. There are two courses at the club, both lined with desert boulders and saguaro; the Monument Course, the better of the two, is so named because of the 14-foot boulder rising off the fairway. Expect to pay at least $155 per person in the high season.

Starfire at Scottsdale Country Club (11500 N. Hayden Rd., 480/948-6000, www.starfiregolfclub.com) is a more centrally located course—head north on Hayden Road and you'll find it—and more reasonably priced than some of the fancier desert courses north of the city. The 27-hole course, lined with eucalyptus and palm trees, was designed by Arnold Palmer and is moderately challenging. Expect to pay about $50 per person during the high season.

TPC of Scottsdale (17020 N. Hayden Rd., 480/585-4334, http://tpc.com/scottsdale/index.html) is where the PGA pros play one of the most popular tournaments of the year in late January; the **FBR Open** (www.phoenixopen.com), formerly the Phoenix Open, is one of the oldest tournaments on the pro tour and draws some of the biggest crowds of any tournament. In the off-season you're likely to see one of the local PGA tour members practicing here. You'll find two exquisite, famous courses—one of them, the Champion's Course, was completely remodeled in 2007. The Scottsdale Princess Resort is linked with the course, and to stay and play here is to engage in the height of luxury and challenging golf, but it's going to cost you. Greens fees will run you about $260 per person in the high season, and about $75 in the deep summer, with discounts for evening play.

ENTERTAINMENT AND EVENTS

Scottsdale is somewhat known as a playground for the beautiful and the rich, and it is that in some quarters—a meat market with a premium on the tanned and tightened, dancing to repetitious beats and peeking into debauched VIP rooms to catch some minor celebrity. But there are a lot of down-to-earth watering holes and scenes here too. Last call is usually 2 A.M., per the state legislature, but many bars and clubs stay open for hours afterward, offering late-night menus and after-hours fun. Dress is generally casual, unless you're going to the highest of the high-end places. Most of the restaurants listed under the Food section double as nightspots as well.

Nightlife

In Scottsdale's Old Town district, **Martini Ranch** (7295 E. Stetson Dr., 480/970-0500, www.martiniranchaz.net) attracts a mid- to upscale crowd, featuring live, mostly local music on its stage, and lots of scantily dressed young women dancing with cologne-scented young men in **The Shaker Room,** a nightclub with DJs and risqué theme nights.

The height of rich and hip Scottsdale nightlife has got to be **The Red Bar and Skybar at the Mondrian Scottsdale** (7959 E. Indian School Rd., www.mondrianscottsdale.com), two enchanting and artfully decorated nightclubs with outdoor patios with fireplaces and covered, secluded cabanas. The best place to see what's really going on in the local music scene is **Club Mardi Gras & VooDoo Lounge** (8040 E. McDowell Rd., 480/970-5707, www.myspace.com/mardigrasbar), a laid-back, unpretentious spot where local musicians are, according to the *Phoenix New Times,* carrying on the desert-rock traditions that made the Valley a pop hotspot in the 1990s, when bands like Gin Blossoms and The Refreshments attracted national audiences. Club Mardi Gras also has DJs and dancing, karaoke, and comedy shows.

Performing Arts

The **Scottsdale Center for the Performing Arts** (7380 E. Second St., 480/994-2787, www.scottsdaleperformingarts.org) is a huge complex of theaters, classrooms, and grassy knolls right downtown. Inside, the **Virginia G. Piper Theater** and a few smaller spaces nearby host a wide range of theater, dance, comedy, and music—mostly classical and jazz. Acts like Laurie Anderson and Arlo Guthrie have performed here, as have jazz legend Dave Brubeck and many others.

Festivals and Events

More than 100 artists, many of them internationally known in art circles, participate in the popular **Arizona Fine Art Expo** (www.arizonafineartexpo.com) from January through March, during which you can stroll in and out of galleries and cabanas set up streetside and watch the artists at work. Also in January, the famous **Barrett-Jackson Antique Auto Auction** (www.barrett-jackson.com) gets under way, selling auction-style the most expensive and spectacular automobiles in existence. Hundreds of white tents go up at Scottsdale Road and the Loop 101 from January through March for the **Celebration of Fine Art** (www.celebrateart.com), while inside juried artists create their works before your eyes and sell them directly.

The **Scottsdale Arabian Horse Show** (www.scottsdaleshow.com) brings equestrian enthusiasts from all over the world to town in February, and in March the **Scottsdale Arts Festival** (www.scottsdaleperformingarts.org) attracts about 10,000 visitors to the Scottsdale Center for the Performing Arts for three days of art sales, demonstrations, and performances.

In April, just before it starts to get hot, the shining stars of the eating scene gather for the **Scottsdale Culinary Festival** (www.scottsdaleculinaryfestival.org).

SHOPPING

If you're a serious shopper with serious money don't miss the upscale centers for which this part of the Valley is famous. Even if you don't have sacks of money, it's fun to walk around these always well-landscaped and fashionable shopping centers, bustling with beautiful people and stocked with luxury items from all over the globe, to get an idea of how the other one percent lives. Scottsdale's busy downtown areas provide the best shopping in town, and nearby **Scottsdale Fashion Square** (7014 E. Camelback Rd., 480/945-5495) is the largest enclosed mall in the Southwest, featuring high-end department stores, boutiques, and restaurants.

The **Borgata** (Scottsdale Rd. and Lincoln, 602/953-6311, www.borgata.com, 10 A.M.–7 P.M. Mon.–Sat., noon–6 P.M. Sun.) is an upscale shopping center with dozens of shops and boutiques featuring high-end shoes, clothing, and accessories; there are several galleries and home-decor shops with handcrafted artisan furniture and many one-of-a-kind finds. **Kierland Commons** (Scottsdale Rd. and Greenway Pkwy., 480/348-1577, www.kierlandcommons.com, 10 A.M.–9 P.M. Mon.–Sat., noon–6 P.M. Sun.) has about 70 upmarket shops and eateries, including **Anthropologie, Restoration Hardware,** and **Crate & Barrel.**

The **Shops at Gainey Village** (Scottsdale Rd. and Doubletree, 480/609-6909, www.theshopsgaineyvillage.com, 10 A.M.–6 P.M. Mon.–Sat., noon–6 P.M. Sun.) is perhaps the most stylish of them all, featuring unique boutiques (including a shop for the ultra-pampered dog in your family), interior design shops, furniture stores with custom-made items you won't find anywhere else but you'll have to pay dearly for, contemporary art galleries, and even, because this is Scottsdale, a shop selling "baby couture."

ACCOMMODATIONS

In Scottsdale, world-class accommodations and pampering are available to a great degree, but only to those who have the resources to buy them; those who don't, however, can still find a middle ground here, and there's even a few places for the budget-minded traveler. If you don't mind braving the heat, summer prices at the top resorts and getaways dip down into the real world.

$50-100

The **Motel 6 Scottsdale** (6848 E. Camelback Rd., 480/946-2280, www.motel6.com, $69–85) is located right downtown and close to everything; it features a pool ringed by palm trees and a breakfast place where it's hard to get a table on the weekends. The **Comfort Suites** (3275 Civic Center Blvd., 480/946-1111, www .comfortinn.com, $60–85) is also centrally located and one of the few options here for the budget-minded traveler looking for something clean, basic, and comfortable.

$100-250

The **3 Palms** (7707 E. McDowell Rd., 888/444-4683, www.scottsdale-resort-hotels .com, $83–342 d) is one of the middle-brow resort-style accommodations in Scottsdale, offering most of the comforts and style of the more expensive places with just a slightly less ritzy sheen. This boutique hotel has cool contemporary interior design in all the rooms, and a large pool area perfect for lounging in the hot sun while sipping drinks. Another relatively affordable place is the **Chaparral Suites Resort** (5001 N. Scottsdale Rd., 480/949-1414, www.chaparral suites.com, $109–229 d), which has comfortable rooms and a lush central courtyard and pool area. The **FireSky Resort & Spa** (4925 N. Scottsdale Rd., 480/945-7666, www .fireskyresort.com, $109–369 d) is a sumptuous, garden-like place downtown with all kinds of secluded and secret spots—lagoons and hot tubs and cozy cabanas—leather chairs and flat-screen TVs in the rooms, and a full-service spa.

Over $250

The ◖ **Hotel Valley Ho** (6850 E. Main St., 480/248-2000 www.hotelvalleyho.com, $250–350 d) recalls the days of the mid-20th-century high-end hipster style, with a Trader Vics on-site and rooms decorated like Frank Sinatra's pad in *The Tender Trap.* The **Mondrian Scottsdale** (7353 East Indian School Rd., 480/308-1100, www.mondrian scottsdale.com, $295–495 d) is a playpen for the rich and famous, or just the rich and glamorous, with rooms like art installations and courtyards behind its high city walls that hold manicured jungles and oasis hideaways; service, food, and spa treatments here match the world's top destinations. You definitely get what you pay for.

FOOD

Scottsdale has many of the Valley's most posh restaurants, and the scene is always changing and evolving. You'll find enough variety here to make your head and your palate spin. It's not all high-toned and intimidating, though; most of the best restaurants here are serious about food and design and service, but they don't take themselves too seriously. Many of Scottsdale's restaurants serve late-night menus and have busy bars as well as packed dining rooms. Reservations are always a good idea.

Brunch

Mickey's Hangover Lounge (4312 N. Brown Ave., 480/425-0111, www.mickeyshangover .com, 4 P.M.–2 A.M. Mon.–Wed., 4 P.M.–3 A.M. Thurs., 4 P.M.–4 A.M. Fri., 10 A.M.–4 A.M. Sat., 10 A.M.–3 P.M. brunch Sat.–Sun., $5–13) is a thrift store–chic clubhouse downtown where you'll always hear Bob Marley on the stereo and where you can order a jug of Mad Dog 20/20 ($10) and put your feet up on the coffee table. If you're not a happy and healthy dissipater (and especially if you are), try Mickey's for brunch on weekends. It serves tasty and creative entrées based on the classic brunch dishes and concocts some of the Valley's best mimosas and Bloody Marys.

American

Cowboy Ciao (7133 E. Stetson Dr., 480/946-3111, www.cowboyciao.com, $10–30, 11:30 A.M.–2:30 P.M. daily, and 5–10 P.M. Sun.–Thurs., 5–11 P.M. Fri.–Sat., $10–30), a standout among Scottsdale's posh eateries, relishes fusions, mixing Italian motifs with cowboy-camp and Old West wood and metal, and serving strange, enticing dishes like elk strip loin and mushroom pan fry. Its take on the grilled cheese, adding brie and pickled tomatoes, is worth the trip itself. The salads and soups here are also particularly good.

AZ 88 (7353 Scottsdale Mall, 480/994-5576, 11:30 A.M.–12:30 A.M. Mon.–Fri., 5 P.M.–12:30 A.M. Sat.–Sun., $7.50–15.50) is an ultra-cool lounge and restaurant with delicious, simple dishes like hamburgers and chicken sandwiches, DJs spinning many nights, and consistently interesting art on the walls, changed out regularly.

Steaks and Chops

Reata Pass Steakhouse (27500 N. Alma School Pkwy., 480/585-7277, 11 A.M.–9 P.M. Tues.–Thurs., 11 A.M.–11 P.M. Fri.–Sat., noon–9 P.M. Sun., closed Mon., $8.95–33.95) is another of Arizona's cowboy-style steakhouses, with rustic, Old West interiors and picnic tables holding beans, corn, ribs, and steaks; these places are always fun, especially for kids. On the site of what used to be a stagecoach stop in the McDowell Mountains, Reata Pass bills itself as the most authentic of the bunch. A more elegant, but still comfortably casual protein-rich meal can be had at Valley favorite **Don & Charlie's** (7501 E. Camelback Rd., 480/990-0900, www.azeats.com/DonAndCharlies/default2. htm, 5–9:30 P.M. Mon.–Sat., 5–9 P.M. Sun., $10.95–44.95), a Chicago-style, old school steakhouse with great prime rib and even better ribs. Pâté and crackers are served when you sit down, and you'll be mesmerized away from the menu by all the unmatched sports memorabilia covering the walls.

Southwestern

Downtown's **Old Town Tortilla Factory** (6910 E. Main St., 480/945-4567, www.oldtown tortillafactory.com, 5–9 P.M. Sun.–Thurs., 5–10 P.M. Fri.–Sat., $12.95–30.95) has an enchanting patio and serves gourmet Southwestern-style creations with pork, fish, chicken, shrimp, and beef. The tortillas are made on-site, come in several different flavors, and are served hot and fresh. The **Tequilaria** inside has shelves of tequila and makes great margaritas. For Southwestern food with a New Mexican flair try **Carlsbad Tavern and Restaurant** (3313 N. Hayden Rd., 480/970-8164, www.carlsbadtavern. com, 11 A.M.–2 A.M. daily, $8–20), where green chilies take over the menu and bats take over the decor. Carlsbad serves hamburgers and sandwiches as well as New Mexican–style dishes.

Seafood

The **Salt Cellar** (550 N. Hayden Rd., 480/947-1963, 5–11 P.M. Mon.–Thurs., 5 P.M.–midnight Fri.–Sat., $19.95–35.95), which actually feels like it's in a cellar, though a very nice one, serves the freshest, best-prepared, top-shelf but not pretentious seafood in the Valley. You can even get five pounds of live Maine lobster ($95) if you so desire.

Polynesian

The interior design at ◖ **Drift Polynesian Restaurant and Tiki Lounge** (4341 N. 75th St., 480/949-8454, 11:30 A.M.–midnight daily, $7–18) is worth a stop in itself, recalling the Tiki-style of the 1960s with an updated grooviness. The food is surprising and delicious; the drinks are umbrella-topped, fruit-filled, and dangerous. The best time to go is during happy hour (4–7 P.M. Mon.–Fri.), when the pu pu platters are flaming and the pink and blue icy drinks are flowing.

Japanese

Sushi on Shea (7000 E. Shea Blvd. #1510, 480/483-7799, www.sushionshea.com, 11 A.M.–11 P.M. daily, $8–20) serves excellent sushi at affordable prices and has hypnotizing fish tanks throughout.

INFORMATION

While you're downtown, stop by the **Scottsdale Convention & Visitors Bureau** (4343 N. Scottsdale Rd. Suite #170, 480/421-1004, www.scottsdalecvb.com) at the Galleria Corporate Center on the corner of Drinkwater and Stetson Avenues for all the Scottsdale-related information and literature you'll ever want. Parking is available either on the street or in the parking structure east of the entrance. Each downtown district runs into the next and is easy to walk to, and there's a **free trolley** (11 A.M.–9 P.M. daily, runs every 10 minutes) that will take you all around the downtown area if you don't like to walk.

GETTING THERE AND AROUND

The best way to get from Phoenix to Scottsdale is to take one of the surface streets east from downtown; that way you'll get to see more of the ground-level city instead of breezing past everything on the freeways. If you take Camelback Road east from downtown Phoenix you'll run right into downtown Scottsdale. If you're heading from Scottsdale to Tempe, take Scottsdale Road south and you'll run right into the college town.

Around the Valley of the Sun

On the far eastern edge of the spreading cityscape, the desert holds a strong line in the Tonto National Forest. In this cactus, creosote, and mesquite wilderness, dashed with fallen slabs and boulders covered in faded-green dry lichen, you will experience the real Central Arizona outback, a rugged and storied stretch of the upper Sonoran Desert. If you have an SUV or a similarly high vehicle (or even, most of the time, a regular car), don't hesitate to drive the Apache Trail (Route 88), a mostly dirt route that takes you deep into the desert, past several man-made lakes to one of the state's huge reclamation-era dams. You can then loop around to U.S. 60, where you'll cruise through several old mining towns and past the jagged Pinal Mountains before heading back into the city. Or detour north for about 40 miles on U.S. 60 from Globe to get a jaw-dropping look at Salt River Canyon. All along the way there are pull-offs and stops, trailheads and historic markers. You can tour these eastern and northeastern reaches of the Valley in one long day, unless you want to hike, then you'll need to mount a separate expedition.

If you're headed to Southern Arizona from the Valley along I-10, veer off the main route for a few hours and visit the mysterious Casa Grande, the largest remaining Hohokam ruin. Or stop at Picacho Peak State Park just off the interstate to hike along a ragged rock spine towering over the desert.

© TIM HULL

a detail from an outbuilding at Casa Grande Ruins National Monument

FRANK LLOYD WRIGHT IN THE VALLEY OF THE SUN

In 1940 Frank Lloyd Wright published an essay in *Arizona Highways* in which he eloquently pleaded for a different kind of architecture for the desert, one not based on previous models but on the unique colors and contours of the desert itself: "The ever advancing human threat to the integral beauty of Arizona might be avoided if the architect would only go to school in the desert . . . ," he wrote, "and humbly learn harmonious contrasts or sympathetic treatments that would, thus, quietly, belong."

Certainly the best of the very few real-world examples of what Wright had in mind is his own **Taliesin West,** Wright's most famous desertland building. He designed a few other distinctive structures in the valley, and some of them are accessible to fans of the nation's greatest architect. In addition to a church and an auditorium, Wright built nine private homes in the valley, eight of which still exist. One of the finest of his private homes was a small bungalow Wright designed for his friend Raymond Carlson, then the editor of *Arizona Highways.*

Many critics and scholars include the 1928 **Arizona Biltmore** (2400 E. Missouri St., Phoenix), then as now the state's most stylish resort, on the short list of public structures Wright designed in the valley. Though the architect of record is his former apprentice, Albert Chase McArthur, Wright was paid a consulting fee on the project and left his mark on the design, as anyone with even a passing knowledge of Wright's quirks and obsessions will see during a stroll around the magnificent "Jewel of the Desert."

Wright created the design for the North Valley's **First Christian Church** (6750 N. Seventh Ave., 602/246-9206, www.fccphx.com) in 1950 as part of the Classical University commission that never got off the ground. In 1972, church leaders obtained the unused plans and started construction on the sanctuary, considered by many the best example of Wright's church architecture. You can stop in for a look around, or attend one of the services held Sundays at 9 A.M. and 10:30 A.M.

Wright originally designed Arizona State University's **Grady Gammage Memorial Auditorium** (1200 S. Forest Ave., Tempe, 480/965-5062) as an opera house for Baghdad, Iraq. In 1957, when Wright was 90 years old, the king of Iraq commissioned him to design several public buildings in Baghdad. Unfortunately, the king was killed the next year, so the project fell apart. Later, the design for the Baghdad opera house was changed a bit to become Gammage Auditorium. It is not one of the critics' favorites – a bit puffy and sappy for some tastes – but the acoustics, as in all of Wright's performance spaces, are absolutely perfect.

Journalist Lawrence Cheek wrote a slim but comprehensive book about Wright's desert work, *Frank Lloyd Wright in Arizona* (Rio Nuevo, 2006), that should be read by anybody interested in Wright's westerly masterpieces.

About 60 miles northwest of the city on U.S. 60 you'll find the old mining town of Wickenburg, which still has a bit of Old West charm. Continue north on Route 89 for a twisting and scenic, mostly two-lane drive through the chaparral and scrub midlands, through a lush ranching region, and on up to the pine forests of Prescott. And if you're taking the quick route to the northland along I-17, consider stopping at Arcosanti, an ongoing experiment in architecture and living.

THE SUPERSTITION MOUNTAINS

These rugged desert mountains rise to about 5,000 feet off the desert floor and are the main component of the 160,000-acre **Superstition Wilderness Area** on the Tonto National Forest. The Superstitions pale in comparison to other Arizona mountains both in elevation and diversity, but they are an ideal place to get an introduction to the Sonoran Desert and spend some time in a wilderness close to the city. The trails are rocky, and some are quite worn in places; the landscape is rough, gray-green desert, rugged and hot and crowded with mobs of saguaro reaching into the always clear blue and huge sky, and carpeted with creosote, brittlebush, prickly pear, and all the other desert familiars. In February and March, especially after a winter of plentiful rainfall, and from April through June, large patches of the desert pop open with purple, red, yellow, and blue—everything that was waiting dormant explodes into bloom. This is the best time to be in the Superstitions. Don't go in the deep summer.

It is possible to get very far away from the city and everything else by going far into the wilderness area. Most, however, stick to the well-trod but still impressive sights along the popular **Peralta Trail,** a moderately difficult, approximately six-mile round-trip hike that leads to a saddle with a fine view of Weavers Needle, a fantastically eroded butte. From Phoenix take U.S. 60 east through Gold Canyon, then turn east on Peralta Road and drive about eight miles to the trailhead for the Peralta and the **Dutchman's Trail,** on which you can take an 18-mile journey through the wilderness area. Expect to pay a $6 per vehicle user fee on the Tonto. For more on hiking in the Superstitions, check out the Tonto National Forest's trail guide at www.fs.fed.us/r3/tonto/wilderness/wilderness-superstition-index.shtml. The folks at **Superstition Search and Rescue** (480/350-3993, www.superstition-sar.org) keep an excellent website with trail descriptions, maps, and information on desert hiking safety.

Lost Dutchman State Park

A stop at this small state park at the base of the Superstitions (6109 N. Apache Trail, 480/982-4485, www.pr.state.az.us/Parks/parkhtml/dutchman.html, sunrise–10 P.M. daily, $5 per vehicle) is a good way for families and day hikers to see the range and to spend some time walking around the desert on relatively easy trails. The park has 70 campsites ($12–15, no hookups) with showers, as well as tables and grills perfect for picnics. The **Treasure Loop Trail** is an easy way to see the park and get an idea of what the desert is like at about 2,000 feet. It's a 2.4-mile round-trip, moderate and well marked, starting and beginning at either picnic area. Using the **Siphon Draw Trail,** you can climb up to about 5,000 feet, first to a high overlook spot called The Flatiron and then on to the top of Superstition Peak, a hard five-mile round-trip hike that rewards the tough with some striking desert views.

Superstition Mountain Museum

This small local-history museum at the beginning of the Apache Trail just outside of Apache Junction (4087 N. Apache Trail, 480/983-4888, www.superstitionmountainmuseum.org, 9 A.M.–4 P.M. daily) makes for an interesting stop if you have an extra half hour to an hour. The displays on local mining legends, especially the infamous whopper about the **Lost Dutchman Mine** (which people hunt for still today, believing that 1890s prospector and "Dutchman" Jacob Waltz died before revealing the route to the world's richest gold mine somewhere deep in the Superstitions), and other Old West history lessons will enhance and contextualize the backcountry drive you're about to take.

◖ THE APACHE TRAIL AND VICINITY

A tour of the Apache Trail (Route 88) and the Old West Highway (U.S. 60), a 120-mile round-trip loop along the wild edges of the sprawl-choked Valley, begins just outside Apache Junction and eventually winds around the Superstition Mountains to Roosevelt Dam, then on through the Pinal Mountains and a few old mining towns.

The route follows in places the course of the Salt River, the damming of which first made all that sprawl possible. But it also created several desert lakes, each improbably beautiful surrounded by an arid army of saguaros peering down from jagged-rock cliffs into the mirage-like waters, wondering what all the fuss is about. The Apache Trail itself came about as a result of the dam, built as it was to cart materials and workers to and from the great

© TIM HULL

The construction of Roosevelt Dam made irrigation farming in the Valley of the Sun predictable and profitable.

construction site, though the route had been regularly traversed by native inhabitants long before the reclamation project began.

Goldfield

Heading out of Apache Junction, the trail passes this Old West–show tourist trap (4650 N. Mammoth Mine Rd., 480/983-0333, www.goldfieldghosttown.com, 10 A.M.–5 P.M. daily), a rebuilt 1890s town on the site of what used to be a mining camp with about 5,000 people, settled after gold was discovered in the Superstitions and depopulated soon after the mining stopped. It's a kind of a mining-camp theme park now, with a working narrow-gauge railroad, theme shops along a boardwalk main street, a couple of cowboy-style restaurants, a saloon, a mine tour, gold panning, staged gunfights, and Jeep tours into the Superstitions. Kids will likely enjoy this attraction; everybody else should move on down the trail.

Canyon Lake and Tortilla Flat

The smallest of the Salt River Project lakes, and the first you come to along the trail is Canyon Lake, with 950 surface acres and 28 miles of shoreline. The headquarters here is the **Canyon Lake Marina and Campground** (Rte. 88, 480/288-9233, www.canyonlakemarina .com), which has a restaurant and campground with sites for tents and RVs with hookups, tables, grills, fire rings, and showers. In normal times you're allowed to ride personal watercraft and water ski on Canyon Lake, and there's even an excursion steamboat and dinner cruise; however, you should check the Tonto National Forest Website (www.fs.fed.us/r3/ tonto/home.shtml) before making any plans to boat on Canyon Lake, as it has lately gone through some drawdowns due to dam maintenance nearby, which may see it closed to all recreation for a time.

Across the trail from the lake there's an old saloon at Tortilla Flat, which was once a stage stop and is now a . . . well, a stage stop—only now its burgers and beers and saddle-topped barstools are popular with Harley riders, who haunt the trail in large numbers on the weekends.

Saguaro guard a cliff dwelling built by the Salado people in the desert east of Phoenix, along the Apache Trail.

Apache Lake

Continuing on the trail, a saguaro and scrub forest spreads out on either side, boulders strewn about and rising from the earth, the Superstitions looming like the petrified rock remains of giant jagged teeth; then the route descends precipitously just before it turns to dirt and washboards near spectacular Fish Creek Canyon, where you'll probably want to stop and take a few photos. Then it's on to the next of the desert lakes, Apache Lake, where the **Apache Lake Marina and Resort** (Rte. 88, 928/467-2511, www.apachelake.com) rents clean and basic lakeside rooms at the **Apache Lake Motel** ($90–105 d), including suites with kitchenettes. The 17-mile long lake is popular with Phoenicians who enjoy water skiing, riding personal watercraft, and fishing for small- and largemouth bass.

Roosevelt Dam and Roosevelt Lake

After Apache Lake, the dirt trail follows a narrow band of river below the dam, then climbs up a bit and that sheer rock wall holding back the river comes into sight. You can stop here and read some plaques about the dam and look at it from a promontory. Then the road passes a large bridge over the dam and the highway heading north to Payson and the Rim Country. The largest of the Salt River Lakes with a peak fill of 22,000 surface acres, Roosevelt Lake can be accessed through the **Roosevelt Lake Marina** (Rte. 88, 928/467-2245, www.rlmaz.com/rlmaz .html, $6 day use, $4 boat fee, $10 camping, first-come first-served). There are four motels near the lake and an RV park. You can rent a boat here, skid around on personal watercraft, or explore hidden coves and fishing spots.

Tonto National Monument

Pass Roosevelt Lake and turn at the sign to get to Tonto National Monument (8 A.M.–5 P.M. daily, $3), a picturesque cliffside ruin once inhabited by the Salado people from about 1150 to 1450. It's so well preserved it appears as if—from far away, at least—people could still live here in the cool shade of a natural rock alcove high above the saguaro and cholla. The paved **Lower Ruin** trail is about a mile and is open to the public; a ranger-guided tour of the **Upper Ruin,** a three-mile round-trip hike, is offered November–April; call ahead for reservations. The visitors center below the ruin has some interesting artifacts of the Salado, and a good bit of information on this often-overlooked tribe.

Globe and Superior

Follow Route 88 through several old Central Arizona mining towns, and then back west on a scenic stretch of U.S. 60 called the Old West Highway. Both Globe and Superior, in the shadow of the rocky Pinal Mountains, have quaint old downtowns that have yet to be discovered by hippies and artists and shop owners and shoppers—sort of like Bisbee before the craft boom. They are mostly boarded up now but seem ripe for discovery, especially Superior, which has a few really cool but disused buildings (long ago fancy hotels and shops) that could be expensively hipped up for the ever-growing retro-loving crowd.

In Globe, the kids will have fun climbing around the largely rebuilt Hohokam and Salado ruins at **Besh-Ba-Gowah Archaeological Park** (1324 Jess Hayes Rd., 928/425-0320, 8 A.M.–5 P.M. daily, $3, kids under 11 free). Unlike most ruins in Arizona, these modest reconstructed pit houses and courtyards are open for scrambling and exploring, and there's a small but interesting museum with exhibits on the lifestyles of those long-lost tribes.

If you're feeling hungry, try the Mexican food at **Guayo's on the Trail** (Junction U.S. 60 in Globe, 928/425-9969, 10:30 A.M.–9 P.M. daily, $5–17), which serves up outstanding traditional Mexican food based on old family recipes. This casual place has been around for going on 40 years, and it's very popular with Apache Trail travelers, especially the motorcycle crowd.

© ELIZABETH JANG

Kids love to climb and explore in the rebuilt Hohokam and Salado settlement at Besh-Ba-Gowah Archaeological Park in Globe.

Salt River Canyon

Take a detour north on Route 77 (which becomes U.S. 60) from Globe along the edge of the Apache Mountains for about 40 miles to spectacular **Salt River Canyon,** one of the more impressive roadside natural wonders in a state chock-full of them. Once used as a hideout by the Apache during the Indian wars, this 2,000-foot-deep jagged desert gorge is where the Salt River runs free and wild. There's a parking area before the bridge where you can learn about the canyon and take pictures, and easy paved trails lead down to the flowing river. If you've got a four-wheel drive, you can head off on a riverside Jeep trail and explore the canyon in more depth. The traffic along Route 77 near the canyon bridge can get heavy and frustrating, especially on the weekends.

Boyce-Thompson Arboretum State Park

A stroll around this unique arboretum (37615 U.S. 60, 520/689-2811, www.pr.state.az.us/Parks/parkhtml/boyce.html, 8 A.M.–5 P.M. daily

© TIM HULL

Boyce-Thompson Arboretum has dozens of cactus varieties in its cactus garden.

Oct.–Apr., 6 A.M.–3 P.M. daily May–Sept., $7.50 adults, $3 kids 5–12) is the perfect capstone to an Apache Trail tour. Just three miles west of Superior along U.S. 60, the arboretum was developed in the early 20th century by wealthy do-gooder and mining magnate Col. William Boyce Thompson. He built his own dreamland here, a kind of desert country Hearst Castle, and endeavored to grow several different ecosystems on his property. Here you can walk on well-trod and easy paths leading through otherworldly cactus gardens, across a cottonwood-covered stream, along the shores of a desert lake, and even through an Australian eucalyptus forest, all surrounded by the huge, telltale boulder-mountains of the Central Arizona outback. This is not recommended in summer.

FROM PHOENIX TO TUCSON

The small towns southeast of the metro area are a snapshot of rural America in a state of flux, adapting to the city's spread and trying to hold on to some kind of identity as commuters move in and take over. The southeast, known to most Arizonans as the area you have to drive through to get from Phoenix to Tucson, was once dedicated to agriculture, though anymore many of those fields are covered not with cotton but with stuccoed homes and RV parks. The area is prone to blowing dust storms, especially during the summer rainy season.

◀ Casa Grande Ruins National Monument

This ancient and fragile, molded-mud apartment building just outside of the old farming town of Coolidge (1100 West Ruins Dr., 520/723-3172, www.nps.gov/cagr/, 8 A.M.–5 P.M. daily, $5 adults, kids under 15 free), an easy 10- to 15-minute detour off I-10 (Exit 211 halfway between Phoenix and Tucson—watch for signs) is all that remains of one of the largest prehistoric structures ever built in North America.

There are still a lot of unanswered questions about how and why Casa Grande grew to dominate the Salt River Valley and beyond at its peak in about 1350, and even more

© TIM HULL

The Hohokam great house ruin at Casa Grande Ruins National Monument is protected from the elements by a large roof structure.

questions about what caused its catastrophic decline around 1450. It's an amazing sight to see nonetheless—almost like a huge, human-sized sand castle covered by a towering metal roof to keep out the elements. The monument's excellent museum interprets and explains what we do know about the Hohokam, those ancient arid-land agriculturists who inspired the Valley's modern-day settlers to attempt to turn the desert into an Eden.

Picacho Peak State Park

This small state park (just off I-10, exit 219, 520/466-3183, www.pr.state.az.us/Parks/parkhtml/picacho.html, 8 A.M.–10 P.M. daily, trails close at sunset) about 40 miles north of Tucson and 60 miles south of Phoenix sits in the shadow of a dramatic 1,500-foot rock up-cropping in the middle of an otherwise mostly flat desert plain. Picacho Peak has always been a natural landmark in this part of the state, and nearby, in 1862, soldiers fought Arizona's only Civil War battle, an event reenacted at the park

every year. There are several good trails that lead up and along the rough spine of the peak; the area is particularly popular in spring, when the bajada stretching out from the cliffsides is often carpeted with multicolored wildflowers. Try the two-mile round-trip **Hunter Trail,** a rather difficult and steep route to the top that begins on the north side and requires negotiation of steel cables anchored into the rock in some places. The three-mile round-trip **Sunset Vista Trail** is a bit easier but longer, starting on the south side and heading to the top. Either way, the views from the top are amazing and well worth the climb.

WICKENBURG

This old mining town northwest of the Valley on U.S. 60 still has a bit of Old West charm and makes for a fun day trip from Phoenix or a couple of hours' detour during a drive north. If you're headed to Prescott from Phoenix, consider taking the back way along U.S. 60 through Wickenburg, then on to Route 89 north, cruising along a twisting rural two-lane through a sleepy but scenic mining and ranching region that most visitors miss.

Sights

Fans of Western Art will want to spend an hour or so at the **Desert Caballeros Western Museum** (1 N. Frontier St., 928/684-2272, www.westernmuseum.org. 10 A.M.–5 P.M. Mon.–Sat., noon–4 P.M. Sun., closed Mon. June–Aug., $7.50), a very decent regional art museum that has some unique exhibits on life in the Old West.

Hikers and birders shouldn't miss the beautiful riparian area at the **Hassayampa River Preserve** (7–11 A.M. Fri.–Sun. in summer, 8 A.M.–5 P.M. Wed.–Sun. in winter, $5), run by the Nature Conservancy, where you can walk along the creek beneath cottonwoods and willows and watch for all manner of water-loving birds darting among the bushes.

Food

A good place to stop for lunch in Wickenburg is **Anita's Cocina** (57 N. Valentine Dr.,

928/684-5777, 6:30 A.M.–9 P.M. daily, $5–10), a popular place with locals where they serve delicious and inexpensive Mexican favorites in a casual atmosphere.

NORTH ON I-17

If you've got a little time to spare during a drive north to Prescott, Sedona, or Flagstaff along I-17, stop by **Rock Springs Café** (35769 S. Old Black Canyon Hwy., I-17 Exit 242, 623/374-5794, www.rockspringscafe.com), an old cowboy-style saloon, historic general store, soda fountain, and café that serves locally famous hamburgers, steaks, barbecue, and homemade pies that you'll want send home in a refrigerated crate. The whole place has a kind of dark, wood-and-stone air of historic authenticity, and it's been the site of one dusty travelers' wayside or another since the late 19th century. On the first Saturday of the month October–June Rock Springs Café puts on a **Hogs 'n Heat Barbecue and Nut Fry,** featuring "mountain oysters" from local cattle, live country music, and plenty of draft beer.

A little farther north, as the ever-reaching imprint of the Valley's insatiable growth begins to disappear and the midland desert scrublands open up wide, veer off at the Cordes Junction exit (Exit 262) and follow the signs to take a tour of the fascinating "urban laboratory" being built by architect and artist Paolo Soleri and his followers at **Arcosanti** (928/632-7135, www.arcosanti.org, 10 A.M.–4 P.M. daily, $8). It looks a bit like the buildings on Luke Skywalker's home planet of Tatooine, and the sweeping high-desert locale adds to its evocative otherworldliness. The approximately one-hour tour takes you through the settlement, as a guide explains the history and philosophy of the project. There's a small café and a gift shop where you can buy one of the world-famous handmade bells that support this ongoing experiment in "Arcology"—an architectural theory that seeks to lessen our imprint on the earth by bringing together architecture and ecology.

Arcosanti Vaults, viewed from the north, are the mid-point of the Arcosanti site and design.

Information and Services

TOURIST INFORMATION

The Downtown Phoenix Visitor Center (125 2nd Street, 877/225-5749, www.visitphoenix.com, 8 A.M.–5 P.M. Mon.–Fri.) has stacks of information and literature, and a helpful staff will answer all your questions. In central Phoenix along the Camelback Corridor, stop by the **Biltmore Visitor Information Center** (24th St. and Camelback), or call the visitor information hotline (602/252-5588) for assistance.

BURTON BARR CENTRAL LIBRARY

This architectural gem in downtown Phoenix has Internet access, a free wireless network, and gorgeous views of the city (1221 N. Central Ave., 602/262-4636, www.phoenixpubliclibrary.com, 9 A.M.–9 P.M. Mon.–Thurs., 9 A.M.–6 P.M. Fri.–Sat., noon–6 P.M. Sun., free).

MEDIA

The two best newspapers in the Valley, and in the state for that matter, are the daily **Arizona Republic** (www.azcentral.com), the largest newspaper in Arizona, and the weekly **Phoenix New Times** (www.newtimes.com), which is the best source for investigative reporting, off-center opinions, and cultural coverage.

HOSPITALS AND EMERGENCY SERVICES

If you get hurt in the Valley or have any kind of emergency medical situation, the simplest thing to do is call 9-1-1. There are several top-notch hospitals around the Valley, and many of them have satellite centers in every major subregion around the basin. **St. Joseph's Hospital and Medical Center** (350 West Thomas Rd., 602/406-3000, www.stjosephs-phx.org) is a Catholic hospital started by the Sisters of Mercy in the late 19th century and is consistently ranked one of the top hospitals in Arizona. It operates a Level 1 Trauma Center, one of just a few in Arizona.

St. Luke's Medical Center (1800 E. Van Buren, 602/251-8100, www.stlukesmedcenter.com) is located near downtown Phoenix and has an updated and state-of-the-art emergency room that includes an innovative Chest Pain Emergency Center dedicated to preventing heart attacks. **Maricopa Medical Center** (2601 E. Roosevelt St., 602/344-5011, www.mihs.org) is one the nation's top hospitals, offering a full range of services including a Level 1 Trauma Center and an infant ICU.

Getting There and Around

All the information below applies to the entire Valley of the Sun, not just Phoenix proper. If you spend time in the sprawling Valley you'll soon realize that it is easier viewed as one big city rather than many mid-sized cities. While the cities around the Valley each have something unique to offer, in terms of getting there and around the differences are negligible. If you're going to be in the Valley more than a day, you are going to need a car. The bus system is reliable and comfortable, but it is not realistic to employ it for sightseeing tours. In the coming years the Valley will join other major world metro areas by improving its public transportation system (in the near term a light rail system is under construction), but for now and for the foreseeable future, to really see the city you'll need a car.

BY AIR

Phoenix Sky Harbor International Airport (3400 E. Sky Harbor Blvd., 602/273-3300, www.phoenix.gov/skyharborairport/) is one of the Southwest's largest, with three terminals served by 23 domestic and international airlines. If you're traveling to Arizona by air, you will likely land at Sky Harbor. The airport is just three miles east of downtown and easy to find. There's a free shuttle system that will take you between terminals. The airport offers free wireless Internet access throughout.

BY BUS

Valley Metro (602/253-5000, www.valley metro.org), the Valley's public transportation authority, is making strides all the time, and the first leg of a new light rail system was due to open for passengers in December 2008. For information and updates check out www .valleymetro.org. Valley Metro's bus service ($1.25 per ride) goes everywhere, including Glendale, Scottsdale, Tempe, and Mesa.

Shuttles

Valley Metro (602/253-5000, www.valley metro.org) operates several free local shuttles in some of the more popular areas. There's one around Mill Avenue and A.S.U. in Tempe called **Flash** (7 A.M.–8 P.M. daily every 15 minutes); a trolley-style service in downtown Scottsdale (11 A.M.–9 P.M. daily every 10 minutes); and a downtown-area shuttle called **Dash** (6:30 A.M.–11 P.M. Mon.–Fri. every 6–18 minutes, depending on time of day).

There are several shuttle companies that offer curb-to-curb rides from the airport to anywhere around the Valley. Shuttle rides will generally cost $15–20 per person to neighborhoods around the central valley, and more to the outer

regions. Try **Phoenix Shuttle** (877/604-6004, www.phoenixshuttle.com) for service around the Valley and **Arizona Shuttle** (800/888-2749, www.arizonashuttle.com) for shuttle rides to and from Sky Harbor and Tucson.

BY CAR

You must have a vehicle to tour the Valley of the Sun and Arizona—there is simply no way around it. Sky Harbor makes it easy to rent one by providing a free **Rental Car Shuttle** from the baggage claim at each terminal to the **Rental Car Center** (1805 E. Sky Harbor Circle South, 602/683-3741), just west of the airport. All the major rental companies are represented at the center, including **Hertz** (602/267-8822 or 800/654-3131, www.hertz.com) and **Budget** (800/527-7000, www.budget.com).

Taxis

Three taxicab companies contract with Sky Harbor to provide transportation at a set rate ($5 first mile, $2 each additional mile, $20 per hour traffic delay, $15 minimum fare, $1 per trip surcharge): **AAA Cab** (602/437-4000), **Allstate** (602/275-8888), and **Discount** (602/266-1110).

You can get a taxi to take you anywhere in the Valley; however, considering the long distances involved, they can get expensive pretty quick. On the weekends you'll find taxis waiting outside of popular drinking and partying areas like downtown Phoenix, Scottsdale, and Tempe, but most of the time you're going to have call a company and arrange for a pick-up. Ultimately, it's not really an efficient way of getting around the Valley.

TUCSON AND SOUTHERN ARIZONA

The Sonoran Desert is a deceptive landscape. The soft greens and yellows can appear monotonous, yet stop and look closely and they reveal staggering variety. It rains here only rarely, yet there is a season, popularly called the monsoon season but more accurately termed the summer rainy season, when this so-called arid land is positively lush. Once a year, in the spring, the land bursts with otherwise dormant wildflowers, like a one-night-only command performance. The region is dominated by desert, a flat land stretching out like a vast forgotten sea, yet increase your elevation into one of the region's Sky Islands and you will be hunting for tropical birds in a misty creek bed, or, if you go high enough, clamping on a pair of skis.

So it is with the culture in Tucson and Southern Arizona. If ever there was a melting pot in America it bubbles here, its heat source being the triple-digit days come July. Traveling the region it is difficult to escape constant reminders that not too long ago this land was considered not the southern end of the United States but rather the northern end of Mexico. The Anglo and Hispanic settlers have since come to terms with each other for the most part, and their mixing has created a unique culture that can only be described as Southwestern. While this true Southwestern experience can be experienced and studied in a few other places, nowhere is it more authentic and at the same time more dynamic than in Southern Arizona. There is proof of this in the region's art, music, and writing, all of which thrive on the arid climate and cultural complexity.

A short drive south, you'll experience the dynamic border region with all its bustling, and sometimes tragic, color. Go east and you'll find the remains of the Old West at its most iconic. Look a little closer and you'll find the new as well, in the artists and artisans who find Southern Arizona's quaint towns like Tubac and Bisbee so inviting. This is a fascinating, exotic region, and one you might find yourself happily lost in.

PLANNING YOUR TIME

You can do Tucson and Southern Arizona in one busy week; to sample some of the Sky Island trails and hideaways, take two weeks. The best times to visit are March through May and September through November. It is very hot on the desert in summer and perfect in the mountains, and in July and August count on near-daily late afternoon thunderstorms. Though hot and humid during the day, the months of the monsoon are a wonderful time to be alive in the Sonoran Desert. It's best to use Tucson as a base and explore the outlying areas by car unless you have more than a week or two to explore. All of the major sights in this region are within a few hours of the city.

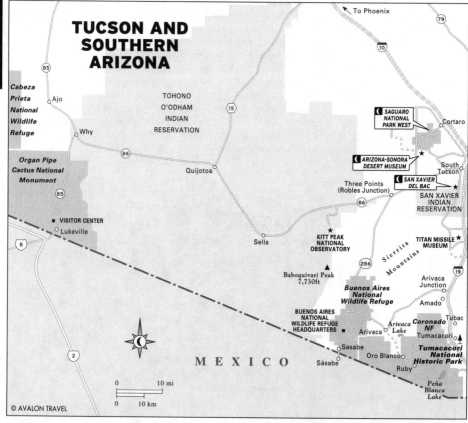

© TIM HULL

Many of the "standing up rocks" at Chiricahua National Monument appear to be precariously doing so.

SOUTHERN ARIZONA

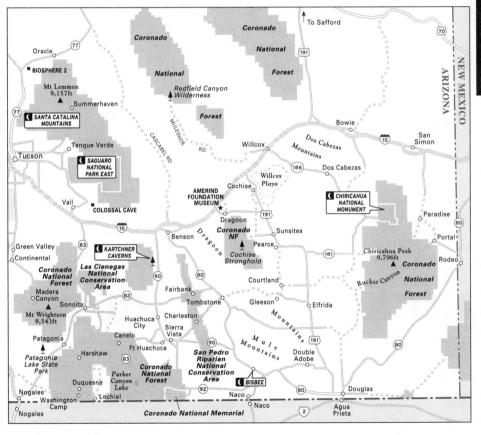

HIGHLIGHTS

(Arizona-Sonora Desert Museum: See the region's wonders up close – mountain lions, wolves, bighorn sheep, and other rare Sonoran natives (page 85).

(Saguaro National Park: Drive, walk, or ride a bike through the Sonoran Desert's unique saguaro forests (page 86).

(Santa Catalina Mountains: Drive to the top of a sky-island peak and cool off in the high green forests (page 90).

(San Xavier del Bac: See Arizona's answer to the Sistine Chapel, a white jewel of a mission on the desert plain (page 94).

(Kartchner Caverns: Enter an otherworldly cave still being formed by slowly dripping water (page 122).

(Bisbee: Explore an old mining boomtown, now an enclave for artists and antique shops (page 126).

(Chiricahua National Monument: Marvel at the "Land of Standing Up Rocks," a forest of hoodoos and twisted rock high in the evergreen mountains (page 129).

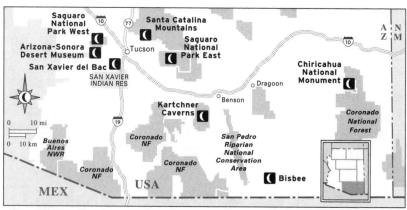

LOOK FOR **(** TO FIND RECOMMENDED SIGHTS, ACTIVITIES, DINING, AND LODGING.

Tucson and Vicinity

Tucson isn't a big city but it's fairly cosmopolitan, and it's surrounded by one of the most exotic landscapes in America. It has more gourmet restaurants, world-class resorts, boutique hotels, and bed-and-breakfasts than most cities its size. Its streets are lined with one-of-a-kind shops and unique art galleries, and its many historic neighborhoods show off romantic Southwestern-style urban and residential architecture. Tucson is many things at once: a college town with hip bars and lounges and a fertile music scene that mixes country, rock, and mariachi; a resort town where one can be pampered beyond reason, rejuvenating the soul or lounging in a big fluffy bathrobe poolside with a margarita; and a hometown, where many families date back a hundred years or more, and the natives—Mexican, Anglo, and Native American alike—hold on to a kernel of truth and authenticity while the city grows and sprawls with new arrivals, all of them looking for the good life here in the sunbelt.

Pima County, which comprises Greater Tucson, has only about a million residents. And yet, Tucson is one of those places everybody's heard of, and it welcomes some three million tourists annually, many of them "snowbirds" from Wisconsin, Michigan, and Canada—retirees looking for a temperate, weatherless place to relax. Its setting is its major draw. In the great Sonoran Desert, one's preconceived notions about arid lands—shifting sand dunes, not a spot of green for days on end—will be shattered forever upon arrival. Mesquite and green-skinned Palo Verde trees grow among tall, multi-armed, hundred-year-old saguaro, squat barrel cactus, red-fruited prickly pear, and sword-like agaves. In the spring, the whole desert bursts with color as dormant wildflowers come back to life. This desert, contrary to popular belief, is humming and crackling and scuttling with life—even in the summer, when the unrelenting sun cooks the land at 110°F.

For more than 200 years Tucson has been spreading across an arid river valley crowded with saguaro and hidden by looming, jagged mountain ranges. It was 1775 when the mud-walled Presidio San Augustine del Tucson first rose out of the dust, founded by an Irishman working for the Spanish crown. But long before that, the ancient Hohokam culture farmed this once-lush river valley, and the remains of their efforts can still be seen here today. In the 1700s, the Jesuits, led by the tough, adventuring Father Kino, established San Xavier del Bac, a mission church, just south of town in the Santa Cruz Valley. It still sits bright white—like a dove, they say—against the soft greens and yellows of the Sonoran desert and ever-blue and -clear Arizona sky, and mass is still celebrated inside the church's dark, cool

SOUTHERN ARIZONA

©TIM HULL

the Old Pueblo seen from Sentinel Hill

SOUTHERN ARIZONA

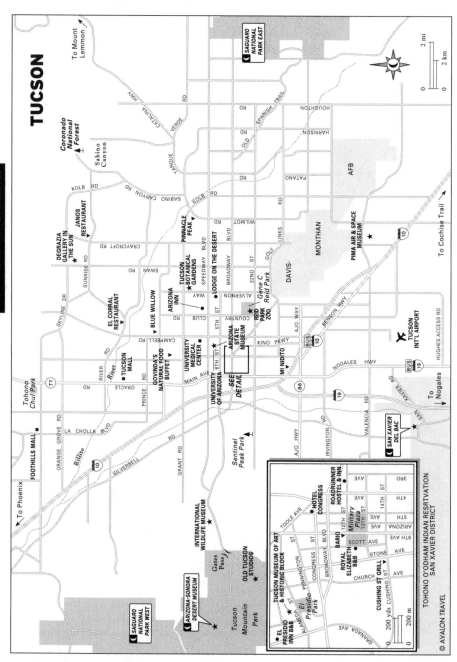

TUCSON

To Mount Lemmon

Coronado National Forest

Sabino Canyon

SAGUARO NATIONAL PARK EAST

To Cochise Trail

To Phoenix

Tohono Chul Park

FOOTHILLS MALL

JANOS RESTAURANT

DEGRAZIA GALLERY IN THE SUN

EL CORRAL RESTAURANT

PINNACLE PEAK

BLUE WILLOW

Tucson BOTANICAL GARDENS

ARIZONA INN

LODGE ON THE DESERT

TUCSON MALL

GOVINDA'S NATURAL FOOD BUFFET

UNIVERSITY MEDICAL CENTER

ARIZONA STATE MUSEUM

UNIVERSITY OF ARIZONA

Gene C Reid Park

REID PARK ZOO

MI NIDITO

PIMA AIR & SPACE MUSEUM

DAVIS-MONTHAN AFB

TUCSON INT'L AIRPORT

Hughes Access Rd

Sentinel Peak Park

INTERNATIONAL WILDLIFE MUSEUM

OLD TUCSON STUDIOS

Gates Pass

Tucson Mountain Park

ARIZONA-SONORA DESERT MUSEUM

SAGUARO NATIONAL PARK WEST

SAN XAVIER DEL BAC

To Nogales

Detail

EL PRESIDIO INN B&B

TUCSON MUSEUM OF ART & HISTORIC BLOCK

El Presidio Park

ROYAL ELIZABETH B&B

HOTEL CONGRESS

ROADRUNNER HOSTEL & INN

Military Plaza

BARIO

CUSHING ST GRILL

TOHONO O'ODHAM INDIAN RESRTVATION
SAN XAVIER DISTRICT

© AVALON TRAVEL

0   200 yds
0   200 m

interior daily. Until the 1850s, the Old Pueblo, as Tucson is fondly called by its many fiercely committed lifers, wasn't even part of the United States. The dusty, mud-street village was the far northern outpost of the Spanish Empire, and then it was Mexico's northernmost holding until the Gadsden Purchase made it part of the United States. While Tucson is all-American now, it still retains an exotic feel, and the cultural influence of Mexico, just 60 miles or so to the south, is everywhere.

Though the heat stays around for four or even five months out of the year, it's a simple, easy trade for two perfect springs. The first comes in actual spring, beginning in late February and holding until May. Tucson's "second spring" occurs while most of the rest of the nation is experiencing fall: from October to late December the temperatures stay in the 70s and 80s; the sky is clear, and everybody is playing outdoors. Even in the summer, which lasts from early May until late September, it's easy to find respite. Just head north for about an hour, twisting slowly up into the Santa Catalina Mountains, one of Southern Arizona's famed Sky Island mountain ranges, where you'll soon find yourself hiking among tall pines and rustic mountain cabins.

ORIENTATION

As it is with most Southwestern cities of a certain size, the Tucson metropolitan area encompasses several small towns as well as the City of Tucson proper. In this section of the book, sights, accommodations, and restaurants are listed according to their proximity to downtown, which remains at least the sentimental heart of the city and will likely become even more than that in the future as long-term plans to reenergize the area are realized under the city's ambitious and long-suffering Rio Nuevo project.

Native Tucsonans have tried to hold onto a semblance of the small, funky city character that once dominated the Old Pueblo, and there are still no real freeways in the city as a result. I-10 provides the only quick throughway, and I-19 is the primary route south to the Santa Cruz Valley. Most of the time, plan to slog along busy surface streets. Traffic is moved along with some speed, however, thanks to the left arrow lights at most major intersections.

The main commercial corridors run west to east—22nd Street, Broadway Boulevard, Speedway Boulevard, and Grant Road. Dozens of hotels, motels, and restaurants can be found along any of these main roads in the city's midtown section, bordered roughly on the east by Swan Road and on the west by I-10. South Tucson is a separate incorporated city, a mile square, south of downtown Tucson.

North of the city, on Oracle Road/Route 77, are the small towns of Oracle, Oro Valley, and Catalina, all nestled in the backside foothills of the Santa Rita Mountains. To the southeast is the old mining and ranching district of Vail and the Rincon Valley, now peppered with suburban housing developments, and beyond that the communities along the Cochise Trail. South on I-19 are the big open-pit copper mines, the bedroom community of Sahuarita, the retirement haven of Green Valley, the artist's colony and shops of Tubac, and then on to the U.S.-Mexico Border.

Tucson itself is surrounded by mountains, with the mighty Santa Catalinas to the north, the Rincon Mountains to the east and the Tucson Mountains to the west. Far south in the Santa Cruz Valley along I-19 are the Santa Rita Mountains. If you remember that the Santa Catalinas, the most imposing range around the valley, are to the north, it isn't too difficult to navigate Tucson. A major road construction project is expected to keep most of the I-10 exits around Tucson closed on a revolving basis until 2010. If you're coming into town from the north or the east, keep an eye out for instructions on which exits are open.

DOWNTOWN

Downtown Tucson, where the city first rose from the desert, isn't the community center it once was. The general area can be expanded to include 4th Avenue and the historic neighborhoods of El Presidio, Armory Park, Barrio Historico, and those around the University of Arizona, all of which are pedestrian-

DOWNTOWN'S HISTORIC NEIGHBORHOODS

The **El Presidio Historic District** is where Tucson began as a place of human habitation, a mixture of adobe row houses and Victorian mansions that is several chapters in the city's history writ in architecture. The district is bounded roughly by Granada on the west, 6th Street on the north, Church Street on the east, and Alameda Street on the south.

Though turned back to desert now, the Royal Presidio de San Agustin del Tucson once stood here, the farthest north the Spanish crown dared to go. The presidio, or fort, had 12-foot-high adobe walls and covered 11 acres, housing a small contingent of soldiers and their families, a population that spent a good deal of its time fearing and fighting Apaches. Much later archeologists discovered that the fort had been built close to a Hohokam site that flourished from about 700–900, proving humans

had made their lives on the banks of the Santa Cruz River for as long as nearly anywhere else in the union. A self-guided tour pamphlet of this district and other downtown-area historic sights is available at the Tucson Visitors Center at La Placita.

When the Americans took over in 1856, the fort was dismantled, its walls used to build homes and businesses for new arrivals. As more Anglos settled in, the district became a mixture of adobe row houses and Eastern-style mansions for early 20th century Tucson's rich and powerful. Many of these old mansions and adobes have been restored and now serve as offices and private residences.

On the district's western end, the 80-year-old **Pima County Courthouse's** (115 N. Church St., 8:30 A.M.–noon and 1–5 P.M. weekdays) sea-green, tiled dome is a landmark of the Old

Pima County Courthouse's dome is a landmark of Tucson's skyline.

Pueblo's modest skyline, and it's worth a walk around the grounds of the city's government beehive to take in the Spanish Colonial revival touches and, on weekdays, to see downtown at its most industrious. On the weekends, especially in the summer, you'll likely find the area mostly deserted but still inviting. Walk across the front courtyard through a few arches and you'll be in **El Presidio Park** with its fountains and memorial to the Mormon Battalion, which occupied the presidio briefly in late 1846.

The photogenic Sonoran-style row houses in the **Barrio Historico District** on the southwest edge of downtown are well adapted to the desert environment. Their front entrances hug the property line (unlike their Anglo counterparts with large front and back yards) to make space for central courtyards hidden from the street, which provide a shaded outdoor living space within the home. Many of the adobes here have been lovingly and colorfully restored and now serve as offices, working galleries, and private residences. Sometimes called Barrio Viejo (the Old Neighborhood), the barrio has been on the National Register of Historic Places since the 1970s. It dates from the mid-1850s and, as its dominant architecture suggests, has traditionally been a Mexican enclave. Many similar neighborhoods once sprawled out to the edge of the El Presidio District, a large quarter referred to as Barrio Libre (Free Neighborhood), due either to the anything-goes atmosphere in some corners or because the Mexican population was mostly left alone to follow its own rules and culture. Much of the quarter was razed in the late 1960s to make way for the "urban renewal" program that built the **Tucson Convention Center** (260 South Church Ave., 520/791-4101).

An especially haunting sight here is the **El Tiradito Shrine** (221 S. Main Ave.). Roadside shrines are common in Southern Arizona even in the most out-of-the-way places, but only one is dedicated to a folk-saint who was, by the church's standards, an unredeemed sinner. El Tiradito (The Castaway) dates to the 1870s, when Juan Oliveras, a young shepherd,

fell in love with his mother-in-law and the two gave in to an illicit passion. They were discovered by her ax-wielding husband, who killed Oliveras and tossed his dead body away on the land that now holds the shrine (such is the tradition, anyway). The church wouldn't allow the doomed lover to be buried on consecrated land, so the people of the barrio interred him where he was "cast away" and erected a shrine. Some say that if you make a wish at the shrine by night and leave a lit candle, and you find it still burning in the morning, your wish will come true – this is why it's sometimes called the "Wishing Shrine."

The **Arizona Historical Society Sosa-Carrillo-Fremont House Museum** (151 S. Granada Ave., 520/622-0956, 10 A.M.-4 P.M. Wed.-Sat., $3 adults, $2 seniors and kids 12-18, under 12 free), on the grounds of the convention center, exhibits artifacts and tells the history of Tucson's Hispanic founding families in a circa-1880 adobe house once leased to the territorial governor. Facing Stone Avenue on the eastern edge of the barrio is **St. Augustine Cathedral** (192 S. Stone Ave., 520/623-6351, www.staugustinecathedral.com), dedicated to Tucson's patron saint. Built in 1896 and remodeled several times over the years, the church has yucca, saguaro, and horned toads carved into its stone facade and celebrates a mass accompanied by mariachi at 8 A.M. Sunday.

For walking tours of downtown, try Alan Kruse of **KruseArizona Tours** (4517 E. Patricia Pl., 520/881-1638, www.KruseArizona.com, $15 per person); he dresses in period costume for a two-hour walk around downtown and serves pastry and coffee. Similarly, Julia Benites Arriola of the **Arizona Historical Society** (949 E. 2nd St., 520/622-0956, $10 per person) serves Mexican pastries and hot beverages on her colorful two-hour tour. The **Tucson Museum of Art and Historic Block** (520/624-2333, ext. 104, mhayes@tucsonarts.com, 10 A.M.-4 P.M. Mon.-Sat., and noon-4 P.M. Sun.) offers a 2.5-hour tour for $10, by reservation.

friendly—something rare in the Southwestern cityscape. This rather large area is the heart of Tucson, even if downtown proper's reformation as a tourist draw and mixed-use urban center has lagged a bit in recent years.

Tucson Museum of Art and Historic Block

The Tucson Museum of Art's (140 N. Main Ave., 520/624-2333, www.tucsonmuseumof art.org, 10 A.M.–4 P.M., Tues.–Sat., noon–4 P.M. Sun., $8 general admission, $6 seniors, $3 students) permanent collection is heavy with the mysterious artifacts of the Americas prior to Columbus's arrival in the New World, the art of the American West, and contemporary art with a Latin flavor. This is a good place to introduce yourself to that tri-cultural mixing that makes Southern Arizona unique. Five historic homes built in the last half of the 19th century survive next to the museum.

Just beyond the museum's wide Main Avenue entrance is the oldest of the Historic Block's buildings (and probably the oldest building in Tucson), **La Casa Cordova,** its two west rooms built several years before the Gadsden Purchase made Tucson part of the United States in 1854. A representative example of the style of Mexican townhouse that once lined the city's core, with its central courtyard and entrance right on the street, the Cordova house's design is mirrored in the block of adobe row houses that make up **Old Town Artisans** (9:30 A.M.–5:30 P.M. Mon.–Sat., 11 A.M.–5 P.M. Sun. Sept.–May; 10 A.M.–4 P.M. Mon.–Sat., 11 A.M.–4 P.M. Sun. June–Aug.), a group of artisan shops, galleries, and a restaurant on the east side of Main Avenue.

A shady courtyard behind the museum's main building, **The Plaza of Pioneers,** has a wall honoring Tucson pioneers from the Spanish, Mexican, and territorial eras. Café a la C'Art (150 N. Main Ave., 520/628-8533 or 520/318-4700, 11 A.M.–3 P.M. Mon.–Fri.) offers sandwiches, soups, and salads in an alfresco atmosphere off the plaza, and there are murals and sculptures worth a look here as well.

Arizona Historical Society Museum Downtown

Until shopping malls began to proliferate in midtown starting in the 1960s, downtown Tucson was the commercial and social heart of the city, a fact that this small museum (Wells Fargo Building, 140 N. Stone Ave., 520/770-1473, www.arizonahistoricalsociety .org, 10 A.M.–4 P.M. weekdays, $3 adults, $2 students 12–18 and seniors) celebrates. While there are ongoing attempts to revitalize downtown through a project called Rio Nuevo, it's unlikely the once bustling, mixed-use area will ever return to its former glory, when locally owned department stores, barber shops, boutiques, hotels, restaurants, and theaters lined the narrow streets, the sidewalks crowded with people working, shopping, living, and playing all within the same few blocks.

The museum, tucked away in a few rooms off the lobby of the Wells Fargo building on Stone Avenue—a still-busy, business-minded downtown district crowded on the weekdays but largely deserted after 5 P.M. Friday— shows artifacts from the early days of downtown through to its desertion, with large, rare photographs and saved ephemera from different eras of the city's history. An especially interesting installation tells the history of the Dillinger gang's capture in Tucson in the 1930s.

Fourth Avenue District

Lined with chic thrift-stores, exotic clothing boutiques, smoke shops, ethnic food restaurants, and cocktail lounges, this is an ideal place to people-watch, and there are some really good places to eat and treasures to be found in the quirky shops. Beware the young men and women of the bohemian persuasion who spend their days panhandling along the street. Twice a year, in fall and spring, the area closes to vehicle traffic for a street fair featuring artisan booths, concerts, and greasy food galore. Fourth Avenue is between downtown and the University District, just a short walk from campus, and on Friday and Saturday nights expect hoards of college kids out looking for inebriation. It's best to avoid driving in this area on weekend nights altogether.

The **Old Pueblo Trolley** (520/792-1802, 6–10 P.M. Fri., noon–midnight Sat., $1 each way, 50 cents for kids 6–12), an historic electric streetcar, runs from 4th Avenue to University Boulevard and on to UA's Main Gate. The trolley also runs noon–6 P.M. on Sunday, when the fare drops to $0.25 each way for everyone. You can board the trolley at various marked stops along the route.

WEST OF DOWNTOWN

Take Speedway Boulevard west under I-10. The road becomes Gate's Pass Road, and then turns into Kinney Road. Follow the signs to each of the following sights, some of Tucson's most representative attractions. You can do it in one long day, though the Desert Museum and Saguaro National Park stand up to a full day each. To get to the Desert Museum, take Speedway Boulevard west for about 12 miles through the desert and then turn right onto Kinney Road. The International Wildlife Museum, which can be easily skipped, is along the way, and Old Tucson is nearby as well.

International Wildlife Museum

A privately operated natural history museum heavy on the taxidermy, the International Wildlife Museum (4800 W. Gates Pass Rd., 520/617-1439, www.thewildlifemuseum.org, 9 A.M.–5 P.M. weekdays, 9 A.M.–6 P.M., Sat.–Sun., $7 adults, $5.50 seniors/military/students, $2.50 kids 4–12, kids under 3 free) has more than 400 mammals, birds, and insects from all corners of the globe in settings made to look like natural habitat. The museum offers rotating special exhibitions related to worldwide wildlife issues.

(Arizona-Sonora Desert Museum

A big part of the fun of a visit to the Arizona-Sonora Desert Museum (2021 North Kinney Rd., 520/883-2702, www.desertmuseum .org, 7:30 A.M.–5 P.M. daily Mar.–Sept., 7:30 A.M.–10 P.M. Sat. June–Aug., 8:30 A.M. –5 P.M.

© TIM HULL

There are some really strange-looking cacti at the Arizona-Sonora Desert Museum.

daily Oct.–Feb., no entry after 4:15 P.M., $12 adults, $4 kids 6–12, kids under 5 free) is the getting there. Driving west out of Tucson over dramatic Gate's Pass, you'll see thousands of sentinel-like saguaros standing tall on the hot, rocky ground below, surrounded by pipe cleaner-like ocotillo and fuzzy cholla, creosote, and prickly pear.

But the saguaro forests of Tucson Mountain Park and Saguaro National Park West, both of which surround the Desert Museum, are only one of several distinctive desert life zones you'll see and learn about at this world-famous museum and zoo, where native mammals, birds, reptiles, amphibians, fish, and arthropods live in displays mimicking their open-desert habitats.

This is the best place to learn about both the general structure and the minute details of the surrounding desert, and probably your only realistic chance to see all of the unique creatures that call it home.

Easy trails wind through the beautiful 21-acre preserve, passing exhibits on semidesert grasslands and mountain woodlands similar to those surrounding and growing on the Sonoran Desert's high mountain ranges. The Desert Loop Trail leads through a lowland scrub and cacti landscape with javelina and coyote. In Cat Canyon, a bespeckled ocelot sleeps in the shade and a bobcat lounges on the rocks. A mountain lion can bee seen close up through a viewing window, and a black bear strolls along a man-made stream and sleeps on a rock promontory. There are also rare Mexican wolves, white-tailed deer, bighorn sheep, and adorable prairie dogs with which to commune.

A riparian habitat has beavers and otters, water-lovers that were once abundant in the Southwest. There's a desert garden exhibit, a cactus and succulent garden, and a butterfly and wildflower display. There are also displays on desert fish, dunes, and a walk-in aviary that holds dozens of native birds. Docents are scattered throughout the complex to help with questions and give presentations on special topics. All this, plus a restaurant, snack bars, and a gift shop that sells excellent Pueblo Indian crafts make the Desert Museum Tucson's very best attraction. If you're planning on doing any exploring in the desert, do so after a trip to the Desert Museum, where you'll get a comprehensive mini-course in desert ecology.

Old Tucson Studios

Since 1939 Old Tucson (201 S. Kinney Rd., 520/883-0100, www.oldtucson.com, 10 A.M.–6 P.M. daily, $16.95 adults, $10.95, kids 4–11) has been the setting for more than 400 film productions, the majority of them Westerns. It was originally constructed to make the film *Arizona,* starring Jean Arthur and William Holden, which tells the story of Tucson's territorial days.

In the 1950s, impresario Bob Shelton bought the disused property and rebuilt its circa 1860s town, again drawing productions west from Hollywood, several starring Shelton's friend John Wayne. It remained popular as a movie set as long as Westerns were popular at the box office, and so went through boom and bust periods along with the genre. Shelton added gunfight shows and other family-oriented tourist attractions to ride out the lean times. Today a rebuilt Old Tucson (the town burned to the ground in the 1990s) concentrates on re-creating a moviehouse version of the Old West for tourists.

Make sure to check out the collection of vintage posters from the films produced at the studio. Tours talk about the history of the studio and the stars who walked its dusty streets, and musical acts and vaudeville-style revues go on all day. There are several restaurants on-site, including **Big Jake's,** which serves up good barbecue and beans, and **El Vaquero,** offering Southwestern-style entrées and a wide variety of specialty drinks. Unless you're a Western-film buff, Old Tucson is a little stale. If you're into the genre you'll find the film-related aspects worth a look. Kids might enjoy it, but the entry price is rather expensive for what you get.

◖ SAGUARO NATIONAL PARK

This is where the icon of arid America holds court. The split Saguaro National Park (www .nps.gov/sagu, 7 A.M.–sunset daily, visitors

© TIM HULL

SOUTHERN ARIZONA

Saguaro National Park's eastern section, backed by the Santa Catalina Mountains

centers open 9 A.M.–5 P.M. daily, $10 per car, receipt valid for seven days, good at both sections) has a western section at the base of the Tucson Mountains and a larger eastern section at the base of the Rincon Mountains. Both are worth visiting, but if you have time only for one go to the eastern section, which is older and larger. (Then again, there are a few other sights around the western portion, while the eastern is a bit on its own, save for nearby Colossal Cave.) Together they protect about 91,300 acres of magnificent Sonoran Desert landscape, including large and crowded saguaro forests surrounded by a thick underbrush of ocotillo, prickly pear, cholla, mesquite, and palo verde. If you want to see an accessible and wondrous example of the Sonoran Desert at its best, there are few better places to go.

The saguaro (pronounced sa-WAH-ro) is much more than a strange-looking plant to the native inhabitants of the Sonoran Desert, be they cactus wrens, coyotes, screech owls, or Tohono O'odham tribespeople. It is so supremely adapted to the arid environment, in which moisture from the sky comes but twice a year, that it anchors an entire busy community of living things, providing food and shelter to all sorts of desert creatures.

The great cactus-tree grows slowly, and only during the summer rainy season. After living, shaded and protected by a mesquite tree, for 15 years, a saguaro is still only about a foot tall. But, then again, these green, ribbed giants can live to be 150 years old or more, so there's really no hurry. Not until it reaches 75 years old does a saguaro even begin to sprout its identifying arms; so when you see a tall and fat one with many arms—and there are many in both sections of the park—know that it is a venerable old guy, deserving of respect and awe.

Tucson Mountains District

The place to start your tour of the western park is the **Red Hills Visitor Center** (2700 N. Kinney Rd., 520/733-5158), where you can learn about the ancient symbiotic friendship between the Tohono O'odham and the saguaro. Here you'll find a guide to the park's 40 miles of trails, and you can also book a tour with a naturalist and peruse the bookstore stocked with titles on local history and nature.

A good way to see the park, especially in the

heat of summer, is to drive the six-mile **Bajada Loop** through a thick saguaro forest. The route is graded dirt and it can get dusty, but you can also walk or bike the loop. Or you can drive the loop and stop at the **Valley View Overlook Trail,** an easy one-mile round-trip trail off the loop road that rises to an expansive view of the Avra Valley and the saguaro-lined desert and the skulking rock mountains. A half-mile round-trip walk to the **Signal Hill Picnic Area** offers a look at ancient petroglyphs. Both trails can be accessed off the Bajada Loop drive and are well marked. There are also a few very short, paved walks around the visitors center featuring interpretive signs about the saguaro and other desert fauna.

Rincon Mountains District

The eastern portion of the park (3693 S. Old Spanish Trail, 520/733-5153) is backed by the 8,600-foot Rincon Mountains. The visitors center has a bookstore and exhibits about the desert. The easiest way to see this section is to stroll, bike, or drive very slowly along the paved **Cactus Forest Drive,** an eight-mile one-way that begins at the visitors center and winds up and across the bajada. The desert here is gorgeous, especially after a rainstorm or early in the morning during the bloom months. There are more than 100 miles of trails here, including one that goes to Rincon Peak above 8,000 feet. The park's newspaper guide has a full description of the major trails.

UNIVERSITY OF ARIZONA

Since it was founded in 1885 as the first institution of higher learning in the Arizona Territory, the University of Arizona's fate and that of its host pueblo have been inextricably linked. It's difficult to imagine what Tucson would be without the shady central campus. A "Public-Ivy" land-grant school that has educated countless Arizona leaders and citizens, UA has nearly 37,000 students (more than the number of residents of most Arizona towns) and is active in the U.S. space program, specifically in Mars exploration. Not surprisingly, the school is world-renowned for its arid land

research and has an allopathic medical school founded by best-selling healer-doctor Andrew Weil. It's not always easy to find parking on campus, and it's impossible during sporting events. Visitors can pay to park at the Park Avenue Garage at the corner of Park and Helen Street, and at the Main Gate Parking Garage at Euclid Avenue and E. 2nd Street.

Arizona Historical Society Museum

Just south of the main gate wall along North Campus Drive is the largest of the Arizona Historical Society's (49 E. 2nd St., 520/628-5774, www.arizonahistorical society.org, 10 A.M.–4 P.M. Mon.–Sat., $5 adults, $4 students 12–18 and seniors) three Tucson museums. Exhibits include a full-scale reproduction of the cramped canvas-tent home early miners lived in, and a walk through a dark underground mine. There's also an old Studebaker on display; this make of car was once so popular with Arizona's sheriffs that the car company sent an author to the young state to write a public relations pamphlet that included exciting stories of frontier law enforcement. This in an interesting stop for Arizona history buffs, and there are several hands-on exhibits for the kids.

Arizona State Museum

Established in 1893, the Arizona State Museum (1013 E. University Blvd., 520/621-6302, www .statemuseum.arizona.edu, 10 A.M.–5 P.M. Mon.–Sat., noon–5 P.M. Sun., $3 per person suggested donation) is the oldest anthropology museum in the Southwest. Here you'll find several rooms of fascinating displays on the state's various Native American tribes and the world's largest collection of Southwest Indian pottery, including many contemporary pieces that prove pottery-making is certainly not a lost art.

University of Arizona Museum of Art

This art museum's (UA campus near Park Ave. and Speedway Blvd., 520/621-7567, http:// artmuseum.arizona.edu, 9 A.M.–5 P.M. Tues.– Fri., noon–4 P.M. Sat.–Sun., closed Mon. and

UA holidays, free) permanent collection has mostly minor (but still worth seeing) works by Tintoretto, Piazzetta, Goya, Bruegel, Rodin, Picasso, Hopper, Pollock, Rothko, O'Keeffe and many more. Asian and Latin American traditions are also well represented. Special shows often feature the work of well-known local artists and artists from Mexico. The museum has an impressive collection of Spanish Medieval Art, the signature piece of which is the 26-panel **Retablo of Ciudad Rodrigo,** an altarpiece depicting the sweep of Biblical events from Genesis through the life of Jesus Christ to the Last Judgment. Unfortunately, the altarpiece was sent to the Kimbell Museum of Art in Fort Worth, Texas, for conservation in 2006 and won't be back on display for some time.

Center for Creative Photography

UA's Center for Creative Photography (1030 N. Olive Rd., 520/621-7968, www.creative photography.org, 9 A.M.–5 P.M. Mon.–Fri., noon–5 P.M. Sat.–Sun., free) has one of the largest photography collections in the world; it holds the archives of Ansel Adams, Edward Weston, and dozens more major artists. The Center mounts a few exhibitions a year so it's a good idea to check the website before traveling to see what's on display. You can even make an appointment to personally view a few of the 80,000 prints accessible to the public (520/621-7968).

EAST AND NORTH OF DOWNTOWN

East of downtown is Tucson's populous midtown section, where there are many hotels and restaurants; the Reid Park Zoo is part of a sprawling midtown green area called Reid Park, a great place to catch a pick-up soccer game or have a picnic. The north end of Tucson, on the bajada and the foothills of the Santa Catalinas, is known for its mission-revival and Spanish Colonial homes, many of them designed by famed architect Josiah Joesler, and its high-end accommodations. The mighty mountains, reaching 10,000 feet and hosting an entirely different world from the desert

below, rise northeast of downtown and are easily reached by taking Grant east from midtown to Tanque Verde (Catalina Highway), then the Mt. Lemmon Highway north into the range.

Reid Park Zoo

Take Broadway Boulevard east to Randolph Way at Reid Park to Tucson's small but prestigious zoo (1100 S. Randolph Way, 520/791-4022, www.tucsonzoo.org, 9 A.M.–4 P.M. daily, $6 adults, $4 seniors, kids 2–14 $2). The zoo specializes in anteater research, and there are several of these strange beasts to look at here. There's also a polar bear, Boris, who seems to be very happy living in what you'd think would be the absolute opposite circumstances in which a polar bear would want to find himself. Not so, zookeepers say. The arctic, a cold desert, is actually drier than Tucson, so as long they keep the air conditioning pumping and his water hole cold he'll be staying for years.

Make sure to take the kids to the giraffe habitat, where for $1 they can buy some treats to feed the long-necked residents, who stick out their long, purple tongues, dripping with saliva, to capture the treat—much to the squealing delight of the feeders. A gift shop sells all kinds of zoo-related stuffed animals, shirts, and books, and a fast-food style eatery serves hamburgers, corn dogs, and the like.

If you get there early enough you might catch a glimpse of the elegant black jaguars, sisters born at a wildlife park outside of Phoenix, lounging in the cool of the morning. The zoo is small enough that little kids aren't likely to get too tired out. Plan about three hours, less if you don't have kids.

Tucson Botanical Gardens

Gardeners and anybody who appreciates beauty should stop at this midtown oasis for a few hours (2150 N. Alvernon Way, 520/326-9686, www.tucsonbotanical.org, 8:30 A.M.–4:30 P.M. daily, $7 adults, $3 kids 4–12). Flat walking trails wind around the nearly six-acre property, which feels secluded and hidden away even though it's right in the path of busy midtown. There are benches throughout on which to sit and contemplate the various gardens—16 in all, each one showcasing a different gardening tradition. Especially lovely is the Mexican-influenced garden, *Nuestro Jardín* (Our Garden), with its shrine of the Virgin of Guadalupe and found items. A cactus and succulent garden has examples of cacti not just from the nearby deserts but also from around the world, and the xeriscape garden demonstrates how you can grow desert-adapted plants without using a lot of water.

If you go between October and March you'll get to see **Butterfly Magic,** a live tropical butterfly exhibit. Call ahead for times and availability. For the price of admission you can take advantage of one of several tours of the gardens. Different tours are offered throughout the month, and not every tour is offered every day, so it's best to call ahead or check the website. The **Garden Gallery** has rotating art shows that can be viewed 8:30 A.M.–4:30 pm daily.

Tohono Chul Park

This 49-acre desert preserve (7366 N. Paseo del Norte, 520/742-6455, www.tohonochulpark .org, 8 A.M.–5 P.M. daily, $5 adults, $4 seniors, $3 students, $2 children 5–12, kids under 5 free) is worth the short drive north on Oracle Road out into Tucson's sprawl. Turn left on Ina Road, and then right on Paseo del Norte and you'll find native-plant gardens with easy trails punctuated by interpretive signs. The **Ethnobotanical Garden,** with rows of maize and other crops once planted by the O'odham and the Spanish settlers, demonstrates the different methods used by each group to coax subsistence out of the dry ground.

Kids will love the miniature stream, in which they can float little boats shaped like fish in the **Garden for Children,** where they can also see some old desert tortoises lolling about. If you stay quiet and sit by one of the many fountains or other water features on the grounds, you might get a glimpse of the many bobcats or javelina that call the preserve home. One night a year, in June or July, the garden's **Night-blooming Cereus** comes to life,

an event so rare and spectacular that there's a hotline (520/575-8468) for visitors to keep up-to-date on the expected bloom.

There are gift shops and galleries on the property, and exhibits generally feature Native American and Hispanic folk and fine arts. Don't miss the locally famous scones at the **Tohono Chul Park Tea Room** (520/797-1222, 8 A.M.–5 P.M. daily, $2.95–12), a perfect place to lounge after exploring the grounds.

DeGrazia Gallery in the Sun

Ettore "Ted" DeGrazia created some of the most enduring impressionistic visions of the Southwest. A native of Southern Arizona, DeGrazia attended the UA and published his first work in *Arizona Highways* magazine. He went on to study in Mexico with muralists Diego Rivera and Jose Clemente Orozco. He died in 1982 at the age of 73, but the DeGrazia Foundation carries on his memory at the Gallery in the Sun (6300 N. Swan Rd., 520/299-9191, http://degrazia.org, 10 A.M.–4 P.M. daily, free), DeGrazia's first studio and gallery in Tucson, built in honor of Padre Kino and dedicated to Our Lady of Guadalupe. A mission on the grounds features DeGrazia murals, with a roof open to the sky. The gallery has a gift shop stocked with DeGrazia reproductions for sale.

◖ Santa Catalina Mountains

In the arid basin and range territory, most living goes on in the basins, while most of the longing targets the cool, arboreal heights of the ranges. A range's relative accessibility usually determines the long-term happiness of the population sweating away on lower ground, so it stands to reason that Tucson's residents, living as they do in the shadow of the Santa Catalina Mountains, are quite content.

About 30 miles, an hour or so up a twisty, paved two-lane from the desert floor northeast of midtown, and you're at nearly 10,000 feet—the trip, it is often said, is like traveling from Mexico to Canada in one short scenic drive. It wasn't until the 1930s that Tucsonans could reach the cool heights in great numbers. It was then that former U.S. Post Master General Frank Hitchcock called in some federal favors and secured money and convict labor to begin building a road into the mountains. The indomitable Civilian Conservation Corps eventually finished the job, and in the 1940s real estate agents began selling lots in what is now **Winterhaven,** a little cabin village at 7,840 feet with a few gift shops and cafés. Just up a bit from the village are the 22 runs of **Ski Valley** (10300 Ski Run Rd., 520/576-1321, snow report 520/576-1400, 9 A.M.–4 P.M. daily, $11–32), the nation's southernmost ski hill.

The season runs, roughly, from mid-December to early April in a good year. The chairlift operates year-round, and it's fun to ride it to the green and cool mountaintop in the summer while the rest of the world sweats below.

There are dozens of trails on the range, and there are several public bathrooms, campgrounds, and lookout points. It's a good idea to stop at the **Palisade Visitor Center** (520/749-8700, 8:30 A.M.–4:40 P.M. daily) at 7,200 feet, which has trail maps, a bookstore, and displays about the mountain's ecology. There's a $5 per car user fee to go up

FIRE ON FROG MOUNTAIN

The Coronado National Forest had barred campfires and smoking by mid-June of 2003, saying it would take just one careless spark to send flames surging through the brush-choked, bone-dry **Santa Catalina Mountains.**

But the precautions weren't enough to keep the worst from happening. On June 17, 2003, a hiker dropped a cigarette on the Aspen Loop Trail in the range's Pusch Ridge Wilderness. A month later, 84,750 acres had turned black, and 333 structures, including much of the mountain village **Summerhaven,** had turned to ash. It cost $16.3 million to put the fire out; it was finally "contained" (stopped from spreading to new ground) on July 15.

At its peak some 1,270 firefighters and support workers battled the blaze, and half a dozen air-tankers rumbled through great plumes of black smoke to drop their deep-red fire retardant on the forest. The smoke, and at night the flames, were visible across Southern Arizona, especially in Tucson, where residents sat outside on hot nights to watch the mountains burn.

President George Bush declared the fire a federal disaster on July 14, and a month later he visited the Santa Catalina Mountains. By August 2, when the public was allowed back on **Mount Lemmon** to survey the damage for the first time, Summerhaven's residents had already started to rebuild, and later came a

promise of funding help from Pima County. Crews began mulching and reseeding the burned areas from the air before the fire was even out, rehabilitation that would continue until the spring of 2004.

More than five years on and the mountain is alive with new growth, though it looks much different than it did before the fire. Especially in Mount Lemmon's upper reaches, trails lead through large stands of burnt-out husks, and you can't help but get black smudges on your arms and hands if you lean on one for balance. Summerhaven promised to come back better than ever, and the village these days now has a just-built look where it used to seem like an inevitable part of the mountain environment. As everything in nature runs in cycles, Summerhaven may be just starting to look snug and lived-in again in another 60 years or so, just about time for another historic conflagration.

A few months after life got back to normal in Tucson, a young college student was charged with making false statements to law enforcement. Police had questioned the young man about allegations that he'd been smoking in the area where investigators believed the fire had started, on the day it started. He originally denied the accusation but later pleaded guilty to lying to police. He was sentenced to six months of probation and 200 hours of community service.

the mountain, paid at a fee station along the road, or you can buy a annual pass for $20, which will allow you to access the Catalinas, the Santa Rita Mountains in the Santa Cruz Valley, and Sabino Canyon as many times as you like for one year.

Expect not to be alone when you're exploring the Catalinas; this is an extremely popular area among locals for picnicking and hiking, especially in the spring and summer. That being said, while the weekends are sometimes bumper-to-bumper, on weekdays, even in the summer, it's possible to avoid large crowds.

Sabino Canyon

Though in the range's foothills, Sabino Canyon is inextricably linked to the Santa Catalinas because without the mountains there would be very little water to fill up Sabino Creek, and without Sabino Creek this Edenic desert canyon would be just another rugged notch dominated by saguaro.

As it is, though, Sabino Creek starts as springs high up in the mountains, gathering snowmelt and runoff as it descends into the foothills, where it rushes through Sabino Canyon with sometimes-deadly vigor, creating a riparian oasis of cottonwoods, willow, walnut, sycamore, and ash, while saguaro, barrel cactus, prickly pear, and cholla dominate the rocky canyon slopes away from the creek's influence. It is a truly spectacular place that should not be missed.

Sabino Canyon Recreation Area, about 13 miles northeast of downtown Tucson, is easily accessible, user-friendly in the extreme, and heavily used—best estimates say 1.25 million people visit every year. Many locals use the canyon's trail system for daily exercise, and hikers, picnickers, and sightseers usually pack the canyon on any given day in any given season.

A paved road rises nearly four miles up into the canyon, crossing the nearly always running creek in several places. During Southern Arizona's summer and winter rainy seasons, it is nearly impossible to cross the small overflowing bridges without getting your feet wet. The Forest Service closed the road to cars in 1978.

It's a relatively easy walk along the road to the top of the canyon and access to trails that go far into the Santa Catalinas. If you don't feel like walking, the **Sabino Canyon Shuttle** (520/749-2861, www.sabinocanyon.com, $7.50 adults, $3 kids 3–12, under 2 free) runs 45-minute, narrated trips into the canyon all day, pausing at nine stops along the way to take on or let off hikers at various trailheads. From July through mid-December the shuttle runs 9 A.M.–4 P.M. weekdays and 9 A.M.–4:30 P.M. on weekends and holidays. From mid-December to June it runs 9 A.M.–4:30 P.M. daily.

From the last tram stop 3.8 miles up in the canyon, hikers can get off and take an easy stroll down the road, crossing the creek at nearly every turn, or try the **Phoneline Trail** winding along the canyon slopes and overlooking the riparian beauty below. Perhaps the most popular trail in the entire Tucson Valley is the hike through nearby **Bear Canyon** to **Seven Falls,** a wonderful series of waterfalls and collecting pools. You can access the **Bear Canyon Trail** from just outside the visitor center, or take the shuttle to a trailhead 1.5 miles on. To the falls it's a total of 3.8 miles one-way, and worth every step. The Bear Canyon shuttle leaves the visitor center every hour on the hour, 9 A.M.–4 P.M. daily ($3 for adults, $1 kids 3–12).

The **Sabino Canyon Visitors Center and Bookstore** (520/749-8700, www.fs.fed .us/r3/coronado/forest/recreation/camping/ sites/sabino.shtml, 8 A.M.–4:30 P.M. Mon.– Fri., 8:30 A.M.–4:30 P.M. Sat.–Sun.) has trail guides and sells gifts and books. There are bathrooms, drinking fountains, and dozens of tucked-away picnic areas throughout the canyon, and many of the trails link-up with one another, so it is easy to cobble together a loop hike that will take you through all of the various life zones. The canyon is open from sunup to sundown every day, and bikes are allowed in the canyon only before 9 A.M. and after 5 P.M., never on Wednesday and Saturday, and never on trails that lead into the **Pusch Ridge Wilderness Area.**

To get to the canyon from midtown take

Speedway Boulevard east until it turns into Tanque Verde Road, then turn north on Sabino Canyon Road to the Recreation Area, just north of Sunrise Road. There's $5-per-car fee for one day, or $10 for a week. An annual pass can be had for $20.

Catalina State Park

This popular desert reserve (State Hwy. 77, mile marker 81, 520/628-5798, www .azstateparks.com/Parks/parkhtml/catalina. html, 5 A.M.–10 P.M. daily, $5 per car) just north of Tucson in the saguaro-dotted foothills of the Santa Catalinas is heavily used, especially on weekends. Hikers shouldn't be surprised to pass large families carrying coolers and bags of chips up the trail.

The 5,500-acre park has eight trails—most of them easy to moderate—picnic areas, charcoal grills, and a small gift shop. It's an easily accessible place to see the desert, lush here thanks to the runoff and snowmelt that barrels down from the mountains through boulder-strewn washes. In the early spring and late summer there are many natural pools that fill up with runoff, some of them deep enough to be called swimming holes.

The seven-mile **Romero Canyon Trail** will take you to an array of natural pools—and you don't have to hike the whole trail to get there. If you want to get off the beaten track a little, veer right about a mile into the trail near a bench and pick your way down into the wash, then head up the wash following a footpath that leads to some out-of-the-way, less used pools. For an easy walk, take the 0.5-mile round-trip **Romero Ruin Interpretive Trail** to an ancient Hohokam site. The ranger station/gift shop has a guide to all the park's trails, some of which link up to other trails all the way up into the mountains.

Biosphere 2

In the early 1990s eight scientists took up residence in this (32540 S. Biosphere Rd., 520/838-6200, www.b2science.org, 9 A.M.–4 P.M. daily, $20 adults, $13 kids 6–12) 3.14-acre simulation of the earth (which would,

of course, be Biosphere 1) in hopes of lasting two years and gaining important knowledge about how humans will survive in the future. They weren't able to remain self-contained owing to problems with the food supply, but two members of the team fell in love at least. The unique laboratory may yet save the world, however, as the UA is now running experiments under the dome and researching ways to combat climate change.

While the science is fascinating—there are actually small savannas, rainforests, deserts, and even an ocean under the glass—many who take the tour seem more fascinated by the doomed experiments in togetherness. Indeed, the tour takes you into the "Biospherians'" apartments and kitchen, and through their garden, and guides field more questions on this part of the tour than all the others. The tour lasts about 45 minutes and is not handicap accessible. The Biosphere is in a beautiful 35-acre desert setting about 30 minutes north of Tucson near the small town of Oracle.

SOUTH OF DOWNTOWN

Head south from downtown and you reach South Tucson, a largely Latino community incorporated as a separate city. The airport is farther south, and to the southeast is the Pima Air and Space Museum, on the southwest edge of Davis Monthan Airforce Base. To the southwest, reached via I-19, is San Xavier del Bac.

Pima Air and Space Museum

One of the largest museums of its kind in the West, the Pima Air and Space Museum (6000 E. Valencia Rd., 520/574-0462, www.pimaair .org, 9 A.M.–5 P.M. daily, $11.75 adults, $9.75 seniors/military, $8 kids 7–12, kids 6 and under free) has interesting exhibits and an impressive number of decommissioned aircraft that tell the story of our fascination with defying gravity. Nearly 300 rare airplanes, many of them military, rest on the grounds and in six different hangars.

The Air and Space Museum is operated by the same group that operates the Titan Missile Museum near Green Valley, and for one price you can see both attractions. War plane enthusiasts will have to take the hour-long bus tour to the **Aerospace Maintenance and Regeneration Center (AMARC)** to see the hundreds of dust-gathering planes ending their days in this "boneyard."

San Xavier del Bac

Founded in 1692 by Father Eusebio Francisco Kino and then built slowly over decades by other priests, missionaries, and natives, the mission sits pure white against the perpetually blue sky about nine miles south of Tucson on the Tohono O'odham's San Xavier Indian Reservation. It is considered by many to be the foremost example of mission architecture remaining in the United States, blending elements of Moorish, Byzantine, and late Mexican Renaissance architecture.

Few Arizona landmarks have received as much worldwide attention as the "White Dove of the Desert" (1950 W. San Xavier Rd.,

520/294-2624, www.sanxaviermission.org, 8 A.M.–5 P.M. daily, free/donations encouraged), which has been called America's answer to the Sistine Chapel. Mass is still celebrated daily in the church (check website for times), but non-Catholic visitors are encouraged and welcomed.

Most days there are tables and booths set up in the mission's plaza selling burritos, fry bread, and other delicious eats, and across the wide plaza to the south is **San Xavier Plaza,** with a snack bar and several shops selling Native American crafts.

Statues and paintings of St. Francis Xavier and the Virgin of Guadalupe decorate the cool, dark interior of the domed church. A continuous videotape about the mission runs throughout the day as a self-guided tour, and there's a gift shop on-site that sells religious items and books about the history of the mission and the region. A small museum presents the history of the area's native inhabitants and

First built in the 1690s by Father Eusebio Francisco Kino, San Xavier del Bac is constantly undergoing reconstruction.

the interior of San Xavier del Bac, America's Sistine Chapel

the construction and ongoing rehabilitation of the mission. The mission is continually being worked on, but the seemingly ever-present scaffolding doesn't detract too much from its grandeur.

ENTERTAINMENT AND EVENTS

Tucson's nightlife and entertainment scene is casual and mixed, drawing drunken college kids, post-college slackers and go-getters, thirty-something urban workers, hip parents who still haunt the alt-rock shows, and professors and professionals of indeterminate age. There's really something for everybody out there. For upscale watering holes, try the bars at the restaurants detailed under *Fine Dining* in the *Food* section of this chapter. There is no smoking in bars or restaurants in Tucson, but most have built outdoor patios to accommodate smokers. For a generation Arizona's bars closed at 1 A.M., but a few years ago the State Legislature put off last call until 2 A.M.;

however, many bars close much earlier on weekdays.

Theaters and Live Music

From the 1930s to the 1970s, the **Fox Theatre** (17 W. Congress St., 520/624-1515, www.foxtucsontheatre.org, box office open 11 A.M.–6 P.M. Mon.–Fri., 11 A.M.–2 P.M. Sat.) was the place to go in Tucson to see Hollywood's latest offering, and the theater's art deco style nearly matched the glamour on the screen. Along with many other once-famous and much-used buildings in downtown, the Fox fell into disrepair until the late 1990s, when a group formed to raise money to refurbish the old movie house. Now the theater, beautifully restored to its original grandeur, shows classic films several times a month and hosts concerts and events.

The **Rialto** (318 E. Congress St., 520/740-1000, www.rialtotheatre.com, box office open noon–6 P.M. Mon.–Fri.) is a cool old theater with a balcony; its stage regularly hosts the best alt-rock and alt-country touring bands, acts like Ryan Adams, Son Volt, and Shooter Jennings. Across Congress Street from the Hotel Congress downtown, the theater originally opened in 1920 and served over the years as a vaudeville house, silent movie theater, and a porno theater, among other things. Now it operates as a nonprofit organization showing the best concerts in town.

The **Temple of Music and Art** (330 S. Scott Ave., 520/884-4875) is a beautiful old theater and play house built in 1927 downtown. It is the main stage for the Arizona Theatre Company and hosts concerts and shows throughout the year.

Nightlife

Tucson's most vibrant nightlife takes place on three blocks within easy walking, or stumbling, distance of each other: Congress Street downtown, 4th Avenue, and Main Gate Square near the UA. There are always plenty of cabs waiting around outside the bars in these neighborhoods, especially on the weekends. When school's in session these areas are fairly packed

SOUTHERN ARIZONA

© TIM HULL

with scantily clad young women and boys in flip-flops and baseball caps (a large contingent of the UA's student body is from California).

That doesn't mean that townies don't go out; in fact, a bartender at the Hotel Congress' **Tap Room** (311 East Congress St., 520/622-8848, www.hotelcongress.com) said that it's just as busy during Spring Break and summer as it is when the students are in town. This cramped old cowboy bar (it has been around since 1919) still packs them in, especially when a band is playing at **Club Congress,** the city's premier spot for touring alternative rock and country bands. Most nights if there's not a band playing at Club Congress, there's a DJ and dancing.

Head west from the Hotel Congress along Congress Street and you'll find several bars and clubs, many of them with dancing, billiards, and DJs. As downtown revitalization moves along in fits and starts, the names and owners of downtown watering holes change fairly regularly. Eventually the higher rents that will inevitably come with revitalization are sure to gentrify and chainify the area, but for now the bars here are mostly locally owned and offer venues for all sorts of local music. One relatively long-lasting, super-cool drinking place on Congress is **Vaudeville Cabaret** (110 E. Congress St., 520/622-3535, www.vaudeville cabaret.com, call for hours), with an artful interior and paintings so good they nearly distract from the eclectic march of bands from around the region that regularly play this venue.

After you've done Congress, take a short stroll over to 4th Avenue, where you'll find the **Shanty** (401 E. 9th St., 520/623-2664, 12 P.M.–1 A.M. Mon.–Wed., noon–2 A.M. Thurs.–Sat., 12 P.M.–12 A.M. Sun.) an old railroad workers' bar turned Irish pub turned college kid hangout. A large patio lined with greenery is usually crowded on the weekends with, as in most Tucson bars, a mixture of the young and the not-so-young, all drinking together. A little farther along 4th you'll find **Plush** (340 E. 6th St., 520/798-1302, call for hours), a well-appointed, comfortable club frequented by downtown artists and musicians, hipsters, and students. Plush is the place on

4th to experience Tucson's vibrant music scene, as well as nationally known alternative rock and alternative country acts. There are often acts playing in the front living-room area and on a stage in the back; there's also a patio for smoking.

Also on 4th, **IBT's** (616 N. 4th Ave., 520/882-3053, www.ibts.net, noon–2 A.M. daily) is Tucson's most popular gay bar, a much bigger place than it looks to be from the outside. Follow the revelers toward the back and you'll find a dance floor and a smoking patio.

Dancing

El Parador (2744 E. Broadway, 520/881-2744, www.elparadortucson.com, 4–9 P.M. Mon.–Thurs., 4–10 P.M. Fri.–Sat., brunch 10:30 A.M.–2 P.M. Sun.) has salsa dancing with a live band 10 P.M.–2 A.M. and dance lessons every Friday beginning at 10:15 P.M. Every second and fourth Saturday of the month, a live salsa band performs 10 P.M.–2 A.M., and there is a disc jockey and dancing 10 P.M.–2 A.M. on the first and third Saturdays.

Cactus Moon Café (5460 E. Broadway Blvd., 520/748-0049), is where the cowboys and cowgirls, urban or otherwise, hang out. It has a huge central dance floor surrounded by booths and tables, and a cavernous space that can fit hundreds of Western-clad revelers. It's not all line-dancing and honky-tonk shuffling, though; DJs will mix up the broadcast with disco and urban dance music as well. A large UA student contingent is usually in-house on the weekends.

Film

If you want to see the latest Hollywood blockbuster or just about any other film in wide release try one of the 20 screens at midtown's **Century El Con** (3601 E. Broadway, 520/202-3343). The best theater in town is **The Loft Cinema** (3233 E. Speedway Blvd., 520/795-0844, www.loftcinema.com), which shows art-house foreign films, and free showings of classic films on Sunday afternoons and Monday nights. There's always something worth seeing at this remodeled old theater, and you can buy a beer and a slice of fancy pizza to go with all the soul-searching on the big screen.

Comedy

Touring stand-up comedians from around the country stop at **Laffs Comedy Club** (2900 E. Broadway Ste. 154, 520/323-8669, www.laffs comedyclub.com), with show times at 8 P.M. Thursday, 8 P.M. and 10:30 P.M. Friday, and 7 P.M. and 9:30 P.M. Saturday. It costs $7 to get in Thursday, and $10 Friday and Saturday.

Performing Arts

The **Arizona Theatre Company** (330 S. Scott Ave., 520/622-2823) puts on an excellent season of plays September–May at the Temple of Music and Art, and the **Arizona Opera** (520/293-4336, www.azopera.org) presents some of the best regional opera in the country October–April at the TCC Music Hall (260 S. Church Ave.). The **Tucson Symphony** (520/882-8585, www.tucsonsymphony.org) holds concerts September–May at the TCC Music Hall.

Casinos

The completely refurbished **Desert Diamond Casino & Hotel** on Tucson's south side (7350 S. Nogales Hwy., 520/294-7777 or 866/332-9467, www.desertdiamondcasino .com), operated by the Tohono O'odham, has slot machines, blackjack, poker, keno, and bingo, as well as a grill and a Chinese restaurant, and a new hotel that opened in late 2007. Take I-19 south to Pima Mine Road and you'll discover the other **Desert Diamond Casino** (520/294-7777, www.desertdiamondcasino .com) operated by the Tohono O'odham. It has slot machines, blackjack, poker, keno, and bingo, and serves home-style meals at an all-you-can eat buffet. **The Agave Restaurant** serves wonderful, eclectic lunches and dinners 11 A.M.–9 P.M. daily. There's a constant stream of talent moving through Desert Diamond's intimate concert theater, which has hosted top-name acts like Willie Nelson and Bob Dylan.

West of I-19 on Valencia Road the Pascua Yaqui Tribe operates **Casino Del Sol** (800/344-9435, www.casinodelsol.com), a Mediterranean-influenced funland with poker, slots, bingo, blackjack, and keno. The complex has several places to eat and drink, including the delicious **Bellissimo**, which serves continental cuisine dinners daily 5–11 P.M. Stick around after the gaming for a concert in the casino's amphitheater, which regularly hosts major touring acts.

Events

In January the multicultural **Family Arts Festival** (Tucson Pima Arts Council, 520/624-0595,www.familyartsfestival.org) features exhibits, concerts, and performances. February is dominated by the biggest local event of them all, **Tucson Gem & Mineral Show** (520/322-5773, www.tgms.org), which brings thousands of visitors to the Old Pueblo. The busy month also welcomes the **La Fiesta de Los Vaqueros** (800/964-5662, www.tucson rodeo.com), Tucson's famed rodeo and parade—the longest non-mechanized parade in the world. The **Southwest Indian Art Fair and Market** (520/621-6302, www.state museum.arizona.edu) in February brings the region's top jewelers, potters, weavers, and carvers from the Navajo, Hopi, Zuni, and other tribes. March brings the "Boys of Spring" back to town as **MLB Spring Training** (866/672-1343, www.cactus-league.com) gets under way, and civil war enthusiasts recreate the Battle of Picacho Pass during the **Civil War in the Southwest** (www.pr.state.az.us/Parks/ parkhtml/picacho.html). Also in March, the Tohono O'odham hold their annual gathering at Mission San Xavier del Bac during the **Wa:k Powwow** (520/294-5727, www.pow wows.com). Cinephiles file into town in April to catch the **Arizona International Film Festival** (520/628-1737, www.azmac.org).

The Tucson Kitchen Musicians put on their signature event, the always fun (and free) **Tucson Folk Festival** (www.tkma.org) in May. With the heat of June comes prayers and dances for rain on **Dia de San Juan,** a series of festivals and rituals celebrating John the Baptist and the saint's historical relationship with the desert's summer rainy season. Ski Valley on Mt. Lemmon celebrates **Oktoberfest on Mt. Lemmon** (520/885-1181) a month early in September. In October the **Tucson Culinary Festival** (www.tucson culinaryfestival.com) features top local and national chefs and lots of good food. Also during the Halloween month, Old Tucson Studios hosts its popular annual horror show called **Nightfall** (520/883-0100, www.nightfallaz .com). November features the non-motorized parade through downtown called the **All Soul's Procession,** featuring giant puppets and other Mexican-inspired folk traditions.

SHOPPING

David Puddy asked it on Seinfeld: "What can you get at the Gap in Rome that you can't get at the Gap on 5th Avenue?" Use this as your mantra while shopping in Tucson and Southern Arizona.

The Old Pueblo has all the chains, more so than most midsized cities. But if you spend your time at the Gap you're going to miss a unique shopping experience—a chance to find that treasure that has eluded you, to return home with an authentic artifact.

You'll find merchants with Mexican imports, folk arts, Western Americana, and Indian jewelry; boutiques with clothes you'll find nowhere else, and galleries featuring the work of artists from Tucson and the rest of the world.

Take a short drive south to Tubac—an artist's village that caters to, or better yet exists for, the discriminating treasure hunter—then on across the border to Nogales, Sonora, and you'll find items you never knew you had to have. A brief scenic journey east and you're among the antique stores and artisan boutiques of old-town Bisbee.

Fear not, shopping in Southern Arizona isn't just for the moneyed (it helps, though). There are finds for everyone, and for every budget.

Shopping Centers

Main Gate Square (University Blvd.,

520/622-8613, www.maingatesquare.com) is right next to the University of Arizona and so is frequented by students. There are 52 stores and restaurants on this block, including **Urban Outfitters** and **Landmark Clothing & Shoes.** This is a good place to walk around and have lunch, and there's always something new opening or moving in. Be careful about parking; instead of braving the back-in-only metered parking, go to the **Main Gate Parking Garage** (815 E. 2nd St.) and leave your car in shade and safety.

The ideal upscale shopping experience can be found in the foothills at Skyline Drive and Campbell Avenue. **La Encantada** (2905 E. Skyline Dr. Ste. 279, 520/299-3556, 10 A.M.–7 P.M. Mon.–Wed., 10 A.M.–8 P.M. Thurs.–Sat., 11 A.M.–6 P.M. Sun.) has posh shops like **Tiffany & Co., Luis Vuitton, Crate & Barrel,** and dozens more in a lush, two-level outdoor setting. Also in the foothills but more for the value-minded shopper is the **Foothills Mall** (7401 N. La Cholla Blvd., 520/219-0650, www.shopfoothillsmall.com, 10 A.M.–9 P.M. Mon.–Sat., 11 A.M.–6 P.M. Sun.), with more than 90 stores, many of them designer outlets. Here you'll find the **Nike Factory Store, Off 5th-Saks Fifth Avenue Outlet,** a Levi's **Outlet** and many more. Plus, there's no city sales tax here. Take I-10 north to the Ina Road exit and then head east to La Cholla Boulevard.

Park Place Mall (5870 E. Broadway Blvd., 520/748-1222, www.parkplacemall.com, 10 A.M.–9 P.M. Mon.–Thurs., 10 A.M.–10 P.M. Fri., 8 A.M.–10 P.M. Sat., 11 A.M.–6 P.M. Sun.) at the eastern edge of midtown has big anchor department stores like **Dillard's** and **Macy's** and popular shops like **Abercrombie & Fitch.** On the city's north side, the **Tucson Mall** (4500 N. Oracle Rd., 520/293-7330, www.tucsonmall.com, 10 A.M.–9 P.M. Mon.–Thurs., 10 A.M.–10 P.M. Fri., 8 A.M.–10 P.M. Sat., 11 A.M.–6 P.M. Sun.) has a similar lineup, along with **Arizona Avenue,** a row of specialty shops selling Arizona- and Western-themed merchandise. From downtown take Oracle north until you see the mall.

Specialty Shops

Vintage clothing for New Bohemians is how the founder of **The Buffalo Exchange** (2001 E. Speedway, 520/795-0508, 10 A.M.–8 P.M. Mon.–Fri., 10 A.M.–7 P.M. Sat., 11 A.M.–6 P.M. Sun.) describes her first store in Tucson. Now the chain has spread throughout the country to college towns and bohemian enclaves from Tempe to Brooklyn, but it all started in midtown Tucson in the early 1970s. This boutique, which has several Tucson locations including a store dedicated to children's clothes, offers some of the most unique used clothes you'll ever find.

If you're looking for a unique treasure to commemorate your trip to the desert, try the shops along **4th Avenue,** especially **Del Sol** (435 N. 4th Ave., 9 A.M.–6 P.M. Sun.–Tues., 9 A.M.–9 P.M. Wed.–Sat.), which has some one-of-a-kind items made in Tucson. For the best in Indian art and artifacts, Spanish Colonial furniture, and jewelry, check out **Morning Star Traders** (2020 E. Speedway, 520/881-2112, www.morningstartraders.com), but call ahead for operating hours. If you're looking for general antiques, there are several treasure-trove stores along Grant Avenue near Tucson Boulevard.

Books, Maps, and Outdoor Supplies

Book lovers can't miss **Bookmans** (6230 E. Speedway Rd., 520/748-9555, 9 A.M.–10 P.M. daily), a Southern Arizona original, which now has clones throughout the state. There are three Bookmans stores in Tucson, all of them featuring thousands of used books, CDs, videos, DVDs, and video games, but the relatively new Speedway location has become the firm's flagship store. Prices are cheap compared to smaller, boutique-style used book stores, and the selection is absolutely without compare. This is one of the West's best used bookstores.

Clues Unlimited (123 South Eastbourne, 520/326-8533, www.cluesunlimited.com, 9 A.M.–5 P.M. Mon.–Sat., noon–5 P.M. Sun.) sells mysteries exclusively, including an unparalleled selection of British imports. It's in **Broadway Village** at the corner of Broadway and Country Club, which has several unique boutiques and eateries.

For books on Arizona's history and wildlands, all the maps you could ever want, and the flags of every country in the world, go to **Tucson's Map & Flag Center** (3239 N. First Ave., 520/887-4234, www.tucsonmaps.com, 8 A.M.–5:30 P.M. Mon.–Fri., 9 A.M.–5:30 P.M. Sat.).

You'll find topographical maps and hiking guides, bedrolls, backpacks, outdoor clothing, and everything else one needs while outfitting for a desert adventure, including a large selection of mountaineering equipment, at **The Summit Hut** (5045 E. Speedway Blvd., 520/325-1554, www.summithut.com, 9 A.M.–8 P.M. Mon.–Fri., 9 A.M.–6:30 P.M. Sat., 10 A.M.–6:30 P.M. Sun.).

PARKS AND RECREATION

The best park in the city is **Reid Park**, with its tennis courts, golf course, soccer fields, lakes, and a two-mile, paved loop-trail used by walkers, runners, and bikers. The park is about three miles east of downtown on Randolph Way—head toward the corner of Alvernon Way and Broadway Boulevard and you can't miss it. Call **Tucson City Parks and Recreation** (520/791-4873) for more information. On the edges of the city you'll find parks that are more like nature preserves. For those of us who would rather watch than do, there's Spring Training baseball and the exciting UA sports teams.

Sentinel Peak

Also called "A" Mountain for the large white—or, since 9-11, red, white, and blue—"A" repainted on its face every year by University of Arizona students (a tradition that began in 1915), **Sentinel Peak** (498 S. Sentinel Peak Rd., 8 A.M.–8 P.M. Mon.–Sat., 8 A.M.–6 P.M. Sun.) served the early populations of the Tucson valley with spring water and black basalt. When Father Kino first rode into the valley in the 1690s, he found the native population living in the small peak's shadow, and it was surely an important landmark in the basin for eons before that. During the presidio days it earned its name as a promontory from which soldiers would scan the desert for Apaches.

Now there's a park on the peak, reached by a paved, winding road to the top. Take Congress Street west under I-10 and follow the signs. There are a few short trails around the park, a little rock shelter to sit under, charcoal barbecues, and some great views of the valley.

Tucson Mountain Park

This 20,000-acre desert preserve surrounding the Arizona-Sonoran Desert Museum and Old Tucson (www.pima.gov/nrpr/places/parkpgs/tucs_mtpk, 7 A.M.–10 P.M. daily) has cactus-lined trails for hiking, biking, and horseback riding and features one of the largest saguaro stands in the world. Make sure to drive over **Gates Pass,** a rugged overlook accessed by driving west on Speedway Boulevard until it turns into Gates Pass Road.

The 5.5-mile desert-country **David Yetman Trail,** named for the host of the PBS show *The Desert Speaks,* is a popular trail. The five-mile **Gates Pass Trail** also offers some spectacular views. If you want to stay the night at the park, the **Gilbert Ray Campground** (8451 W. McCain Loop, off Kinney Rd., 520/883-4200, $10–20) has sites with RV hookups, picnic tables, restrooms, and a dumping station.

Spectator Sports

The biggest sports draw in the region are the teams of the University of Arizona. With perennial powerhouses in basketball, volleyball, and baseball, and a Pac-10 football team that is expected to hold its own in a tough division, there's always something to cheer for on campus. For ticket information call the UA's McKale Center (520/621-2287), www.arizonaathletics.com). Don't expect it to be easy.

Every March Major League Baseball brings **Spring Training** and **Cactus League Baseball** to Tucson. The **Chicago White Sox** and the **Arizona Diamondbacks** play at Tucson Electric Park (2500 E. Ajo Way, 520/434-1000), and the **Colorado Rockies** work out at Hi Corbett Field at Reid Park (520/327-9467).

In February, the PGA and Tiger Woods

stop off in Tucson for the **Accenture Match Play Championships** (888/603-7600, www.worldgolfchampionships.com) at Dove Mountain, bringing along the world's top 64 golfers to battle it out for an oversized $8 million check.

ACCOMMODATIONS

Tucson has a wide variety of chain hotels in all price ranges. There are also several one-of-a-kind, Tucson-only places to stay. If you are budget-minded, cruise along the I-10 frontage road just west of downtown, where you'll find a row of chains, a few of them a bit shabby; however, if the annual Gem and Mineral Show is in session (Jan. 26–Feb. 11), this stretch is choked with displays and getting a room will be impossible. Plan on paying more for a room anywhere in the city during the Gem Show. It's a good idea to make reservations most times during the year, though in the summer you're likely to find vacancies galore and prices cheaper than during the cooler, busier months.

$50-100

The only hostel in Tucson is the **Roadrunner Hostel and Inn** (346 E. 12th St., 520/628-4709, cell 520/940-7280, roadrunr@dakotacom.net, $24 for dorm, $48 for private room), which offers free linens and blankets, showers, laundry, and a large kitchen for guests to use. **Motel 6** (960 S. Freeway, 520/628-1339, www.motel6.com, $37–59 d) is the old standby of budget travelers the world over; this one has a heated pool. **Roadway Inn** (1248 N. Stone Ave. 520/622-6446, $65–95 d) is an inexpensive but clean chain located close to downtown and the University of Arizona; it features a complimentary breakfast, cable, and a pool.

The **Hotel Congress** (311 E. Congress St., 800/722-8848, reservations@hotelcongress.com, $49–109 d), known to locals and history buffs as the hotel where members of John Dillinger's gang were arrested (Dillinger was captured at a nearby home), is a historic downtown hotel that offers charm and atmosphere. Built in 1919 and remodeled only slightly since then, it's listed on the National

Historic Register. Beware the noise most nights coming from the Club Congress downstairs (it's not too bad, but there is a thumping that comes through the walls). The club is a venue for alternative bands and alt-country bands from across the nation, and the Tap Room bar will make you feel like a cowboy on his day off. The Cup Café off the beautiful old lobby has an eclectic mix of gourmet and Southwestern-style food for breakfast, lunch, and dinner.

The **Doubletree Hotel at Reid Park** (445 S. Alvernon Way, 520/881-4200, $79–289 d) is right across the street from the sprawling urban park, near golf courses, the zoo, and pretty much everything else in midtown. The hotel has a heated pool, exercise room, tennis courts, high-speed Internet, and two restaurants. The **Smuggler's Inn** (6350 E. Speedway Blvd., 520/296-3292, $79 d) is an eastside institution set amidst lush gardens and lagoons. It's not as fancy as it used to seem, what with all the glittering new chains around, but it's still an affordable and memorable place to stay, offering rooms with patios overlooking the gardens, a pool and spa, and proximity to many restaurants.

Another historic Old Pueblo hotel is the **Lodge on the Desert** (306 N. Alvernon Way, 520/325-3366, www.lodgeonthedesert .com, $94–309 d), built on what in 1936 was still the desert but is now midtown. Beautiful grounds, a pool and spa, and top-notch dining among a historic atmosphere make the lodge a memorable place to stay. In the summer of 2008, the lodge was undergoing a major expansion project, adding 65 rooms. Construction is expected to be complete by early 2009. Not as quaint and memorable but still quite comfortable is the **Windmill Suites at St. Phillips Plaza** (4250 N. Campbell Ave., 520/577-0007, www.wind millinns.com, $79–189 d), located in an upscale shopping plaza with art galleries and a day spa; the hotel offers free coffee and continental breakfast, a heated pool, whirlpool, bike rentals, a lending library, and wireless Internet.

Over $100

If you are looking for a relatively affordable urban compound, **Embassy Suites Williams** Center (5335 E. Broadway, 520/573-0700 or 800/362-2779, www.hilton.com, $99–249 d) offers rooms with kitchenettes and refrigerators, a pool and spa, free happy hour and breakfast, exercise room, and high-speed Internet, located in midtown close to everything. The **Arizona Inn** (2200 E. Elm St., 520/325-1541 or 800/933-1093, www.arizona inn.com, $149–300 d) is a true Tucson landmark. Founded in 1930 by Isabella Greenway, Arizona's first female member of Congress, the inn has 86 rooms on 14 acres of gardens and beautifully landscaped grounds in the heart of the city. All rooms have writing desks, refrigerators, televisions, DVD players, high-speed Internet, bathrobes, and much more. Rooms range from standard suites to deluxe suites. A stay at this elegant hideaway in the middle of town includes complimentary afternoon tea, ice cream by the pool, nightly music in the Audubon Bar, free use of a well-stocked library, a 60-foot heated outdoor pool, and clay tennis courts.

The beautiful (**El Presidio Inn Bed & Breakfast** (297 N. Main Ave., 520/623-6151 or 800/349-6151, $120–150 d), in the Julius Kruttschnitt House, built in 1886 and remodeled over the years with various architectural styles, is one of the city's best small inns, with a cool garden courtyard setting in the historic heart of town. The **Royal Elizabeth Bed and Breakfast Inn** (204 S. Scott, 877/670-9022, www.royalelizabeth.com) is in a beautiful home known as the Blenman House, built in 1878 in Tucson's El Presidio District. It's now on the National Register of Historic Places. There are six large rooms to choose from, all elegantly decorated in an old-world style, with big sweeping beds and footed stand-alone bathtubs. There's also a heated pool and spa and immaculate grounds. Rates run $155–285 a night, with a two-night minimum on weekends. The **Sam Hughes Inn** (2020 E. 7th St., 520/861-2191, www.samhughesinn .com, $105–130 d) is nestled in the historic residential neighborhood that gives it its name. The home was built in 1931 in the Spanish style so popular around Tucson, and offers four rooms, each uniquely decorated. Sam

TUCSON RESORTS

Visitors and émigrés have sought healing in Southern Arizona since at least the early 19th century. Any tubercular patient lucky enough to flee the crowded, disease-ridden tenements of the Northeast or the malarial bottomlands of the South was invariably advised to seek the high and dry air of the Southwest. Nineteenth century medicine being what it was, physicians had little else but this general, somewhat specious advice to offer the scores of Americans who suffered from TB, fevers, dysentery, and other ailments of the chest and the blood.

Scholar Billy Jones, in his book *Health-Seekers in the Southwest 1817-1900*, estimates that some 20-25 percent of those who moved to the Southwest during the great migrations of the 19th and 20th centuries did so hoping to cure some ailment, creating a kind of "Health Frontier." In Tucson this resulted in the haphazard construction of vast tent-cities on the outskirts of town, populated by consumptives and often destitute men and women not long for the world.

Medical science has since cured most of the diseases that once brought sickly travelers to the desert, but that hasn't stopped today's visitors from seeking health of a different breed. Tucson has long rivaled its ritzy northern neighbors Scottsdale and Sedona as a place where the afflicted, both physically and psychically, can find solace – usually very expensive solace.

Canyon Ranch (8600 E. Rockcliff Rd., 520/749-9000 or 800/742-9000, www.canyonranch.com), perhaps Tucson's most famous resort, is representative of what the other top resorts offer. Here you can not only pamper yourself silly with spa treatments (an activity sure to lead to optimum, albeit temporary, good health), but then it's off to appointments with a staff nutritionist, chiropractor, acupuncturist, and internist. A personal trainer will work with you on keeping in shape long-term, while a meditation class will help you get in tune with your spirituality. After one of your three gourmet (but healthy) meals every day, you can attend lectures and classes on various topics in healthful living.

For an experience reportedly so meaningful, it's not surprising that you're going to have spend accordingly. A minimum three-night stay at Canyon Ranch is going to set you back $2,600-5,020 per person, depending on accommodations. That's all-inclusive, however; for that price you get three gourmet meals a day, spa treatments galore, consultations with all the medical professionals on staff, and unlimited activities. The high season at Canyon Ranch is September 23-June 7th, after which, as it is with all Tucson's resorts, prices drop rather dramatically.

It's no wonder that guests often come away from a few days at a Tucson spa with a new outlook on life. One young woman who spent three days at **Miraval, Life in Balance Resort & Spa** (5000 E. Via Estancia Miraval, Catalina, 520/825-4000 or 800/232-3969, www.miravalresorts.com), a favorite spot of no less an authority on living life to the fullest than Oprah Winfrey, said that she thinks of her life as having two general periods: before Miraval, and after Miraval.

Hacienda del Sol Guest Ranch Resort (5601 N. Hacienda del Sol Rd., 520/299-1501 or 800/728-6514, www.haciendadelsol.com) offers casitas for $495 a night, and a historic courtyard room goes for $175 a night on the weekdays. **Loews Ventana Canyon Resort** (7000 N. Resort Dr., 520/299-2020 or 800/234-5117, www.loewshotels.com/hotels/tucson, $345-495 d) was rated number 31 of the Top 100 golf resorts in the nation by *Conde Nast Traveler*. The resort has a popular star-gazing program and a desert setting you won't soon forget. There's also **The Westin La Paloma Resort & Spa** (3800 E. Sunrise Dr., 800/937-8461, westinlapalomaresort.com, $299-489 d) and the **Westward Look Resort** (245 E. Ina Rd., 520/297-1151 or 800/722-2500, www.westwardlook.com $139-339 d), which promises health seekers, just as the desert has done for generations, a "rejuvenating resort environment inspired by the beauty of its pristine natural surroundings."

Hughes is centrally located just a few blocks from the University of Arizona. The **Catalina Park B&B** (309 E. 1st St., 520/792-4541 or 800/792-4885, www.catalinaparkinn.com, $106–166 d) in the West University Historic District was built in 1927 and has beautiful mixed gardens with many native plants. There are six rooms, two of which are detached from the main house. This inn is close to the UA, downtown, and midtown. Wireless Internet throughout the property makes it a great place for combining business and pleasure. The inn is closed in July and August.

FOOD

Tucson is famous for its Mexican restaurants, most of them serving Sonoran-style food. The Old Pueblo is full of non-Mexican dining as well, including some high-end places that would be the envy of any town, anywhere. But you can't come to the border region without sampling the local tastes, and herein you will find the best restaurants at which to do just that.

Diners and Delis

The B-line (621 N. 4th Ave., 520/882-7575, 7:30 A.M.–10 P.M. Tues.–Sat., 7:30 A.M.–8 P.M. Sun.) has huge breakfast burritos, a full coffee bar, and free wireless Internet. Make sure to check out the art on the walls. **Bison Witches Deli and Bar** (326 N. 4th Ave., 520/740-1541, 11 A.M.–midnight daily for kitchen, until 2 A.M. for bar, $2.75–7) has overstuffed sandwiches, soup in bread bowls, and good beers on tap. It gets a little crowded on the weekends but is worth the wait.

If you want a creative deli-style sandwich or a slice of stone-fired pizza try **Time Market** (444 E. University Blvd., 520/622-0761, 9 A.M.–8 P.M., daily) between 4th Avenue and the University. The **Rincon Market** (2513 Sixth St., 520/327-6653, 7 A.M.–10 P.M. Mon.–Fri, 7 A.M.–8 P.M. Sat., 8 A.M.–8 P.M. Sun.) has delicious sandwiches and a nightly entrée, usually served to go. On the weekends there's a fabulous, but crowded, omelette bar.

The best greasy spoon in Tucson, and perhaps the greasiest, is **Frank's/Francisco's** (3843 E. Pima, 520/881-2710, 6 A.M.–2 P.M. and 5–10 P.M. Mon.–Thurs., 6 A.M.–2 P.M. and 5 P.M.–midnight Fri., 7 A.M.–2 P.M. and 5 P.M.–midnight Sat., 8 A.M.–2 P.M. and 5–10 P.M. Sun., $1.40–9), whose motto is "Elegant Dining Elsewhere." You can sit at a rickety table or belly up to the bar and watch your hash browns cook on the grill. The breakfast menu has all you'd expect, with the addition of Mexican favorites that come highly recommended. There's nothing like getting all spiced up early in the morning. At night Frank's becomes Francisco's and serves Michoacán-style Mexican food and gives away free slow-cooked pinto beans to go.

The locally beloved **Beyond Bread** (3026 N. Campbell Ave., 520/322-9965; 6260 E. Speedway Blvd., 520/747-7477, www.beyond bread.com, 6:30 A.M.–8 P.M. Mon.–Fri., 7 A.M.–8 P.M. Sat., $2.50–7.50) consistently scores Best Breakfast and Best Sandwich honors on the city's many "Best of Tucson" lists. Most nights the only place to eat open downtown is the **The Grill** (100 E. Congress St., 520/623-7621, open 24 hrs., $2–12), a favorite with the city's bohemians and music scenesters. Try the tater tots, but don't expect prompt service or a lot of small talk from the staff.

American

The **Cup Café** (311 E. Congress St., 520/798-1618, 7 A.M.–10 P.M. Sun.–Thurs., 7 A.M.–11 P.M. Fri.–Sat., $3.50–24) serves an eclectic blend of American food with a dash of several ethnic traditions. Inside the Hotel Congress downtown, The Cup is a popular weekend breakfast destination but is a perfect choice for lunch and dinner anytime. Dishes may jump from hummus to nachos, with entrées like borracho (drunk) pork tenderloin, marinated in tequila and chipotles, served with a sweet potato gratin, country green beans, and a red onion marmalade.

The **Cushing Street Grill** (198 W. Cushing St., 520/622-7984, www.cushingstreet.com, 11 A.M.–midnight daily, 4 P.M.–close in summer, $3.50–18), on the edge of the Barrio Historico, has been operating out of its

SOUTHERN ARIZONA

circa-1860s historic building since 1972. It's a nice space, with garden patio dining available when the weather permits, which is most of the time. The place is known for its carefully made mojito ($8), concocted with loads of fresh mint. Many of the entrees have a Southwestern flair—try the "gulf tacos" with fish fresh from the Sea of Cortez, just a few hundred miles south. Reservations are recommended.

If you want a gourmet meal but don't feel like taking off your swimsuit, go to **Feast** (4122 E. Speedway Blvd., 520/326-9363 or 520/326-6500, www.eatatfeast.com, 11 A.M.–9 P.M. Tues.–Sun., $3.25–17.50) for its "tasteful takeout." There's nothing like eating smoked Angus prime rib with a sherry-and-roasted garlic glaze and blue cheese scalloped potatoes on the bed while watching a movie. The menu changes monthly.

Huge and delicious omelettes can be had at the **Blue Willow** (2616 N. Campbell Ave., 520/327-7577, 7 A.M.–9 P.M. Mon.–Thurs., 8 A.M.–10 P.M. Sat., 8 A.M.–9 P.M. Sun.; $8–12), serving out of a cute old house with a large covered patio in Campbell Avenue's busy commercial district. The emphasis here is on fresh, homemade, and all natural. A gift shop sells funny stickers, buttons, and knickknacks about politics and gender issues.

Fine Dining

Located downtown on the bottom level of the historic Oddfellows Hall building, 🄲 **Barrio** (135 S. 6th Ave., 520/629-0191, www.barrio foodanddrink.com, 11 A.M.–9 P.M. Mon., 11 A.M.–10 P.M. Tues.–Thurs., 11 A.M.–midnight Fri., noon–midnight Sat., 5–9 P.M. Sun., $8.50–28) offers a true dining experience in an elegant space. With fresh fish and beef specials and unique desserts, as well as a full bar and private, romantic booths, Barrio is the ideal place for a special couple's night out. Try the venison rubbed with a dry barbecue, pan-seared and served on a bed of shoestring potatoes. Barrio also offers a well-stocked wine list and specialty drinks. This place is perfect for a post- or pre-theater or opera dinner (both

venues are located nearby), or a long, luxurious lunch.

Kingfisher (2564 E. Grant Rd., 520/323-7739, www.kingfishertucson.com, 11 A.M.–3 P.M., Mon.–Fri. and 5–10 P.M. daily, $8–24) has fresh seafood and serves 15 different varieties of oyster. Every summer the chef creates a "Road Trip" of regional American cuisine and takes diners on a culinary journey, switching to a different region and a new menu every two weeks. A limited menu is served for late-night diners, and there's live jazz and blues on some nights.

Janos Restaurant (3770 E. Sunrise Drive, 520/615-6100, www.janos.com, 5:30–9:00 P.M. Mon.–Thurs., 5:30–9:30 P.M. Fri.–Sat., $15–50) may be the most famous restaurant in Tucson, with its celebrity chef Janos Wilder. It's a bit of a drive up into the tony foothills to sample this place, but gourmands won't want to miss it. The menu is all over the globe, offering green tea–smoked duck, stir-fried bok choy, and cinnamon-spiced pears right next to Oaxacan lamb barbacoa with green corn tamale pie. You might have to go back more than once. Wilder calls his adjacent **J Bar** (3770 E. Sunrise Dr., 520/615-6100, www.janos. com, 5–9:30 P.M. Mon.–Sat., happy hour 5–6:30 P.M. Mon.–Sat., $6–28) "a Latin Grill," and his carne asada in cilantro adobo is an interesting variation on a Sonoran-style favorite. J Bar also has a whole host of creative drinks and a daily happy hour, though you'll find the drink prices higher at J Bar's happy hour than they are at most places during regular hour.

Also serving up a delicious fusion of tastes is **Terra Cotta** (3500 E. Sunrise Dr., 520/577-8100, www.cafeterracotta.com, lunch 11:30 A.M.–3 P.M. Mon.–Fri., dinner from 4 P.M. daily, brunch 10 A.M.–3 P.M. Sun., dinner and brunch only in summer, $6–26), another of the foothills restaurants giving Tucson a good name these days in food circles. "Innovative regional flavors" is how the owners describe their style. They have sought to make their fare truly Southwestern, which means using ingredients native to the American

Southwest, Northern Mexico, and farther south. The grilled New York strip steak with Oaxacan barbecue sauce, tobacco onions, and garlic mashed potatoes is a meal you'll dream about long after it's done, and the wood-fired pizzas and creative starters are delightful.

Asian

Karuna's Thai Plate (1917 E. Grant Rd., 520/325-4129, noon–3 P.M. and 5–9 P.M., Tues.–Thurs., noon–3 P.M. and 5–10 P.M. Fri.–Sat., 5–9 P.M. Sun., $5–15) has a daily buffet and delicious, reasonably priced entrées. **Sushi-Cho** (1830 E. Broadway Blvd., 520/628-8800, 11 A.M.–2:30 P.M. and 5–10 P.M. Mon.–Fri., 5–10 P.M. Sat.) has some of the freshest, best-prepared sushi in town. **Guilin Healthy Chinese Restaurant** (3250 E. Speedway Blvd., 520/320-7768, 11 A.M.–9 P.M. Mon.–Thurs., 11 A.M.–10 P.M. Fri., 11:30 A.M.–9:30 P.M. Sat., 11:30 A.M.–9 P.M. Sun., $10–14) has many dishes for vegetarians.

Steaks and Chops

◖ **El Corral Restaurant** (2201 E. River Rd., 520/299-6092, www.elcorraltucson.com, 5–10 P.M. Mon.–Thurs., 4:30–10 P.M. Fri.–Sun., $8.95–18.95) in the foothills along River Road has the best prime rib in town, served with beans and great starters, and pictures on the walls and other memorabilia of the great movie cowboys.

The cowboy steaks at **Pinnacle Peak** (6541 E. Tanque Verde Rd., 520/296-0911, www.pinnaclepeaktucson.com, 5–10 P.M. Mon.–Fri., 4:30–10 P.M. Sat.–Sun, $4.95–18.95) are huge and served with delicious beans, and while you're waiting for your table you can look around the kitschy Old West town outside the steakhouse.

Mexican

Rosa's (1750 E. Fort Lowell Rd. #164, 520/325-0362, www.rosasmexicanfood.com, 11 A.M.–10 P.M. daily, $2.50–10.50) is a favorite of Willie Nelson, who comes to town every now and again, and pictures of his visits

are all over the walls. You'll probably have to wait to get a seat at ◖ **Mi Nidito** (1813 S. 4th Ave., 520/622-5081, www.minidito.net, 11 A.M.–10:30 P.M. Wed.–Fri. and Sun., 11 A.M.–2 A.M. Fri.–Sat., $2.50–10.90), Bill Clinton's favorite place—he ate here when he came to town during his presidency, sampling pretty much one of everything, and his order is preserved as a special on the menu—it's worth the wait. **Café Poca Cosa** (110 E. Pennington St., 520/622-6400, http://pocacosatucson.com, 11 A.M.–9 P.M. Tues.–Thurs., 11 A.M.–10 P.M. Fri.–Sat.) has an always-changing menu featuring some of the most exciting Mexican recipes around.

El Charro Café (311 N. Court Ave., 520/622-1922, www.elcharrocafe.com, 11 A.M.–9 P.M. Mon.–Thurs. and Sun., 11 A.M.–10 P.M. Fri.–Sat., $6–18) makes the city's most beloved Mexican food in a building once lived in by Julias Finn, a French stonemason who came to Tucson to work on the cathedral. The restaurant has a bar, **¡Toma!,** with half-price drinks and appetizers (delicious Mexican favorites like cheese crisps and quesadillas) 3–6 P.M. daily.

Pizza

Magpies Gourmet Pizza (605 N. 4th Ave., 520/628-1661, www.magpiespizza.com, 11 A.M.–10 P.M. Mon.–Wed., 11 A.M.–11 P.M. Thurs.–Sat., $3–25) is a sure bet, having won the *Tucson Weekly*'s Best of Tucson poll every year since 1989.

Greek/Mediterranean

◖ **Ali Baba** (2545 E. Speedway Blvd. #125, 520/319-2559, 11 A.M.–8 P.M. Mon.–Sat., noon–8 P.M. Sun., $3–9) serves the city's best Mediterranean food in an ultra-casual environment.

Vegetarian

The best vegetarian eats in town can be found at **Govinda's Natural Food Buffet** (711 E. Blacklidge Dr., 520/792-0630, www.govindasoftucson.com, 11:30 A.M.–2:30 P.M. Wed.–Sat.,

5–9 P.M. Tues.–Sat., brunch 11 A.M.–2:30 P.M. Sun., $2–10), offering all-you-can-eat vegetarian dishes, many of them vegan; on Thursday nights everything is vegan, and on Tuesdays authentic Indian food is served.

GETTING THERE AND AROUND
Air
Tucson International Airport (520/573-8000, www.tucsonairport.org) hosts 12 different airlines making approximately 75 departures everyday. If you book a flight directly into Tucson it may be slightly more expensive than flying into Sky Harbor in Phoenix, but TIA is a much less hectic port. To get there from midtown take Campbell Avenue, which turns into Kino Parkway south of Broadway. Follow road signs to Benson Highway, which leads to Tucson Boulevard and the airport entrance. There are always cabs waiting just outside the main entrance; expect to pay about $20 for a ride to midtown.

Car Rental
If you're flying into Tucson and don't have friends or relatives to chauffeur you around a typically sprawling Southwestern city, you'll need to rent a car. The airport has several counters from which to choose. If you're booking ahead try the locally owned **Adobe Car & Van Rental of Tucson** (3150 E. Grant Rd., 520/320-1495 or 888/471-7951), which has free pick-up service.

Cabs and Shuttles
Cab rides can get expensive in Tucson because everything is so spread out. Expect to spend about $15 for a ride from midtown to restaurants and bars downtown or on 4th Avenue. There are plenty of rides to choose from. Try **AAA Yellow Cab Co./Fiesta Taxi** (520/624-6611 or 520/399-6062), or **All State Cab Company** (520/798-1111 or 520/887-9000). **Arizona Stagecoach** (520/881-4111 or 520/889-1000, www.azstage coach.com) runs a door-to-door 24-hour shuttle to and from TIA, and **Arizona Shuttle**

Service (520/795-6771 or 520/795-6775, www.arizonashuttle.com) offers 18 daily trips between TIA and Phoenix's Sky Harbor Airport.

Buses and Trains
For bus service from Tucson to all points on the map there's the **Greyhound Bus Station** (471 W. Congress, east of I-10, 520/792-3475, www.greyhound.com). The **Amtrak Station** is downtown (400 N. Toole Ave., 520/623-4442, www.amtrak.com).

Public Transportation
The City of Tucson operates the **Sun Tran** (4220 S. Park Ave., 520/623-4301, www.sun tran.com) bus line. It has stops all over the Old Pueblo and operates 6 A.M.–7 P.M. weekdays and 8 A.M.–5 P.M. weekends. Full fare is $1, with kids under five riding free.

INFORMATION AND SERVICES
Visitors Center
Make sure to stop by the **Metropolitan Tucson Convention and Visitors Bureau** (110 S. Church, Ste. 7199, 520/624-1817, 8 A.M.–5 P.M.). The bureau produces a helpful guide to the city you can pick up at the office or out in front during off hours. There are scores of tourist pamphlets for the perusing. Park in the metered parking on Church Avenue in front of the Technicolor **La Placita**, which houses the bureau and a few shops and cafés.

Forest Contacts
Most of the public lands around Tucson and Southern Arizona are administered by **Coronado National Forest.** The forest's main office in Tucson (300 W. Congress St., 520/388-8300, www.fs.fed.us/r3/coronado, 8 A.M.–4:30 P.M. Mon.–Fri.) can direct you to a specific field office.

The **Bureau of Land Management** (12661 E. Broadway, 520/258-7200, www.az.blm .gov, 8 A.M.–4 P.M. Mon–Fri.) monitors much of the public land that is not within the national forest.

If you have any trouble with wild animals or need to report a poaching incident, call the **Arizona Game & Fish Department** (555 N. Greasewood Rd., 520/628-5376, www.azgfd .gov, 8 A.M.–5 P.M. Mon.–Fri.).

Hospitals

Dial 9-1-1 for emergencies anywhere in Southern Arizona. **University Medical Center** (1501 N. Campbell Ave., 520/694-0111) has the region's only Level 1 trauma center, so if you are seriously hurt anywhere in Southern Arizona you are likely to be treated by the capable staff there.

Media

The morning daily newspaper **The Arizona Daily Star** (azstarnet.com) has a local focus but isn't provincial by any means. The weekly alternative tabloid **Tucson Weekly** (www .tucsonweekly.com) is the place to go for news on arts, entertainment, politics, and local news. You'll find it free throughout the city.

The Santa Cruz Valley

Heading south out of Tucson on I-19 you enter the Santa Cruz Valley, a storied landscape through which the Spanish took some of their first steps into the vast north.

This is the land of the trailblazing Father Eusebio Kino, who in the later 1600s traveled through Pimeria Alta, the "land of the upper Pima," as the Spanish called this region, referring to one of the many native populations that called the valley home for eons before Europeans arrived. The Tohono O'odham also live here, formerly called the Papago, whose San Xavier Indian Reservation stretches out west of the Interstate. Kino, a Jesuit with a penchant for roughing it, founded several missions in Pimeria Alta, two of which, on the Arizona side of the border, still stand and still hold masses. One of the oldest continually inhabited villages in the New World can be found at Tubac, now an artist colony and tourist stop where they celebrate the legacy of the Basque adventurer Juan Bautista de Anza, the younger, who attempted to tame the valley of its hostile Apaches and eventually led the expedition west that established San Francisco, California.

The valley has always been a ranching area, even during Kino's time, and after the Gadsden Purchase several Anglo ranches were established and thrived for generations. Much of the former ranch land has been sold to establish conservation areas and wildlife refuges in this rare ecosystem. During the Cold War, intercontinental ballistic missiles (ICBMs) were cocked and ready in underground missile silos throughout the valley, an era celebrated with a museum. The area has also long been home to large open-pit copper mines, and the towering tailings piles rise like ziggurats to the west of the retirement community of Green Valley. And in Ambos Nogales, the name meaning, roughly, both Nogales, you'll witness the teaming U.S.-Mexico border region in all its fascinating chaos.

The Santa Rita Mountains to the east attract subtropical birds on the move from Mexico and points farther south to their sky island heights, a fact that in turn attracts birding enthusiasts from around the world. You can hike to the top of 9,000-foot Mt. Wrightson and see the whole world on a clear day, or stay in one Madera Canyon's small lodges and take a tour of an observatory where scientists are trying to discover the beginnings of the universe.

GREEN VALLEY/SAHUARITA

Sahuarita is a bedroom community about 15 miles south of Tucson, the site of the largest pecan-growing operation in the world. Green Valley is one of Arizona's best retirement communities, home to about 25,000 year-round residents and many more part-time snowbirds from the frozen north. Together the two towns

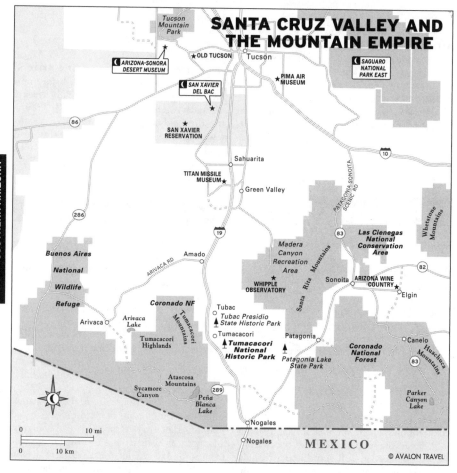

SANTA CRUZ VALLEY AND THE MOUNTAIN EMPIRE

© AVALON TRAVEL

make up a relatively large population center between the dry Santa Cruz River to the east and the copper mines to the west.

Asarco Mineral Discovery Center

Take exit 80 off I-19 and drive west of the casino to reach this illuminating sight (1421 W. Pima Mine Rd., Sahuarita, 520/625-8233, www.mineraldiscovery.com, 9 A.M.–5 P.M. Tues.–Sat., exhibitions free, mine tour $6 adults, $4 kids 5–12). The Discovery Center, using exhibits, old mining equipment, and films, explains how all the huge piles of dirt flanking the valley's west side got there.

The copper in the Santa Cruz Valley is of the porphyry variety, meaning it's very low grade and takes a lot of earth-moving to get at; a one-hour bus tour offered five times a day on Tuesday, Thursday, and Saturday will take you up into the hills to the sprawling Mission Mine to show you how it's done. From the bus you'll see the vast pit and the post-apocalyptic landscape created by large-scale copper mining, and you'll drive through a working mill.

Back at the Discovery Center a gift shop sells souvenirs.

Titan Missile Museum

This deactivated missile site (1580 W. Duval Mine Rd., Sahuarita, 520/625-7736, www .pimaair.org, 9 A.M.–5 P.M. daily, $8.50 adults, $5 kids 7–12), one of several missile facilities staffed with underground-dwelling Cold Warriors in what was once referred to as the Titan Valley, had its Titan II aimed squarely at the USSR from 1963 to 1982. The site was decommissioned in 1986 and became a National Historic Landmark in 1994.

The one-hour tour takes you deep underground, and volunteer guides, some of them former crew members, explain what daily life was like working at the silo. The highlight of the tour for many is seeing an actual Titan II still waiting there in the launch duct. Guides also simulate the launch sequence that crewmembers hoped they would never have to complete. The visitors center provides context with a Cold War timeline and artifacts from the era, and a gift shop sells souvenirs and books.

Food, Shopping, and Accommodations

Drive east on Sahuarita Road past the pecan groves—roll down your windows and feel how much cooler the trees make the air— and you'll come to the **Pecan Store** (1625 E. Sahuarita Rd., Sahuarita, 520/791-2062 or 800/327-3226, www.pecanstore.com, 9 A.M.–5 P.M. Mon.–Sat.), an outlet of Farmers Investment Corp., which operates the largest integrated pecan growing and packaging operation in the world (some 400,000 trees on 5,000 acres) and sells, of course, pecans and pecan accessories.

If you're staying a while in Green Valley, try the **Inn at San Ignacio** (1861 W. Demetrie Loop, Green Valley, 520/393-5700, www .innatsanignacio.com), which has villa rooms and condo-style suites with kitchenettes, cable, and Internet access. The inn is near several golf courses and offers special deals for birders. There are also several chain hotels just off the Interstate in Green Valley and Sahuarita.

SANTA RITA MOUNTAINS

Black bears, mountain lions, ringtailed cats, deer, and too many birds to count call this sky island range home, where mining and logging once were legitimate pursuits but now outdoor recreation rules. The range's highest peak is 9,453-foot Mount Wrightson. Most visitors to the Santa Ritas head to Madera Canyon and its trails to the peak's summit.

Madera Canyon

A classic example of a Maderan pine-oak woodland, Madera Canyon is the part-time home to many subtropical bird species that stop off on their migrations north to mate along a cool mountain creek in conditions not dissimilar from more tropical climes to the south. Consequently the canyon is a kind of Mecca for serious birders fulfilling their life lists. It

During the summer rainy season, usually small Madera Creek becomes a torrent.

SOUTHERN ARIZONA

© TIM HULL

The peak of Mount Wrightson, the highest point in the Santa Rita Mountains, rises to nearly 10,000 feet.

is one of a very few places in North America one can see the fat green-and-red elegant trogan, a relative of the Quetzal and the source of much thrill and consternation for birders visiting from points far away. The great variety of hummingbird species flitting about the canyon also draws visitors from far and wide.

A paved two-lane leads from the desert floor up to about 6,000 feet, where well-used and relatively steep trails climb the slopes of **Mount Wrightson** all the way to its bare and rocky, 9,453-foot peak. The most popular trail to the top is the 10.8-mile round-trip **Old Baldy Trail,** which is fairly steep but much shorter than the more gradual, 16-mile round-trip **Super Trail.** Both trails are well marked, heavily used, and start near the Mount Wrightson Picnic Area at the top of the canyon. Both trails also take you over **Josephine Saddle,** at about 7,000 feet, and **Baldy Saddle** at more than 8,000 feet just below the peak, which make good places to stop and rest. At Josephine Saddle make sure to look at the makeshift memorial to a group of Boy Scouts that got caught in a snowstorm on the mountain in the 1950s

and never returned. If you're coming up the Super Trail, stop and rest at Sprung Spring just before you reach the saddle, which has delicious mountain water trickling from a spigot.

To see the lushness that a little trickling water can inspire hit the 5.8-mile **Bog Spring-Kent Spring Loop,** which leads over some old mining roads in the lower reaches of the canyon onto some fairly steep and skinny trails along a windswept ridge, providing some pretty spectacular views of the valley below. The trail eventually leads deep into the forest, where sycamores thrive on the edges of green and spongy clearings. Also try the 4.4-mile one-way **Nature Trail,** a strenuous but easy way to see the entire canyon, from the desert grasslands at its entrance at the **Proctor Parking Area,** where you can pick up the trail, all the way up to the woodlands at the top. Small signs along the way point out notable flora and fauna, and the highest point on the trail, high above the canyon floor, offers a unique perspective.

The average summertime temperature in the canyon is about 85°F, about 15–20°F cooler on any given summer day than it is down in the valley. It gets cold in the high country October–April, and it regularly snows up there in deep winter. Madera Canyon is an extremely popular day-use area and hiking destination for Tucson and Santa Cruz Valley residents, so expect to see quite a few people on the trails and using the three developed picnic areas, all of which have tables, bathrooms, and charcoal grills. You can pick up a trail map at any of the lodges in the canyon, or you can get one at the welcome station at the canyon's entrance, but it is staffed irregularly. There's a $5 per car user fee, or you can purchase a $20 annual pass.

Mount Hopkins Fred Lawrence Whipple Observatory

The Smithsonian Institution operates this observatory atop 8,550-foot Mount Hopkins, where astronomers take advantage of the dark Southern Arizona sky to scan space for very faint objects. The MMT, the largest single-mirror telescope in North America, is one of four you can see up close during a six-hour tour of the facility offered Monday, Wednesday, and Friday, mid-March through November ($7 adults, $2.50 kids 6–12, no children under 6). It's a good idea to call ahead for reservations far in advance. The visitors center near Amado (520/670-5707, http://cfa-www.harvard.edu/flwo, 8:30 A.M.–4:30 P.M. Mon.–Fri.) has displays about the work being done on the mountain and the history of the telescope.

Accommodations and Camping

Madera Canyon used to be dotted with summer homes and getaway cabins, but beginning in the 1970s the U.S. Forest Service tore them down and converted the treasured ecosystem into a federal recreation area. Now only a scattered few homes remain on historic mining claims. Three of the lasting structures are lodges that welcome visitors year-round. As you're driving up the canyon's only road, first you come upon the **Santa Rita Lodge** (520/625-8746, www.santaritalodge.com, $85–98 d), offering several casitas and freestanding cabins with private decks. The Lodge, the oldest in the canyon, has beautiful grounds along Madera Creek and

attracts birds with feeders and provides benches for viewing. There's also a gift shop, but no food, so bring your own or plan to eat in Green Valley about 12 miles away. March through May the lodge can fix you up with an experienced birding guide by appointment. Tours start early and last about four hours ($20 per person).

Next you'll see the A-frame **Madera Kubo** (520/625-2908, www.maderakubo.com, $95 d), which has four cozy cabins and a gift shop, but no food. Near the top of the canyon is the ◖ **Chuparosa Inn** (520/393-7370, www.chuparosainn.com, $130–150 d), with three beautiful rooms, a great bird-watching area, a barbecue, and friendly hosts. The Chuparosa serves a hearty continental breakfast, but you're on your own for lunch and dinner. If you prefer to rough it, the **Bog Springs Campground** (turn left off Madera Canyon Road at sign, 520/281-2296, www.fs.fed.us/r3/coronado/forest/recreation/camping/sites/bog_springs.shtml) has campsites, $10 year-round, on a first-come first-served basis.

Information

The area is managed by the Coronado National Forest's Nogales Ranger District (303 Old Tucson Rd,, Nogales, I-19 Ruby Rd. exit, then turn east, 520/281-2296, 8 A.M.–4:30 P.M. Mon.–Fri.). The Forest's main office in Tucson has information on this area as well.

BUENOS AIRES WILDLIFE REFUGE

This remote 118,000-acre refuge preserves large swaths of endangered semidesert grassland, home to the pronghorn. The refuge's flagship program was once the reintroduction of the rare masked bobwhite quail to the grasslands, but the program was transferred to a private organization in 2007. Its proximity to the U.S.-Mexico Border has caused some trouble on the refuge, and portions are indefinitely closed to the public because of smuggling activity.

One the most accessible portions of the refuge is the **Arivaca Cienega,** a swamp-like desert wetland just outside the tiny village of **Arivaca.** The easy two-mile loop trail includes boardwalks over the wetter portions, and birds, frogs, and snakes abound. Take Arivaca Road about 20 miles from I-19 Exit 48 until you see the sign for the Cienega, just east of Arivaca. At the western end of town turn at the "Y" and drive 2.5 miles to Arivaca Creek, also managed by the refuge, where there's easy creekside hiking among cottonwood and mesquite. Far off to the northwest in the Baboquivari Mountains is Brown Canyon, a riparian area accessible only with a guide and by appointment.

To get to refuge headquarters (P.O. Box 109, Sasabe, AZ 86633, 520/823-4251, www.fws.gov/southwest/refuges/arizona/buenosaires/index.html, 7:30 A.M.–4 P.M. daily, closed weekends June 1–Aug. 15) go through Arivaca to Highway 286, head south four miles, then turn left at milepost 7.5. There's also a satellite office in downtown Arivaca next to the mercantile that's open intermittently.

TUBAC AND TUMACACORI

These two villages along the Santa Cruz are steeped in the history of the Spanish adventures in Pimeria Alta. Padre Kino established the mission at Tumacacori in 1691, and Tubac, a Piman village, became a mission farm and ranch. By the 1730s Spanish colonists had arrived from the south to farm and ranch the fertile river valley. In 1751 the violent Piman revolt convinced the Spanish crown to establish the Presidio San Ignacio de Tubac, which was founded the next year. The famous Basque Juan Bautista de Anza II was the second commander of the presidio, and in 1776 he led the first of two overland journeys to establish a fort at San Francisco, California, taking along about 60 colonists from Tubac. In 1860 silver strikes nearby briefly made Tubac the largest town in the Arizona Territory. It eventually fell into obscurity, but was discovered again as an artist's colony during the second half of the 20th century, and today its many galleries and shops are a draw for tourists and locals alike.

Crowds flock to Tubac during the weeklong **Tubac Festival of the Arts** in February, during which artisans and artists from around the country set up booths. Music and the smell of greasy, delicious food fill the village.

Tubac Presidio State Historic Park

Arizona's first state park, founded in 1959, preserves the history and foundations of the Presidio San Ignacio de Tubac (520/398-2252, www.pr.state.az.us, 8 A.M.–5 P.M. daily, $3 adults over 14, $1 kids 7–13). You can see the fort's original foundation and peruse a museum that explains what life was like for the natives, settlers, and soldiers. Guided tours and hands-on interpretation programs are available on request. The park's annual **Anza Days** celebration around the third week of October honors the fort's most famous commander with historical re-creations, music, and food. The Tubaquenos, a historical re-enactment society, put on living history demonstrations at the park 1–4 P.M. Sunday October–March.

Tumacacori National Historic Park

Padre Kino founded the **Mission San Jose de Tumacacori** in 1691, and much of it still stands today on this 310-acre national park (three miles south of Tubac on the east-side Frontage Rd., 520/398-2341, www.nps.gov/tuma, 9 A.M.–5 P.M. daily, $3 adults over 16). You can explore the mission and its grounds, which include an old graveyard, an orchard, and a re-created Piman shelter. A museum tells the history of the mission and Pimeria Alta, and most days you can buy tortillas and refried beans made right before your eyes in the traditional fashion. A gift shop sells a wide assortment of books on local history.

The mission at Tumacacori still holds masses on holidays, but the two other missions protected by the park are mostly in ruins. The ruins of mission **San Cayetano de Calabazas,** normally closed to the public, can be visited on monthly guided tours for $10 per person. Reservations are required (520/398-2341).

THE WESTERN DESERT

Southwest of Tucson, the vast, desert homeland of the Tohono O'odham Indians stretches out, a hot wasteland where few dare to venture.

You can head out to this 4,400-square-mile borderland reservation via Highway 286 west of Tucson, but there isn't much out here except gorgeous, mostly untouched desert. Straddling the border, the reservation is a popular, albeit deadly, corridor for illegal migrants heading north, and dozens die crossing the reservation every year. Only the O'odham know how to live out here.

About 90 minutes west of Tucson along Highways 86 and 386 (follow the signs) you'll find another of Southern Arizona's famous observatories. **Kitt Peak National Observatory** (520/318-8726, www.noao.edu, 9 A.M.-3:45 P.M. daily, $2 suggested donation) operates 23 telescopes – the world's largest collection – atop the 6,875-foot peak in the reservation's Quinlan Mountains. Docent-led tours are available at 10 A.M., 11:30 A.M., and 1:30 P.M. and last about an hour ($2 adults, $1 kids over 6), or you can pick up a pamphlet and take a self-guided tour. The visitors center has exhibits on astronomy, and a gift shop selling star- and planet-related items and O'odham baskets.

Far off to the west look for 7,700-foot Baboquivari Peak, the home of I'itoi, the tribe's sacred "elder brother" god. The reservation capital, **Sells,** is a small outpost about 58 miles southwest of Tucson on Highway 86.

There's a supermarket, a few businesses, offices, and a school. During the first weekend in February O'odham cowboys join in the **All Indian Rodeo and Fair,** during which locals set up food booths, play music, march in a parade, dance, and show off and sell their crafts.

Continue through the thick desert west on Highway 86 and you'll hit **Ajo,** a copper mining community with a few restaurants and a good place to see the scars strip mining leaves open on the land. South of Ajo on Highway 85, past the tiny town of **Why,** you'll find **Organ Pipe Cactus National Monument.** This rugged, beautiful monument along the border protects what amounts to pretty much all of the Organ Pipe cacti in North America, along with many other species of cactus, and is a popular area for seeing spring wildflowers in bloom. It has in the past been named one of the most dangerous national monuments in the country. This area is a major drug smuggling corridor and sees its share of illegal migrants, too. The **Kris Eggle Visitor Center** (520/387-6849), named for a ranger who was killed during a shootout with drug smugglers, is open daily from 8 A.M.-5 P.M. There's a campground with 208 sites, drinking water, but no hookups or facilities ($12 per night). The 21-mile Ajo Mountain Drive, on a twisty dirt road that's usually passable, will take you into the monument's center, where you can see the goofy, many-armed cactus up close.

Juan Bautista de Anza National Historic Trail

There's a 4.5-mile portion of the route used to take colonists and their stock animals from Northern Mexico to Northern California in 1775–1776 between the presidio and the mission that makes for an easy and shady riverside hike, though there's often a lot of trash along the route as a result of illegal migration and seasonal flooding of the northward flowing Santa Cruz River. The route crosses private ranch land, and you're bound to see cattle. It leads from just outside the state park to just outside the national park, or vice versa, and is a route historically used to travel between the two landmarks.

Shopping

Tubac has more than 100 shops and galleries, many of them selling Mexican and South American imports. The village has two bookstores, a year-round Christmas gallery, and several little shops whose wares simply must be seen. Pick up an illustrated map of the shopping district at any of the shops or at the visitors center.

Accommodations

Tubac Golf Resort and Spa (1 Avenue de Otero, 520/398-2211, www.tubacgolfresort .com, $140–265 d) is a historic, upscale resort and golf course with casitas and rooms of various sizes and styles, two restaurants, a pool, hot tub, and other amenities. Over the last several years the resort has been going through a $40 million restoration. Check the website for great package deals; prices drop considerably in summer. The **Tubac Country Inn** (12 Burruel St., 520/398-3178, www.tubaccountryinn.com, $85–155 d) is situated right in the heart of the village and offers suites with kitchenettes, TVs, and wireless Internet.

Food

Open since 1944 and still run by the same family, **Wisdom's Café** (1931 E. Frontage Rd., 520/398-2397, www.wisdomscafe.com, noon–3 P.M. and 5–8 P.M. Mon.–Sat. $5–12) may be the best restaurant in the Santa Cruz Valley, serving Mexican food from handed-down family recipes. Don't miss the famous fruit burrito for dessert. Head south on the Frontage Road toward the mission and look for the big chicken statue out front.

AMADO

You'll know you've made it to Amado, a former ranching center, when you see the building-sized cow skull on the west-side of I-19 about 10 miles south of Green Valley, Exit 48. The skull serves as the facade for the **Longhorn Grill** (520/398-3955, lunch and dinner daily), which serves southwestern food, ribs, and even pizza. Across the street a statute of a Hereford much smaller than the skull announces the locally beloved **Cow Palace Restaurant** (520/398-1999, www.cowpalacerestaurant .com, breakfast, lunch, and dinner daily), serving a wide variety of favorites from chicken fried steak to spaghetti; and if you hang out in the bar long enough there's a pretty good chance you'll meet a real live cowboy.

Information

A good place to start your Tubac visit is the

This lush riparian canyon in the Tumacacori Highlands supports a rich array of life.

© TIM HULL

Tubac-Santa Cruz Visitor Center (4 Plaza Rd., 520/398-0007, www.toursantacruz.com, 9 A.M.–4 P.M. Mon.–Fri., 10 A.M.–4 P.M. Sat.–Sun.), just to the left as you enter the village by the big Tubac sign.

Tumacacori Highlands

This huge wilderness of semidesert grasslands, rugged mountains, and riparian canyons west of the valley can best be accessed using the Ruby Road, I-19 Exit 12 just north of Nogales. West about 11 miles is **Pena Blanca Lake,** where bass and catfish can be lured in but not eaten because of high mercury content. There's a boat ramp and trail around the lake. Branch off on Forest Road 39 for the **White Rock Campground,** which has sites year-round, but no water ($5). Continue another five miles along Forest Road 39 to the trailhead for the **Atascosa Lookout Trail.** The popular, steep trail to the 6,255-foot peak, a six-mile round-trip, takes you to a decommissioned fire lookout which, for a few months in 1968, was manned by writer **Edward Abbey.**

There's a sign pointing to the trailhead for the **Sycamore Canyon Trail** on Forest Road 39 about 10 miles in from Pena Blanca Lake. This trail leads deep into a watered canyon, with steep walls dotted with saguaro, white sycamore trees shading the creek bed, and jagged rocks jutting out from above. It's a five-mile hike one-way to the U.S.-Mexico Border, marked by a barbed-wire fence. The trail isn't always well marked, as the creek often overtakes it, and you will certainly have to wade in parts. During the rainy season some sections may be impassable. The canyon is a major corridor for drug smuggling, and you are likely to see a lot of trash and other evidence of the trade.

AMBOS NOGALES

Ambos Nogales, roughly meaning "both Nogaleses," is the local name for this region of the U.S./Mexico border. Nogales, Arizona, is a somewhat sleepy government and produce warehousing town with about 25,000 souls,

while the sprawling industrial city Nogales, Mexico just across the border teems with more than 500,000 residents. Most visitors stick to the tourist-friendly blocks just across the border. A good portion of the nation's produce passes through the port of entry in Nogales, Arizona, as does a large amount of illegal drugs.

Nogales, Arizona

This small town named, like its cross-border sister, for the walnut trees that once thrived in the area, has long been Santa Cruz County's seat, and the beautiful old neoclassical, shiny-domed **Santa Cruz County Courthouse** (2150 North Congress Dr.), built in 1904 out of stone quarried locally lends it a historic feel that belies the constant comings and goings of a border town. The **Old City Hall** building, built in 1914, now houses the **Pimeria Alta Historical Society** (Grand Ave. and Crawford St., 520/287-4621, 10 A.M.–4 P.M. Wed.–Sun), with several interesting exhibits and artifacts on the history of the region. The town's historic downtown along **Morley Avenue** has a few stores that were established in the early 1900s and are still being run by descendants of pioneer merchants.

ACCOMMODATIONS

There are several chain hotels in Nogales, Arizona, along Mariposa Road and along Grand Avenue, both major thoroughfares. If you're looking for something special there's the historic **Hacienda Corona de Guevavi** (348 South River Rd., 520/287-6503 www.hacienda corona.com), a historic inn along the Santa Cruz that once hosted John Wayne and other stars. The inn features murals by Salvador Corona, a famous artist and bullfighter, and offers B&B-style rooms and stand-alone *casitas*. It has a swimming pool and offers horseback riding, stargazing, and many other activities.

FOOD

With dozens of authentic Mexican restaurants within an easy walk across the border, don't spend too much time eating on the Arizona side. If you insist on eating in Arizona, try the steaks and Sonoran-style food at **Las Vigas Steak Ranch** (180 W Loma St. at Fiesta Market off arroyo Blvd., 520/287-6641), or the excellent Mexican food at **Cocina La Ley** (226 W. 3rd St., 520/287-4555).

Crossing the Border

Nogales, Mexico is a modern factory and produce-shipping center, but it's also a very popular tourist destination. It's easy to get there: Just walk across the international border in downtown, Nogales, Arizona, after parking at one of the many pay lots (about $4 per day) near the port-of-entry. There's a tourist area of about a square mile just south of the border, with restaurants, curio shops, and drugstores. You can drive into Mexico, but the lines of cars driving north into the United States are long and slow. If you need a ride there are cabs everywhere and the drivers speak English; they, like everyone else who deals with tourists, take U.S. cash. Prices are generally low, and some of the street vendors will bargain with you.

FOOD

The main north–south street is Obregon, two blocks west of the border crossing station. Popular restaurants include **La Roca,** east of the railroad tracks in downtown; **El Toro,** a steakhouse, about two miles south of the border on Lopez Mateos; and **La Palapa,** a no-frills seafood place 1.5 miles south on Lopez Mateos. **The Oasis** has an outdoor balcony overlooking where two main thoroughfares, Lopez Mateos and Obregon, merge, reminiscent of Times Square, but much smaller. Sit there, enjoy shrimp in a warm cheese sauce, and watch the traffic. And yes, you can drink the water, but most restaurants will put a bottle of it on your table.

Information

For visitor information go to the **Nogales-Santa Cruz Chamber of Commerce** (23 W. Kino Park Way, 520/287-3685, www .nogaleschamber.com).

There's a U.S. Consulate (in Mexico tel. 01/631-311-8150 or 01/631-313-4797, from U.S. tel. 011/52-631-313-48-20, 8 A.M.–5 P.M. Mon.–Fri., closed weekends) in Nogales, Sonora, on Calle San Jose, about five miles south of the border. If you get in trouble on the weekend, there's a consulate officer who checks the Nogales, Mexico jail daily—Monday through Friday.

Although it's hassle-free to enter Mexico, coming back can present problems: Starting in mid-2009 American citizens will need a passport to return to the United States via land and sea. (A passport is already required for air travel from Mexico to the United States.) Until then, two forms of identification, such as a birth certificate and a state-issued driver's license or ID card, will suffice.

THE MOUNTAIN EMPIRE: PATAGONIA, SONOITA AND ELGIN

With an average elevation between 4,000 and 5,000 feet, and average annual rainfall around 20 inches, the grasslands and creek beds of the "Mountain Empire" on the eastern side of the Santa Rita range are much cooler than Tucson, and the landscape is unlike any other in Arizona. The towns here are tiny, but they serve an increasingly popular tourist spot, so little out-of-the-way inns are plentiful. In Patagonia, the largest town in the area with only about 800 people, there's a yellow train depot in the center of town, built in 1900, and a nearby butterfly garden. A few shops sell unique locally made items and other treasures.

Getting There and Around

There are two ways to get to the grassland seas and cottonwood forests of the Mountain Empire, an historic ranching and mining district between the Santa Rita, Patagonia, Mustang, and Huachuca Mountains. If you're coming from the Santa Cruz Valley, take Highway 82 from Nogales 19 miles southeast

© TIM HULL

SOUTHERN ARIZONA

Roadside shrines like this one near Patagonia can be found throughout Southern Arizona and Northern Mexico.

to Patagonia and then on to Sonoita, where Highway 83 branches off north to I-10. If you're coming from Tucson, take I-10 east to Highway 83.

Telles Grotto Shrine

Just southwest of Patagonia along Highway 82, near Milepost 15.9, there's shrine built into the rock face of the mountain. It's worth taking a few minutes to climb the steps and take a peek inside, where there will likely be candles burning and messages written to the dead. The shrine was built in the 1940s by the Telles family, whose matriarch vowed she would construct and keep up the shrine if her five boys returned safely from World War II. They did, and the shrine is still in use today.

Patagonia Lake State Park

About seven miles south of Patagonia on Highway 82 is Southern Arizona's largest lake, 2.5-mile-long Patagonia Lake (400 Patagonia Lake Rd., 520/287-6965, 8 A.M.–10 P.M. daily), where you can fish for bass, bluegill, and catfish,

and camp, rent a boat, swim and lay around Boulder Beach, water ski (though not on weekends), and hike around the 5,000-acre Sonoita Creek State Natural Area. The campground has 72 campsites and 34 hookups ($15 w/ no hookup, $22 w/ water and electric), and there are boat launches, restrooms, showers, a dump station, and a camp supply store. In March crowds head to the park to see the annual Mariachi Festival. From Nogales head 12 miles northeast on Highway 82, then turn left at the sign and drive four miles to park entrance.

Patagonia-Sonoita Creek Preserve

The Nature Conservancy protects a Fremont cottonwood-Gooding willow riparian forest—one of the best and last remaining examples of this lush landscape in Arizona—on about 750 acres along perennial Sonoita Creek (520/394-2400, www.nature.org/arizona, 7:30 A.M.–4 P.M. Wed.–Sun. Oct.–March, 6:30 A.M.–4 P.M. Wed.–Sun. Apr.–Sept., $5 per person). This small green paradise has six miles of easy trails leading trough the forest,

© TIM HULL

A group of equestrians winds through scrubby foothills on the eastern side of the Santa Rita Mountains in Southern Arizona.

with its 100-foot tall, 130-year-old cotton-woods—the biggest and oldest in the country—and along the creek. The birding here is excellent, and it's not uncommon to see deer, bobcats, toads, and frogs in this verdant preserve. Friendly Conservancy volunteers lead nature walks every Saturday morning at 9 A.M. This is an extremely rare ecosystem, one that was once abundant in Southern Arizona but now has all but disappeared.

Accommodations, Food, and Information

The Sonoita Inn (3243 Hwy. 82, Sonoita, 520/455-5935, www.sonoitainn.com) at the crossroads of Highways 82 and 83 has 18 rooms with Western ambience, all with great views of the grasslands and mountains.

There has been a proliferation of bed-and-breakfasts in this area over the last several years. You can find brochures for most of them at **Mariposa Books** (436 Naugle Ave., 520/394-9186), a great bookstore in Patagonia with a **tourist information** desk.

The Velvet Elvis Pizza Co. (292 Naugle Ave., Patagonia, 520/394-2102, www.velvetelvispizza.com, 11:30 A.M.–8:30 P.M. Thurs.–Sun.) serves delicious gourmet pizza and has interesting pictures of The King and the Virgin. The **Steak Out Restaurant & Saloon** (at the junction of Rte. 82 and Rte. 83, Sonoita, 520/455-5205, 5–9 P.M. Mon.–Thurs., 5–10 P.M. Fri., 11 A.M.–10 P.M. Sat.–Sun.) has delicious steaks and ribs.

Wine Country

With soil and growing conditions often likened to those in Burgundy, France, the Sonoita-Elgin grasslands are becoming a well-known and well-reviewed winemaking region. It's fun to drive through the open landscape sampling wines, but consider taking along a designated driver.

In Sonoita just east of the crossroads on the east side of Highway 82 is the **Dos Cabezas Wineworks** (3248 Hwy. 82, 520/455-5141) is open for tasting 10:30 A.M.–4:30 P.M. Fri.–Sun. The tasting room and gift shop at **Sonoita Vineyards** (Elgin-Canelo Rd., 520/455-5893, www.sonoitavineyards.com), located three miles south of Elgin, is open 10 A.M.–4 P.M. daily. Also along the Elgin Road is **Callaghan Vineyards** (336 Elgin Rd., 520/455-5322, www.callaghan vineyards.com, tasting room 11 A.M.–3 P.M. Fri.–Sun.). The **Village of Elgin Winery** (471 Elgin Rd., 520/455-9309, www.elgin wines.com) has tasting daily 10 A.M.–5 P.M.,

and the **Rancho Rossa Vinyards** (201 Cattle Ranch Ln., Elgin, 520/455-0700, www .ranchrossa.com) is open 10:30 A.M.–3:30 P.M., Sat.–Sun., and Fridays as well from December to March. In April locals turn out in Elgin for the annual **Blessing of the Vine Festival.** Check www.elginwines.com for details.

The Cochise Trail

The small towns in Southern Arizona offer many sights and attractions, mostly of the Old West variety, and are good bases for exploring the spectacular natural areas around them, mostly of the riparian and mountainous variety.

Named after the indomitable Apache Chief Cochise, who waged war against the United States in the 1860s and 1870s, the region was also home to probably the most famous Apache of them all, the warrior and medicine man Geronimo, who was the last of his kind to

surrender to the reservation. Miners, ranchers, cowboys, outlaws, and even a few gunfighters lived here, too, and their brief reign is still celebrated in touristy Tombstone. But many people come for the vistas, the birds, and the trails that can be found in the accessible Huachuca and Chiracahua Mountain ranges.

Getting There and Around
The Cochise Trail and its environs are best traveled by car. If you want to avoid the Interstate, a good road trip can be made of heading east

© TIM HULL

The stacked-boulder Dragoon Mountains in southeast Arizona were once the favorite home and hideout of Cochise, the great Apache chief.

SOUTHERN ARIZONA

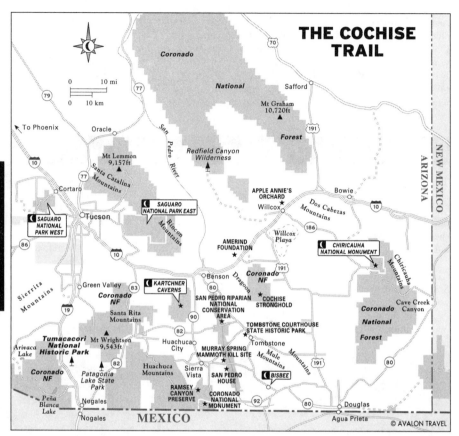

THE COCHISE TRAIL

out of Tucson on I-10, then take Highway 83 south, which will take you through the grasslands of the Mountain Empire to the heights of the Coronado National Memorial (on some dirt roads), into the Huachuca Mountains, and then on to the San Pedro River Valley. Exit at Hwy. 90 or Hwy. 80, or Hwy. 191 to make loop drives to the all the best sights in the area.

Sierra Vista and Fort Huachuca

Much of the war against the Apaches was fought from Fort Huachuca, founded in 1877 in a canyon that had historically served as an escape route for the West's final holdout tribe. Currently the fort is a major center for military intelligence training. Both stories are told at two museums here. The **Fort Huachuca Museum** (Building 41401, 520/533-5736, 9 A.M.–4 P.M. Mon.–Fri., 1–4 P.M. Sat.–Sun., $2 suggested donation) has exhibits about Army life on the Southwestern frontier, the famous battles with the Chiracahua Apaches, and the Buffalo Soldiers—African American cavalrymen whose story is one of the most fascinating of the West. The **U.S. Army Intelligence Museum** (9 A.M.–4 P.M. Mon.–Fri., 1–4 P.M. Sat.–Sun.) tells the 200-year story of Army's underrated intelligence corps. The museum is located two doors down from the Fort Huachuca Museum.

The military town of Sierra Vista, while the largest town in the valley, the fort's host, and sitting at the base of the Huachuca Mountains, has little charm in and of itself. There are a lot of well-known U.S. chain hotels and restaurants, and it's close to the southern end of the San Pedro River. It makes a good base if you're planning on spending some quality time in the mountains, but otherwise it's just a drive-though.

ACCOMMODATIONS AND FOOD

There is no shortage of chain hotels and restaurants in Sierra Vista, especially along Fry Boulevard, the town's main drag. But if you want to stay in the mountains—and who wouldn't?—there are several bed-and-breakfasts nestled in the range's canyons. The riverside **Casa de San Pedro** (8933 S. Yellow Lane, Hereford, 520/366-1300 or 888/257-2050, www.bedandbirds.com, $149–175 d) is a territorial-style home with a central courtyard, a pool, hot tub, and all kinds of activities geared toward birders and nature lovers. **Ramsey Canyon Inn** (29 Ramsey Canyon Road, Hereford, 520/378-3010, www.ramsey canyoninn, $130–150) just outside the Ramsey Canyon Preserve, has six rooms named for hummingbird species, delicious breakfasts, and a setting that can't be beat.

INFORMATION

Check out the **Sierra Vista Convention and Visitors Bureau** (3020 E. Tacoma St., 520/417-6960 or 800/288-3861, 8 A.M.–5 P.M. Mon.–Fri., 9 A.M.–4 P.M. Sat.).

Huachuca Mountains

Ranging in elevation from 3,934 feet at the base to 9,455 feet at the top of Miller Peak, the Huachucas are another of Southern Arizona's signature sky island ranges. You'll see the common transition from semidesert grasslands at the base, up into arid scrub, onto mixed oak forests, and all the way up to cool Ponderosa Pine forests in the higher reaches. There are dozens of trails in the range, and rough roads that lead deep into the outback. If you're looking to put together a backpacking or camping adventure in this range, talk to the staff at the **Coronado National Forest Sierra Vista Ranger District** (5990 S. Hwy. 92, Hereford, 520/378-0311).

Ramsey Canyon

You'll pass the ranger station as you head up to the 300-acre **Ramsey Canyon Preserve,** an easily accessible, stream-influenced canyon protected by the Nature Conservancy (27 Ramsey Canyon Rd., 520/378-2785, www .nature.org, 8 A.M.–5 P.M. daily Mar.–Oct., 9 A.M.–4 P.M. daily Nov.–Feb). This is a very popular area with birders, who come to see the more than 14 species of hummingbird and other avian species that stop over in the cool riparian canyon, fed by babbling Ramsey Creek, protected by high canyon walls, and crowded with sycamores, maples, and columbines.

The upper part of the canyon is within the **Miller Peak Wilderness Area.** Make sure you stop at the Nature Conservancy's excellent visitors center, which has maps, trail guides, books, T-shirts, and helpful, friendly volunteers. It's a good idea to get there early; this area is very popular and the parking lot only has 23 first-come, first-served spaces.

To reach the preserve, take Ramsey Canyon Road west from Highway 92 south of Sierra Vista (six miles south of Fry Boulevard); the preserve is at the end of the road, four miles west of the highway.

Also along Ramsey Canyon Road, before you reach the preserve, you'll find the **Arizona Folklore Preserve,** a quaint little theater along the creek where Arizona State Balladeer and nationally known folkie Dolan Ellis puts on acoustic folk concerts at 2 P.M. on Saturdays and Sundays. The shows are popular, so call ahead (520/378-6165, www.arizonafolklore .com) for a reservation.

Coronado National Memorial

Named in honor of the Spanish Conquistador Francisco Vásquez de Coronado, who trudged north in 1540 searching for the Seven Cities of Cibola—which turned out to be nothing more than a few hardscrabble pueblos—this beautiful landscape along the U.S.-Mexico border, on the southern end of the Huachuca Mountains, has a visitors center (Coronado Memorial Rd., 5 miles from Hwy. 92, 520/366-5515, www.nps.gov/coro, 9 A.M.–5 P.M. daily) with exhibits about its namesake, local history, and natural history. Three miles west of the visitors center there's a scenic overlook at Montezuma Pass, with expansive, windswept views of the San Pedro and San Rafael valleys and Mexico. You can have a picnic here and hike around on a number of trails leading to and from the lookout, but there's no camping allowed. To get there go south on Highway 92 about 20 miles to S. Coronado Memorial Drive, then it's five miles to the visitors center. (At the visitors center you can purchase a map of the Huachucas with all the trails on it for $5.)

San Pedro Riparian National Conservation Area

This 58,000-acre preserve protects some 40 miles of the upper San Pedro River between St. David and the border. There are about 400 species of birds here, 82 mammal species, and 45 reptile and amphibian species, some of which you're likely to see if you stay vigilant and quiet while exploring. Beavers, once plentiful in the now nearly extinct riparian habitats of Southern Arizona, have been reintroduced here. The **Friends of the San Pedro River** have converted a 1930s-era ranch house—in the shade of a beautiful 120-year-old Fremont cottonwood tree—into the **San Pedro House** gift shop and bookstore (9800 Hwy. 90, 520/508-4445, 9:30 A.M.–4:30 P.M. daily), where you can pick up information and pamphlets for a self-guided river walk and other trails, as well as get advice from the volunteers here. You'll also find the **Murray Springs Clovis Site and Trail,** a kind of stone-age butcher shop frequented by Clovis people 8,000–11,000 years ago. Scientists have dug up the fossils of several huge extinct mammals here, some of which are currently housed at the Museum of Natural History in New York.

◖ Kartchner Caverns

Kartchner Caverns (P.O. Box 1849, Benson, AZ 85602, 520/586-2283 for reservations, 520/586-4100 for information, www.azstateparks.com, 7:30 A.M.–6 P.M. daily, free with tour reservation, $5 per vehicle up to four people, $2 each additional person) were discovered in the early 1970s by two cave-loving University of Arizona students. Gary Tenen and Randy Tufts knew right away that they had shimmied down a sink-hole in the Whetstone Mountains into caving immortality, as the small, wet cave—meaning that it is still forming drip by drip, in a very real sense "alive"—is one of the most spectacular water-on-rock formations of its kind. And yet the explorers managed to keep their find a secret for several years in an effort to protect it from cavers less responsible than themselves. They called it Xanadu, after the great English poet Samuel Taylor Coleridge's famous unfinished poem "Kubla Khan," a name given to the Throne Room's 58-foot main column, formed not so much by drips but by torrents of water flowing into the cave over millennia, and the largest cave column in Arizona.

Eventually Tenen and Tufts told the property owners what they'd found, and the Kartchner family quickly joined those who wanted to see the cave preserved. A pre-tour film in the park's **Discovery Center** tells the whole story and explains what makes this cave unique. There's also an interesting museum and a gift shop; just outside the Discovery Center a native plant butterfly garden is worth a stroll.

There are two different tours you can take though the caverns. The **Big Room Tour** (1.5 hours, $23 adults, $13 ages 7–13, no children under 7) is offered only October 15–April 15. During the summer months a large colony of bats returns to the big room, as they have likely done for eons, to give birth to and rear their single pups. The **Rotunda/Throne Room Tour** (1.5 hours, $19 adults, $10 ages 7–13) is offered year-round and is more than enough to satisfy even the most discerning spelunker.

SINGING WIND BOOKSHOP

The ranching country around the tiny town of Benson, in the San Pedro River Valley, isn't the first place you'd expect to find a must-visit Arizona bookstore. But bibliophiles, especially those interested in books about the Southwest, should take the short drive on a dirt road off I-40 and visit Winifred Bundy's **Singing Wind Bookshop** (700 W. Singing Wind Rd., 520/586-2425, 9 A.M.-5 P.M. daily, including most holidays), a store she opened more than 30 years ago in the same ranch house she's lived in for half a century.

Bundy is liable to greet you in her stocking feet with her friendly dog jogging along side. She'll offer to give you the tour – take it. The store is organized rather eccentrically, and Bundy is a great source for recommendations and fun to talk to. The bookstore stocks primarily new books, with a special emphasis on Southwestern history and culture. There's a relatively large and diverse children's section as well.

Bundy learned about the Southwest from the great writer and librarian **Lawrence Clark Powell.** She now publishes several one-of-a-kind editions of his work and also sells tapes of conversations with Powell accompanied by music from Tucson band **Calexico.**

If you plan to buy any books – and it's difficult, many find, to drive all the way out there and not purchase something; there's simply too much great stuff that can't be found elsewhere – take cash or a checkbook. Winifred "doesn't mess with credit cards." She encourages book-lovers to bring lunch and have a picnic on the ranch, and don't miss saying hello to the mule and the beautiful white horse who share a pasture along the road leading to the shop.

From Benson, along I-10 about 40 miles east of Tucson, take 4th Street (the main drag), to Ocotillo Road, then head north about three miles to Singing Wind Road, a dirt road. Turn east onto the road, drive to a green gate (it may or may not be open; if it isn't, open it yourself) and then about a quarter of a mile to the ranch house.

© TIM HULL

Singing Wind Bookshop

Because the cave is still "alive," much is made of its conservation. Visitors are warned repeatedly not to touch any of the formations, and guides are not shy about telling kids to stand back and keep their hands to themselves. The tour information is repetitive if you've just watched the pre-tour movie.

If a tour of the cave isn't enough, the park offers campsites with electric hookups, water, a dump station, and restrooms with showers ($22).

TOMBSTONE

Just outside of the green and lush Mormon village of St. David, Highway 80 rises onto the dry scrubby plane where Ed Schieffelin struck silver in 1879, defying the soldiers who'd predicted he'd find only his own tombstone out there.

The town of the same name became one of the largest, rowdiest, and deceptively sophisticated locales in the Southwest for a time, a place where legends were created daily by overheated newspapermen, and where a 30-second gun fight of dubious legality became a defining frontier myth. These days about 1,600 residents call Tombstone home, many of them retirees or working in some capacity for the town's tourism industry, which attracts visitors, many of them from Europe, year-round.

Boothill Graveyard

Reportedly, many of Tombstone's gunfighters, along with their victims, lay alongside prostitutes, settlers, and obscure passers-through in this hilltop graveyard (7:30 A.M.–6 P.M. daily, donations welcome). You can walk among the more than 300 uniformly bland and refurbished graves, and read short messages on some of them that illuminate what death was like on the frontier. It doesn't feel authentic in the least, despite claims to the contrary, but it is free. Boothill is just off Highway 80 at the north of end of town.

Allen Street/
National Historic District

In danger of losing the federal funding that accompanies National Historic Landmark status (legend in Tombstone has a tendency to trample true history for tourists' sake), the Tombstone city council in 2006 covered Allen Street with dirt to make visiting the town a more "authentic" experience. Closed to cars and lined with wood-plank sidewalks, Western kitsch shops, and even a few genuine historical attractions, Allen Street *is* Tombstone to most. There are several saloons and restaurants here, and faux-gunfighters and saloon girls (some of them with somewhat anachronistic tattoos) mill about next to the working stagecoach replicas of Old Tombstone Historical Tours (520/457-3018, $10 adults, $5 kids). The National Historic District includes several streets off of Allen, including Toughnut Street on the west, Fremont Street on the North, and 6th Street on the south.

Within this historic district you'll find the **Tombstone Epitaph Museum** (5th St., 520/457-2211, 9:30 A.M.–5 P.M. daily), where you can see the original press used to print the perfectly named *Epitaph,* first published in 1880 and still going, and other

the site of the famous gunfight at the OK Corral

printing-related exhibits. The **OK Corral and Historama** (Allen St., 520/457-3456, www .ok-corral.com, 9 A.M.–5 P.M. daily, $7.50 with gunfight, $5.50 without) has all the information you'll need on the famous, albeit short, gunfight between the Earps and Clantons. You can see a rather tired and dusty historical re-enactment of the fight and watch a show, narrated by Vincent Price, on the major events in Tombstone history.

Among the saloons in the district, the **Crystal Palace Saloon** and **Big Nose Kate's Saloon** are worth a look, with Kate's being a fine place to knock back a few and look at all the pictures on the walls if you have the time. Both are on Allen Street. One of the best sights on Allen is the **Bird Cage Theatre** (Allen and 6th Sts., 520/457-3421, 8 A.M.–6 P.M. daily, $6 adults, $5 kids 8–18), an 1881 dance hall, brothel, saloon, theater, and casino that has been spectacularly preserved. A self-guided tour takes you through the building, which looks much as it did when it closed in 1889. On Fremont and 6th Streets the **Tombstone Western Heritage Museum** (520/457-3800, 9 A.M.–5 P.M. Mon.–Sat., 12:30–5 P.M. Sun., $5 adults, $3 kids 8–18) has many relics of Tombstone's past, including a few personal items once owned by the Earps.

Tombstone Courthouse State Historic Park

A more sober treatment of Tombstone's history is presented inside this preserved 1882 courthouse on 3rd and Toughnut Streets (520/457-3311, 8 A.M.–5 P.M. daily, $4 adults, $1 kids 7–13). The museum features artifacts, pictures, and ephemera from the territorial days, and there's a rebuilt gallows in the building's courtyard. Particularly interesting are the two nearly forensic accounts of the gunfight, with slightly differing details.

Rose Tree Inn Museum

Planted way back in 1885, this Lady Banksia, sent all the way from Scotland to Tombstone as a gift, is believed to be the world's largest

© TIM HULL

The gallows still wait for outlaws on the grounds of the Tombstone Courthouse State Historic Park.

rose tree at 8,700 square feet and is listed in the *Guinness Book of Records*. The white blossoms are usually at their best in early April. The small museum exhibits photos and furniture owned by the tree's planter, who moved to the territory in 1880 (4th and Toughnut Sts., 9 A.M.–5 P.M. daily, $3).

Events

In March Tombstone celebrates its founder during **Ed Schieffelin Territorial Days.** In April the **Tombstone Rose Tree Festival** shines the light on the record-making rose tree, and in May Tombstone's most famous citizen gets his own party during **Wyatt Earp Days.** The anniversary of that infamous gunfight warrants a celebration every year in October. Contact the Tombstone Chamber of Commerce (888/457-3929, www.tombstone chamber.com) for more information.

Accommodations

There are a few easy-to-locate chain hotels in

Tombstone and a variety of bed-and-breakfasts. The **Tombstone Boarding House B&B** (108 N. 4th St., 520/457-3716 or 877/225-1319, www.tombstoneboardinghouse.com, $59–89 d) offers comfortable rooms in two adobe houses that date to the 1880s. The **Wild Rose Inn** (101 N. 3rd St., 520/457-3844 or 866/457-3844, $79–89 d, $109 with private bath) is in a Victorian home built in the early 1900s.

Food
Nellie Cashman Restaurant (5th and Toughnut Sts., 520/457-2212, all meals daily) has good American food, and the **Lamplight Room** (198 N. 4th St., 520/457-3716) serves Mexican and American food for breakfast, lunch, and dinner daily. There are several eateries within the historic district, most of the serving cowboy- and Southwestern-style food.

Information
Make sure to stop by the **Visitor Information Center** (4th and Allen Sts., 520/457-3929, 10 A.M.–4 P.M. daily), where you'll find a nearly overwhelming amount of information about the town and its sights.

◖ BISBEE
The most charming town in Cochise County began life in the 1880s as a copper mining camp. Eventually several billion pounds of the useful ore would be taken out of the ground here, and by 1910 Bisbee was said to be the biggest city between the Midwest and West Coast.

Flooding in the 1,000 foot-deep tunnels and the boom-and-bust nature of the mining economy closed the mines by the 1970s, and the town, with its labyrinthine staircases and cozy little bungalows built precariously on the slopes of the Mule Mountains, was nearly moribund when it was discovered by hippies, artists, and artisans, a group that funkified the town into what it is today. Retired miners, retirees from elsewhere, county government

workers, and sons and daughters of the pioneers also call Bisbee home. Old Town is stuffed full of shops, galleries, restaurants, historic landmarks, and some of the best old hotels in the West. Perhaps the most fun to be had in Bisbee comes from just walking around, climbing the scores of off-kilter steps, and exploring its back alleys and narrow streets.

Mining History Sights
Driving in on Highway 80, just after the intersection with Highway 92, you can stop at a turnout along the side of the road and witness the **Lavender Pit Mine** and the huge tailings surrounding the largest open-pit mine in the state, now closed.

Bisbee is still proud of its history as the queen of all mining towns, and you can learn all about it at the **Bisbee Mining and Historical Museum** (Copper Queen Plaza, junction of Main St. and Brewery Gulch, 520/432-7071, www.bisbeemuseum.org, 10 A.M.–4 P.M. daily, $4 adults, $1 kids 4–16), housed in the building formerly occupied by the headquarters of the Copper Queen Consolidated Mining Company. Now an affiliate of the Smithsonian Institution, the museum has exhibits on local history and culture during territorial days, with an emphasis on the history and science of copper mining.

You can see for yourself what it was like descending into the earth every day to coax the ore out of the mountain on the 75-minute **Queen Mine Tour** (478 N. Dart Rd., 520/432-2071 or 866/432-2071, www.cityofbisbee.com/queenminetours, 9 A.M., 10:30 A.M., noon, 2 P.M., and 3:30 P.M. daily, $12 adults, $5 kids 4–15). Retired miners lead these tours and will regale you with stories of what it was really like underground, as you ride deep beneath the earth on a old mine car, wearing a yellow slicker, a hard hat, and headlamp. It's about 47 degrees in the shaft, so think about taking something warm to wear. If you don't want to go under, consider going over on the 90-minute, 11-mile

Surface Tour (departs from the Queen Mine Tour Office daily at 10:30 A.M., noon, 2 P.M., and 3:30 P.M., $10), which takes you through the historic district and shows you the open pit while you sit back in a comfortable van.

Shopping

Old Town Bisbee has dozens of unique shops, and there always seem to be new ones opening. There are jewelry stores, shops selling local and Mexican folk art, a bookstore with both new and used tomes and a large section of books by local authors, a shop that sells only things made out of copper, and several multilevel antique and junk shops that you can get lost in for hours.

Accommodations

There are all manner of accommodations in Bisbee, and bed-and-breakfasts proliferate along the narrow, twisty roads of Old Town.

The **Bisbee Grand Hotel** (61 Main St., 520/432-5900 or 800/421-1909, www.bisbee grandhotel.net, $79–175 d) is in a Victorian building in Old Town. It offers small, well-decorated rooms with private baths, and a full breakfast is served on the veranda. It has wireless Internet and a saloon frequented by tourists and locals. The **The Copper Queen Hotel** (11 Howell Ave., 520/432-2216, www.copper queen.com, $114–176 d) is an institution in Bisbee, built in 1902 and still in beautiful shape, but almost certainly haunted, as anyone in Bisbee will tell you. It has a solar-heated pool, a saloon, and a restaurant.

For a truly unique experience rent one of the 1950s vintage trailers at **Shady Dell RV Park** (1 Old Douglas Rd. 520/432-3567, www.theshadydell.com, $45–145 d), each beautifully refurbished and decorated. Many have interiors of polished chrome and wood and include black-and-white TVs and phonographs complete with 45 singles from the era. Located on the premises is **Dot's Diner** (520/432-1112, 7 A.M.–2:30 P.M. daily), a ready-made 10-stool diner from the 1950s where you can get great food.

Food

Café Roka (35 Main St. downtown, 520/432-5153, www.caferoka.com, 5–9 P.M. Wed.–Sat., $14–24) has some of the best Italian food around with a tasteful, elegant multilevel interior. **Winchester's** (inside Copper Queen Hotel, 11 Howell Ave., 520/432-1910, 7–10:30 A.M., 11 A.M.–2:30 P.M., and 5:30–9 P.M., $9–23) at the Copper Queen serves delicious American food and other dishes, and its breakfast is especially good.

The Stock Exchange Saloon (15 Brewery Ave., 520/432-1333, 11 A.M.–1:30 A.M. daily) has great sandwiches and salads for lunch and steaks and other rib-sticking fare for dinner. **Café Cornucopia** (14 Main St., 520/432-4820, 10 A.M.–4 P.M. daily) is a perfect place for lunch, with scrumptious sandwiches, soups, salads, and baked goods.

Information

Bisbee Chamber of Commerce & Visitor Center (1 Main St., Copper Queen Plaza, 520/432-5421 or 866/224-7233, www.bisbee arizona.com, 9 A.M.–5 P.M. Mon.–Fri., 10 A.M.–4 P.M. Sat.–Sun.) you'll find brochures on self-guided walking tours and loads of information on what to do and see.

Parking isn't easy, especially on weekends, so it's a good idea to find a space, stick with it, and explore the town on foot.

Douglas

This old smelter town on the border was once a frequent stop for bigwigs in the Phelps Dodge Mining Company, and as such has several historic buildings constructed in the late 19th and 20th centuries, the best of which is the still-operating **Gadsden Hotel** (1046 G Ave., 520/364-4481, www.hotelgadsden.com, $50–100 d), built in 1912 so executives could live in luxury out here on the frontier. The town is pretty quiet these days, and the surrounding countryside is plagued by drug- and people-smuggling activity. It's worth a stop to see the five-story hotel, with its Italian-marble staircase, Tiffany glass, and stained-glass murals. You can walk through the small downtown Historic Business District along G Avenue and look at the fine old buildings, many of them rare standing examples of various early-20th-century architectural style.

WILLCOX AND VICINITY

Though the former railroad and ranching town has seen better days, the canyons, mountains, and grasslands around Willcox are worth the 80-mile drive east on I-10 from Tucson. Willcox today has a few boarded up buildings and abandoned motels along its main thoroughfare, but its historic downtown holds some interest and is worth a mosey. The famous singing cowboy Rex Allen grew up in the area; a museum and an annual festival honor that fact. Willcox is also known as the place where Wyatt's brother, Warren Earp, met with a bullet in 1900, later to be buried in the Historic Willcox Cemetery.

Historic Downtown/ Railroad Avenue

This area used to be where life in Willcox happened, and even today it's the most interesting part of town. There's a shady, grassy park with a big bronze statue of native son Rex Allen, and across the street on Railroad Avenue the singing cowboy's life and career are celebrated at the **Rex Allen Arizona Cowboy Museum** (150 N. Railroad Ave., 520/384-4583 or 877/234-4111, 10 A.M.–4 P.M. daily, $2 single, $3 couple, $5 family), which also displays a **Cowboy Hall of Fame** honoring area ranchers and cowboys. Just down the sidewalk a bit is the **Willcox Commercial Store,** which claims to be the oldest continually operating store in the state. The **Willcox Rex Allen Theater** (520/384-4244), a 1935 art deco movie house, still runs new movies daily, and at the end of Railroad Avenue is the **Southern Pacific Depot,** built way back in 1880 and now used by the City of Willcox. The depot's lobby has exhibits on the history of the area and the railroad, and Rex Allen narrates a video played on a loop (8:30 A.M.–4:30 P.M.

Mon.–Fri.). The small town honors its most famous native with **Rex Allen Days** the first week in October every year.

Just around the corner from Railroad Avenue, the **Chiricahua Regional Museum** (127 E. Maley, 520/384-3971, 10 A.M.–4 P.M. Mon.–Sat.) exhibits mining artifacts, weapons used by Native Americans and the cavalry, and rocks and minerals found in the region. There's also an excellent display on the history of the Apaches.

Apple Annie's Orchard

The Sulphur Springs Valley outside of Willcox has the perfect growing conditions for the apple, peach, pear, and Asian pear orchards at Apple Annie's (2081 N. Hardy Rd., Willcox, 520/384-2084, www.appleannies .com, 8 A.M.–5:30 P.M. daily July 3–Oct. 31). From July to late October every year people flock to the "U-Pick" farm to pick and purchase fruit by the bucketful. The farm also

You can pick your own fruit right off the trees at Apple Annie's Orchard.

© TIM HULL

SOUTHERN ARIZONA

serves delicious hamburgers and cowboy beans for lunch, and you can buy all kinds of home-made preserves, sauces, condiments, and pies in the farm store. Take I-10 to exit 340, turn west on Ft. Grant Road and travel 5.5 miles to the Apple Annie's sign.

Amerind Foundation

On your way east on I-10, get off at the Dragoon Exit (318) to visit this excellent lit-tle museum (520/586-3666, www.amerind .org, 10 A.M.–4 P.M. daily, closed Mon.–Tues. June–Sept., $4 adults, $3 kids 12–18) in beautiful Texas Canyon. Established in 1937, the Amerind Foundation (a contraction of American and Indian) preserves and studies Native American cultures from prehistory all the way to the Chiricahua Apache and beyond. It is commonly thought to hold one of the best private ethnological collections in the nation. The museum is fascinating, and the location, among the imposing boul-ders of Texas Canyon, makes it well worth the stop.

Cochise Stronghold

A bit farther east on I-10, at Exit 331, takes you to the former hideout of Cochise and his band in the strange Dragoon Mountains. Head southeast on Highway 191, then west nine miles on Ironwood Road. The last four miles are on a dirt road. The great Apache chief is said to be buried somewhere out here, but nobody knows precisely where. Looking around it seems an ideal place to hide, with plenty of bluffs from which to watch the plains for the oncoming army. There are a few easy trails at the Stronghold, includ-ing a short nature trail and a paved history trail with information about the Chiricahua Apache. A few campsites ($12) are shel-tered by the same high boulders that once kept the Chiricahua hidden. If you want to hike deeper into the canyon, try the six-mile round-trip Cochise Stronghold Trail that veers off the nature trail.

© TIM HULL

SOUTHERN ARIZONA

The Dragoon Mountains provided an ideal hideout for the Chiricahua.

◖ Chiricahua National Monument

This place simply has to be seen to be be-lieved. Precarious rock spires jut into the sky in this strange, wonderful landscape, called the "Land of Standing Up Rocks" by the Apache. About 38 miles southeast of Willcox (120 from Tucson) on Highway 186, the National Monument (520/824-3560, www.nps.gov/chir, 8 A.M.–4:30 P.M. daily, $5 adults over 16) protects one of the most unusual areas in Arizona. There's a visi-tors center two miles from the monument entrance on Bonita Canyon Road, a paved two-lane road you can drive six gorgeous miles up to **Massai Point** and one of the most spectacular overlooks this side of the Grand Canyon. The visitors center has an excellent free guide with information on all the trails within the monument, their length, and how to find the trailheads, and there's a

© TIM HULL

hoodoos in the "Land of Standing Up Rocks"

free hikers' shuttle available. You can camp at the Bonita Campground a half mile from the visitors center for $12 per night (no hookups). Bring your own food and water to this special place because none is available for miles in any direction. For information and advice on getting out into the less accessible regions of the Chiricahua range, contact the **Douglas Ranger District** (1192 W. Saddleview Rd., 520/364-3468, 8 A.M.–4:30 P.M. Mon.–Fri.), 2.2 miles north of Highway 80 on Highway 191 in Douglas.

FLAGSTAFF AND NORTH-CENTRAL ARIZONA

Before and after the advent of air-conditioning, Arizona's north-central transition zones and coniferous mountain highlands made the long five-month summers livable for desert dwellers, who spent the hot months establishing "mountain clubs" in the cool of Prescott and Payson and the White Mountains.

Between Prescott—a quaint, Midwestern-style town with a colorful, Old West history—and Flagstaff—one of the Colorado Plateau's capital cities and the hub of the northland—you'll find the famed Red Rock Country, one of the world's most celebrated landscapes.

Posh Sedona sits at the center of a red, pink, and green-dotted geologic canvas, with the green bursts of Oak Creek Canyon and the often ignored but gorgeous Verde Valley right nearby. Just to the north is the Mogollon Rim,

a 200-mile-long cliff that marks the southern border of the vast plateau. The Rim, as it's called locally, drops 2,000 feet in some places and provides some inspiring views. Those same views inspired the likes of the writer Zane Grey, who called the region home on occasion.

Exploring this region you'll find a different Arizona, one that most of the clichéd ideas about the state don't account for. Don't miss contemplating the ruins of the Sinagua culture scattered all over this land. And bring your hiking boots, mountain bikes, skis, canoes, kayaks, and tents; this is outdoor country at its best. But there are also cleaner and more comfortable things to do: Sedona, Flagstaff, Prescott, Jerome, and other towns in the region offer unique accommodations and dining, as well as a variety of shops and

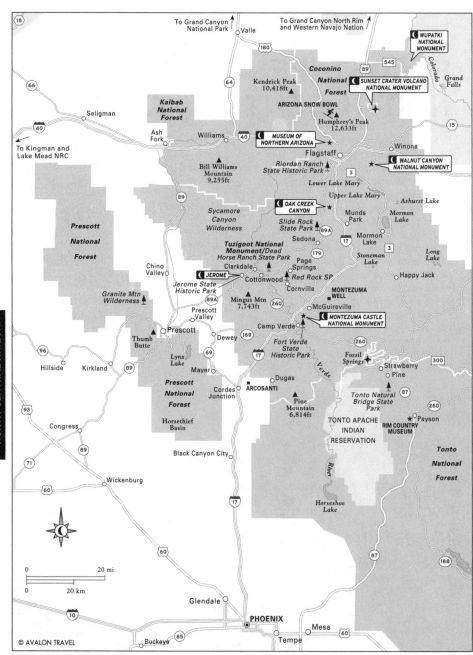

NORTH-CENTRAL ARIZONA

© AVALON TRAVEL

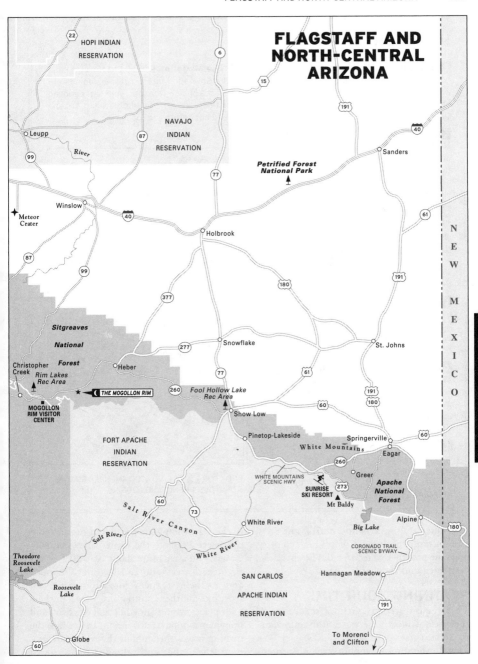

FLAGSTAFF AND NORTH-CENTRAL ARIZONA

NORTH-CENTRAL ARIZONA

HIGHLIGHTS

◖ **Museum of Northern Arizona:** Don't miss the Colorado Plateau's premier museum, where you'll learn about the plants, animals, geology and people that make the northlands such a fascinating landscape (page 138).

◖ **Sunset Crater Volcano and Wupatki National Monuments:** Explore the foothills of a silent black-rock crater and the architectural wonders of the Northern Sinagua golden age – 800 year-old red-rock apartment buildings rising from the dry scrublands (page 145).

◖ **Walnut Canyon National Monument:** Hike above a diversely vegetated canyon, moving from desert to forest in one short walk, past high-wall ruins built of stacked and mortared stone, while far below petrified sand dunes swirl and a ribbon of water flows through lush bottomlands (page 148).

◖ **Jerome:** Discover a haunted old mining town clinging to the side of a mineral-laden hill, now home to bed-and-breakfasts, hotels, eclectic restaurants, and one-of-a-kind boutiques (page 160).

◖ **Montezuma Castle National Monument:** See the mysterious ruins of the Southern Sinagua culture's highpoint – a cliff-wall castle molded out of limestone and cozy apartments clinging to the walls above a rare sinkhole (page 164).

◖ **Oak Creek Canyon:** Drive along a shady creekside with red-and- white-rock walls towering on each side, where birds, butterflies, and people flock to the babbling water sliding over pink slickrock (page 175).

◖ **The Mogollon Rim:** Sit on the very edge of the Colorado Plateau overlooking a deep-green sea of pine-tree tops, your legs dangling over the high cliff and all of lowland Arizona spread out before you (page 178).

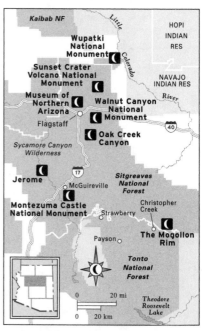

LOOK FOR ◖ TO FIND RECOMMENDED SIGHTS, ACTIVITIES, DINING, AND LODGING.

boutiques selling arts and crafts, antiques, and souvenirs of the arid West's high country, once the province of miners and lumberjacks, cattlemen and shepherds.

PLANNING YOUR TIME

This region attracts visitors regardless of the season, mostly because, unlike lowland Arizona, this region actually has a few seasons. In the summer months, the pine forests of the transition zone are a cool respite from the desert: Prescott, the Verde Valley, and Rim Country on average are about 10 to 20°F cooler than the lower Sonoran life zones. Flagstaff and, to the east, the White Mountains, can seem like another country altogether; in these high places winter snowfall makes skiing and snowplay a popular attraction. In the fall, the turning leaves throughout the region are glorious; the orange and yellow of the scattered deciduous trees look like fire-flares among the dominant stands of ponderosa pine.

A comprehensive trip to the region, one touching on all its charms and sights and including backcountry hikes and off-the-track exploring, would take about two weeks. A week would suffice to see everything, indulge your sensual whims, and explore the pinelands, red rocks, and mountaintops a bit.

A Northland Road Trip

This is ideal road-trip country, its scenic treasures nearly always represented not only deep in the wilderness but right there on the roadside, too. Starting from Phoenix, the most scenic road trip, and one on which you'll hit all the wonders and sights, goes first to Prescott, where you'll pick up Highway 89A, twisting up and over Mingus Mountain through Jerome, then down the other side to the Verde Valley. After seeing the ruins and lush riverine spectacle of Verde country, take 89A to Sedona, through Oak Creek Canyon, and up to Flagstaff, where it becomes Highway 89 and leads to Wupatki and Sunset Crater. Then head south to I-40 and east to Walnut Canyon. Continue on the Interstate to Winslow, where you'll pickup Route 87 south through the pines to Payson and Tonto Natural Bridge, just below the Mogollon Rim. After exploring below the rim, take Forest Road 300 (a dirt road but easily traversed) across the rim to Route 260 (if you want to skip the dirt road backcountry pick up Route 260 in Payson), which becomes the White Mountain Scenic Highway and leads through the high forest and meadow country to Route 191, the Coronado Trail. Slowly twist and turn down the forest-lined, two-lane trail, through the tiny mountain towns, down to the desert grasslands of southeastern Arizona. Then take I-10 west through Tucson and back to Phoenix. If you don't stop too long at any one place, such a drive-through, best-of-the-region's scenery road trip makes for a memorable and busy long weekend.

Flagstaff and Vicinity

The San Francisco Peaks, Arizona's tallest mountains and the Olympus of the Hopi Katsina, watch over this highland hub, the long-ago waterless home of the Sinagua and the Colorado Plateau's Arizona-side capital. Cinder-rocks from centuries of volcanic activity crunch perpetually beneath your feet here, and the town's scent is a potpourri of pine sap, wet leaves, and wood smoke mixing with incense, patchouli oil, train smoke, and beer. The redbrick, railroad-era downtown sits at around 7,000 feet, and the whole area from mountains to meadows is covered under about 100 inches of snow every year. In the summer it's mild, in the 70s and 80s mostly, but it gets cool and then cold pretty fast from September to December, when, in wet years, the first snow falls. In the deep winter and on into early April daytime temperatures are cold, and nighttime lows dip well below freezing.

Always a crossroads, it is especially so these days, thriving as a tourism gateway to the Grand Canyon, Indian Country, and the Colorado Plateau. It is also a college town attracting students from all over the world, and a major pull-off along I-40. Despite all that, it has managed to retain a good bit of its small mountain-town charm and Old West-through-Route 66 character. Its picturesque qualities, combined with its myriad opportunities for outdoor adventuring, make Flagstaff a major northland tourist draw in its own right.

Flagstaff's founding, including its rather literal naming legend, date to July 4, 1876. A group of New England émigrés, guided by one of those famous mountain men who had stalked the region for years already, camped nearby at a perpetual spring long known to wilderness loners and indigenous residents. In honor of the birthday happening back in the states, the Yankees stripped a skinny pine of its branches and attached a U.S. flag at the top,

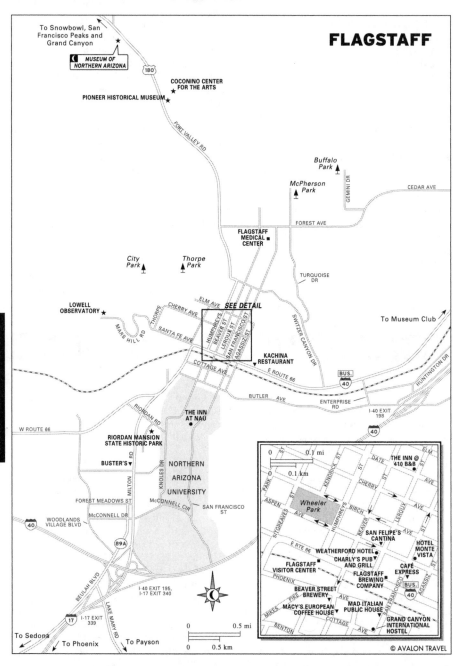

FLAGSTAFF

To Snowbowl, San Francisco Peaks and Grand Canyon

MUSEUM OF NORTHERN ARIZONA

180

COCONINO CENTER FOR THE ARTS

PIONEER HISTORICAL MUSEUM

FORT VALLEY RD

Buffalo Park

McPherson Park

GEMINI DR

CEDAR AVE

FOREST AVE

FLAGSTAFF MEDICAL CENTER

City Park

Thorpe Park

TURQUOISE DR

LOWELL OBSERVATORY

ELM AVE

SEE DETAIL

CHERRY AVE

HUMPHREYS ST

BEAVER ST

LEROUX ST

SAN FRANCISCO ST

AGASSIZ ST

THORPE

SANTA FE AVE

MARS HILL RD

SWITZER CANYON DR

To Museum Club

KACHINA RESTAURANT

COTTAGE AVE

E ROUTE 66

BUS. 40

BUTLER AVE

ENTERPRISE RD

HUNTINGTON DR

I-40 EXIT 198

RIORDAN RD

THE INN AT NAU

W ROUTE 66

RIORDAN MANSION STATE HISTORIC PARK

BUSTER'S

KNOLES DR

NORTHERN ARIZONA UNIVERSITY

40

I-40 EXIT

FOREST MEADOWS ST

MILTON

McCONNELL DR

McCONNELL CIR

SAN FRANCISCO ST

WOODLANDS VILLAGE BLVD

89A

BEULAH BLVD

LAKE MARY RD

I-40 EXIT 195, I-17 EXIT 340

17

I-17 EXIT 339

To Sedona   To Phoenix   To Payson

0   0.5 mi

0   0.5 km

Detail

0   ST   0.1 mi

0   0.1 km

PARK ST

DATE ST

KENDRICK ST

CHERRY ST

THE INN @ 410 B&B

ELM AVE

ASPEN AVE

SITGREAVES AVE

Wheeler Park

HUMPHREYS ST

BEAVER ST

BIRCH AVE

LEROUX ST

AVE

SAN FELIPE'S CANTINA

HOTEL MONTE VISTA

E RTE 66

WEATHERFORD HOTEL

CHARLY'S PUB AND GRILL

SAN FRANCISCO ST

AGASSIZ ST

CAFÉ EXPRESS

FLAGSTAFF VISITOR CENTER

PHOENIX AVE

FLAGSTAFF BREWING COMPANY

BUS. 40

BEAVER STREET BREWERY

PIKE AVE

MIKES PIKE

MACY'S EUROPEAN COFFEE HOUSE

MAD ITALIAN PUBLIC HOUSE

COTTAGE AVE

BENTON

GRAND CANYON INTERNATIONAL HOSTEL

© AVALON TRAVEL

A view of the northland from 11,500 feet up in the San Francisco Peaks above Flagstaff.

thus marking the spring and naming (as it was a flag-staff) a new stop along the trail. The outpost really didn't get going until the Santa Fe Railroad arrived in the 1880s, establishing the present-day downtown area and allowing for the ranching and lumber industries to exploit the surrounding forests and grasslands. Though tourism and the service industry are the town's major lifelines these days, the railroad is still very much a part of Flagstaff. As many as 80 trains a day chug through the heart of town, dividing it in two and often stopping traffic. The wail of train-horns is so ubiquitous that many residents don't even notice it anymore. There's something romantic and evocative, almost emotional, about being in a warm bed on a cool, star-bright forest night and hearing the plaintive whine of a westbound train.

SIGHTS
Historic Downtown District

Flagstaff has managed to hold on to many of its historic downtown buildings, short redbrick high-rises and quaint storefronts that served the needs of the railway and its passengers, housed and kept Route 66's argonauts, and marked the social and commercial heart of the town for generations. Any more, few residents would have occasion to go downtown to purchase a staple, unless healing crystals or wind chimes are integral to their lifestyle. Recent upgrades, which thankfully didn't completely corporatize the downtown, have made the fact that the area remains vibrant only to draw tourists, eaters, drinkers, and strollers more explicit than ever. Such is the fate of many old railroad and territorial downtowns throughout the West, but it has largely been a happy fate for Flagstaff. The downtown is a pleasant place to be any time of year, and the traveler will find myriad places to eat and to drink and to hunt for all manner of artistic and handmade treasures. Take a half a day or so—better it be later in the day to include some time to belly up to one of the downtown bars—and walk along Humphrey Street, Beaver Street, Leroux Street, San Francisco Street, and Route 66 across from the train depot, ducking in and out of shops, galleries, watering holes, and eateries. Head south of the tracks to the old Southside neighborhood, where there are more shops, restaurants, and bars near the Northern Arizona State University campus.

Riordan Mansion State Historic Park

Here's a great American success story that would have come off perfect in Technicolor: Two brothers, Michael and Timothy Riordan, make it big on the Western frontier denuding the Arizona northland of its harvestable lumber. The boys are rich and powerful and run in Flagstaff's founding circles, helping to build a lasting American community out of a rough, arid wilderness. The close brothers marry close sisters, Caroline and Elizabeth Metz, and the two fledgling families get on so well that they decide to build a 40-room, 13,000-square-foot Arts and Crafts–style masterpiece and live in it together. They hire El Tovar Hotel designer Charles Whittlesy to design two mansions in one, each shooting off in separate directions

NORTH-CENTRAL ARIZONA

like wings and linked by a pool hall and communal space. Then they decorate their majestic home with Stickley furniture, stained glass, and enough elegant, craftsman-style detail to draw crowds of visitors for the next 100 years. And everybody lives happily ever after.

The rock-and-log mansion, sprawling amidst a stand of pines in the middle of Flagstaff's commercial section and abutting the NAU campus, is now a state park (off Milton Rd. at 409 W. Riordan Rd., 928/779-4395, 8:30 A.M.–5 P.M. daily, $6 adults, $2.50 kids 7–13) that offers tours of this Arts and Crafts treasure, one of the best examples of the distinctive Anglo architecture that left a stylish stamp on the Southwest in the late 19th and early 20th centuries. Only a small portion of the structure is included in the tour, but it's full of original furniture and displays about the family and life in Flagstaff's formative years. The six-acre pine-needle blanket around the mansion has some great picnic spots.

Lowell Observatory

This hilltop campus (1400 W. Mars Hill Rd., 928/774-3358, www.lowell.edu, noon–5 P.M. Nov.–Feb., 9 A.M.–5 P.M. Mar.–Oct., stargazing starts at 7:30 P.M. Wed., Fri., and Sat. Sept.–May, 8 P.M. Mon.–Sat. June–Aug., $6 adults over 17, $3 kids 5–17) just west of downtown, occupied by tall straight pines and a few small white-domed structures with round concrete bases, has had a good deal of influence over the science of astronomy since its founders began searching the clear rural skies over Flagstaff in 1894. The historic viewpoint has had something to do with contemporary ideas about the beginnings of the universe as well.

It was here between 1912 and 1914 that Vesto Slipher discovered that the universe's galaxies are moving away from the earth, a phenomenon measured by changes in the light spectrum called redshifts. This in turn helped Edwin Hubble and others confirm that the universe is expanding, thus providing the first observable evidence for the Big Bang. Another

historic distinction came a few years later in 1930, when then 24-year-old Clyde Tombaugh looked out from atop Mars Hill and discovered the former planet, now dwarf-planet, Pluto.

Today the campus welcomes the public with 45-minute tours offered on the hour 10 A.M.–4 P.M. in summer and 1–4 P.M. in winter. The tours include a look through a solar telescope to view spots and flares on the sun, a duck into the cramped Pluto Telescope building, and a walk past a 350-foot-long model of the solar system. The **Steele Visitor Center** shows a movie about the observatory and interesting exhibits on astronomy. If you visit at night you can take part in galactic viewing sessions with staff astronomers.

Though smaller and less sleek and impressive than the more state-of-the-art telescopes in Southern Arizona, Lowell is worth the trip for its historical import (it's one of the oldest observatories in the nation, deemed a federal Historic Landmark in 1965), and for its picturesque location in the shadowy pines there at the border of Flagstaff's Thorpe Park. Don't miss checking out **Percival Lowell's tomb,** a neoclassical, observatory-shaped mausoleum that honors the observatory's founder, whose popular writings led many Americans to suspect that there was a series of observable canals, and by implication life, on Mars.

◖ Museum of Northern Arizona

A couple of well-educated and adventurous Easterners, Mary and Harold Colton, an artist and a zoologist who first came to Northern Arizona to climb mountains on their honeymoon, founded this essential museum (U.S. 180 three miles north of downtown, 928/774-5213, www.musnaz.org, 9 A.M.–5 P.M. daily, $5 adults over 17, $2 kids 7–17) in 1928 to preserve and encourage the indigenous arts and crafts of the Colorado Plateau. Since then it has become the cultural and scientific centerpoint of the Four Corners region, collecting, interpreting, and displaying the natural history, art, and artifacts of timeless landscapes and timeworn human cultures.

The museum's main building is itself a

warm, elegant, dark-wood and river-rock work of art set amidst the pines along the shallow Rio de Flag, with Arts and Crafts–era touches like the handmade Hopi-tile borders around the main entrance, fired on commission by the famous Hopi potter Sadie Adams in the 1930s. Inside there are comprehensive exhibits on the Four Corners region's ancient and current biomes and its buried and blowing strata, and one of the better introductions to Ancestral Puebloan and Puebloan cultures you'll find, with displays on the Basketmakers through the Anasazi and up to the Hopi of today. Volunteer docents stroll about and are eager to discuss and supplement any of the exhibits. The collection of Pueblo Indian pottery, jewelry, kachinas, and basketry is the museum's high point, and the galleries showing contemporary Hopi and Pueblo art, including oil paintings, watercolors, and sculpture, tend to open one's eyes to the vibrancy of the great plateau's current cultural moment.

Those who appreciate design should make a point to stroll into the **Branigar/Chase Discovery Center** lounge to see the Arts and Crafts flourishes in this cozy living-room setting. Just across the highway, those interested in the more narrowly focused history of Flagstaff should check out the **Arizona Historical Society's Pioneer Museum** (U.S. 180, 928/774-6272, 9 A.M.–5 P.M. Mon.–Sat.). Also right nearby and worth a look is the **Coconino Center for the Arts** (928/779-2300, www .culturalpartners.org, 11 A.M.–5 P.M. Tues.– Sat.), where local and regional artists display and sell their work.

ENTERTAINMENT AND EVENTS
Nightlife

Most of Flagstaff's favorite nightspots can be found downtown. The nightlife here is naturally full of college students, but you'll find older locals and many tourists getting into the mix regularly. The hip **Monte Vista Lounge** (100 N. San Francisco St., 928/774-2403) is a good place to sip cocktails and lounge around, with live music on the weekends.

TRAIN HIGH: NAU'S CENTER FOR HIGH-ALTITUDE TRAINING

What do Ian Thorpe, the great Australian swimming star, and the athletes of the Egyptian Volleyball Federation have in common? They've both trained at Northern Arizona University's **Center for High Altitude Training** (928/523-4444, www .hastc.nau.edu), an elite facility where top-level athletes from all over the world are pushed to their limits in Flagstaff's clean, thin, 7,000-foot-high air.

The perceived benefits of training in high altitudes are by no means universally accepted, though many upper echelon athletes swear by it. While it's true that as the body works to adjust to getting less oxygen in higher altitudes, it makes adaptive changes and increases red blood cell production, at the same time it's harder to train with the same intensity at 7,000 feet as one would during sea-level workout. Consequently, while performance at high altitudes is likely to be less than spectacular, upon returning to sea level some athletes find their times greatly improved. For speed skaters and sprint runners, the decreased resistance of the thin air makes for times faster than those at sea level.

The center opened in 1984 and since then has become one of the top high-altitude training centers in the world. Beginning with the 1986 Olympic games in Atlanta, 191 Olympic and Paralympic medals have gone to athletes who've trained at the center – a total of about 5,000 athletes from 40 different countries, including China, Germany, and, of course, the U.S. The center is also one of only nine training facilities in the nation to be designated an official Olympic training facility by the U.S. Olympic Committee.

Plus, those Flagstaff residents and visitors who are fans of sports with more international renown than American appeal have plenty of chances for celebrity sighting.

You're bound to see college kids dancing on the bartops at **San Felipe's Cantina** (103 N. Leroux St., 928/779-6000), a Mexican beach–themed joint that is extremely popular with the NAU party crowd. More sedate and drawing a slightly older crowd is **Charley's Pub** (23 N. Leroux St., 928/779-1919), the town's favorite spot for live blues and other music. The rooftop bar at the **Mad Italian Public House** (101 S. San Francisco St., 928/779-1820) should not be missed, and the pool tables and happy crowds here are great on a weekend night. If you're just looking to kick back a few good beers and talk, the **Flagstaff Brewing Company** (16 E. Route 66, 928/773-1442) is the place to go, and if you're looking to kick up your cowboy boots and line-dance your way through an evening, check out the historic **Museum Club** (3404 E. Route 66, 928/526-9434) east of downtown.

Live Music

Flagstaff's a pretty laid-back town, and it has its share of mountain men, bohemians, and creative types. NAU's more than 20,000 students, many from abroad, help give the old frontier town a dash of do-it-yourself cosmopolitanism. It's not surprising, then, that the area attracts headlining acts and smaller indie favorites to its bars and theaters at a steady clip. If you're a fan of alternative pop, alt-country, classic country, bluegrass, classic rock, and just plain rock and roll, it's a good idea to check the websites of the following venues before making your travel plans. Odds are some funky act you love or have barely heard of will be playing during your visit.

The **Orpheum** (15 W. Aspen St., 928/556-1580, www.orpheumpresents.com), a retro-cool theater and bar that was once Flagstaff's first movie house, hosts practitioners of modern music from Ozomatli to Rob Zombie and shows classic, neoclassic, and first-run movies on special nights each month. **The Pine Mountain Amphitheater** (928/774-0899, www.pinemountainamphitheater.com) out in the pines at Fort Tuthill Park is the region's best outdoor venue and attracts great bands from all over, many of the bluegrass and country persuasion. **Prochnow Auditorium** (928/523-5661 or 888/520-7214) at NAU books national and international acts into an intimate setting.

Events

Flagstaff hosts a variety of cultural events, mostly during its cool springs and warm summers. In March the **Flagstaff Mountain Film Festival** (www.flagstaffmountainfilms.com) screens the year's best independent films with an environmental, outdoor adventure, and social justice bent. In April, world-renowned authors come to town for lectures, signings, readings, and panel discussions at the **Northern Arizona Book Festival** (928/380-8682, www.nazbookfestival.org).

The **Museum of Northern Arizona Heritage Program** (928/774-5213, www.musnaz.org) puts on several important and well-attended cultural festivals each year, featuring native arts and crafts markets, food, history displays, and entertainment: The **Hopi Festival of Arts and Culture** in early July; The **Navajo Festival of Arts and Culture** in early August; and, in late October, **Celebración de la Gente,** marking Dia de los Muertos, the Day of the Dead. In late May, the museum puts on the **Zuni Festival of Arts and Culture.** The second week in September, just before it starts to get cold in the north country, Flagstaff ushers in **Route 66 Days** (928/607-2347, www.flagstaffroute66days.com), celebrated with a parade, a classic car show, and all manner of special activities along the downtown portion of the Mother Road.

SHOPPING

The best place to shop for distinctive gifts, souvenirs, decorations, clothes, and outdoor gear is Flagstaff's historic downtown. You'll find Native American arts and crafts, western wear, New Age items, art galleries specializing in handmade objects, antiques stores, and three really good outdoor gear shops: **Peace Surplus** (14 W. Route 66, 928/779-4521) with all kinds of military surplus outdoor and survival gear;

Babbitt's (12 E. Aspen, 928/774-4775), selling top-notch wilderness trekking and fly fishing gear from a famous old building with a famous old northland name; and **Aspen Sports** (15 N. San Francisco St., 928/779-1935), which sells the best in outdoor, hiking, skiing, and trekking gear.

Bookmans (1520 S. Riordan Ranch Rd., 928/774-0005), Arizona's original used-media supercenter, is the best bookstore in Northern Arizona bar none, with a huge selection of used books, music, and DVDs.

SPORTS AND RECREATION
Hiking

Head north on Highway 180 eight miles to the San Francisco Peaks for the best hikes in the area. There are dozens of lesser hikes around the peaks, but the most memorable, essential hike in these sylvan volcano lands is the **Humphrey's Peak Trail.** The tough hike leads to the highest reaches of Humphrey's Peak at 12,633 feet—the very top of Arizona and perhaps nearby to the sacred realms wherein the Hopi Kachina dwell and watch. The nine-mile round-trip is very strenuous but beautiful. The trail moves through a shady Aspen forest and then up above the tree line to a windy and rocky alpine stretch. Be careful of altitude sickness if you're a habituated lowlander. The trailhead is just beyond the ski lift at the Snow Bowl complex, on Snow Bowl Road (Forest Road 516). The **Kachina Trail,** which begins at the dead-end of Snow owl Road, is a less vertical walk and is popular with locals. It's a 10-mile round-trip stroll along mostly flat land—you're at 9,500 feet anyway . . . why go up any more?—through thick stands of conifers and aspens and sweeping views at every corner. This is a particularly beautiful route in the fall, with fiery yellows and reds everywhere.

Contact the **Coconino National Forest** (1824 S. Thompson St., 928/527-3600) for information on hiking in the peaks and see www.fs.fed.us/r3/coconino/recreation/peaks/rec_peaks.shtml for other hikes in the volcanic highlands.

Mountain Biking

Mountain biking is very popular in Flagstaff, and many of its trails are up-and-down exciting and technical to the point of mental exhaustion. Enthusiasts will want to head straightaway to the series of moderate-to-difficult, inter-connected trails of the **Mount Elden Trail System** east of town along Highway 89. There are enough loops and mountainside single-tracks in this area to keep you busy for a while.

Actually, the very first thing you'll want to do is head to one of the downtown outdoor stores, Bookman's, or **Absolute Bikes** (200 E. Rte. 66, 928/779-5969, www.absolutebikes.net), Flagstaff's biking headquarters, and pick up a copy of the essential *Cosmic Ray's* guide to the area's trails (and to all of Arizona's mountain biking trails, for that matter). It's the single best book on northland biking and should already be in the collection of any serious Southwestern rider. The folks at Absolute Bikes will also rent you a tough mountain bike ($40–70 per day, reserve 72 hours in advance) and help you decide which trail to hit.

Snowbowl

This ski lodge on the slopes of the San Francisco Peaks (Take Highway 180 north to Snow Bowl Rd., 928/779-1951, www.snowbowl.com) offers skiers and snowboarders over 2,300 feet of vertical drop and 32 scenic trails that cover 777 acres. In wet years the first snow usually falls in December, but in recent, drought-ridden years the snow has stayed away until late in the season. The resort is involved in protracted litigation with Native Americans over man-made snow. The Hopi and other tribes consider the mountains sacred and don't want the skiers there at all, let alone the effrontery of man-made snow on the mighty peaks for the sake of recreation profits.

In the summer, the ski-lift becomes the **Skyride** (928/779-1951, www.snowbowl.com, $10 adults over 12, $6 kids 8–12), lifting passengers slowly up to 11,500 feet, where you need a jacket in July and the hazy flatland

HIGHEST TOILET IN ARIZONA   ELEV. 11.500 FT.

© TIM HULL

The ski lift at Snowbowl, in the San Francisco Peaks near Flagstaff, takes you up 11,500 feet to the highest toilet in Arizona.

stretches out for eternity. The Snowbowl also has several mountain **disc golf** courses. In fact, the peaks hosted the 2005 World Championships for that increasingly popular sport.

Flagstaff Nordic Center

This complex of trails and sledding hills (Hwy. 180 north 15 miles to mile marker 232, 928/220-0550, www.flagstaffnordic center.com) is a popular place for cross-country skiing, sledding, snowshoeing, and all manner of snow play as long as there's snow on the Coconino National Forest at the base of the peaks. Equipment rental, lessons, and races are available.

Plateau Lakes

Several lakes dot the volcanic plateau south of Flagstaff, including **Mormon Lake,** the state's largest natural lake. Though shrinking and even sometimes dry altogether due

to drought, Mormon Lake is a beautiful body of water set amidst the green pines and junipers of the plateau, ideal for spring and summer boating, fishing, and even windsurfing. In the winter, the plateau country is popular with cross-country skiers and snowmobile enthusiasts. There are also plenty of lakeside hiking trails and mountain bike routes nearby, and myriad opportunities for bird-watching and wildlife-viewing, including herds of elk that call the plateau home.

To reach Flagstaff's lake district, head south out of town on Lake Mary Road. Along the way you'll pass several smaller lakes—**Lower and Upper Lake Mary, Marshall Lake,** and **Ashurst Lake**—before reaching Mormon Lake via Forest Road 90, about 30 miles from town. The **Dairy Springs and Double Springs Campgrounds** ($14 per night, open May through mid-October) offer spots with drinking water and vault toilets. Nearby, **Mormon Lake Lodge** (928/354-2227, www.forever

lodging.com, $50–185) has comfortable log cabins of various sizes to rent and has a 74-spot RV park as well. There's a delicious steakhouse and saloon with rustic Western ambience, serving forest explorers since the 1920s, and the lodge rents horses and mountains bikes.

For more on hiking, biking, fishing, and boating opportunities on the plateau, contact the **The Peaks/Mormon Lake Ranger Districts** (5075 N. Hwy 89, 928/527-3600, www.fs.fed.us/r3/coconino/recreation/mormon_lake/index.shtml, 8 A.M.–4:30 P.M. Mon.–Fri.).

ACCOMMODATIONS

Flagstaff, being an Interstate town close to several world-renowned sights (i.e., the Grand Canyon), has all the chains. A good value and a unique experience can be had at one of the historic downtown hotels like the Weatherford or the Hotel Monte Vista.

Under $50

The **Grand Canyon International Hostel** (19 S. San Francisco St., 888/442-2696, www.grandcanyonhostel.com, $20–45) is a clean and friendly place to stay on the cheap, located in an old 1930s building downtown in which you're likely to meet some lasting friends, many of them foreign tourists tramping around the Colorado Plateau. The hostel offers bunk-style sleeping arrangements and private rooms, mostly shared bathrooms, a self-serve kitchen, Internet access, free breakfast, and a chance to join in on tours of the region. It's a cozy, welcoming hippie-home-style place to stay.

$50-100

The **G Weatherford Hotel** (29 N. Leroux St., 928/779-1919, www.weatherfordhotel.com, $65–105 d) is one of two historic hotels downtown. It's basic but romantic, if you're into stepping back in time when you head off to bed. There are no TVs or phones in the rooms, and the whole place is a little creaky,

but the location and the history make this a fun place to rest, especially with the bar and grill downstairs.

The **G Hotel Monte Vista** (100 N. San Francisco, 928/779-6971 or 800/545-3068, www.hotelmontevista.com, $50–160 d), the other historic downtown hotel, is a bit swankier. The redbrick high-rise, built in 1927, once served high-class and famous travelers heading west on the Santa Fe Line. These days it offers rooms that have historic charm but are still comfortable and convenient, with cable TV and private bathrooms. There's a hip cocktail lounge downstairs and, like many of the grand old railroad hotels, there are lots of tales to be heard about the Hollywood greats who stayed here and the restless ghosts who stayed behind.

The **Ski Lift Lodge** (6355 Hwy. 180, 928/774-0729 or 800/472-3599, $59–85 d) has simple, cabin-style rooms out in the forest beneath the San Francisco Peaks. It's dark out there, and you can see all the stars in the universe on many nights. This lodge is a good bet if you're skiing or engaging in other snow-related activities.

Over $100

The **Embassy Suites** (706 S. Milton, 928/774-4333, www.embassysuitesflagstaff.com, $99–139 d) offers a cozy and tasteful compound in the center of commercial Flagstaff, with a pool and hot tub, free made-to-order breakfast, and a complimentary nightly cocktail hour in its leather-chair lounge. This place is perfect for families: A relatively inexpensive suite offers two large beds in one room, a hide-a-bed in another, TVs in both, and a refrigerator. For a touch of wilderness adventure with all the comforts of an in-town hotel, try the **Arizona Mountain Inn** (4200 Lake Mary Rd., 928/774-8959, www.arizonamountaininn.com, $85–410), offering 17 rustic but comfortable cabins in the pines outside of town near Lake Mary, each with wood-burning stove, kitchen, and outdoor grill.

The Inn at 410 Bed and Breakfast (410 N. Leroux St., 928/774-0088 or 888/774-2008, www.inn410.com, $150–210 d) has 10 artfully decorated rooms in a classic old home in a quiet, tree-lined neighborhood just off downtown. This is a wonderful little place, with so much detail and stylishness. Breakfasts are interesting and filling, often with a Southwestern tinge, and tea is served every afternoon. You certainly can't go wrong with this award-winning place, one of the best B&Bs in the state. The **Starlight Pines Bed and Breakfast** (3380 E. Lockett Rd., 928/527-1912 or 800/752-1912, www.starlightpinesbb.com, $119–149) is located about three miles from town in the forest at the foot of Mt. Elden, offering four rooms stuffed with antiques in a Victorian-era home. There's a porch swing, claw-foot bathtubs perfect for bubble baths, and fresh-cut flowers in every room, but no TVs. They'll even bring your breakfast to your room for you.

FOOD

Flagstaff has some excellent restaurants, an inordinate number for its size owing to the cosmopolitan make-up of its population.

American

There's something about drinking a dark, handcrafted pint of beer in the piney mountain heights that makes one feel as good as can be—maybe it's the alcohol mixed with the altitude. The best place to get that feeling is the **Beaver Street Brewery** (11 S. Beaver St., 928/779-0079, www.beaverstreetbrewery.com, 11:30 A.M.–1 A.M. daily, $7–18), where excellent beers are made on-site, and there's delicious, hearty food of the bar and grill variety. **Brandy's Restaurant and Bakery** (1500 E. Cedar Ave. #40, 928/779-2187, www.brandysrestaurant.com, 6:30 A.M.–9 P.M. Tues.–Sat., 6:30 A.M.–2:30 P.M. Sun.–Mon., $7–14) often wins the Best Breakfast honors from readers of the local newspaper, and those readers know what they're talking about. The homemade breads and bagels make everything else somehow taste better. Try the Eggs Brandy, two poached eggs on a homemade bagel smothered in Hollandaise

sauce. Brandy's serves an eclectic mix of sandwiches, soups, and salads for lunch, and a creative menu of entrées for dinner—the chili-balsamic-marinated steak is particularly good. **Buster's** (1800 S. Milton Rd., 928/774-5155, 11:30 A.M.–10 P.M. daily, $5–23) has been a local favorite for years, serving up good steaks and burgers and such, and offering the hangover-assuring Buster Bowl to any hard-drinking college student who happens in. Downtown, **Charly's Pub and Grill** (23 N. Leroux St., inside the Weatherford Hotel, 928/779-1919, www.weatherfordhotel.com, 11 A.M.–10 P.M. Mon.–Fri., 11 A.M.–11 P.M. Fri.–Sat., $5–15) is a great place for lunch, with thick sandwiches and great soups. **Josephine's Modern American Bistro** (503 N. Humphrey's St., 928/779-3400, www.josephinesrestaurant.com, 11 A.M.–2:30 P.M. Mon.–Fri. and 5–9 P.M. Mon.–Sat., $8–30) offers a creative fusion of tastes for lunch and dinner, like the roasted pepper and hummus grilled cheese sandwich and the chili relleno with sundried cranberry guacamole, from a cozy historic home near downtown.

Mexican

The **Kachina Downtown Restaurant** (522 E. Route 66, 928/779-1944, 11 A.M.–8 P.M. Sun.–Mon., 10 A.M.–9 P.M. Tues.–Thurs., 10 A.M.–9:30 P.M. Fri.–Sat., $6–18) is a good place for good old Sonoran dishes at a fair price.

Asian

The **Himalayan Grill** (801 S. Milton Ave., Suite A, 928/213-5444, 11 A.M.–2:30 P.M. and 5–10 P.M. daily, $8–20) serves excellent Indian food, and a special Himalayan Margarita, mixed an icy blue.

Sakura (1175 W. Route 66 in the Radisson Woodlands Hotel, 928/773-9118, 11:30 A.M.–2 P.M. Mon.–Sat. and 5–10 P.M. daily, $8–30) is a favorite with locals for sushi and teppanyaki, often busy on the weekends.

Italian

NiMarco's Pizza (101 S. Beaver St., 928/779-2691, 11 A.M.–9 P.M. daily, $5–20) in the Southside neighborhood serves the best pizza in town in a casual space and will deliver to most hotels.

Vegetarian

◖ Café Express (16 N. San Francisco St., 928/774-0541, 7 A.M.–9 P.M. daily, $2–8) is a favorite with Flagstaff's new bohemians and a gathering place for college students and locals alike, with excellent, all-natural creations and a laid-back atmosphere downtown. **Macy's European Coffee House** (14 S. Beaver St., 928/774-2243, 6 A.M.–10 P.M. daily, $5–10) south of the tracks is the best place to get coffee and a quick vegetarian bite to eat, or just hang out and watch the locals file in and out, many of them dreadlocked and hippified.

INFORMATION

The **Flagstaff Visitor Center** (1 E. Route 66, 928/774-9541, www.flagstaffarizona.org, 8 A.M.–7 P.M. Mon.–Sat.), located in the old train depot in the center of town, has all kinds of information on Flagstaff and the surrounding areas.

GETTING THERE AND AROUND

The best and, really, the only easy way to see Flagstaff and the surrounding country is by car. From Phoenix, take I-17 north for about 2.5 hours (146 miles) and you're in another world.

Air

Flagstaff's small **Pulliam Airport** (928/556-1234), located about five miles south of downtown, offers several daily flights to and from Sky Harbor in Phoenix.

Train, Bus, and Tours

Amtrak's Southwest Chief Route, which mirrors the old Santa Fe Railway's Super Chief Route of the grand Fred Harvey days, stops twice daily (one eastbound, one westbound) at Flagstaff's classic downtown depot (1 E. Route 66, 800/872-7245), the former Santa Fe headquarters and also the town's visitors center (800/842-7293). The route crosses the

country from Chicago to L.A., dipping into the Southwest through northern New Mexico and northern Arizona.

Inside the depot, you can hire **Open Road Tours** (800/766-7117, www.openroadtours .com) to guide and shuttle you in comfort all over the region. Right nearby you can catch a **Greyhound Bus** (800/231-2222, www.grey hound.com) to just about anywhere.

Public Transportation

Flagstaff's city bus, the **Mountain Line** (928/779-6624, $1 per ride), runs 6 A.M.–10 P.M. weekdays and 7 A.M.–8 P.M. weekends to stops all over town.

◖ SUNSET CRATER VOLCANO AND WUPATKI NATIONAL MONUMENTS

Sunset Crater Volcano isn't really a volcano at all anymore, but a nearly perfectly conical pile of cinder and ash that built up around the former volcano's main vent. Sunset Crater erupted,

The barren lava fields below Sunset Crater Volcano, near Flagstaff, host only hardy flora and fauna.

probably several different times, between 1049 and 1100. The eruptions transformed this particularly arid portion of the not exactly lush Colorado Plateau, and now huge cinder barrens, as surprising as an alien world the first time you see them, stretch out along the loop road leading through these popular national monuments. You can't climb the crater-cone anymore, years of scarring by the crowds saw to that, but you can walk across the main lava field at the crater's base, a cinder field with scattered dwarfed, crooked pines and bursts of rough-rock adapted flowers and shrubs, all the while craning up at the 1,000-foot-high, 2,550-foot-wide cone.

Along with turning its immediate environs into a scorched but beautiful wasteland, the volcano's eruptions may have inadvertently helped human culture thrive for a brief time in this formidable environment, the subject and object of Sunset Crater's sister monument, Wupatki. The series of eruptions spewed about a ton of ashfall over 88 square miles, and closer to the source the ash created a kind of rich mulch that, combined with a few years of above average rainfall, may have stimulated a spike in population growth and cultural influence. Archeological findings in the area suggest that the five pueblos in the shadow of the crater, especially the large Wupatki,

WHO WERE THE SINAGUA AND WHERE DID THEY GO?

They left their architecture and masonry all over North-Central Arizona, from the redrock apartment buildings rising from the cinder plains below the San Francisco Peaks, to the sandstone cliff hideouts of Walnut Canyon, to the limestone castles in the lush, easy-living Verde Valley, to the brick-stone rooms leaning against Sedona's redwalls.

We don't really know what they called themselves, but we call them, according to tradition more than anything else, the Sinagua, Spanish for "without water" – a name that alludes to that given by early Spanish explorers to this region of pine-covered highlands still stuck somehow in aridity: *Sierra Sin Agua* (mountains without water).

Their cultural development followed a pattern similar to that of the Ancestral Puebloans in the Four Corners region. They first lived in pit houses bolstered by wooden beams, and made a living from small-scale dryland farming, hunting, and gathering piñon nuts and other land-given seasonal delicacies. They made strong and stylish baskets and pottery (though they didn't decorate theirs in the manner of the Anasazi and others); they were weavers, craftsmen, and traders.

Around A.D. 700 a branch of the Sinagua migrated below the Mogollon Rim to the Verde

Valley and began living the good life next to fish-filled rivers and streams that flowed all year round; these migrants are now called the Southern Sinagua, and the ones that stayed behind are called the Northern Sinagua. When, around A.D. 1064, the volcano that is now Sunset Crater, northeast of Flagstaff, erupted, there were Sinagua villages well within reach of its spewing ash and lava, though archeologists have found evidence that nearby pithouses had been disassembled and moved just before the eruption, leading to the assumption that they probably knew the big one was coming.

The eruption would not be the end of the Sinagua – quite the contrary. Though the reasons why are debated – it could have been that crops grew to surplus because a post-eruption cinder mulch made the land more fertile; or it could be that the years following the big blow were wetter than normal; or it could be a bit of both – after the eruption Sinagua culture began to become more complex, and soon it would go through a boomtime. From roughly 1130 to 1400 or so, Sinagua culture flourished as the Sinagualands became an important stop in a trade network that included Mexico to the south, the Four Corners to the north, and beyond. At pueblo-style ruins dating from this era, archeologists have found shells, copper

were at the center of a trading crossroads and the most important population center for 50 miles or more, with about 2,000 people living within a day's walk from the sprawling red-rock apartment building by 1190. Times seem to have been good for about 150 years here, and then, owing to a variety of factors, everybody left. The Hopi and other Pueblo people consider Wupatki a sacred place, one more in a series of former homes their ancestors kept during their long migrations to Black Mesa. Today you can walk among the red and pink ruins, standing on jutting patios and looking out over the dry land, wondering what that waterless life was like, and marveling at the adaptive, architectural, and artistic genius of those who came before.

Visiting the Monuments

The monuments sit side by side on an arid, clump-grass sweep with humps of volcanic remains and colored with pine stands and, if you're lucky, blankets of yellow wildflowers, about 12 miles north of Flagstaff along Highway 89. Turn onto the Sunset Crater-Wupatki Loop Road, which will lead you across the cinder barrens, through the forest, and out onto the red-dirt plains and the ruins, and then back to Highway 89. One ticket is good for both monuments.

bells, and Macaw bones, all from Mexico. Sinagua architecture became more Puebloan, and villages often had Mexican-style ball courts and Kivas similar to those of the Anasazi. It is from this era that the famous ruins protected throughout this region date.

Then it all ended. Owing to drought, disease, war, civil strife, a combination of any one or all of these, or some other strange tragedy we will never learn about, by the early 1400s the Sinagua culture was on the run. By 1425, even the seemingly lucky farmers of the Verde Valley had abandoned their castles, the survivors and stragglers mixing with other tribes, their kind never to be seen again. Lucky for us they were such good builders.

NORTH-CENTRAL ARIZONA

© TIM HULL

The Sinagua people built this stone and mortar room, one of many in Walnut Canyon near Flagstaff.

© TIM HULL

The Sinagua built this red-stone apartment-style building on the plains north of Flagstaff.

Heading north from Flagstaff, you'll get to the **Sunset Crater Volcano Visitor Center** (928/526-0502, www.nps.gov/sucr/, 9 A.M.–5 P.M. daily Nov.–Apr., 8 A.M.–5 P.M. daily May–Oct., $5 for seven-day pass, kids under 16 free) first, about two miles from the junction. Take a few minutes to look over the small museum and gift shop; there are several displays about volcanoes and the history of the region. Pick up the guidebook ($1 or free if you recycle it) to the one-mile loop **Lava Flow Trail** out onto the **Bonito Lava Flow** and head up the road a bit to the trailhead. This is an easy walk among the cinder barrens, a strange landscape with a kind of ruined beauty about it—only squat pines will grow, but there are surprising flushes of life throughout, small niches in which color can find a foothold. The trail skirts the base of the great crater-cone and takes about an hour or so.

Another 16 miles on the loop road and you're at the **Wupatki Visitor Center** (928/679-2365, www.nps.gov/wupa, 9 A.M.–5 P.M. daily Nov.–Apr., 8 A.M.–5 P.M.

daily May–Oct., $5 for seven-day pass, kids under 16 free), a total of 21 miles from the junction, near the last of the five pueblos, the titular Wupatki. The other pueblos are before Wupatki, reached by two separate short trails, each with its own parking lot along the loop road. At Wupatki, you can purchase a guide ($1 or free if you recycle it) to the half-mile **Wupatki Pueblo Trail,** which leads around the village complex and back to the visitors center. If you don't have time to see all five pueblos, head straight to Wupatki, the biggest and best of them all.

◖ WALNUT CANYON NATIONAL MONUMENT

Not far from Wupatki, another group of Sinagua farmed the forested rim and built stacked limestone-and-clay apartments into the cliffsides of Walnut Canyon, a 20-mile-long, 400-foot-deep gathering of nearly every North American life zone in one relatively small wonderland. Near the rim, a huge island of rock juts out of the canyon innards, around which residents constructed their cells, most of them facing south and east to gather warmth. Depending on how much sunlight any one side of the island received, the Sinagua could count on several seasons of food gathering, from cactus fruit to piñon nuts to wild grapes. A creek snakes through the canyon's green bottomlands, encouraging cottonwoods and willows. The Sinagua lived in this high, dry Eden for about 125 years, leaving finally for good around 1250. This is an enchanting, mysterious place that should not be missed.

Visiting the Monument

Take I-40 east from Flagstaff for 7.5 miles to Exit 204, then it's 3 miles south to the canyon rim and the **Walnut Canyon Visitor Center** (928/526-3367, www.nps.gov/waca/, 9 A.M.–5 P.M. daily Nov.–Apr., 8 A.M.–5 P.M. daily May–Oct., $5 for seven-day pass, kids under 16 free), where there are a few displays, a small gift shop, and a spectacular window-view of the canyon. An hour or more on the **Island Trail,** a one-mile loop past 25 cliff dwellings (close enough to touch and examine up close) and into several different biomes high above the riparian bottomlands, is essential to a visit here, but it's not entirely easy; you must climb down (and back up) 240 rock-hewn steps to get to the island, descending 185 feet. Once you're on the island, though, it's an easy, mostly flat walk, and one that you won't soon forget. There's also a short trail up on the rim with some great views.

Prescott and the Verde Valley

Here you'll find the true transition zone, the no-man's-land of ecotones—points of species contact—between the high forests and the low deserts. Dry chaparral brushlands climb the rocky mountains to become dry ponderosa pine forests, and it's not surprising to see clumps of cactus the entire way up. The whole region, even its most forgotten outbacks, is crisscrossed by trails and roads left over from the old mining days. Head up and over the mountains and you'll find a lush river valley, fed by the perpetual Verde River, and the golden-age ruins of a lost tribe. There's a lot to do and see in the central transition zones, especially if the history of the Old West, highland outdoor adventuring, and poking around for artistic treasures are of any interest to you.

PRESCOTT

President Abraham Lincoln signed the bill that created the Arizona Territory in 1863, separating Arizonaland from the vast frontier to the north of Mexico City called New Mexico. Around the same time it was decided to found the administrative capital of the new territory in a clime more northerly than that confederate hotbed down in Tucson, then one of the largest population centers in the region. A group of federal appointees headed out for the rocky, chaparral-clogged midlands and the skinny pine forests around a mile high, near placer-laden Hassayampa Creek and the Bradshaw Mountains, both objects of desire for gold and silver miners who couldn't make a go of it in crowded California.

They eventually built the capital as a strange but functional Midwestern church town–meets–rowdy mining camp amalgam that today, long after the little mountain-nestled burg consciously turned from extraction and ranching to tourism for its supper, brings in droves of Phoenicians and other desert-dwellers on weekends and holidays, each of them looking for something that has been left behind and forgotten out in the unrecognizable valley sprawl.

With more than 700 buildings on the National Register of Historic Places and a rough Old West history full of political chicanery and violence to back up its sometimes heavy-handed marketing, the town has much to recommend it to tourists, especially those

© TIM HULL

The neoclassical Yavapai County Courthouse is one of several buildings in downtown Prescott that evoke nostalgia for small-town America.

fascinated by the 19th-century Anglo West and Victorian architecture. Thus Prescott has become "Everybody's Hometown," a slogan printed on signs and flags throughout the Middle-American-picturesque downtown. The town has a sizable population of well-off retirees and a hard-to-miss group of young back-to-nature bohemian residents, many of them students at Prescott College, a private Liberal Arts college specializing in environmental studies.

Prescott enjoys the further distinction of being "Arizona's Christmas City." Every year, just after Thanksgiving, the huge neoclassical courthouse downtown is decked in semi-gaudy Christmas decorations and illuminated during a crisp nighttime ceremony, attendance at which would make even a lifelong big city resident nostalgic for small-town life.

Prescott's most lasting draw for those living down the hill and elsewhere is its four-season climate—warm in summer, perfect in spring, cool in fall, and cold, sometimes even snowy, in winter—which over the generations

has prompted the desert folk to build getaway cabins and then dream homes in the cool piney hills around the town. The Prescott National Forest hugs the outskirts of town in a sappy embrace, traversed by hundreds of trails and ideal for all manner of outdoor retreats and recreation.

Downtown and the Courthouse Plaza

Most of Prescott's charm and interest is centered on a few blocks in the downtown area (Gurley, Montezuma, Cortez, and Goodwin Streets), among dozens of shops, boutiques, antique stores, and art galleries (many of them with an Old West theme, and most in the middle- to high-end of the price range), and the town's best restaurants and bars, most of them frequented by visitors and locals alike. The whole scene surrounds the big stone, tall-pillared courthouse, built in 1916 out of locally quarried stone, and its grassy grounds lined by imported trees; there's always something going on—square-dancing, craft shows,

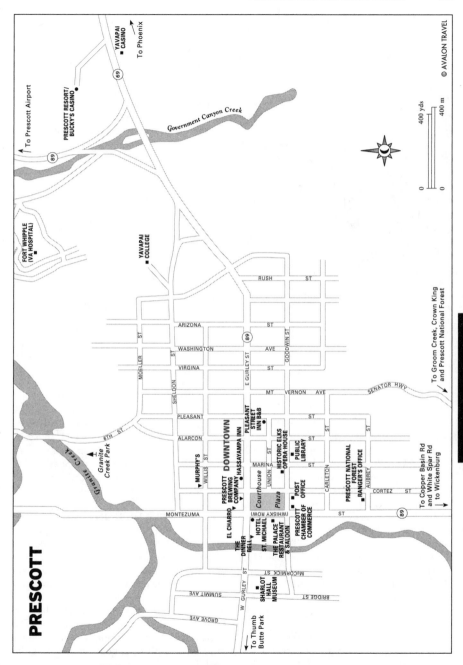

PRESCOTT

To Prescott Airport

FORT WHIPPLE
(VA HOSPITAL)

YAVAPAI
CASINO
To Phoenix

PRESCOTT RESORT/
BUCKY'S CASINO

Government Canyon Creek

© AVALON TRAVEL

YAVAPAI
COLLEGE

RUSH   ST

ARIZONA   ST

WASHINGTON   AVE

VIRGINA   ST

MOELLER   ST

SHELDON   ST

MT   VERNON   AVE

SENATOR HWY

GOODWIN ST

E GURLEY ST

PLEASANT   ST

ALARCON   ST

8TH   ST

Granite Creek Park

Granite Creek

DOWNTOWN

PLEASANT
STREET
INN B&B

HISTORIC ELKS
OPERA HOUSE

PUBLIC
LIBRARY

PRESCOTT NATIONAL
FOREST
RANGER'S OFFICE

MURPHY'S

PRESCOTT
BREWING
COMPANY

HASSAYAMPA INN

WILLIS   ST

MARINA   ST

UNION   ST

CARLETON   ST

AUBREY   ST

CORTEZ   ST

Courthouse

Plaza

POST
OFFICE

MONTEZUMA   ST

EL CHARRO

THE DINNER
BELL

HOTEL
ST. MICHAEL

THE PALACE
RESTAURANT
& SALOON

PRESCOTT
CHAMBER OF
COMMERCE

WHISKY ROW

SHARLOT
HALL
MUSEUM

W. GURLEY   ST

McCORMICK ST

BRIDGE ST

SUMMIT AVE

GROVE AVE

To Thumb
Butte Park

To Groom Creek, Crown King
and Prescott National Forest

To Copper Basin Rd
and White Spar Rd
to Wickenburg

0   400 yds

0   400 m

NORTH-CENTRAL ARIZONA

© TIM HULL

Roughrider Buckey O'Neill, who died fighting with Teddy Roosevelt's famous band, was once the mayor of Prescott.

live theater, a few families or couples lounging on the grass with a picnic, kids playing with Frisbees and Hacky Sacks, and exercisers doing laps on the cobblestone walkways, led quickly by their dogs.

Large bronze statues grace three sides of the plaza: a cowboy supine fireside with his horse watching over him, a lifelike war memorial with sinewy soldiers, and a huge equestrian scene featuring Bucky O'Neill, frontier renaissance man and Spanish-American War victim. This famous area landmark was sculpted by Solon Borglum, whose brother Gutzon sculpted Mount Rushmore. Downtown is definitely the place to be in Prescott, and you could spend an entire day and night just strolling around, shopping, eating, drinking, people-watching, looking at old buildings, and sucking in the clean mile-high air, never bothering to see the rest of the town, which is much bigger (population 40,000) than the quaint plaza and downtown suggest.

While no longer the capital of the entire territory, Prescott is the Yavapai County seat, and

as such the downtown's government buildings can get busy on weekdays. On weekends the road- and foot-traffic slows a bit, but not significantly. Tourists and day-trippers crowd the center of town, especially during summer and during the many festivals and shows held on the plaza throughout the year. There are parking spaces all along the downtown streets, and a public garage just west of the plaza on Gurley Street. It's best to find a parking space and keep it as long as you can.

Sharlot Hall Museum

Named for its brilliant founder, a writer, editor, poet, and historian in a time when Western women didn't usually do such things, this local-history museum (two blocks west of the Plaza on Gurley St., 928/445-3122, www .sharlot.org, 10 A.M.–5 P.M. Mon.–Sat., noon–4 P.M. Sun., $5 adults, free kids under 18) has beautiful grounds and interesting exhibits on the town's wild frontier days, balanced by a good portion of the quotidian details and artifacts of hard, complex daily life on the Southwestern edge of civilization. The grassy complex, spread over three acres with rose gardens and re-creations of frontier-style structures, features the refurbished Victorian gem called the **Bashford House,** and the log-cabin residence of the state's first governor. A rose garden honors Prescott's pioneer women, the fascinating biographies of which are available for perusal in a file at the museum. It's an easy walk from downtown to the Sharlot Hall Museum, worth it if only to see the pretty green grounds and the mansions of another age.

FORT WHIPPLE MUSEUM

The Sharlot Hall Museum also operates the small Fort Whipple Museum (Bldg. 11, Veterans Administration campus, 500 N. Hwy. 89, 928/445-3122, 10 A.M.–4 P.M., Thurs.–Sat., free) about four miles north of downtown on the tree-lined campus of the VA Hospital, formerly home to Fort Whipple, a major base for General Crook's war against the Apache. The museum, housed in an old Victorian house once used as officers' quarters, displays the

NORTH-CENTRAL ARIZONA

memorabilia and daily items of frontier military life and puts on historical re-enactments one Saturday a month.

Smoki Museum

For 70 years, from 1920 to 1990, the builders of this little puebloesque building (147 N. Arizona St., 928/445-1230, www.smokimuseum.org,

---

HOW PRESCOTT GOT ITS NAME

Though not really a literary incubator of any note, Prescott is curiously named after an esteemed New England man of letters, historian William Hickling Prescott (1796-1859).

Though Prescott had died long before the remote little camp in the Arizona's thirsty central mountains acquired his famous name, his work, especially his bestselling *History of the Conquest of Mexico*, published in 1843 to universal acclaim, was much on the minds of the party sent to found Arizona's territorial capital. While on the trail toward the territory, the officials, many of whom, like most learned men of their time, were fans of Prescott's work, passed the time reading the reports of Lt. Amiel Weeks Whipple, who'd trekked through the region with the railroad's 35th Parallel Survey about a decade earlier.

In his writings, the lieutenant suggests several times that what is now North-Central Arizona may actually be that vague land to the "northwest" from where, as Prescott had written, the ancient Aztecs hailed before they conquered the Valley of Mexico. Somehow the suggestion stuck, and so did the name. Likewise, two of downtown Prescott's main streets were given famous names from the conquest: Montezuma St. and Cortez St.

Don't expect most native residents to know this little tale, though you can always tell a longtimer when he or she questions your pronunciation of their cryptically named hometown. "It's not Prescott, it's Preskit," goes the common corrective.

---

10 A.M.–4 P.M. Tues.–Sat., 1–4 P.M. Sun., $5 adults, kids under 12 free) a few miles west of downtown off Gurley Street, a group of Prescott businessmen called the Smoki People, covered their half-naked bodies in a shade of brownish-red and sold tickets to an annual fairground performance of dances and ceremonies based on Hopi religion, including even the famous Snake Dance with its live props. A corresponding museum preserved and displayed some excellent examples of Puebloan, Navajo, and Yavapai arts, crafts, and artifacts, and items from tribes throughout the West. Not exactly a politically correct organization, the Smoki People were protested out of existence in 1990 by the Hopi, who were fed up with having their sacred culture co-opted, and, as they saw it, mocked, by Anglos. The whole story is told through a fascinating and frank exhibit in the museum, now dedicated to interpreting the Smoki phenomenon, which was extremely popular among locals for many years, and preserving some wonderful treasures collected over the years. This is a quirky and illuminating attraction, and the building itself should be seen by lovers of unique structures. The museum is part of the Prescott Armory Historic District, which includes nearby Ken Lindley Field, the old Prescott National Guard Armory, and the Citizens' Cemetery, each of which will be of at least passing interest to history buffs and old-building enthusiasts.

The Phippen Museum of Western Art

Prescott's only art museum (4701 Hwy. 89 North, 928/778-1385, www.phippenart museum.org, 10 A.M.–4 P.M. Tues.–Sat, 1–4 P.M. Sun., $5 adults, kids under 12 free) is an essential stop for those who appreciate the Cowboy Artists of America school of painting and bronze sculpture. The museum's namesake, the artist George Phippen, was that famous group's co-founder and first president, and the collection features many of the luminaries of the movement, as well as Native American arts and crafts and about four special, Western-related exhibits every year. The drive out to the hilltop museum is as stimulating as all the oil paintings of cattle drives and bronze bucking broncos inside put together. The building overlooks a little dry-grass valley just past the strangely piled giant boulders of Granite Dells and the reedy confines of Watson Lake nearby, a scenic seven miles north from downtown.

Entertainment and Events

Every Saturday night from May to September a group of big-smile players puts on the silly, dinner-theater style musical and comedy variety show **The Arizona Revue—That's Entertainment** ($20 adults, $10 kids), and at Christmas the show takes on a holiday sheen. The best thing about the Arizona Revue is its venue, the **Historic Elks Opera House** (888/858-3557) on Gurley Street downtown, leaning on Elks Hill right across from the Hassayampa Inn. The stylish old opera house, which still has a good bit of its grandeur, also books other acts throughout the year, mostly in a similar vein.

The Courthouse Plaza hosts several large shows and festivals every year, including the **Mountain Artist Guild Spring Festival** in mid-May and the **Phippen Museum Western Art Show & Sale** over Memorial Day weekend, both big events in the regional Western art world. June brings the kooky and colorful **Tsunami on the Square,** a performance festival that has costumed characters and street theater taking over the downtown sidewalks. Also in June, major touring acts show up in town for the **Prescott Bluegrass Festival.** Prescott is famous, and used to be a bit infamous, for the wild public revelry of the Fourth of July weekend, when **Prescott Frontier Days and the World's Oldest Rodeo** puts the populace and the many visitors in the mood to party. In August the **Mountain Artists Summer Festival** hits the plaza, and just up the road literary cowpunchers get together and put on readings and performances at the Sharlot Hall Museum's **Annual Cowboy Poets Gathering.**

NIGHTLIFE

While these days there are more galleries and boutiques than saloons, gambling halls, and brothels along the short stretch of Montezuma Street known since territorial days as **Whiskey Row,** downtown is still the best place to party in Prescott. Besides the Palace and the other saloons along "the row," there's **Moctezuma's,** (144 S. Montezuma St., 928/445-1244) a dance place that draws a young crowd. A block south, toward the quieter end of Montezuma, you'll find **Coyote Joe's,** (214 S. Montezuma St., 928/778-9570, www.coyotejoesgrill.com) a locals' bar with a great happy hour, strong beer selection, and delicious bar eats. Same goes for the **Prescott Brewing Company** (130 W. Gurley St., 928/771-2795, www.prescottbrewingcompany .com) across from the Plaza on the north side of the square. To kick back with the wilderness crowd, try **Lizzard's Lounge** (120 N. Cortez, 928/778-2244) just off the downtown on Cortez. Nearly every bar along the row and the surrounding blocks features live entertainment on the weekends, mostly of the bar-band or country-rambler variety, many from out of state. You can have a lot of fun in Prescott's bars and saloons, and there are some weekend nights during the summer when the whole town seems to be joining in the party going on downtown. It's on such special, hazy nights that one gets a tiny glimpse into what Saturday night must've been like during those raucous, forgetful territorial days.

Shopping

Prescott is well known as a place to find antiques, art, and that unique, indescribable item you always knew you needed but never could find. Downtown is the best place to search for such treasures. The streets flanking the Courthouse Plaza (Gurley, Montezuma, Cortez and Goodwin Streets) and continuing on for several blocks in every direction are crowded with shops and boutiques and galleries selling cowboy-style Western art, Mexican folk arts, handmade jewelry and crafts, gifts, Western clothing, and even high-style, contemporary furniture and home decorations. **Cortez Street** especially is a kind of antiques

Once a debauched row of drinking and gambling dens, this stretch of downtown Prescott is now a mixture of bars, boutiques, and restaurants.

row, with several big stores stacked with the fascinating leftovers of past generations, the members of which usually constructed their daily-life items to last and to look beautiful and stylish while dong so. There's really no need to venture out of the downtown to shop for souvenirs, but if you're looking for the big chains head north out of town on Gurley to Highway 69 toward Prescott Valley and you'll see a few large strip malls with all the usual conveniences, restaurants, and stores. A little farther on is the **Prescott Gateway Mall** (928/442-3659), a large complex with major department stores and all kinds of mall shops and chain stores.

Sports and Recreation

The **Prescott National Forest,** more than a million acres of desert scrub, chaparral, piñon, juniper, and pine carpeting rolling hills, dry-grass flatlands, and rocky mountains, is the western edge of the largest Ponderosa Pine forest in the world, the beginning of the great Arizona Pine Belt that stretches across and below the Mogollon Rim all the way to New Mexico.

Just a few miles from downtown, the forest around Prescott is a perfect place for a high-altitude hike over pine needle–strewn trails, an afternoon picnic, a cool-breeze glide across a tucked-away forest lake, or an overnight camping trip beneath the tall, sap-scented woods. The forest has long been used for small-scale mining, ranching, and outdoor recreation, and in some places it shows its wear and tear. There are more homes on this forest than one usually sees on federal land, mostly owing to the fact that owners of mining claims are allowed to build on public lands, and there are a lot of still-active mining claims in those mineraled mountains. Old mining and logging roads are now used by mountain bikers and hikers, and, in some areas, off-road vehicle enthusiasts.

The forest's headquarters just off downtown (344 S. Cortez St., 928/443-8000, www.fs.fed .us/r3/prescott, 8 A.M.–4:30 P.M. Mon.–Fri.) has a kiosk with free single-sheet descriptions and maps of every trail on the forest. It's really

© TIM HULL

the Prescott National Forest seen from the top of Spruce Mountain

a good idea to stop here if you're going to be doing anything on the forest—there's simply too much information to pass up. Staff rangers at the office can help you with any questions.

Lynx Lake Recreation Area ($2 parking, 6 A.M.–9 P.M. for day use), just north of town off Highway 69, is a 55-acre lake surrounded by Ponderosa Pines and stocked with trout. You can float your own boat out on the lake and fish, or rent a craft and gear at the **Lynx Lake Store and Marina** (928/778-0720). The surrounding forest has several hiking and biking trails. The 4.3-mile hike to Salida Gulch will get you to the **Gold Pan Day Use Area,** where you can engage in the bent-over occupation that put the forest around Prescott on the map. The area has two basic campgrounds ($10 per night, no reservations).

In the forest just outside town along Senator Highway is **Goldwater Lake,** a popular place for picnicking, kayaking, and canoeing. Out along Highway 89, about five miles north of downtown, **Watson Lake** is surrounded by giant otherworldly boulder piles, an area

called **Granite Dells.** The five-mile **Peavine Trail,** an old railroad right-of-way that takes you through the heart of the amazing rock piles, is a highlight of this area and can be hiked or biked with ease. If you didn't bring your mountain bike, you can rent one right near the trailhead from **Encore Performance** (2929 N. Hwy. 89, 928/778-7910, www.epf guzzi.com/peavine/, 9 A.M.–5:30 P.M. Tues.–Sat., $12 per hour). If you forgot your canoe or kayak, or if you want to try either of these activities for the first time, call **Prescott Outdoors, LLC** (928/925-1410 for Watson Lake, 928/925-8858 for Goldwater Lake, open spring and summer only).

Granite Basin Recreation Area ($2 parking fee) is a boulder-and-pine wilderness west of town off of Iron Springs Road, the home of 7,600-foot-high Granite Mountain, the stained sheer-rock face of which is a preferred residence of peregrine falcons. The area has a small lake with fishing and a popular, basic campground ($10, no hookups or reservations), as well as miles of hiking and biking trails.

HIKING AND MOUNTAIN BIKING

You could spend years hiking and biking the Prescott National Forest and still not get to every trail and hidden, trickling-water canyon. If you've got years to spare, go down to the forest headquarters, pick up all of the handy free maps, and get hiking. If you have only a few days, however, try one of the popular and beautiful hikes described below. Most forest trails that aren't in a Wilderness Area are open to hikers, bikers, and horseback riders; all trails are closed to motorized vehicles unless expressly set aside for off-road recreation. For bike repair, rental, and equipment, see **Ironclad Bicycles** (710 White Spar Rd., 928/776-1755).

The five-mile Peavine Trail through Granite Dells is definitely a recommended hike if you only have time for one or two adventures, as is the steep but relatively easy two-mile hike up to a saddle at the base of **Thumb Butte,** providing awesome views of the town all nestled among the pines. Several trails around the popular **Thumb Butte Picnic Area** (three miles west of downtown on Gurley Street, which becomes Thumb Butte Road) lead into the forest, along creeksides, and off to highlands from which you can see the San Francisco Peaks way up north. The **North Thumb Butte Trails** are all short, but a significant loop around the whole area can be cobbled together from the disparate routes. To reach other trails around Thumb Butte, or to take a scenic back-road tour of the area in your car (best if it's high-clearance) or on your mountain bike, head past the picnic area and take the **Thumb Butte Loop Road,** a 20-mile route around the Thumb that ends up on White Spar Road, taking you through the high pine lands and past some amazing lookouts. The road has hiking trails and old Jeep roads all along it, each of them leading deep into the shady forest.

The four-mile one-way hike up to the big boulders waiting atop **Granite Mountain** (three miles west of downtown off Iron Springs Rd., $2 parking fee) is highly recommended for those who don't mind a steep trudge. It's one of the most popular trails in the Prescott area, and

for good reason. Peregrine falcons nest on the mountain's rock face, so bring binoculars. The trail winds up the mountain from a manzanita and piñon forest up through to the pine and on up to the rocky peak at 7,600 feet. It gets pretty cold in the early spring, fall, and winter, and there's likely to be snowpack in the higher regions in the winter. This is a Wilderness Area, so no mountain bikes are allowed, and some of the areas around the cliff face are closed in spring and winter so the falcons can go about their nesting in peace.

Probably the best all-around hike in the Prescott forest, the **Groom Creek Loop Trail** extends through the forest and up more than 1,000 feet to the top of Spruce Mountain, where there's a fire lookout and a few promontories from which you can just about see the top of every tree in the land. The winding single track heading downhill makes this a wild ride on a mountain bike, nearly worth the difficult climb up. Head out Senator Highway via Mt. Vernon Avenue, lined with intricate old Victorian homes, for about six miles until you see the sign for Groom Creek Horse Camp. The trailhead parking lot is on the east side of the road.

Accommodations

A tourist haven, Prescott has many chain hotels, one or two of them nearly upscale, not a few smaller independents, and a growing number of bed-and-breakfast establishments. Most of the accommodations can be found along Gurley Street from one end of town to the other. The Tourist Information Center (800/266-7534) downtown has reams of pamphlets and brochures on various area accommodations. It's best to make reservations before arriving, especially in the summer.

UNDER $50

Pine View Motel (500 Copper Basin Rd., 928/445-4660, $35–45 d) is a great bargain just outside of the downtown area, along Copper Basin Road on the way out into the forest. The rooms are basic and clean, some of them with kitchenettes.

YOUR OWN CABIN IN THE PINEBELT

Ever dreamed of having your own secluded cabin deep in the woods, accessible only by an unmarked jeep-trail, watched over every dark wilderness night by a riot of smeared-sky stars?

The U.S. Forest Service in Arizona has a unique program called a **Room With A View** (877/444-6777, www.reserveusa.com for reservations), through which they rent out remote cabins and ranch houses, most of them former ranger residences, to anyone who wants to stay a few nights deep in the wilderness on a relatively comfortable bed. You bring your own dishes, utensils, sheets and blankets, but most of the cabins have running water, flush toilets, showers, stoves and outside barbecue grills and picnic tables. This program provides a rare opportunity to see what it was like homesteading in the Southwestern pinebelt, only with a lot more comfort and convenience.

Listed below are the Room With a View properties in North-Central Arizona, each of them worth considering as your own personal hideout in the forest.

Horsethief Cabin ($109 per night, sleeps up to six people, available May 1–Nov. 30) is in the pine-covered Bradshaw Mountains above Prescott, near the old mining camp Crown King (where there's a saloon and a store). The cabin is next to small Horsethief Basin Lake, which is stocked with catfish and bass, and close to dozens of forest trails. The **Towers Mountain Cabin** ($109, sleeps up to four people, available April 1–Nov. 30), in the Prescott National Forest sits at 7,628 feet above Crown King, right next to an active fire lookout tower. **Sycamore Cabin** ($109 per night, sleeps up to eight people, available year-round), in the Prescott National Forest's Verde District, was built by the Civilian Conservation Corps in 1936 and has gas heating and a swamp cooler. There's a horseshoe pit out by the barbecue grill and picnic table, and cool Sycamore Creek, lined with cottonwoods, runs right behind. The **Crescent Moon Ranch** ($209 per night, sleeps up to 10 people, available year-round), in the Coconino National Forest near Sedona, sits at the base of Cathedral Rock on the banks of Oak Creek. It's a large three-bedroom, three-bath ranching house with an enclosed Arizona Room. There are hiking trails nearby, bass and trout in the creek, and rare birds — maybe even a beaver or a river otter — hanging around streamside. Up on the Mogollon Rim in the Coconino National Forest you'll find **Fernow Cabin** (928/526-0866, $75-100 depending on season, sleeps up to eight, available year-round), a cozy little loghouse with two bedrooms and a loft, tucked into the high forest, waiting...

$100-200

The historic **Hotel St. Michael** (205 W. Gurley St., 928/776-1999, www.stmichaelhotel.com, $69–129 d) is right downtown on the corner of Whiskey Row and Gurley Street, a redbrick reminder of another era. Built in 1901 with gargoyles staring down from its facade, the hotel has an excellent bistro and coffeehouse on its street level and individually decorated rooms, cable TV, and air-conditioning. The comfortable, old building still operates an elevator installed in 1925. A room comes with breakfast in the bistro.

The **Hotel Vendome** (230 S. Cortez St., 928/776-0900 or 888/468-3583, www .vendomehotel.com, $99–179 d) is a delightful, finely detailed place to stay in one of Prescott's central, tree-lined neighborhoods, with beautiful relics of the Victorian heyday on every lot. Within easy walking distance to downtown, the Vendome, a Registered Historic Landmark, offers rooms with big bathtubs and all the comforts you could ever want and still feel good about yourself.

As historic Prescott hotels go, however, The ◖ **Hassayampa Inn** (122 E. Gurley St., 928/778-9434, www.hassayampainn.com, $104–244 d) is the star. Built in 1927 atop Elks Hill, a high-class gateway to downtown, the landmark hotel has a kind of redbrick, modified Spanish Colonial Revival style, with a bell tower and a covered passageway from the street to the lobby doors. Off the lobby there's a great restaurant, The Peacock Room, and a cozy dark-wood lounge where a jazz band often plays. The rooms are old and a little creaky but have TVs and air-conditioning.

The **Prescott Pines Bed and Breakfast** (902 White Spar Rd., 928/445-7270, www.prescottpinesinn.com, $90–135 d) sits on the edge of the forest and offers Victorian country-style charm and some amazing breakfasts, surrounded by roses and grass and the color pink. The **Pleasant St. Inn Bed and Breakfast** (142 S. Pleasant St., 928/445-4774, www.pleasantbandb.com, $125–175 d), just a few blocks from downtown, is in a Victorian home built in 1906, a romantic reminder of the aesthetic and cultural origins of the Anglos who "civilized" North-Central Arizona after the railroad arrived.

Food
DINERS AND LUNCH SPOTS
For the best breakfast in town, and a hearty lunch in the New American Diner style, head to (**The Dinner Bell** (321 W. Gurley, 928/445-9888, $3–6, cash only), two blocks west of the Plaza, a favorite with locals for generations. If you're a working person, an old-timer, or a longtime local, enter via the front door and take up a booth or a barstool in the diner portion. Everybody else, take the plank walkway along the side of the building and sit in the back, an artsy addition that offers creekside eating in a more bohemian milieu—same menu for both rooms. **El Charro** (120 N. Montezuma St., 928/445-7130, www.elcharrorestaurant.com, 11 A.M.–9 P.M. daily, $5–10), a casual Mexican place downtown that's been serving great Sonoran-style food since 1959, is a favorite spot among locals for an inexpensive and delicious lunch or dinner, with maybe a few margaritas on the side.

DINNER
If you prefer beer, don't miss the **Prescott Brewing Company** (130 W. Gurley St.,

928/771-2795, www.prescottbrewingcompany.com, 11 A.M.–10 P.M. Mon.–Thurs., 11 A.M.–11 P.M. Fri.–Sat., $7–15), right across Gurley from the Courthouse Plaza. While serving rib-sticking pub fare like bangers and mash and shepherds pie, along with a wide assortment of lighter dishes, the "brewpub," as it's called locally, brews up some of the best beers in the territory. It's bound to get a little loud in there in the weekends, but nothing like it used to get during the wild days down at the **The Palace Restaurant and Saloon** (120 S. Montezuma St., 928/541-1996, www.historicpalace.com, 11 A.M.–9:30 P.M. Mon.–Thurs., 11 A.M.–10:30 P.M. Fri.–Sat., $7–11 lunch, $14–28 dinner), though back then it was simply called the Palace, and it was known throughout the region as a rowdy and fun place to be on a weekend night (or a weeknight, for that matter). Though the old heavy-wood bar remains, and it can still get a little rowdy with drunk tourists and locals mixing together, the Palace is today mostly a good restaurant with sandwiches, burgers and salads for lunch and steak, prime rib, fish and other dishes for dinner. Everybody's partied at the Palace, from the Earp brothers to Steve McQueen. At least three-quarters of the fun of a visit is looking at all the artifacts and memorabilia on the walls of days much more exciting than our own.

The **Peacock Room** (122 E. Gurley, 928/778-9434, www.hassayampainn.com/html/dining.html, breakfast, lunch, and dinner daily, $5–10 lunch, $14–32 dinner) inside the Hassayampa Inn is a great place for a long lazy lunch or a romantic, candle-lit dinner. Puffy booths line the walls, art-deco lines define the interior, and the chef serves up good steak, lamb, and fish dishes, along with Southwestern-tinged specials like Sonoran pork osso buco. **Murphy's** (201 N. Cortez, 928/445-4044, www.cyberfork.com/murphys, 11 A.M.–3:00 P.M. daily, 4–10 P.M. weekdays, 4–11 P.M. Fri.–Sat., $8–15 lunch, $17–46 dinner) is a local favorite for prime-rib, seafood, and a slow drink in a cozy, private booth. The bar serves delicious pub-style eats (3–4 P.M.).

Information and Services

The **Prescott Chamber of Commerce** (117 W. Goodwin Street, 928/445-2000 or 800/266-7534, www.prescott.org, 9 A.M.–5 P.M. Mon.–Fri., 10 A.M.–2 P.M. Sat.–Sun.) has friendly volunteers and tons of free information on the area. A volunteer offers free guided historical tours of the downtown at 10 A.M. Friday–Sunday out of the Chamber building.

THE VERDE VALLEY

In the Verde Valley—an ancient oasis fed and greened by water falling headlong off the Mogollon Rim—you can't walk a mile without seeing some fallen ruin or artifact left behind by the conquistadores, miners, agriculturists and speculators who've been drawn to this fertile valley and its surrounding mountains over the centuries. Most people came here after rumors of ore; others grew crops and orchards and raised livestock. The area continues to grow at a steady pace, as more and more refugees from the Phoenix sprawl hunt out the remaining rural enclaves. It's still rather quiet here, though that is likely to change in the next decade or so. The area has long been known for one ruin in particular, the spectacular, if misnamed, Montezuma Castle. This must be seen. There's a good bit of outdoor fun to be had in the valley, including tubing and boating down still-wild stretches of the Verde River, and hiking into beautiful Sycamore Canyon. But, even before you reach the valley you'll get a chance to shop, eat, and stay in some memorable stores, restaurants, and hotels in Jerome, a former copper boomtown that is too cool to pass up.

Mingus Mountain

The best way to start a tour of the Verde Valley is to drive up and over the mountain that watches over it from the west, 7,743-foot Mingus Mountain, part of the Black Hills range. Take Highway 89A from the mountain's base—either from the Verde Valley on the eastside or Prescott Valley on the west—and slowly negotiate the switchbacked two-lane road, towered over by cliffs and overlooking deep, pine-swept draws. It's one of the most scenically stunning drives in the region, usually taking about an hour to go the 30 miles or so over the mountain, through the old mining metropolis of Jerome, and down the other side. The drive is understandably popular with motorcycle enthusiasts and sports-car pilots, so you might have to pull over and let some of the more hasty pass. Near the top of the mountain, you'll find **Mingus Mountain Recreation Area,** where there's a few high forest campgrounds (basic spots, $10, no reservations) and the eight-mile round-trip hike along the **Woodchute Trail** into the Woodchute Wilderness and up around to the north side of Woodchute Mountain, from which the long-ago boomtown Jerome got the wood to build itself. It's a pretty easy hike through an open pine and juniper forest that allows for some spectacular views. If you don't feel like hiking but still want to see the valley from way up high, head about three miles on the dirt road to the recreation area, where there's a promontory from which you can see mile after hazy mile spreading out in various shades of green and brown, as you sit high up in the clouds on a granite outcropping.

◖ Jerome

More than 1,000 years ago the Sinagua took minerals out of the cliffs Jerome would one day cling to, engaging in primitive small-scale mining for precious stones and paints. This established the primary use of Cleopatra Hill, where Spanish conquistadores, too, would dig for what was precious to their culture—gold and silver. But it wasn't until copper became one of the most useful metals of the modern age that the "Million Dollar Copper Camp" really got going. At its zenith in the 1920s, it would boast some 15,000 residents.

Throughout the late 19th and early 20th centuries, Jerome was known for its moral subjectivity; prostitution and other common territorial sins were tolerated, albeit regulated, well into the 1940s. Mining, no matter what mineral you're after, is always going to be a boom and bust enterprise, and by the 1950s the bust

© TIM HULL

Jerome, a hillside town of artists and artisans in North-Central Arizona, was once a busy and profitable copper mining boom town.

had descended and Phelps Dodge left, never to return. The town turned ghostly by 1953, when it had less than 50 full-time residents and a lot of abandoned and moldering homes, hotels, and shops. By the 1970s, however, hippies, artists, drop-outs, and crafters had found the picturesque old town and began its resurgence as a colorfully populated hilltop village of creative people, the kind of funky tourist haven and hideaway one finds all over the old mining frontier. Today dozens of shops, many of them carrying one-of-a-kind creations made by Jerome's bevy of resident artists and artisans, line the narrow, twisting streets through town, and saloonesque bars, historic boutique hotels, and New American eateries occupy the old buildings that once served as saloons, hardware stores, hospitals, and hotels during the town's busy mining years, when the pits were worked around the clock. A couple of hours walking Jerome's streets, shopping for nowhere-else gifts and souvenirs, and eating at one of its excellent restaurants, is a fine way to spend an Arizona day.

JEROME HISTORICAL SOCIETY MUSEUM

This small local history museum (200 Main St., 928/634-5477, 9 A.M.–5 P.M. daily, $2, kids free)

has exhibits on Jerome's exciting and sometimes violent history. It has ephemera and artifacts from the town's various eras, from its boom days through the big bust in the 1950s and beyond. There's a hefty touch of the lurid here, with a lot about violence and illicit sex and the social consequences of each—the most fascinating displays in the building, naturally. There's also a small gift shop that sells books on the history of Jerome and souvenirs of the region.

JEROME STATE HISTORIC PARK

The Douglas family ruled mining in Jerome for decades, and in 1916 patriarch James "Rawhide Jimmy" Douglas built this palatial adobe house above his Little Daisy Mine, the better to welcome mine investors and company officials to town with the kind of style and comfort not always expected in western wild lands. The mansion (Douglas Rd. off 89A, 928/635-5381, www.pr.state.az.us/Parks/parkhtml/jerome.html, 8:30 A.M.–5 P.M. daily, $3 adults, kids under 14 free) is now a state park dedicated to Jerome's history, and it's worth a visit just to see the building; the library has been beautifully restored and evokes what it was like to live comfortably and richly in an otherwise rough mining town. There are also several interesting displays on Jerome's history, and a lot of rusty old mining equipment sitting around the grounds. A short video, narrated by a friendly ghost, tells the story of Jerome, and a cool 3-D model of the town shows what the tunnels looked like under it.

SHOPPING

There are dozens of shops, boutiques, galleries, and antique stores in Jerome, and there are always new ones opening up as the tourist traffic through town increases. Along with all the usual shops with gifts and crafts and a Southwestern flare, you'll find contemporary fine art, hand-made wines, fudge, pottery, copper and turquoise jewelry, and all sorts of other treasures in Jerome, where shopping is really the primary activity. Make sure to check out the amazing collection of kaleidoscopes at **Nelly Bly** (136 Main St., 928/634-0255, www.nellieblyscopes.com). Stick to Main Street to find most of the shops, while others can be found on Clark Street, Hill Street, and Jerome Avenue.

NIGHTLIFE

While these days nothing like it used to be back when Jerome was known as one of the "wickedest" places in the territory, and certainly far from what it was in the 70s and 80s, when, according to legend, illegal narcotics were regularly ingested from the town's bar-tops, Jerome's nightlife can still get a little rowdy, and therefore fun. The **Spirit Room Bar** (166 Main St., 928/634-8809, 11 A.M.–1 A.M. daily) offers deep cocktails and live music Saturday and Sunday afternoons and into the night.

ACCOMMODATIONS

Jerome has several boutique hotels and bed-and-breakfast inns, most of them in wonderfully refurbished historic buildings with at least one or two ghosts in residence.

 ◖ Jerome Grand Hotel (200 Hill St., 928/634-8200, www.jeromegrandhotel.net, $100–185 d) used to be a hospital, and from the outside has the character of an old sanatorium, perched on a hill and heavy with secrets; inside

the rooms are tastefully decorated and comfortable, with nice showers and tubs, TVs, and views of the valley below. The **Conner Hotel of Jerome** (164 main St., 928/634-5006, www.connorhotel.com, $95–155 d) has been around in one form or another in the same location since 1898, a high-class establishment for boomtown visitors. Today it's a charming, comfortable place to stay in downtown Jerome, with twelve rooms, each with TV, mini-fridge, private bath, and wireless Internet. The **Mile High Inn** (309 Main St., 928/634-5094, www.jeromemilehighinn.com, $85–120 d), a comfy place occupying a redbrick storefront on Main St., has five rooms individually decorated with a Southwestern-Victorian style, not all with private baths—though the innkeepers guarantee a private bath Thursday–Sunday.

FOOD

Mile High Grill & Spirits (309 Main St., 928/634-5094, breakfast, lunch, and dinner daily, $5–12) serves great breakfasts until noon, and steaks, prime rib, sandwiches, and salads for lunch and dinner. The bar has a great beer selection and serves some unique, locally-inspired specialty drinks. The walls are decorated with the work of local artists. Sit at one of the window tables and watch people walk by while you kick back a few cold ones. Or you could sit at one of the candle-lit tables overlooking the Verde Valley at **◖ The Asylum** (200 Hill St., 928/639-3197, www.theasylum.biz, 11 A.M.–3 P.M. and 5–9 P.M. daily, $8–13 lunch, $18–26 dinner) up on a hill inside the Jerome Grand Hotel. The restaurant bills itself as "a restaurant on the fringe," meaning, one assumes, cooking on the cutting edge of New American cuisine. The menu has an interesting mix of the familiar and the exotic fused together to create some delicious meals, and the wine selection is as impressive as the elegant, view-centered interior.

Clarkdale and the Verde Canyon Railway

Founded in 1912 by the United Verde Copper Company for workers at a nearby smelter,

Clarkdale remains largely unreconstructed today, though the smelter and the company shut down long ago. It's said that the quiet town was the first master-planned community in Arizona, a state that would one day suffer from a surfeit of that breed. There's not much here save the **The Verde Canyon Railroad** (300 North Broadway, 800/320-0718, www .verdecanyonrr.com, $54–119), an excursion train that runs on tracks formerly used to bring ore from Jerome to the smelter in Clarkdale. The four-hour round-trip ride takes its passengers from Clarkdale to Perkinsville Ranch and back, snaking through Verde Canyon, an inaccessible, bald eagle-populated notch with ochre cliffs towering on one side and the green river meandering on the other. It's a slow but unforgettable route, at one point disappearing into a dark, 680-foot tunnel. There's a small café and a gift shop at the Clarkdale depot.

The least expensive fare is an Adult Coach ticket at $54, which is a basic and comfortable ride through the spectacular canyon. A first-class ticket starts at $79.95 and includes open-air viewing cars, a complementary glass of champagne, supremely comfortable seats and a full bar. For $119 you can book passage on the Grape Escape Train, which includes a wine tasting party featuring four or five different wines and foods to complement the varietals.

Tuzigoot National Monument

Just outside of Clarkdale, **Tuzigoot National Monument** (off of Broadway between Clarkdale and Old Town Cottonwood, 928/634-5564, www.nps.gov/tuzi/, 8 A.M.–6 P.M. in summer, 8 A.M.–5 P.M. in winter, $5 adults, kids under 16 free), a 120-room, stacked-stone pueblo ruin on top of a hill overlooking the lush river valley, is the first of three federally protected sites in the Verde Valley that preserve what remains of the disappeared Sinagua culture. A museum has some good exhibits on Sinagua culture and the natural history of the area. You can walk up to the roof of the building and see the green valley with Sinagua eyes. Not as dramatic as Montezuma Castle or Well, but an important sight nonetheless.

Old Town Cottonwood

This pleasant and short stretch of Highway 89A (Main Street) through downtown Cottonwood, just a few miles east of the road to Tuzigoot,

© TIM HULL

The Sinagua built this pueblo-style hilltop village in the Verde Valley.

was once the commercial and social heart of the valley. Some of the old buildings remain, others have been rebuilt and replaced several times over the generations. Along the clean, refurbished sidewalks there are a few shops, antique stores, cafes, and galleries, and a couple of really good restaurants. The Old Town area is on the National Register of Historic Places, and is worth a brief stroll and maybe a stop for lunch or dinner. The **Old Town Café** (1025 N. Main St., 928/634-5980, 8 A.M.–3 P.M. Tues.–Sat., $3.50–9.50) has decadent European-style pastries, filling sandwiches, quiche, Greek salad, and excellent coffee. The 1950s-style **Willy's Burgers and Shakes** (794 N. Main St., 928/634-6648, 11 A.M.–3 P.M. daily, $6–9) offers awesome versions of the American street-food staples for which it is named. For those who like burgers but not meat, they offer a wonderful veggie burger, and fried potato fans shouldn't miss the sweet potato fries.

Dead Horse Ranch State Park

This near-jungle of a state park (675 Dead Horse Ranch Rd., Cottonwood, 928/634-5283, www.azstateparks.com, opens at 8 A.M. daily, $6 per car up to four people) just a few blocks from Old Town Cottonwood provides easy access to the riparian wonders of the Verde River. Here you can walk streamside for miles, below weeping cottonwoods and hanging willows, and through all kinds of vines and branches teeming out of proportion. You'll completely forget that you are in the arid West here. If you want to camp and fish one of the man-made lagoons, there are dozens of spots with hook-ups, bathrooms and showers ($12–19 per night). But the park is best used for a riverside day-trip, a few hours spent exploring the source of all life in the valley, maybe with a picnic and some bird watching. The best hike is the 1.5 mile loop along the **Verde River Greenway,** a six-mile stretch of lush life along the Verde between the Tuzigoot and Bridgeport bridges meant to preserve the riparian ecosystem, one of only a few remaining in the state. Unlike the park's creepy name, the Verde River Greenway's name is descriptive to perfection—that's exactly what

it is, a green-way, and it is all the more beautiful for being so rare and threatened.

Fort Verde Historic Park

One of several outposts in the central highlands from which General Crook battled the Apache and others, this historic park (off I-17 near Camp Verde, 928/567-3275, 8 A.M.–5 P.M. daily, adults $2, kids under 14 free) will be of interest to history lovers and those wondering what a poor soldier's life was like serving on the very edge of the known world. You can stroll the grounds and look into a few old buildings set up with original fort artifacts, furniture, and daily-life items that give one a feeling for late 19th century Anglo-West life and a connection to the officers, surgeons, and enlisted men who must have wondered every day how they got all the way out here.

◖ Montezuma Castle National Monument

If you only have time to make one stop in the Verde Valley, make it the Montezuma Castle National Monument (I-17 exit

a Sinagua limestone cliff dwelling in the Verde Valley

© TIM HULL

289, 928/567-3322, www.nps.gov/moca/, 8 A.M.–5 P.M. daily, 8 A.M.–6 P.M. daily in summer, $5 for 7-day pass, kids under 16 free). The five-story, twenty-room limestone castle, built in about A.D. 1200, looks down on Beaver Creek and the former farmlands of its builders from an improbable niche in the cliffside. It seems like it *was* a castle of some kind, the home of a ruler or a god; but it was more likely the apartment-style shelter for a group of Sinagua who found the creek and the sheltered cliffs to their liking. There's not much to do here other than walk along the short trail and look up at the ruin, but it is something that really should be seen. Imagine being the first explorer to come upon the abandoned castle—it's easy to do so; when you walk out of the small visitor center and behold the cliffside for the first time, it's a breath-catching moment.

MONTEZUMA WELL

The Montezuma Well (take I-17 exit 293, 928/567-4521, 8 A.M.–6 P.M. daily June–Aug.,

---

THE VERDE BACKCOUNTRY: FOSSIL SPRINGS AND VERDE HOT SPRINGS

Forest Road 708, also known as the Fossil Creek Road, is a 26-mile dusty washboard of a road below the Mogollon Rim, deep in the river valley outback between Camp Verde and Strawberry. Take this out-of-the-way route to find deep collecting pools for swimming, warm smooth rocks for sunbathing, and a tough but beautiful semi-desert hike. Or, detour off down to the banks of the Verde and take a short walk along the river past a decommissioned power plant to the ruins of an old resort, its hot springs still spilling and steaming out of the ground.

Fossil Springs: Take Route 260 from either Camp Verde or Strawberry and then turn on Forest Road 708. About five miles from Strawberry look for the sign that says Fossil Creek Trail. It's a tough and steep, eight-mile round-trip hike that drops more than 1,300 feet, but once you see where it leads all will be forgiven. Fossil Springs flows interminably, at a constant 72°F, 20,000 gallons a minute into a series of inviting pools at the bottom of a deep canyon.

Verde Hot Springs: If you're looking for an easier hike, take Forest Road 502 off of Forest Road 708 (signed from the west but not the east), about twelve miles from Strawberry. Drive about 6.5 miles south to the Verde, where the old power plant molders, and take a short hike against the river flow along the road beyond the ruined plant. After about a mile you'll see the ruined baths of the old Verde Hot Springs Resort across the green river, now a hidden public art gallery decorated with generations of graffiti and wall-paintings. It's not likely that the baths are cleaned too often, and you might, on any given day, run into a few naked or nearly naked refugees from the world, drinking beer and enjoying the solitude of one of the stranger of the famous Verde Valley ruins.

the ruins of an old hot spring resort along the Verde River

© TIM HULL

8 A.M.–5P.M. Sept.–May, free), a sister monument just up the interstate from the castle, is often overlooked, but it's a fascinating, quiet stop that will leave you in a bit of awe at nature's strangeness. The "well" is actually a sinkhole into which 1.5 million gallons of 74°F spring water has flowed daily for untold stretches of flowing time, ringed by rough cliffs into which the Sinagua built apartments. You can walk a short, twisting path down to the water's edge and explore the rock-wall rooms.

Beaver Creek Recreation Area

If you find the streamside red rocks of Sedona and Oak Creek too busy, try this rather out-of-the-way oasis at the dirt-road end of Highway 179 after it moves past I-17. Here red-rock banks and tree-shade await, lining Wet Beaver Creek. The warm red-rock slabs provide perfect jumping boards into the pools along the creek, great for splashing around and soaking your feet. There's a campground here with nice creekside spots if you can't bear to leave this beautiful spot.

V-BAR-V RANCH PETROGLYPH SITE

Just up the road from the creek are some of the best petroglyphs in the state at the V-Bar-V Ranch (928/282-4119, www.redrockcountry .org, 9:30 A.M.–3:30 P.M. Fri.–Mon.). Most of the hundreds of rock-carved symbols, creatures, and mysteries were created between A.D. 900 and A.D. 1300 by the Sinagua. Fans of the art form should not miss this sight.

Accommodations and Food

While the valley has some affordable and comfortable places to stay and a few great places to eat, its proximity to better dining and sleeping in Jerome and Sedona make it easy to skip over when it comes to food and accommodations.

That being said, the **Little Daisy Motel** (34 S. Main St., Cottonwood, 928/634-7865, www.littledaisy.com, $50–55 d) is a clean little place with basic rooms, friendly hosts and a very agreeable bill at the end of your stay. If you feel like gambling and watching classic-rock reunion gigs, check out the **The Lodge at Cliff**

Castle (333 Middle Verde Rd., Camp Verde, 928/567-6711, www.cliffcastlecasino.net, $70–110 d) at Cliff Castle Casino in Camp Verde, just before the turn off to Montezuma Castle, hence the name.

For lunch or dinner try **Nic's Italian Steak & Crab House** (925 North Main Street, Cottonwood 928/634-9626, 5–10 P.M. daily, $8–29). Nic serves some tasty Italian dishes, as well as steaks and seafood, and offers homemade bread and a good wine list, though not as good as the list at the **Verde Valley Wine Company & Recovery Room Restaurant** (401 S. Calvary Way, Cottonwood, 928/639-9463, 11 A.M.–5 P.M. daily $8–28), serving everything from Zinfandel Wine Burgers to bacon-wrapped filet mignon in a shiny modern interior. They also have a wine shop.

For those who have to have delicious mounds of Mexican food wherever they travel, try **La Casa Bonita** (991 S. Main St., Cottonwood, 928/634-7018, 11 A.M.–10 P.M. Sun.–Thurs., 11 A.M.–11 P.M. Fri.–Sat., $8–15).

Sports and Recreation

Along with an aforementioned stroll along the Verde River Greenway, **hikers** should make it a point not to leave the valley before taking a jaunt into the **Sycamore Canyon Wilderness Area,** one of Arizona's most beloved and beautiful natural treasures, often called, as are other lesser canyons in the state, "the other grand canyon." It is the state's second largest canyon and one of the first to enjoy federal wilderness protection.

You can reach the southern rim of the canyon by taking the road to Tuzigoot and then turning left after the bridge on Sycamore Canyon Road, then heading about 10 miles to the rim.

The best day-trip into the canyon from this end starts at the Parsons Trailhead on the rim. You descend about 500 feet into the bottomlands, where you'll walk along the creek, with cottonwood and willow and other water-loving flora all around, deep collector pools catching falling leaves in the fall, the riverside shade lifesaving in the summer, and dark high walls towering over you, closing in ever tighter. You can back-pack through the entire 11-mile canyon bottom, but the day-use portion of the Parsons Trail ends about 4 miles in at a deep pool—the spring that feeds the creek From there return the way you came, climbing back up to the rim. Expect to get your feet wet crossing the creek in a few places, and expect to not want to leave the canyon bottom and return to dry reality.

The **Verde River Scenic Area** is a wild stretch of the river that is popular with canoers, kayakers, and other **boating** types. The beautiful, sometimes rough and rapid stretch from Beasly Flat to Childs offers a true river adventure. The best way to prepare for a trip is to get a hold of the **Boater's Guide to the Verde River,** which you can download for free at www.fs.fed.us/r3/coconino/recreation/ red_rock/verde-river-boat.shtml. Or contact the **Verde Ranger District** (300 E. Hwy. 260, Camp Verde, 928/567-4121).

Sedona and Red Rock Country

SEDONA

Second only to Grand Canyon as a favorite Arizona destination, Sedona and its red rocks resemble the great gorge in several ways. Like the canyon, Sedona's rare beauty is the result of geologic circumstance—the slow work of wind, rain, trickling water, and the predictable restless rocking of the Colorado Plateau. The little resort town sits at the base of the plateau, and its red-rock monuments, sit dramatically alone rising into the light-blue sky. The monuments were once a part of the plateau, the connection eaten away by erosion, that ingenious sculptor that makes all of Arizona its medium, over millions of years. High concentrations of iron-oxide, or rust, in the sediment layers stain the rock-statues many shades of red as a finishing flourish. The result is one of the most beautiful and sought-after landscapes on earth.

Also like the canyon, this landscape seems so otherworldly that it's a struggle not to go a little beyond yourself here. For most, all other

© TIM HULL

the cliffs of Sedona seen from Schnebly Hill Road

NORTH-CENTRAL ARIZONA

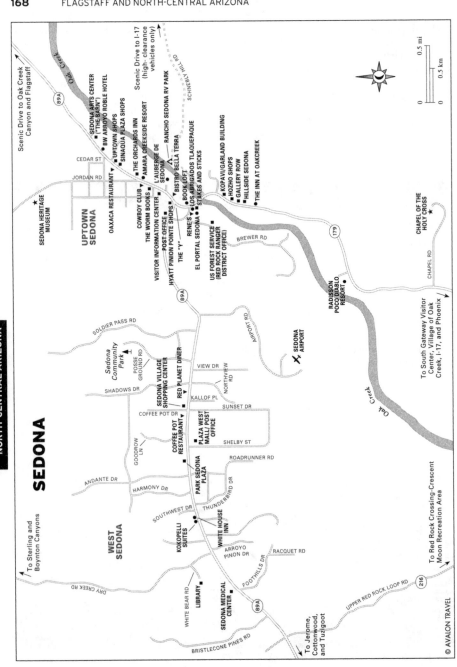

SEDONA

Scenic Drive to Oak Creek Canyon and Flagstaff

Oak Creek

89A

Scenic Drive to I-17 (high- clearance vehicles only)

SCHNEBLY HILL RD

SEDONA ARTS CENTER ("THE BARN")
BW ARROYO ROBLE HOTEL
UPTOWN SHOPS
SINAGUA PLAZA SHOPS
THE ORCHARDS INN
AMARA CREEKSIDE RESORT
L'AUBERGE DE SEDONA
RANCHO SEDONA RV PARK
BISTRO BELLA TERRA
BOOK LOFT
LOS ABRIGADOS TLAQUEPAQUE
STAKES AND STICKS
KOPAVI/GARLAND BUILDING
HOZHO SHOPS
GALLERY ROW
HILLSIDE SEDONA
THE INN AT OAKCREEK

CEDAR ST
JORDAN RD

SEDONA HERITAGE MUSEUM ★

UPTOWN SEDONA

OAXACA RESTAURANT ▼
COWBOY CLUB ■
THE WORM BOOKS ■
POST OFFICE ■
VISITOR INFORMATION CENTER ■
THE "Y"
RENE'S ■
EL PORTAL SEDONA ■
HYATT PIÑON POINTE SHOPS
US FOREST SERVICE (RED ROCK RANGER DISTRICT OFFICE)

BREWER RD

179

CHAPEL OF THE HOLY CROSS ★

CHAPEL RD

89A

RADISSON POCO DIABLO RESORT ●

To South Gateway Visitor Center, Village of Oak Creek, I-17, and Phoenix

SOLDIER PASS RD

Sedona Community Park
POSSE GROUND RD
SEDONA VILLAGE SHOPPING CENTER
RED PLANET DINER ▼
VIEW DR
NORTHVIEW RD
SHADOWS DR
KALLOF PL
SUNSET DR
COFFEE POT DR
COFFEE POT RESTAURANT ▼
PLAZA WEST MALL/POST OFFICE
SHELBY ST
GOODROW LN
PARK SEDONA PLAZA
ROADRUNNER RD
ANDANTE DR
HARMONY DR
SOUTHWEST DR
THUNDERBIRD DR
WHITE HOUSE INN
KOKOPELLI SUITES
ARROYO PIÑON DR
RACQUET RD
FOOTHILLS DR

SEDONA AIRPORT ✈
AIRPORT RD

Oak Creek

To Red Rock Crossing-Crescent Moon Recreation Area

WEST SEDONA

To Sterling and Boynton Canyons

DRY CREEK RD

WHITE BEAR RD
LIBRARY
SEDONA MEDICAL CENTER
89A
UPPER RED ROCK LOOP RD
216

To Jerome, Cottonwood, and Tuzigoot

BRISTLECONE PINES RD

0   0.5 mi
0   0.5 km

© AVALON TRAVEL

explanations fail, which can explain why the spiritual instincts come alive for many who visit, and why there are hordes of spiritual entrepreneurs ready to exploit those instincts. Here you can stay in extreme comfort, bordering on the decadent, or rough it to a certain degree. You can purchase a world-class work of art, and jostle through the backcountry in a pink jeep. There will be crowds, but it is worth braving them, if only for an afternoon, to see this special place.

Orientation

Despite its international reputation as a life-list destination, Sedona is really just a small, somewhat rural town that happens to be stuck in a geologic wonderland. Of course, it has more art galleries, crystal shops, and bistros than most small towns, but there are actually only about 10,000 year-round residents here, though some four million tourists come to the red rocks every year, searching for one thing or another.

Since it's a small town with a huge transient population, driving and parking in Sedona can be an adventure; nonetheless, it's easy to find your way around. The first thing you have to know is that there are four or five distinct zones in and around Sedona, all of them accessible using just two connecting roads. Route 89A runs right through the heart of town and on north to Oak Creek Canyon and eventually to Flagstaff. The portion of this road north of its junction with Route 179, the town's main intersection, called the "Y" among locals, is called Uptown. The stretch of 89A prior to the Y is called West Sedona. Route 179 heads southwest from the "Y" and continues through the red rocks, eventually intersecting with I-17. The stretch of Route 179 between Schnebly Hill Road and Canyon Dr. is called Gallery Row. The Village of Oak Creek is about five miles southwest of Sedona along Route 179.

Sights

Nature is the main attraction here, covered in more depth in the Red Rock Country section

Chapel of the Holy Cross

below. All of Sedona and its environs qualify as a "sight," so to speak. Still, you'll want to make sure you get a look at the famous **Chapel of the Holy Cross** (three miles south of the "Y" at Chapel Rd., 9 A.M.–5 P.M. Mon.–Sat., 10 A.M.–5 P.M. Sun., free), part of the Roman Catholic Diocese of Phoenix. The towering, cross-faced chapel appears to be emerging full born from a red-rock cradle southwest of town (and supposedly near a vortex). In keeping with the self-conscious spiritual vibe in Sedona, many visitors come here to quietly commune with the view, encouraging the emotion all that stained sandstone inspires.

To learn a little local history, at least from the Anglo point of view, check out the **Sedona Heritage Museum** (735 Jordan Rd., 928/282-7038, www.sedonamuseum.org, 11 A.M.–3 P.M. daily, $3) in Uptown's **Jordan Historical Park,** where there's an old fruit orchard and a few disused artifacts from the agricultural past. The museum features an historic cabin, built in the 1930s by fruit growers, and now restored with some original furnishings, wherein is told the story of early Sedona from the 1880s on. The best exhibit is the **Movie Room,** all about the many films that have been made amid the red rocks (Zane Grey's *Call of the Canyon, Johnny Guitar,* etc.).

Events

The red rocks make a good backdrop for just about any kind of activity, and music bouncing off the sun drenched buttes just seems to sound better. Each September for nearly 30 years now the best Jazz artists in the world have gathered here to play the **Sedona Jazz on the Rocks** (928/282-1985, www.sedonajazz.com) festival and to prove that theory. September is a great time to be in the northland, like a second spring; if you are a jazz fan you should plan your life accordingly. The same applies to classical music lovers, who will appreciate the usually stellar line-up that late August brings to the **Red Rocks Music Festival** (602/787-1577 or 877/733-7257, www.redrocksmusicfestival .com) every year. Cinephiles will enjoy drinking wine with indie film stars during the **Sedona International Film Festival** (928/282 1177, www.sedonafilmfestival.com), five days in late February and early March filled with cutting-edge and independent films with discussions and workshops on the same. The plastic arts take over in October, with the renowned **Sedona Arts Festival** (928/204-9456, www .sedonaartsfestival.org) and the **Sedona Plein Air Festival** (928/282-3809 or 888/954-4442, www.sedonapleinairfestival.com).

Nightlife

Sipping wine amid the scenery and doing all manner of things by candle- and star-light are the particular habits of nocturnal Sedona, mostly a couple's time and romantic to an absurd degree. If you're looking to be around people, have a few drinks and some conversation, try the **Rooftop Cantina** at Oaxaca and **Stakes & Sticks** (160 Portal Lane, 928/204-7849) adjacent to Tlaquepaque, which has more than 20 flat screen TVs showing mostly spots, off-track betting, and the more laid-back **Shef's Bar** (www.shefsbar.com) inside.

Shopping and Galleries

Contemporary eclectic, mid-to-high-end arts and crafts with a fetish for the Southwestern legendary, Native American jewelry and spiritual objects, Mexican colors and religious items, or a heavy-framed painting of a cowboy sleeping next to a campfire, his worn old hat pulled down a bit over his eyes…This is pretty much what you'll find in Sedona's many shopping districts, though there are notable exceptions. After a while one boutique, gallery, and fancy "trading post" tends to meld into the next. It's great fun, and probably the second most popular activity here, just below staring dumbfounded at the rocks. It's doubtless even more fun if you have the wallet to afford the best pieces, which, sadly, always cost the most, and sometimes even more than that.

Start at the **Uptown Shops** (N. Hwy 89), the original Sedona shopping district. Both sides of Highway 89 have several levels of little touristy shops, souvenir stands, boutiques and jewelry stores. If you feel like going hiking and didn't plan for it, look for **Sedona Outdoors** (270 N. Hwy. 89A Ste 5, 928/203-0641, 9 A.M.–8 P.M. daily), where you can get pretty much any gear you need and a lot you probably don't. Next, head to the high-end **Shops at Hyatt Piñon Pointe** (at the "Y," 928/204-8828, www .theshopsathyattpinonpointe.com), where the shoe-loving shopper can lose their mind at **Marchesa's Fine Shoe's Salon.** Don't miss what is arguably Sedona's best gallery, **Visions Fine Art Gallery,** which has a more varied collection than just about anybody in town. After Piñon Pointe, it's on to Sedona's true shopping treasure, **Tlaquepaque Arts & Crafts Village** (336 Highway 179, 928/282.4838, www.tlaq .com) an enchanting collection of Mexican-style courtyards with all kinds of unique shops and the best restaurant in town, **René at Tlaquepaque.** There's even a little white stucco chapel in the "village," as if you're in an upscale version of Old Mexico, with beautiful stained-glass and a mural above the altar. There are more than 40 shops and galleries among the courtyards and shade trees here, including **The Storyteller Bookstore**

(928/282-2144, 10 A.M.–5 P.M. daily), specializing in Southwestern books, and **Feliz Navidad** (928/282-2752, www.feliz navidadsedona.com, 10 A.M.–5 P.M. daily), dedicated to Christmas ornaments with a Mexican aesthetic. Next head across the street from Tlaquepaque to **Gallery Row,** where you'll find the best Native American art. **Kopavi** (411 Hwy. 179, Garland Building upstairs, 928/282-4774, 10:30 A.M.–5 P.M. daily) has the best items made by Hopi artists. It is best to call first to make sure they are open. Also check out **Hozho** (431 Hwy. 179, 928/204-2257) for tasteful Southwestern styles. The **Hillside Sedona** (671 Hwy. 179, 928/282-4500, www .hillsidevillages.com) complex is also in this area and deserves a look, especially the **Gallery of Modern Masters** (888/282-3313, www .galleryofmodernmasters.com, 10 A.M.–8 P.M. daily) which has some spectacular pieces by some of the all time greats.

VILLAGE OF OAK CREEK
If you haven't had enough shopping yet, head about five miles south on Highway 179 and explore the relatively new shops at the beautiful **Tequa Festival Marketplace** (7000 Hwy. 179, 928/284-4699, www.tequa.net) and, perhaps for the first and only time during your visit to Sedona, find a bargain at the **Oak Creek Factory Outlets** (6601 S. Hwy 179, 928/284-2150).

Accommodations
There are dozens of hotels and resorts in Sedona, some of them like little towns themselves. There are a few bargains, but you could spend hundreds, even thousands a night if you wanted to, and you generally get what you pay for. Some of the resorts are outlandishly well-appointed, with golf courses and all kinds of spa treatments, workshops, and spiritual rituals. For easy booking, try the free **Sedona Central Reservations** (800/445-4128, www .sedonacentralreservations.com).

$50-100
The **Whitehouse Inn** (2986 W. Hwy. 89A,

928/282-6680, www.whitehouseinn.netfirms .com, $49–99 d) is an affordable and basic place to stay, not sumptuous or anything, but a clean and central base for a realistic visit without the huge price tag, mud bathes, and chakra healing. Same goes for the **Sedona Village Lodge** (105 Bellrock Plaza, 800/890-052, www.sedonalodge.com, $49–79 d), which is clean and basic, and the **Matterhorn Inn** (230 Apple Ave., 800/372-8207, www.matterhorn inn.com, $79–159 d), which is highly recommended, centrally located and comfy.

$100-200
The **Wildflower Inn** (6086 Hwy. 179, 888/494-5335, www.sedonawildflowerinn .com, $99–159 d) in the Village of Oak Creek looks out at Bell Rock and offers rooms with fireplaces, and in-room whirlpool tubs—a little bit of decadence at a relatively affordable price. The **Orchards Inn** (254 N. Highway 89 A, 928/282-2405 or 800/341-5931, www .orchardsinn.com $99–200 d) has wonderful rooms, many with fireplaces and patios with views of the red rocks, a tasteful, cozy lobby—one of the best affordable places in Uptown. The **Kokopelli Suites** (3119 W. Hwy. 89A, 800/789-7393, www.kokopellisuites.com, $109–239) offers two-room suites with kitchens and is great for families.

$200 AND ABOVE
Amara Creekside Resort (310 N. Hwy. 89, 928/282-4828, www.amararesort.com, $189–409 d) is one of those Sedona places you've heard about; lovely beyond reason, intimidating yet tasteful, this retreat on the banks of Oak Creek has a full-service spa and all the other amenities you'd expect from a five-diamond hideaway. Also along the creek is **The Inn on Oak Creek** (556 Hwy 179, 928/282-7896 or 800/499-7896, www.innon oakcreek.com, $185–295 d), an enchanting bed-and-breakfast that seems a world away from the bustle. The **El Portal Sedona** (95 Portal Lane, 800/313-0017, www.elportal sedona.com, $250–550 d) is an amazing 12-room hacienda in the rustic-elegant style,

with deep comfort, great food, and furniture you'll want to pack up and take home.

Food

A favorite with the locals, the **☾ Coffee Pot Restaurant** (2050 W. Hwy. 89A, 928/282-6626, 6 A.M.–2 P.M. daily, $3–10) is great for breakfast and lunch, with filling home-style food in big portions; expect a crowd. The sci-fi aesthetic of the **Red Planet Diner** (1655 W. 89A, 928/282 6070, 11 A.M.–11 P.M. daily, $8–15) is something to see, and the burgers and sandwiches are pretty good too. The **Cowboy Club** (241 N. Hwy. 89A, 928/282-4200, www .cowboyclub.com, 11 A.M.–4 P.M. and 5–10 P.M. daily, $5–27) in Uptown Sedona is a perennial favorite, a Western-style joint with a lot of buffalo meat on the menu and great steaks and other dishes. One of the better Mexican places in the northland is **☾ Oaxaca Restaurant** (321 N. Hwy. 89A, 928/282-4179, www.oaxaca restaurant.com, 8 A.M.–9 P.M. daily, $6–16),

and the **Bistro Bella Terra** (101 N. Hwy. 89A, 928/203-7771, www.bistrobellaterra .com, 11 A.M.–11 P.M. daily, $8–24) is perfect for one of those high-toned Sedona date nights if you're looking for creative, delicious food, a good wine list, and romantic atmosphere. The best place to eat in Sedona is **☾ René at Tlaquepaque** (336 Hwy. 179, 928/282-9225, www.rene-sedona.com, 11:30 A.M.–2:30 P.M. and 5:30–8:30 P.M. daily, $11–16 lunch, $22–42 dinner), with its Mexican courtyard ambience and outrageously tasty food. Try the baked French onion soup and the sweet potato ravioli, or the venison, or the…just try the whole menu, and go back again and again if you can.

Information

The Sedona Chamber of Commerce has a very energetic and organized tourism bureau that operates two well-stocked and well-staffed visitor centers. There's an office in the **Uptown** shopping area that's easy to spot (928/282-7722 or 800/288-7336, www.visitsedona.com, 8 A.M.–5 P.M. Mon.–Sat., 8 A.M.–3 P.M. Sun.) and one at the Tequa Plaza, in the **Village of Oak Creek** southwest of town.

Getting There and Around

You really need to have a car to see Sedona and Red Rock Country right, and it would be ideal to have an SUV or a four-wheel-drive vehicle. A sedan will do just fine though, especially if you plan on booking a jeep tour to see the backcountry. The best way to get to Sedona from out of state is to fly into **Phoenix Sky Harbor,** rent a car there, and drive about 1.5 hours north to the red rocks.

Once you've made it to town, if you don't feel like driving around, hop on the **Sedona Trolley** (928/282-5400, www.sedonatrolly .com, $11 for adults, $5.50 for kids under 12) for two different 55-minute "best-of" tours offered between 10 A.M. and 4 P.M. daily.

RED ROCK COUNTRY

Many of the more representational red-rock buttes, spires, and monuments have names,

PHOTO COURTESY RENÉ AT TLAQUEPAQUE

René at Tlaquepaque

NORTH-CENTRAL ARIZONA

though you might not always see the same figure in the rock that the name implies. Most of the most famous rocks can be seen from the road. Starting on Highway 89A and heading into Sedona from the west, look for **Chimney Rock** off to the north around Harmony Drive. A little farther east and far off to the north is **Coffee Pot Rock,** roughly equivalent with Coffee Pot Drive. Turn at the "Y" and head southwest on Highway 179 to see **Camel Head & Snoopy Rock,** around Canyon Drive, and **Submarine Rock** at Morgan Drive, both off to the east. To the west and nearly to the Village of Oak Creek, around Oak Creek Cliffs Drive, look for **Cathedral Rock,** and just after Indian Cliffs Rd. on the west, check out **Bell Rock.** A good promontory from which to view the whole area is **Airport Mesa,** at the end of Airport Road off Highway 89A.

For all the information on driving, hiking, and biking in Red Rock Country, stop by the **Red Rock Ranger District** (8375 Rte. 179, 928/282-4119 or 928/203-2903, www.fs.fed

.us/r3/coconino, 8 A.M.–4:30 P.M. Mon.–Fri., 8 A.M.– 5 P.M. Sat.–Sun.) visitor center.

RED ROCK PASS

Before you do anything in Red Rock Country, stop by the ranger station or the Sedona visitor center and purchase a **Red Rock Pass,** which you're required to have even if you're only going to be motoring around the rocks stopping every now and again. It only costs $5 per day or $15 for a week, and the money goes for the upkeep of this heavily used national forest.

Hiking

Some rangers complain that the most popular trails around Sedona are getting too worn and overused for their own good, but they are popular for a reason. You can expect to see a lot of other hikers with the same idea as you on the following trails, but they cannot in all good conscience be missed by serious hikers, and they should be walked by even the most casual trekker. A leisurely hike is the best way to see the red rocks up close.

The five-mile round-trip **Sterling Pass to Vultee Arch** trail takes you up about 1,000 feet in a strenuous climb and then back down to a delicate natural rock arch that is supposed to have some kind of power over the body and mind. Probably the best all around hike in Sedona, but a tough climb. The trailhead is seven miles north of Sedona on Highway 89A along the side of the highway. Easier is the very popular **Boyton Canyon Trail,** five miles round-trip to a vortex through the Red Mountain Secret Wilderness, where you'll see canyon walls more than 1,000 feet high and water falls if it's a wet time of year. Head south on Highway 89A from Sedona and turn right on Dry Creek Road, then go left on FR152C for the trailhead. For some streamside hiking try the **West Fork of Oak Creek Trail,** 6.5 miles round-trip, takes you through a riparian wonderland mixed with red rocks and deep greens. Very popular so expect crowds. The trailhead is at mile post 385 along Highway 89A in Oak Creek Canyon. It's an easy, mostly flat hike, but you'll probably get your feet wet crossing the creek a few times.

© ELIZABETH JANG

Coffee Pot Rock

Mountain Biking

First make sure you have your trusty copy of *Cosmic Ray's Fat Tire Tales and Trails Mountain Bike Guide to Arizona* for all the secret and not-so-secret trails and slick rock around Red Rock Country. One of the best biking areas is the **Bell Rock Loops,** a series of red-dirt single tracks among the petrified sand dunes out in the rocks near the Village of Oak Creek. The northland biking authorities at **Absolute Bikes** (6101 Hwy. 179, 928/284-1242 or 877/284-1242, www.absolutebikes.net/sedona, 8 A.M.–6 P.M. Mon.–Fri., 8 A.M.–5 P.M. Sat.–Sun.), located right near the Bell Rock Loops trailhead, can give you some pointers, sell you Cosmic Ray's essential guide, and even rent you a mountain bike.

WHAT'S A VORTEX AND WHY SHOULD YOU CARE?

Hanging around the Sedona Visitor Center in the summer, one hears more than once the suggestions of local volunteers trying to get out-of-towners, especially first time visitors, interested in the little town's story beyond the famous vortexes. "But we came out here from Boston and we want to see the vortexes."

Well, you can't really see them. A vortex, they say, is a place with a special energy, a space in a landscape that gathers energy from all around it, concentrating it, perhaps to be manipulated by someone in touch with the earth's languages. The redrocks around Sedona are said to be rotten with them, and a hike or drive to a vortex site has become the most popular New Age activity here in recent years. Don't worry, you can still get your tarot cards read, have your aura photographed, your past lives remembered and your crystals recharged at storefronts all over town.

The vortex movement, according to Dwight Garner of the *New York Times,* began in 1987, "the year of the Harmonic Convergence when believers flocked to mystical places across the planet, hoping for a global awakening of harmony and love." Reportedly some 5,000 true believers descended on Sedona, obviously one of those "mystical places," probably owing more to its unique scenery more than anything else, and many of them never left. These days there's no shortage of guides who will take you out into the redrocks and introduce you to the vortexes, and perhaps, your spiritual self.

Suzanne McMillan and her staff at **Sedona Vortex Tours** (1385 W. Hwy. 89A, 928/282-2733, sedonavortextours.com, $75-30 per person, 3-5 hours) promise to "teach you how to feel the vortex energy." McMillian has been leading tours since 1988, taking seekers out in vans or on hikes to vortexes and on Medicine Wheel Tours. Linda Summers of **Sedona Spirit Journeys** (928/282-8966, $75 per person for 2.5 hours) has a degree in Native American Studies and guides a "Sedona Vortex Healing Journey," during which she shares the history of the vortex sites and offers "guided meditation, drumming, and a special crystal and Reiki healing energy in the beauty of nature." Cynthia Tierra of **Healing From the Heart** (928/821-0989, www.healingone.net, $100-500 per person, 1-3 hours) has 25 years of experience as a holistic health practitioner and Reiki Master. She will guide you to both well-known and "secret" vortexes, and she gives psychic readings as well. **Sedona Spirit Yoga & Hiking** (928/282-9900, 888/282-9901, www.yogalife.net, $85-155 per person, 3-6 hours), run by Johanna (Maheshvari) Mosca, who calls herself "Madame Vortex," offers guided vortex hikes that include yoga sessions on the redrock buttes.

site of the Bell Rock vortex

© ELIZABETH JANG

Red Rock State Park

The 286-acre Red Rock State Park (Lower Red Rock Loop Rd., 928/282-6907, 8 A.M.–8 P.M. daily in summer, 8 A.M.–6 P.M. in winter, visitor center is open 9 A.M.–6 P.M. daily, $6 per vehicle) is a great place to see Oak Creek, which runs through the park and provides water for huge cottonwoods and willows under which you can lounge and walk. There are all kinds of short streamside hiking trails, and every day at 10 A.M. a ranger leads an hour-long nature walk through the riparian ecosystem. The main thrust here is environmental education, and this is the best place to really get to know the ecology of the area.

Palatki and Honanki

These two small Sinagua ruins in the red rocks are worth a look, but they require a drive into the backcountry and Red Rock Pass. You should make reservations to see **Palatki** (928/282-3854, 9:30 A.M. –3:30 P.M. daily) as parking is limited to 20 cars. To visit the smaller **Honanki,** you don't have to make a reservation. To get to Palatki, the bigger and better of the two and the one that should take precedence, take Highway 89A toward Cottonwood. About three miles past the "Y" in Sedona, turn right on Dry Creek Road. You'll pass several intersections, but there are signs that will tell you which way to go. Just before you reach Palatki, the road bears left and there's a sign pointing you to Honoki. There are volunteers to explain what you're seeing at Palatki, but at Honanki you are on your own.

◖ Oak Creek Canyon

Arguably the most beautiful drive in the state is the twisty, streamside drive north on Highway 89A through Oak Creek Canyon and back up to the plateau. Head north out of Sedona, over the large bridge hovering high over Oak Creek, and just drive and look, slowly, taking great pains not to veer into oncoming traffic as you're craning to see the towering red rocks, topped with white caps and greenery peppered throughout. The creek is so beautiful that you'll want to stop along the side of the road and probably put your feet in. Or you can stop at **Slide Rock State Park** (6871 N. Hwy 89A, 928/282-3034, 8 A.M.6 P.M. daily, $10 per vehicle) and try out the 80-foot natural red rock slide, or walk around the short nature trails, picnic, or just soak in the creek and lay around on the warm rocks. There will likely be crowds in the summer.

Jeep Tours

One of the most famous tour companies in the Southwest, **Pink Jeep Tours** (Hwy. 89A in Uptown Sedona, 800/873-3662, www.pinkjeep. com, 7 A.M.–6 P.M. daily, $45–139) has, for 45 years, operated under a special permit with the forest service to take their gaudy open-air four-wheel drive jeeps out into the redlands, filled with eager and excited tourists. It's pretty much an institution, and the guides are usually friendly, entertaining, and knowledgeable. Unless you have your own four-wheeler, this is the best way to see the red rocks in a vehicle. There are a lot of jeep tour companies in town, but Pink Jeeps in one of the oldest and certainly the best of the bunch.

Rim Country and the White Mountains

The great Arizona pinelands continue east across the Mogollon Rim and past its eastern edge, then they rise and mix with other, shaggier conifers in the high ridges and valleys of the White Mountain range. The range's top peak, 11,420-foot Mt. Baldy, is the highest non-San Francisco Peak mountaintop in the state. Creeks and washes that eventually meet the Salt River fall off these mountains, feeding the river that once, long ago, watered the Salt River Valley, now called the Valley of the Sun and without a river. Phoenicians and their Tucson neighbors have long used these nearly alpine heights as a summer hideout from the desert heat. The practice has been so prevalent for so long, that certain old-timers can

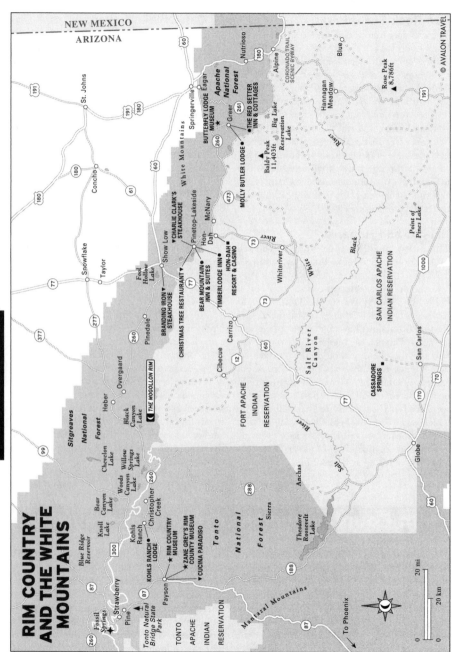

NEW MEXICO
ARIZONA

St. Johns

Apache National Forest

Nutrioso

Blue

Rose Peak 8,786ft

CORONADO TRAIL SCENIC BYWAY

© AVALON TRAVEL

Eagar
Springerville

Alpine

Hannagan Meadow

BUTTERFLY LODGE MUSEUM
Greer
THE RED SETTER INN & COTTAGES

Big Lake

White Mountains

MOLLY BUTLER LODGE
Baldy Peak 11,403ft
Big Lake Reservoir Lake

Concho

Snowflake

Taylor

Show Low
Pinetop-Lakeside
McNary
Hon-Dah

Point of Pines Lake

CHARLIE CLARK'S STEAKHOUSE

Fool Hollow Lake

BRANCHING IRON STEAKHOUSE
CHRISTMAS TREE RESTAURANT
BEAR MOUNTAIN INN & SUITES
TIMBERLODGE INN
HON-DAH RESORT & CASINO

Black River

Whiteriver

San Carlos Apache Indian Reservation

Pinedale

Pinetop

Carrizo

San Carlos

Overgaard

Cibecue

Salt River Canyon

CASSADORE SPRINGS

Heber

THE MOGOLLON RIM

Black Canyon Lake

FORT APACHE INDIAN RESERVATION

Globe

Sitgreaves National Forest

Chevelon Lake

Willow Springs Lake

Woods Canyon Lake

Salt River

Bear Canyon Lake

Christopher Creek

Tonto National Forest

Sierra

Anchas

Theodore Roosevelt Lake

Knoll Lake

Kohls Ranch

Blue Ridge Reservoir

KOHLS RANCH LODGE
RIM COUNTRY MUSEUM
ZANE GREY'S RIM COUNTRY MUSEUM
CUCINA PARADISO

Payson

Fossil Springs
Tonto Natural Bridge State Park
Strawberry
Pine

Mantazal Mountains

To Phoenix

RIM COUNTRY AND THE WHITE MOUNTAINS

TONTO APACHE INDIAN RESERVATION

20 mi

20 km

remember when many of the eligible teenage girls in any given middle-class lowland neighborhood would suddenly be gone, kidnapped to the northland by rich folk needing summer au pairs. Likewise, an Arizona girl could make herself a nice sum lounging by the cool lake with kids all summer. Today there are still quite a few summer homes in the White Mountains, only they are usually bigger and more complex and audacious than they used to be. The area has maintained something of an isolated, almost enchanted feel to it, as if the whole landscape shuts down come winter and is only open and bright for a few months every year. Most of the towns here are tiny and of no particular interest save as picturesque vignettes of rural quietude and glacial change. The White Mountains have long been inhabited by Latter Day Saints, and their influence is everywhere here.

If you're not an outdoor adventure enthusiast, an angler, or a high-country trekker, odds are you'll only want to drive through, stopping at a few interesting roadside shops, admiring a view or a particularly expansive high meadow, spotting elk or pronghorn or even a bear wander-jogging not far off the highway, and eating at one the area's several good restaurants. And what a drive it is. There are two scenic drives in this area—the White Mountain Scenic Highway and the Coronado Trail—two of the state's very best. Following their twisty, meadow-lined routes will take you everywhere you need to be in this green mountain hideaway.

PAYSON AND VICINITY

Even if you've never read any of Zane Grey's more than 130 books, a look at the **Zane Grey Cabin** (700 Green Valley Parkway, 928/474-3483, $2), is a must when you're in the small town of Payson. He loved this area, which he called the Tonto Rim, and came here to write and hunt for many years. The original cabin burned down in the 1990 Dude Fire, but a local group rebuilt it exactly and furnished it according to surviving pictures. There's also a small **Rim Country Museum** next door with

a view of Tonto Natural Bridge near Payson

exhibits on Grey and what life was like for the Anglo pioneers who settled this piney area below the great rim.

Below the Rim

Tucked just below the rim north on Highway 87 from Payson, the tiny towns of **Pine** and **Strawberry** have a few antique stores, lodges, restaurants, and a forest atmosphere. Just west of Highway 87 on Highway 260 you'll pass **Kohls Ranch** and **Christopher Creek,** forested burgs with cabins to rent. Try the **Kohl's Ranch Lodge** (202 S. Kohl's Ranch Lodge Rd., 928/478-4211, $120–350), with its bucolic, mountain-forest setting and creek-side cabins.

Tonto Natural Bridge State Park

The Tonto Natural Bridge State Park (11 miles north of Payson on Highway 87, 928/476-4202, 8 A.M.–7 P.M. daily in summer, $3 per person) is the major stop in Rim Country other than the rim itself. The world's largest natural travertine bridge, the strange and wondrous sight can be hiked to or over on short trails. Though the trail going to the dripping, moss-covered inner bridge is steep going back up, it's short and should really be taken to get the full experience. Hike down and sit on the wet rocks, watching water drip off the bridge's arch high above.

☾ The Mogollon Rim

The 7,000-foot high edge of the Colorado Plateau is responsible for making Arizona the extremely varied land that it is. The trail once used by General Crook to run supplies from Fort Verde to Fort Apache during the Apache wars is now Forest Road 300, also known as the Rim Road. The dirt road (not really rough at all, OK for sedans) parallels the Mogollon Rim, and there are many turnouts where you'll want to get out of the car and walk right up to the Rim and stand on the very edge of the plateau, overlooking the pine seas below.

Drive north out of Payson on Route 87 and you'll see the sign for Forest Road 300. Turn east on Forest Road 300 and drive all the way across the rim to the **Mogollon Rim Visitor Center,** where there's a paved trail and some breathtaking views right at the edge of the White Mountain region, near Highway 260. The drive is about 51 miles one-way. Or

you can make a loop of it by taking Forest Road 321 to Forst Road 96 to Forest Road 95 to Clint's Well on Route 87, about 54 miles round-trip. Along the Rim Road you'll see the effects of the huge, destructive **Dude Fire** in the 1990s—blackened stands of deadwood and new green growth blanketing the ground.

Just to the north of Forest Road 300 is the **Rim Lakes Recreation Area,** a gathering of several small lakes with great fishing, all of them easily accessed off of Forest Road 300—just look for the signs for **Knoll Lake, Bear Canyon Lake, Black Canyon Lake,** and others. These rim lakes are all stuffed with trout and bass, and there are hiking trails all around and between them. There are seven nearby campgrounds ($5–16 per night), or you can pull your rig right to the edge of the rim and sleep there. For more information call the **Apache-Sitgreaves National Forests** (Springerville, 928/333-4301); check out all the rim lake hiking trails at www.fs.fed.us/r3/asnf/.

Accommodations and Food

There are a lot of chain hotels and restaurants around Payson to serve Phoenicians escaping

The Mogollon Rim rises above the forested valley below.

© TIM HULL

a thick stand of aspens on the Mogollon Rim near the General Crook Trail

the heat, as it's a mere 1.5 hour drive from the Valley. Most of the services are along the main route through town.

You can't go wrong staying at the small **Majestic Mountain Inn** (602 E. Hwy. 260, 928/474-6097, $69–150), which has nice, clean rooms, Internet, a heated pool and much more.

Cucina Paradiso (512 N. Beeline Hwy., 928/468-6500, 11 A.M.–2 P.M. and 4–8:30 P.M. daily, $7–19) has excellent northern Italian food and hand-tossed, wood-fired pizza.

SHOW LOW

Show Low, a larger town than most in this region with about 10,000 people, is popular with retirees and heat-birds. It's not one of the more scenic towns in the White Mountains, but it has several chain hotels and a few restaurants. A popular fishing, camping, and picnicing area nearby is **Fools Hollow Lake Recreation Area** (928/537-3680, 5 A.M.–10 P.M. daily, $6 day pass, $12–25 camping), where you'll find a jewel-like blue highland lake surrounded

by tall pines. There's a well-stocked **Visitor Center** (81 E. Deuce of Clubs, 928/537-2326) on the main drag that has a lot of information on the White Mountains region.

Accommodations and Food

Most of the accommodations and restaurants in Show Low can be found along the town's short main drag, Deuce of Clubs.

The **Branding Iron Steakhouse** (573 Deuce of Clubs, 928/537-5151, 11 A.M.–9 P.M. Mon.–Thurs., 11 A.M.–10 P.M. Fri., 4–10 P.M. Sat., $7–15) serves a good cut of meat with all the fixings, perfect for a cold high-country evening. Local favorite **Licano's Mexican Steakhouse** (572 Deuce of Clubs, 928/537-8220, 11 A.M.–9:30 P.M. daily, $4–15) serves excellent Mexican food.

If you're staying overnight, try the **Best Western Paint Pony Lodge** (581 W. Deuce of Clubs, 928/537-5773, $79–110), which has standard rooms and high-speed Internet, and serves a free continental breakfast.

PINETOP-LAKESIDE

This small resort village marks the beginning of the **White Mountain Scenic Road,** otherwise known as Route 260 to the Round Valley. Pinetop-Lakeside, one incorporated community, sits at more than 7,000-feet, a high forest getaway with just 4,000 year-round residents. When the snow melts, however, more than 35,000 call this place home. There are quite a few distinctive shops and not a few restaurants, including a couple of really memorable joints. If you're planning to spend a few days in the White Mountains, Pinetop-Lakeside should be your base. Here you'll find the **White Mountain Trail System,** a series of forest-and-meadow loops ranked as one of the top hikes in the nation.

Accommodations

There are more than 40 hotels, motels, cabins for rent, and country resorts in this tiny sylvan burg, so many that it seems like the whole town is for rent by the night. Check out the **Pinetop-Lakeside Chamber of Commerce**

Visitor Center (102-C W. White Mountain Blvd, 800/573-4031, www.pinetoplakeside chamber.com) for accommodation information. One of the least expensive options is the **Mountain Hacienda Lodge** (Hwy. 260, 928/367-4146, $45–59), a regular motel-style place that looks better with the forest around it—a good bargain, clean and comfortable, with wireless Internet.

Another standard, affordable, and comfortable place to stay is the **Bear Mountain Inn and Suites** (Hwy. 260., 928/368-6600, www.bear mountainpinetop.com, $55–109) with wireless Internet, and suites with cozy, romantic fireplaces—a perfect place to base your ski or hiking weekend. The **Timberlodge Inn** (Hwy. 260, 928/367-4463, www.timberlodge.com, $64–179) has two-room connecting suites with kitchens, cable TV, and free wireless—perfect for families. Just outside of town on the White Mountain Apache Reservation is the gleaming **Hon-Dah Resort & Casino** (at the Jct. of Hwy. 260 and Hwy. 73, 928/369-0299, www .hon-dah.com, $99–190 d), with nice rooms, a great buffet, comedy shows, live bands, dancing, drinking, and, of course, slots, blackjack and poker.

Food

The oldest continually operating restaurant in the White Mountains, **Charlie Clark's Steakhouse** (Hwy. 260, 928/367-4900, www .charlieclarks.com, 5–10 P.M. daily) serves up the best steaks, sea food and prime rib in the area on property that, during prohibition, used to hold a distillery. It's been around since 1938, but it's been upgraded a few times since then, and is now a casual Western-style place that's very popular.

Information

The **Pinetop-Lakeside Chamber of Commerce Visitor Center** (102-C W. White Mountain Blvd, 800/573-4031, www.pinetop lakesidechamber.com, 8:30 A.M.–4:30 P.M. Mon.–Fri., 8:30 A.M.–2:30 P.M. Sat.–Sun.) has all the information you will need on visiting this area.

GREER

Turn south off Highway 260 onto Highway 273 to reach the little village of Greer (www.greer arizona.com), a log-cabin hamlet nestled in the forest and green meadows at 7,000–9,000 feet below the White Mountains, through which flows the Little Colorado River. The area is outlandishly beautiful and picturesque. It could just as well be nestled and snugged in the Alps, and the babbling forks of the river support a lush riparian belt with overgrowing greenery and flat skinny trails along the moss-covered waterway. There are four seasons in Greer, each spectacular. In spring and summer it's perfect for hiking, horseback riding, and laying around in highland meadows, surrounded by colorful wildflowers. In winter the snow comes, and Greer makes a good base for trips to the ski hills and for cross-country expeditions into the forest.

Sights

While the forests and meadows tend to push everything else of interest off the radar, the strange and quaint **Butterfly Lodge Museum** (Hwy. 373 and CR1126, 928/735-7514, www.wmon-line.com/butterflylodge.htm, 10 A.M.–5 P.M. Thurs.–Sun., Memorial Day weekend–Labor Day weekend, $2 adults, $1 youth 12–17, 12 and under free) is worth a look if you're in Greer during the summer. The little log house was once the hunting lodge of James Willard Schultz, an early 20th century writer of adventure stories about the West for magazines, known primarily for his 1907 book *My Life As An Indian*. The home was later used as a studio by Schultz's equally interesting son, Hart Merriam Schultz, or Lone Wolf, a famous Indian painter and artist. The home is set up with all kinds of artifacts and everyday items that show what life was like in this remote green mountain valley years ago. There are several of Lone Wolf's paintings on display, and a gift shop selling the elder Schultz's nostalgic writings.

Hiking

The best hikes in and around Greer are those that lead along the forks of the Little Colorado

River. You can hike to the lower end of Mount Baldy on the **East Fork Trail,** a six-mile one-way trip. Pick up the trailhead where Main Street enters the National Forest on the south end of Greer. The first leg of the hike is pretty steep, but then it evens out and is green and meadowy. If you just want to stroll in the creeping green forest along the forks, head south until the end of the main road and follow the well-worn footpaths along the river. In some places the ground is so spongy and over-grown with greenery that it seems like you're in a rain forest.

Accommodations and Food

There are several lodges in Greer, and a host of cabins for rent, whether for the night or the season. For a complete list check out the official Greer, Arizona website at www.greer arizona.com.

The **Red Setter Inn & Cottages** (8 Main St., 928/735-7216, www.redsetterinn.com, $199 d) is an all-inclusive lodge offering free fly fishing, use of mountain bikes and snow shoes, and free movies; this adults-only resort is tucked in the trees near the creek and offers cabins for rent and bed-and-breakfast-style rooms; the price includes a full breakfast and a sack lunch. The **373 Bar & Grill** at the nearby **Greer Lodge Resort,** run by the same people, serves good breakfasts, lunches and dinners daily.

The historic ◖ **Molly Butler Lodge** (109 Main Street, 928/735-7226 or 866/288-3167, www.mollybutlerlodge.com, $65–115 d) rents cabins for multiple people, great for families; the cabins are a little rustic but comfortable and clean and perfect for the setting; there are no TVs or phone in the rooms but they have them at the lodge, where there's also a fantastic restaurant that's been serving hearty mountain food since 1910. It's open for dinner daily (5–9 P.M., $10–15), serving excellent fish, steaks, chili, prime rib and more.

THE CORONADO TRAIL

Once you reach **Eager-Springerville,** also called Round Valley, a heavily Mormon area with the nation's only domed high school stadium, you'll be on the famed **Coronado Trail,** the route the conquistadores supposedly took on their way to the nonexistent Seven Cities of Cibola. It'll take at least five hours to drive the twisty two-lane road down the mountain to the desert grassland, a distance of about 120 miles. You'll pass the tiny towns of **Alpine, Nutrioso,** and **Hannigans Meadow,** but the scenery is really the attraction here. Don't take this spectacular drive if you get impatient or car sick.

A WHITE MOUNTAIN RECREATION GUIDE

Listed below are some of the best outdoor adventures you can have in this region:

- **Hike Mt. Baldy.** Take Route 260 and Route 273 to the trailhead 10 miles southeast on Route 273, which becomes Forest Road 113. For more information, contact the Springerville Ranger District at 928/333-4372.

- **Hike or mountain bike the White Mountain Trail System.** The trail system includes 11 loop trails near Pinetop-Lakeside. Contact the Lakeside Ranger Station (928/368-5111, www.ci.pinetop-lakeside.az.us/trailsystem.shtml) for more information.

- **Visit the Big Lake Recreation Area.** A half-hour drive from Springerville/Eager, you'll find four campgrounds and great fishing.

- **Cross Country ski at Hannagan's Meadow.** South of Alpine, approximately 45 minute's drive from Springerville/Eagar.

- **Downhill Ski at Sunrise Ski Resort.** (928/735-7669, www.sunrisepark .com)

NAVAJO AND HOPI COUNTRY

Here is the Arizona you often see on posters and in old films: Monument Valley, the Painted Desert, the railroad tracks, and Route 66. This is also the Arizona you rarely see unless you make a concerted effort to do so: The Navajo Nation, the Hopi Mesas, and the hidden, forgotten ruins of an ancient civilization.

From the vast, arid grasslands of the High Desert to the pink and red sandstone guardians of Indian Country, the scenery here gets top billing, but there are also comforts to be had in this region that was once an exotic, longed-for destination for generations of Americans and still is a major draw for those looking for something just a bit off the beaten path.

Here you can gaze at weather-formed canyons with rock features that seem deliberately molded according to a strange, thrilling

aesthetic; hike into Canyon de Chelly (pronounced Canyon de "shay"), a sacred place where pueblo ruins sit below sheer, multicolored walls; or visit the Hopis in their remote mesa-top villages, many of them living no differently than their ancestors did a thousand years ago. This place is not for the lazy, easy-come traveler, but for those looking for something different. The region's challenges, its sometimes foreign feel, only make a trip out here all the more memorable and meaningful.

PLANNING YOUR TIME

You could easily spend five days to a week in this region, hiking the canyons and exploring the ruins, following native guides to out-of-the-way sights, searching for handmade treasures

HIGHLIGHTS

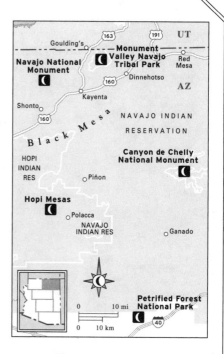

◖ Navajo National Monument: Stand on the edge of sacred Tsegi Canyon and gaze at an ancient city rising out of the flaking, reddish-pink rock, hidden and forgotten in a natural alcove above a green-and-white swipe of bottomland aspen forest (page 190).

◖ Monument Valley Navajo Tribal Park: Drive the sandy red-dirt loop around a barren valley populated by jutting, crumbling stone giants, an awe-inspiring landscape rooted deeply in the American imagination (page 193).

◖ Canyon de Chelly National Monument: Hike to the White House Ruin along a precipitous rock trail hewn out of the cliffside, past a Navajo farm and into the shade of cottonwoods below the sheer canyon walls, circled endlessly by ravens and silence (page 195).

◖ Hopi Mesas: Take a quiet walk through the oldest continually inhabited village on the continent, where past and present bleed together and thousand-year-old traditions are a part of everyday life (page 197).

◖ Petrified Forest National Park: Walk among the smooth-rock remains of a swampy forest, now a parched land strewn with reminders of the earth's unfathomable age and a desert decorated with pastel blues and pinks (page 200).

LOOK FOR ◖ TO FIND RECOMMENDED SIGHTS, ACTIVITIES, DINING, AND LODGING.

and touring all the parks and monuments; however, a long weekend would suffice to hit all of the essentials and to gain an unforgettable impression of Indian Country.

One of the most important things to remember while traveling in Indian Country is that the Navajo and Hopi Nations are on **daylight saving time,** unlike the rest of Arizona. That means that from March through November, the reservations observe Mountain Daylight Saving Time, while the rest of Arizona observes Mountain Standard Time (MST) all year.

GETTING THERE AND AROUND

It's relatively easy to navigate Northeastern Arizona, as long as you have a steady vehicle and a good map. Remember that the distances between stations, much as it was in the old days of the territory, are far, for the most part, so it's important to take advantage of off-road respite when it presents itself.

To reach the high desert railroad towns and the sights nearby, stick to I-40, which is well signed for tourist sights. To reach the Navajo and Hopi reservations from the west,

NAVAJO & HOPI COUNTRY

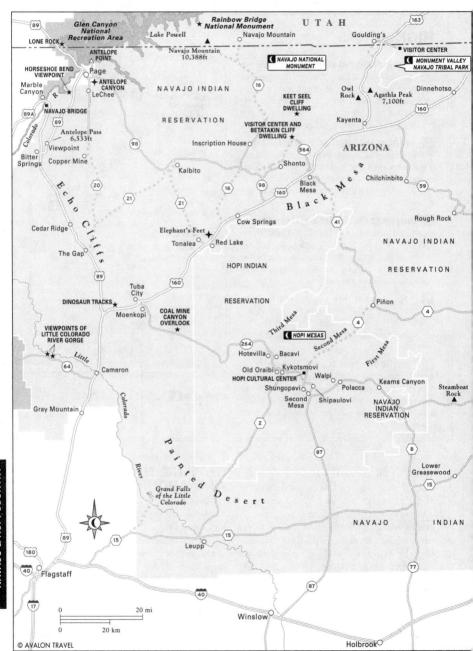

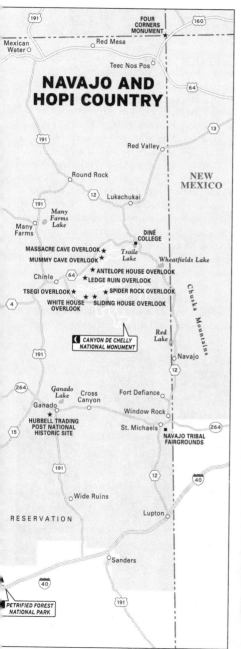

NAVAJO AND HOPI COUNTRY

NEW MEXICO

take Highway 89 north from I-40 at Flagstaff to Cameron, at the entrance to the Navajo Nation. Past Cameron, turn east on Highway 160, which will take you through Tuba City and Kayenta, past the Navajo National Monument and Monument Valley Navajo Tribal Park. Take Highway 191 south from Highway 160 east of Kayenta to reach Chinle and Canyon De Chelly National Monument. From there take Highway 191 farther south to Ganado and the Hubbell Trading Post, and then head east on Highway 264 to Window Rock, the Nation's capital.

If you're entering the Nation from the east take Indian Road 12 north to Window Rock from I-40 and then go north and west to hit the sights.

Hopiland can be reached from the west by way of State Highway 264 from Highway 160 at Tuba City and Moenkopi; from the east, pick up State Highway 264 at Window Rock.

The best map of this area is the American Automobile Association's (AAA) *Indian Country Guide Map.*

The moon rises over Monument Valley in Navajoland.

NAVAJO & HOPI COUNTRY

The Navajo Nation

Though it has been visited by tourists regularly for more than a century, the 27,000-square-mile Navajo Nation still feels like the American outback. This is one of the most isolated, undeveloped regions in the country, a land of red-dirt roads, scrubby gray-green sweeps of arid plane, and pink-rock spires reaching for the persistent, glaring blue-white sky. To visit "Indian Country" one must enter without expectations, and be open and ready for sudden bolts of strange beauty and spiritual recognition.

The appeal of the sprawling Nation is primarily scenic. Understanding this, the Diné have not exploited their homeland for the sake of more dollars and euros. The comforts are few and far between, and the landscape is all the better for it. Moreover, the land here is sacred in a very real sense to the Diné: This is where they live; it is not a tourist attraction but a homeland, a birthright, and a cathedral.

Respectful visitors will find this seemingly empty land to be full of wonder.

But then again the Nation isn't as remote as it seems. Just as it was before paved highways traversed the land, a trip to the reservation today is a journey between springs. The few population centers have all grown up naturally where stores of cool water flow beneath the otherwise parched high desert—semi-green places like Tuba City, Kayenta, Chinle, and Window Rock, the Nation's capital on the eastern border. These towns, while not much to look at—they are no more than dusty accumulations of houses and businesses along the highway, the minor accomplishments of humans dwarfed even more in this land of great rock giants—offer the usual chain hotels (though nearly all rooms are on the expensive side) and some homegrown restaurants serving foods unique to the region.

There are rare opportunities here to go beyond—beyond time when you contemplate

natural hideouts in the rocks of Canyon de Chelly

THE DINÉ

The Diné (the name the Navajo give to themselves, meaning "The People") are the largest and most populous Native American nation. They migrated down from Canada, with their Apache brethren, to the Colorado Plateau about a century before the Spanish arrived from the south, and lived a seminomadic life of hunting, gathering, and raiding that sometimes had them at odds with their neighbors who were sedentary, pueblo-dwelling farmers.

After contact with the Spanish and the Pueblos, the Diné also became pastoralists and farmers, one of many occasions when these resilient people borrowed from another culture to expand their own. As the anthropologist Edward T. Hall explains: "In their natural state all people are highly adaptable, but the Navajos seem to be the most adaptable people on earth – not simply in adapting to new technologies...but in their ability to live with, even absorb into their society, people who are different."

The Nation's modern story is largely one of survival in the face of government antagonism and neglect. In 1863, Col. Kit Carson was sent in to exert government control over the Navajo, loosing a brutal campaign to round-up what remained of the tribe and forcibly march them some 300 miles toward isolation and death at Fort Sumner, New Mexico Territory. This event, called the "Long Walk" in Navajo lore, remains an indelible scar on the collective heart of the Diné, a before-and-after dividing line in the Nation's modern history. About 8,000 Navajo were interred at Fort Sumner; four years later, when the tribe returned to Navajoland, some 5,000 remained.

After years of extreme privation, they eventually returned to their adapting ways, becoming very successful pastoralists, weavers, and artists. They were encouraged and helped by the white traders who found worldwide markets for high-quality Navajo crafts and brought modern goods to the remote reservation. The Diné have thrived and reproduced more than any other Native American group and now, less than 150 years after the Long Walk, they number 298,000 (about 180,000 of whom live on the reservation).

Still, today, despite the presence of large mineral and energy mining operations on their lands, nearly half of all Diné families live below the federal poverty line, and many still live without modern conveniences most of us take for granted. For some this economic reality comes about because they choose to live a traditional Navajo existence; for others it is more about the lack of jobs and opportunity on the reservation, whose economy is often compared to that of a Third World country. Those who leave the reservation often do so to attend college in Flagstaff, Tempe, Tucson, and Albuquerque. Education remains one of the best future hopes for the Nation and a source of pride and advocacy for Navajo leaders. According to a Comprehensive Economic Development Strategy for the Navajo Nation released in 2007, more than 75 percent of female Navajo high school students graduate every year, and 69 percent of males graduate annually. There are some 5,000 Navajo females enrolled in college, and 2,340 Navajo men enrolled in college.

the abandoned cities hanging from the cliffs of Navajo National Monument and Canyon de Chelly, and beyond reality as you watch the sun set over Monument Valley, surrounded by an alien but all too familiar beauty.

For shoppers, collectors, and treasure hunters, the Nation probably has the most working artists this side of Santa Fe. The best and most memorable items—famous Navajo rugs, overlay jewelry, baskets, pottery—can be found and purchased on the artist's doorstep, but you have to keep your eyes open for homemade signs out in all that vastness.

As guests of the Diné, tourists are expected to be respectful and follow a few simple but nonnegotiable rules of the reservation. One should not, however, overreact to these rules in a way that keeps you from interacting with the

NAVAJO & HOPI COUNTRY

friendly and fascinating Navajo people. If you simply remember that you are not in a living diorama—that these are real people with real lives to live—then you should be fine. Think about how you'd feel if strangers showed up and started photographing your house. That being said, it is never appropriate to photograph Diné individuals or their property without first obtaining permission. The federal parks and monuments are an exception, though there are farms in Canyon de Chelly that you can't photograph. This is a hard-and-fast rule, so don't even try it. If you do, expect to have your camera gear confiscated. Also, even though the reservation may seem wild and open at times, it's not appropriate to drive off-road or across the land. The land here provides many a Diné family's livelihood, and it should not be disturbed by visitors. If you are invited to witness a religious ceremony of some kind, all due respect is expected—take off your hat and watch silently, as you would a Catholic mass. Drugs and alcohol are not allowed anywhere on the reservation.

CAMERON

If you're heading north on U.S. 89 from Flagstaff to the Nation, the **Cameron Trading Post** (877/221-0690), while usually crowded with folks on their way to the Grand Canyon, makes for a handy first stop for gas and snacks and a look at the beautiful old bridge that crosses Little Colorado Gorge. There's also a restaurant, a hotel, shops, and a gallery to browse.

TUBA CITY AND VICINITY

The Navajo call it *Tonaneesdizi* (Weaving Water or Water Scattered), due to its many life-giving, underground natural springs that coax greenery out of the rocky ground and make this small town a kind of dusty oasis. For centuries an agricultural center for the Hopi (who would run from the mesas to nearby Moencopi to tend their corn), in the late 1800s the area was settled by Mormons. They named their town after a Hopi leader called Tuuvi, who had become a Latter-day Saint and invited others to

Painted Desert on the Navajo Nation near Tuba City

© TIM HULL

NAVAJO & HOPI COUNTRY

settle here. In 1903 the federal government sent off the settlers because the town was on part of the expanded Navajo Reservation. Today Tuba City, with a population of about 9,000 residents, serves as the administrative and cultural center of the western portion of the reservation. Its location at the junction of Highway 264 and U.S. 160 and proximity to the essential Navajo National Monument makes it a natural stop for travelers. Nearby you can witness the marks ancient beasts have left on the landscape. Tuba City may not look like much—it isn't, really—but there are a few places to eat and stay, and, of course, trading posts to browse.

Sights

Approaching Tuba City from the west (from Highway 89 north from Flagstaff to U.S. 160 east), you'll drive through a wondrous stretch of **Painted Desert,** red, dusty-orange, and gray mounds rising above the ruins of washes, like the humped, craggy backs of buried dinosaurs, with not a shrub in sight. There are

A Navajo guide will show you dinosaur tracks for a fee.

several natural turnoffs along the road to take pictures of this strange landscape. In downtown Tuba City, you'll find the new **Explore Navajo Interactive Museum** (Main St. and Moenave Rd., 928/640-0684, www.explore navajo.com, call for hours, open seasonally). The museum offers interesting displays on Navajo history and culture, created with the assistance of Navajo scholars and artists.

About five miles west of Tuba City on U.S. 160 look for a sign that says **Dinosaur Tracks.** Turn north onto the dirt road and expect to be greeted by one of several Navajo guides who hang around the area, especially during the busy summer season. You can follow one of the friendly guides onto a great red-rock sandstone slab, where eons ago raptors and other creatures that walked this land when it was swampy and fertile were sealed forever in the stone. The guides, many of whom learned details about the tracks from Northern Arizona University archeologists working in the area, will spray water on the dozens of foot- and claw-prints to bring them out of the red rock

The tracks of dinosaurs are embedded in the red rock on this barren stretch of Navajoland.

NAVAJO & HOPI COUNTRY

while explaining exactly what you're seeing. Expect to tip $10–20 for the tour (it seems a bit excessive, but think about sitting out on that hot high desert all day). Off to the northeast look for the lush green hillsides where several Navajo families live off the natural springs for which this area is known. You can also usually find a few booths set up near the tracks selling Navajo crafts.

If you're visiting in October, don't miss the annual **Western Navajo Fair** held at the local fairgrounds, which always draws some great bands and vendors.

Shopping

The **Historic Tuba Trading Post** (Main St. and Moenave Rd., 928/283-5441, 8 A.M.–6 P.M. daily) in downtown Tuba City has been selling native crafts and a vast array of staples since the 1870s. It's still open, offering a great assortment of handmade jewelry, rugs, and other popular Indian Country souvenirs and collectibles. **Van's Trading Post** (928/283-5343, 8 A.M.–8 P.M. daily) along Highway 160 is like a lesser Wal-Mart, half grocery store and half other merchandise like clothing and furniture. There's a coin laundry next door, and a pawn shop is also operated on-site.

Accommodations and Food

The nicest hotel in Tuba City is the **Quality Inn Navajo Nation** (Main St. and Moenave Rd., 928/283-4545, www.qualityinntubacity .com, $78–113 d), right next to the Historic Tuba City Trading Post. The two-story hotel has clean rooms, a gift shop, and wireless Internet, and on the same property is the **Hogan Restaurant** (928/283-5260, breakfast, lunch, and dinner daily), a diner-style place that serves good burgers and fries and Navajo and Mexican favorites. Next door you can even get a cappuccino or a latte and check your e-mail at **Hogan Espresso** Internet cafe (no phone, 7 A.M. –9 P.M. Mon.–Thurs., 7 A.M. –7 P.M. Fri., and 9 A.M. –7 P.M. Sat.–Sun.)

The **Greyhills Inn** (928/283-6271 Ext. 142) is a hostel-style inn located next to Greyhills High School (just east of the junction off Highway 160), and is operated by students as part of a hotel management training program. For about $56 you can get a clean room with two queen beds in a remodeled dormitory. All rooms have TVs and are nonsmoking. You share bathrooms, a kitchen, and a lounge.

A note about reserving a room: Every room in town is booked weeks before the Western Navajo Fair, and expect to pay extra if you manage to book one.

Kate's Café (Edgewater Dr. and Main St., 928/283-6773, www.javansuch.com, 6 A.M.–10 P.M. Mon.–Fri., 7 A.M.–9 P.M. Sat.–Sun., $3–15) is a Navajo-owned restaurant serving Mexican and American food for breakfast, lunch, and dinner. It's inexpensive and delicious, with friendly staff and a comfortable atmosphere, located in the center of town near the Tuba Trading Post.

◧ NAVAJO NATIONAL MONUMENT

Though it's within the Navajo Reservation, beautiful **Tsegi Canyon** was once home to the *Hisatsinom,* ancestors of the Hopi. These Ancestral Puebloans (commonly called Anasazi) are credited with building the three cliffside villages in the canyon—some of the best-preserved and most awe-inspiring ruins in the Southwest. The Hopi, Navajo, Zuni, and Paiute cultures still consider this a sacred place, so only a few short hikes to promontories above the canyon are open to the general public. If you want to explore the area deeper, you can sign up to take guided hikes to two of the ruins with a park ranger.

Only the ruins of the village called Betatakin by the Navajo and Talastima by the Hopi are visible from the canyon rim, tucked in a south-facing natural rock alcove that kept the village cool in the summer and warm in the winter; just below the village is a large aspen forest. Deeper in is Keet Seel, an older and larger village than Betatakin and one of the largest cliff dwellings in the Southwest. It's called Kawestima by the

© TIM HULL

The Anasazi built this cliffdwelling in Tsegi Canyon, now part of Navajo National Monument.

Hopi. **Inscription House,** or Tsu'ovi, is also perched in the canyon, but has been closed to the public since the late 1960s.

Archeologists believe that the Kayenta Anasazi (one of three Ancestral Puebloan subgroups, along with the Chaco Anasazi and the Mesa Verde Anasazi) lived in the canyon as early as A.D. 950, with major building projects getting underway around A.D. 1250. But by A.D. 1300, for reasons only guessed at, all of the villages had been abandoned.

Visiting Navajo National Monument

The park is about 50 miles northeast of Tuba City and some 20 miles southwest of Kayenta. Approaching from either way on U.S. 160, take Route 564 nine miles to the park entrance. Unlike most parks and monuments off the reservation, admission here is free. The **Visitor Center** (928/672-2700, www.nps.gov/nava,

9 A.M.–5 P.M. daily, free) has a gift shop that sells books, T-shirts, hats, and small water bottles, as well as an interesting museum featuring everyday life items used by the Puebloans and found in their left-behind villages.

Just outside the visitors center there are three short hiking trails that allow for optimum viewing of the canyon. The one-mile round-trip **Sandal Trail** is paved and leads to an overlook perfect for viewing the village of Betatakin/Talastima sleeping in its alcove. It's steep going back up and should not be treated lightly just because it's short. Take water, especially in the summer. The 0.8-mile round-trip **Aspen Forest Overlook** descends about 300 feet to provide a good look at the forest below the village, but you can't see the ruins; the **Canyon View Trail** leads 0.6 miles round-trip to a nice view of the ruins near the **Canyon View Campground.**

Camping

The Monument has two small campgrounds, free and open year-round, with spaces available first-come, first-served. Spaces have charcoal grills, but open campfires aren't allowed. The closest place to gear up is the rather spare Black Mesa Trading Post at the junction of Highway 160 and Route 564. It's a good idea to get supplies in either Tuba City or Kayenta before traveling to the Monument for an overnight visit.

Hiking

If viewing Betatakin from the ridgetop isn't enough for you, you can sign up to take one of two hikes into the canyon to explore the ruins up close. The hike to Betatakin is five miles round-trip and takes 3–5 hours to complete. A ranger guides you 700 feet down into the canyon and then on to the ruins. It is a mildly strenuous hike, but memorable for its scenery and not its difficulty. Two hikes are available daily in the summer May–September, leaving from the Visitor Center at 8:20 A.M. and 11:30 A.M. During the rest of the year one hike leaves from the center daily at 10 A.M. It's required that you sign up beforehand with the rangers at the Visitor Center if you want to take the hike.

The trek to **Keet Seel** (which roughly translates to "shattered house"), one of the best preserved ruins in the Southwest, is a bit more involved. It's a 17-mile round-trip trudge through the canyon bottomlands along what is not so much a trail but a meandering stream, complete with several small waterfalls, which you must cross dozens of times. You will get your feet wet early and often on this hike; there's no way to avoid it. Many hikers take along a sturdy pair of hiking sandals and change into them after descending 1,000 feet into the canyon. This is as close as you're likely to get to the ancients. When you arrive at the primitive campground within sight of the ruin, a ranger who lives in a Hogan-shaped log cabin nearby will take you on an hour-long tour of the ruin, which is reached by climbing a steep ladder into a cliffside rock alcove. The ranger will explain all about the Anasazi who once lived in this hidden canyon. Keet Seel was "discovered," for the Anglo world anyway, by the famous Southwestern ruin-hunter Richard Wetherill while he was chasing a runaway burro. If you are a world-champion hiker you might want to go in and out in the same day, but a stay overnight at the campground near the ruins is a memorable experience. (There is no water available at the campground, nor are fires allowed, but there is a compost toilet available.) You have to attend a short orientation meeting either the morning of your hike at 8 a.m. or the afternoon prior at 4 p.m. It's recommended that you arrive the day before so you can get an early start. Though there's a small hotel near the entrance road to the monument, the best place to stay is at one of the chains in Kayenta, about a half-hour drive from the monument. It's a good idea to purchase and pack all your backpacking supplies before arriving on the reservation, as there aren't any good places to do so nearby.

Reservations and a backcountry permit are required for Keet Seel and are limited to 20 persons per day. Call ahead for best results (928/672-2700). The hike is offered daily in the summer, May–September, but after September 15 it's offered every second weekend of the month only.

KAYENTA AND VICINITY

Called *Tohdineeshzhee* (Water Going in Different Directions) by the Diné, Kayenta is the town nearest to Monument Valley and is a good base for a visit to the northern reservation. John Wetherill, who with his brother Richard was one of the first Anglos to explore (and exploit) the Ancestral Puebloan ruins of Mesa Verde and Chaco Canyon, opened a trading post here in 1910. Today it's the only town on the reservation with a U.S.-style township government, home to about 5,000 people, mostly workers in the tourism industry and employees of the Peabody Coal Company, which operates the nearby Black Mesa Mine.

Shopping

The Navajo Arts and Crafts Enterprise has a retail store at Kayenta (928/697-8611, www.gonavajo.com) at the junction of Highways 160 and 163. Operated by Navajos, the company sells all kinds of handmade arts and crafts through a website and at retail outlets in a few reservation towns.

Accommodations and Food

Because it is so close to Monument Valley, there are several nice chain hotels in Kayenta, most of them along Highway 160 as you enter town. The **Hampton Inn** (928/697-3170, $100–150 d) is very comfortable and offers free wireless Internet, a pool, a gift shop, a restaurant, and free continental breakfast. The **Best Western Wetherill Inn** (U.S. 163, 928/697-3231, www.gouldings.com, $59–108 d) has a pool, wireless Internet, a gift shop, and a complimentary breakfast.

The **Blue Coffee Pot Café** (0.25 mile east of U.S. 160 and 163 junction, 928/697-3396, $4–8) serves good American, Navajo, and Mexican food. The **Burger**

King (928/697-3534) on Highway 160 (near the Hampton Inn) has the usual, with the added feature of a **Navajo Code Talkers** exhibit, which you can view as you chow down on your french fries. The ◖ **Amigo Café** (928/697-8448) just north of the junction serves Mexican and American food and is popular with the locals.

◖ MONUMENT VALLEY NAVAJO TRIBAL PARK

If there was any question that this is one of the most celebrated and enticing landscapes in the world, listen to the conversations around you as you visit Monument Valley—and you must visit Monument Valley, if only to prove that all the images you've seen are real. It sounds like "It's a Small World" out on this arid, dusty valley. Italian, German, British, and various Eastern European visitors gather at every lookout, looking for something distinctly Western, or American, in the iconic jutting red rocks.

It was the director John Ford who brought this strange, remote place to the world and made it a stand-in for the West's dueling freedom and danger, most memorably in *The Searchers*. Now, to drive around the park is to enter a thousand car commercials, magazine layouts, road films, and Westerns, a landscape that's comfortably, beautifully familiar even if you're seeing it for the first time.

The Navajo have thankfully not overdeveloped this sacred place—some would argue it's underdeveloped for its potential—so the only way to see the park without a Navajo guide is to drive the 17-mile unpaved loop road (6 A.M.–8:30 P.M. daily May–Sept., 8 A.M.–4:30 P.M. daily Oct.–Apr., $5), which has 11 pull-out scenic views of the rock spires and lonely buttes. Upon entering the park you'll get a map of the drive with the names of each "Monument"—names like Wetherill Mesa, John Ford's Point, and The Thumb. If you can manage it, it's worth arriving about an hour or so before sundown to see the sunset over the valley—you'll wonder how you got

© TIM HULL

dusk at Monument Valley

here, and you'll stay until the lights go out. Be warned, though, that with the constant stream of cars driving the dry, dirt road, the air tends to get dusty.

You're allowed to take photographs here, but only of the natural wonders. Remember to ask permission before taking pictures of any Navajos or their private property. If you want to do more than the drive, contact the **Visitor Center** (435/727-5874 or 435/727-5870, 6 A.M.–8 P.M. May–Sept., 8 A.M.–5 P.M. Oct.–Apr.) to find out about tour operators. Inside the Visitor Center there's a small museum of Navajo culture, a gift shop, and the **View Restaurant** (435/727-3468).

Camping

Campsites are available at the **Mitten View Campground** ($10 per night up to six people, $20 for up to 13, half price Oct.–Apr.) year-round, first-come, first-served. Each site has a table, a grill, a ramada, and trash can, and there are restrooms and coin-operated showers. No hookups are available, but a dump station is open during the summer. Check in at the Visitor Center to get a campsite.

Goulding's Lodge

This compound just outside the park features a hotel with luxury amenities, a campground, a museum, and a trading post selling Navajo crafts. It keeps the name of the first trader to settle in the valley, Harry Goulding, who opened a trading post here in 1928, exchanging staples for Navajo jewelry and rugs. The story goes that in the late 1930s Goulding himself went to Hollywood to convince Ford to come to Monument Valley to film *Stagecoach*.

◖ Goulding's Lodge (435/727-3231, www .gouldings.com, $175–187 d summer, $73–95 d winter) has 62 rooms and 8 family-friendly, multi-room suites with cable TV and DVD players. There's an indoor swimming pool and exercise room, and you can even rent one of the many classic Westerns available and watch it in your room. The **Stagecoach Dining Room** serves American and Navajo

food for breakfast, lunch, and dinner. The well-equipped **Goulding's Campground** offers tent sites for $22 per night and full hookup sites for $36 per night. A camping cabin with a TV, kitchen, and bathroom is available for $69 per night. There's also a convenience store, gas station, coin laundry, car wash, and an indoor pool at the campground.

Goulding's offers tours of the Monument with Navajo guides for $35 (everyone over 8 years old) for 2.5 hours, $45 for 3.5 hours, and $80 per person for an all-day excursion, which includes a cookout lunch.

Four Corners Monument

About 70 miles east on Highway 160 from Kayenta is the only place (928/871-6647, 8 A.M.–5 P.M. Sept.–May, 7 A.M.–8 P.M. June–Aug., $3) in the U.S. where, if you do a little bit of Twister-style contorting, you can exist briefly in four states at once—Arizona, Colorado, New Mexico, and Utah. You're not likely to stay long after you take the obligatory picture. In the summer months there are usually Navajos and others set up selling crafts.

CHINLE AND VICINITY

Like most town names on the arid Navajo Reservation, Ch'inlih refers to moisture, in this case "Water Flowing." There isn't much here for the tourist save a few chain hotels and the gateway to Canyon de Chelly. Chinle has been a center for canyon visitors since the early 20th century, when the famous trader Lorenzo Hubbell operated a stagecoach from the train stop at Gallup to bring tourists to see the ancient cliff dwellings and the other wonders of the canyon.

Accommodations and Food

Chinle makes a good base for exploring the canyon, offering a **Best Western** (928/674-5875, www.canyondechelly.com, $100–120 d) with a pool and restaurant, and a **Holiday Inn** (928/674-5000, www.holiday-inn.com, $100–150 d) with the same. About 14 miles north is **Many Farms,** where you can stay in a dormitory-style hostel run by students. Back in Chinle, there's a small store with a **Subway** inside at the Highway 191 junction, and the ubiquitous **Basha's** supermarket on the main drag sells groceries.

Near the Visitor Center on Canyon de Chelly National Monument is the **Thunderbird Lodge** (3.5 miles east of U.S. 191 on Indian Route 7, 928/674-5841, $65–77 d winter, $102–106 d summer) offers Southwestern-style rooms with Navajo flourishes, a cafeteria-style restaurant, Internet, and tours of the canyon with Navajo guides. Also on the Monument is the **Cottonwood Campground,** a free, first-come, first-served campground with running water and flush toilets in the summer only.

◖ CANYON DE CHELLY NATIONAL MONUMENT

The short but steep hike down a skinny trail hewn out of petrified pink sand dunes to the **White House Ruin** in Canyon de Chelly is one of the highlights of a visit to Indian Country. The trail is the only route to the sandy, shady canyon bottomlands that you can take without a guide, and it offers a rare chance to see Anasazi ruins up close and on your own. Once on the canyon bottom, you pass a traditional Navajo hogan and farm, and the canyon walls, streaked with purple, black, and orange, rise hundreds of feet. Hawks and ravens can be seen circling overhead, black and brown dots high in the bright blue sky. Cavelike hideouts built by natural forces in sandstone alcoves call for you to rest and sit back in their cool shade. Cottonwoods, willows, and peach trees grow in the bottomlands, while piñon pine, juniper, scrub oak, cholla, and prickly pear cling to the sides of the precipitous trail, a dusty-green set against the reddish-pink of the de Chelly Sandstone. While you can also take two scenic drives to see all the canyon's wonders, there is no substitute for hiking in.

Visiting Canyon de Chelly

The Visitors Center (928/674-5500, www .nps.gov/cach, 8 A.M.–5 P.M. daily, free) is a good place to start your visit. Here you can

© TIM HULL

Canyon de Chelly National Monument

the Anasazi White House Ruin in Canyon de Chelly

find out about guided tours (a ranger will give you a comprehensive list if you ask), learn about the history and science of the canyon, and browse a small bookstore stocked well with volumes on the Southwest and the Colorado Plateau. A map of the park's scenic drives is available here for free.

If you plan on hiking the 2.5-mile round-trip trail to the White House Ruin, pick up the trailhead at the **White House Overlook,** the fourth signed stop along the 37-mile round-trip **South Rim Drive.** This route will also take you to the **Spider Rock Overlook,** where you can see the eponymous 800-foot red-rock spire. The 34-mile round-trip North Rim Drive should be done by anyone interested in ruins, as the **Ledge Ruin** and **Antelope House Ruin** are both visible from overlooks.

HUBBELL TRADING POST NATIONAL HISTORIC SITE

When you walk into the rustic building in **Ganado** that has housed the Hubbell Trading Post (928/755-3475, www.nps.gov/hutr,

8 A.M.–6 P.M. in summer, 8 A.M.–5 P.M. in winter, $2 adults over 16 for Hubbell Home Tour) since 1876, you expect to enter a museum or a typical visitors center. Instead, you enter a working trading post that looks much like it did 100 years ago, still selling crafts and staples, still an important commercial spot to the Diné. The area has a fascinating history, and this is the best place to learn about the impact white traders—J. L. Hubbell and his family the most famous and beloved among them—had on Navajo life ways and the reservation economy. You can tour the homestead with a ranger or with a self-guided tour book, and peek into the Hubbell Home, laden with Navajo rugs, old books, and original paintings by the famous artist E. A. Burbank. There's also a small museum and bookstore operated by the National Parks Service.

WINDOW ROCK

The capital of the Navajo Nation is a lot like the other population centers in Navajoland: small, utilitarian, and surrounded by scenery that dwarfs the man-made buildings. The famous rock, a 200-foot-high red sandstone monument with an unlikely 47-foot-diameter wind- and water-chipped hole in it (called *Tseghahodzani* by the Navajo, roughly translating to "The Rock With the Hole In It") stares down from behind the Navajo Tribal Government offices and can be easily viewed. The town has been the center of the Navajo Nation government since the 1930s, and you can tour the **Navajo Nation Council Chambers** and browse the 58,000-square-foot **Navajo Library, Museum, and Visitors Center** (928/871-7941, 8 A.M.–8 P.M. Tues.–Fri., 8 A.M.–5 P.M. Mon. and Sat.) to learn more about Navajo history and life on the reservation. In the shadow of Window Rock is the **Window Rock Navajo Tribal Park** (928/871-6647, 8 A.M.–5 P.M. daily, free), which honors Navajo veterans.

The **Navajo Nation Fair** (928/871-6478) is held every year on the first weekend after Labor Day, swelling the town's population. Don't count on getting a hotel reservation during this event.

Shopping

The headquarters of the **Navajo Arts and Crafts Enterprises** (928/871-4090, 9 A.M.–5 P.M. Mon.–Fri.) and a well-stocked outlet are located east of the junction of Highway 264 and Indian Route 12. The **Chi Hoo Tso Indian Market** at the junction of Route 264 and Indian Route 12 has food booths and artists selling crafts and all sorts of other stuff.

Accommodations and Food

The **Quality Inn Navajo Nation Capital** (48 W. Hwy. 264, 928/871-4108, $64–83 d) offers Wireless internet and a full breakfast. The **Diné Restaurant** inside the Quality Inn (928/871-4108, $10–14) serves American and Navajo food for breakfast, lunch, and dinner and is a popular spot with the locals.

Tourist Information

Contact the **Navajo Tourism Department** (P.O. Box 663, Window Rock, AZ 86515, 928/810-8501, www.discovernavajo.com) for advice and information about traveling in this region.

Hopiland

When you visit Hopi, you step out of normal time into a kind of sacred time in which the *Hisatsinom* still speak to their modern-day descendants, the "People of Peace," and the lessons and stories of the ancients still guide and rule life in the 21st century, the dawning of which has mostly been ignored around Hopiland.

The Hopi are a very religious, conservative people on the whole, and what they really want, it seems, is to be left alone to mark their sacred time and grow their small plots of corn in their washes and valleys—which is a Hopi religious rite in itself. Signs are everywhere on Hopiland pleading with visitors to show respect for the present in this land that seems so rooted in the past. Go to Hopiland if you want to have a quiet, spiritual experience

touring crumbling villages occupied for centuries, interacting with the friendly and creative people whose direct and well-remembered ancestors built and lived in most of the spectacular Pueblo ruins around Indian Country, and searching for artistic treasures built on patterns and narratives laid down before time began.

◖ HOPI MESAS

The Hopis live on three remote mesas on the southern tip of **Black Mesa,** a separate reservation carved out of the southeast portion of Navajoland. There are 10 villages on the mesas, numbered east to west, and the farming community of Moencopi near Tuba City is also considered part of Hopi. Just to the east is Keams Canyon, the center

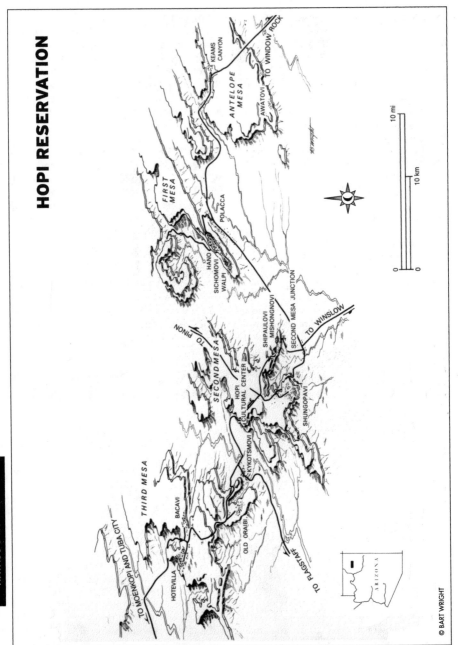

HOPI RESERVATION

© BART WRIGHT

of the federal government's presence on the reservation.

The Hopis do not allow any photography, sketching, or recording on Hopi land, and they don't like it when you enter their villages without first asking a village leader or at least someone at a craft store or gallery. Talk to the folks at the Hopi Cultural Center if you have any questions about the rules. Be respectful, and remember, as it is with the Navajos, the Hopi people are living their lives, not participating in an anthropological experiment. Don't bring any drugs or alcohol onto the reservation, and don't take any pottery shards off of it.

First Mesa

Polacca, just below First Mesa, is one of the younger villages on Hopi, founded in 1890. There are many Hopi and Tewa potters living in Polacca. If you're interested in buying direct from the artists, keep a look out for hand-made signs outside of homes. Next you'll come to **Hano,** founded in the 1680 after the Pueblo Revolt by Tewas from the New Mexico. The Hopi said the fleeing Tewas could stay in exchange for their vigilance in keeping enemies and attackers off the Mesa trails. Hano is the home of the famous Tewa potter **Nampeyo;** in the early 1900s, Fred Harvey convinced Nampeyo to move to the Grand Canyon to demonstrate pottery making for tourists, living in a kind of live diorama at the famous Mary Colter–designed "Hopi House." The area is still a center of pottery making, and artists directly related to Nampeyo—who is credited, even as a Tewa, with beginning a renaissance in Hopi pottery and thus creating a major modern art form and economy—still reside and work here, selling pottery out of their homes.

Just above Hano is **Sichomovi,** founded in 1750 by citizens of **Walpi.** This village has running water and electricity, unlike Walpi, a time warp at the very edge of the mesa founded in the 1600s when villagers moved up the mesa from their village below to escape the predations of their neighbors. The Snake Dance—with real rattlesnakes gathered from around the Mesas—a ritual popular in both the lore

of ethnology and that of Southwestern tourism, is still performed here semiannually but is not usually open to outsiders. If you want to walk through Walpi, stepping back in time hundreds of years, you can arrange for a tour in Sichomovi at **Ponsi Hall** (928/737-2262, 9 A.M.–3 P.M. daily in summer, 10 A.M.–3 P.M. daily in winter, $8 adults, $5 kids under 16).

Second Mesa

Head east on Highway 264 to Second Mesa, where the **Hopi Cultural Center** (928/734-2401, www.hopiculturalcenter.com, 8 A.M.–5 P.M.) has a small museum ($3) featuring blown-up photographs of Hopiland taken in the 19th and early 20th centuries, and displays on Hopi culture. Also on the complex are a restaurant serving traditional Hopi dishes, a hotel, and a few excellent shops. The village of **Shongopavi** on Second Mesa is believed to have been the first Hopi village.

Third Mesa

The village of **Oraibi,** also called Old Oraibi, on Third Mesa sits on what is considered to be the oldest inhabited ground in North America. Twenty-four families still live in the village, which sits at the edge of the mesa and looks out over the hazy flatland sea below. There's no electricity, no running water. "Our elders want no webbing above us and nothing buried in the ground," a Hopi woman who had been born and raised in the village explained. Some villagers have installed solar panels on the roofs of their small homes—each one built next to or on top of the ruin of an older one—to bring a little modern comfort. There are several kivas in the village that look exactly like those seen in the *Hisatsinom* ruins, with their rough ladders sticking out of their trap-door entrances, except these are still in use. A walk around this village, in which people have made lives since at least A.D. 1100, is a strangely humbling experience. You may come away from it wondering why most of us think we need so much stuff to live that elusive good life. Stop in at **Hamana So-o's Arts and Crafts** (928/206-6392) at the entrance to the village before walking around. The friendly couple there will tell you about the history of the village and give you a few rules of etiquette. The villages of **Hotevilla, Bacavi,** and **Kykotsmovi** are also on Third Mesa.

Shopping

The Hopis are world-renowned for their pottery, baskets, overlay jewelry, and kachina dolls. There are dozens of artists on the Hopi reservation making and selling collectible, museum-quality crafts. Look for homemade signs on homes in most of villages advertising crafts for sale. There are also several galleries and shops on Hopiland, including **Gentle Rain Designs** on Third Mesa (Hwy. 264 and Rte. 2, 928/734-8535). On Second Mesa check out the ❰ **Hopi Arts and Crafts Co-Op Guild** (928/734-2463) near the Hopi Cultural Center, and **Shungopavi Village,** which has several galleries worth perusing, including **Hopi Silver Arts and Crafts** (928/734-6695) near the entrance to the village on Highway 264.

Accommodations and Food

There are few services on Hopi, but it isn't far from any of the Navajo towns, and it's close to the High Desert towns as well.

The **Hopi Cultural Center on Second Mesa** is a hotel ($95–100 d Mar.–Oct., slightly cheaper in winter), and restaurant (6 A.M.–9 P.M. daily in summer, 7 A.M.–8 P.M. in winter) that serves American and Hopi food for breakfast, lunch, and dinner. The **Hotevilla Village Co-Op Store** on Third Mesa (928/734-2350) has a convenience store with a gas station, and **The Kykotsmovi Village Store** on Third Mesa (928/734-2456) has a deli and a gas station. **McGee's Store and Café** in Keams Canyon (928/738-2295) has food, arts and crafts, and a gas station.

Information and Services

In case of an emergency, the **Hopi Health Center** (928/937-6000) is located at Keams Canyon, open to non-Indians for emergencies only.

The High Desert

HOLBROOK AND VICINITY

Long ago, by most accounts, Holbrook was a rough and violent cowboy town, then it profited, like everything else in this region, from the railroad and Route 66, back when tourists would necessarily stay a while. These days it's not much more than a convenient gateway and stopover for those visiting the nearby Petrified Forest National Park and Indian Country, offering several chain hotels and mostly fast food. For those interested in both the history of the old and modern west, a trip to the **Navajo County Historical Society's museum** (100 E. Arizona St., 928/524-6558 or 800/524-2459, 8 A.M.–4 P.M., free) in the 1880s Navajo County Court House is a must. Donations are encouraged and rewarded by free chips of petrified wood. It's a strange, crowded place without a lot of context—you feel like you're wandering around

an abandoned government building after the population has died out. Sitting in the old jail, used until the 1970s and still decorated with the graffiti and sketches of its former inmates, is an eerie, almost thrilling experience.

Accommodations and Food

There are a number of chain hotels off I-40 in and around Holbrook, most of them located on Navajo Boulevard, the town's main drag, including a comfortable **Holiday Inn Express** (1308 E. Navajo Blvd., 928/524-1466, $99–119 d) with a small indoor pool, wireless Internet, and continental breakfast.

❰ PETRIFIED FOREST NATIONAL PARK

What once was a swampy forest frequented by ancient oversized reptiles is now a blasted scrubland strewn with multicolored, quartz-

a boulder covered with petroglyphs in the Painted Desert

an ancient log at Petrified Forest National Monument

wrapped logs some 225 million years old, each one possessing a smooth, multicolored splotch or swirl seemingly unique from the rest. You can walk among the logs on several easy, paved trails and view a small ruin and petroglyph-covered rocks (best with binoculars, but there are viewing scopes provided). Then, driving through the pastel-hued badlands of the **Painted Desert,** which, seen from a promontory along the park's 28-mile scenic drive, will take your breath away, stop at the **Painted Desert Inn Museum.** The historical interest in this pueblo revival–style structure is more modern than primordial. Redesigned by Mary Colter, the great genius of Southwestern style and elegance, the Inn was a restaurant and store operated by the Fred Harvey Company just after World War II, and before that it was a rustic, out-of-the-way hotel and taproom built from petrified wood. There's a gift shop and bookstore at the inn now, and you can walk through it and

gaze at the evocative, mysterious murals, full of Hopi mythology and symbolism, painted by Fred Kabotie, the great Hopi artist whom Colter commissioned to decorate the inn's walls. The park's proximity both to a major railroad stop at Winslow and Route 66 have made it a popular Southwestern tourist attraction since the late 19th century, and the lore and style of that golden age of tourism pervades the park with a pleasant nostalgia, adding an extra, unexpected dimension to the overwhelming age all around you.

Visiting the Park

Approaching the park (928/524-6228, www.nps.gov/pefo, 7 A.M.–6 P.M. in summer until Oct. 27, then 8 A.M.–5 P.M. daily, $10 per vehicle for 7 days) from the east, take I-40 to U.S. 180 from Holbrook to south entrance, past numerous shops featuring all things petrified. A paved road leads 28 miles north through the park, past several pull-over points of interest, back to I-40. From the east take I-40 Exit 311 to the north entrance, then head south through the park.

There are two **visitors centers,** one at the south entrance and one at the north, both showing a short movie about the park and passing out free maps of all the stops. At the south entrance there's a ◖ **Fred Harvey Company** restaurant that serves delicious fried chicken, Navajo tacos, and other road-food favorites in a cool Route 66 retro dining room.

WINSLOW AND VICINITY

Winslow has little to inspire a visit, but this small, ex–Route 66, ex-railroad town shouldn't be skipped altogether if you happen to be in the area. Much of its historic downtown remains intact, if not too busy, and there are a few off-track treasures to be found if you have time to walk around. The town seems committed to celebrating the fact that its name appeared in the song "Take It Easy," an Eagles hit co-penned by Jackson Brown. There are

LA POSADA: THE LAST OF THE FRED HARVEY RAILROAD HOTELS

Now owned by Winslow Mayor Allen Affeldt and his wife, the brilliant painter Tina Mion (whose paintings fill the arched hallways of the hotel), **La Posada** (303 E. Second St., Winslow, 928/289-4366, www.laposada.org, $99-149 d) has been beautifully restored and is a reminder of the days when traveling to Indian County was a chic journey taken by the rich and famous and anybody else who could afford it.

This was largely the result of the genius of Fred Harvey. He and his "Harvey Girls" – well-trained, professional young women imported to the West to serve train passengers at Harvey's restaurants along the Sante Fe Railroad's right-of-way – made a trip to this barren, underdeveloped High Desert, an experience quite beyond merely comfortable. The Harvey Company lunch counters and hotel restaurants offered fine dining and fresh, gourmet food prepared by European chefs, and the unmatched service of the Harvey Girls, many of whom ended up marrying their customers. Using the talents of Mary Jane Colter, the Southwest's greatest designer and architect, Harvey built fine hotels in decidedly out-of-the-way places, allowing passengers on the Sante Fe's popular Los Angeles to Chicago line to live well even when stopping in Needles, California and Winslow, Arizona.

Harvey also hired attractive, educated young women who knew their history, anthropology, ethnology, and art as tour guides. Intrepid tourists who could pay, in 1936, about $45 per person were packed into tough but comfortable limousines, along with gourmet box lunches, and driven in style deep into Indian Country. These trips were famously called "Indian Detours" – three days of adventure and exoticism billed, according to surviving marketing pamphlets, as "the most distinctive motor cruise service in the world...off the beaten path in the Great Southwest."

The crowning achievement of the Harvey-Colter partnership came just before the stock market crash with the construction of La Posada (The Resting Place) at Winslow, the headquarters of the Santa Fe Railroad and the gateway to Arizona's Indian Country. Howard Hughes, Sinatra, Einstein, Bob Hope and the Crown Prince of Japan all stayed in Colter's masterpiece, along with many other luminaries of American and world culture. They'd hop off the train right outside the hotel, tour the Hopi Mesas and Navajoland, and then return to the comfort of the Spanish Hacienda-inspired hotel and supreme comfort in a land that knew little of that luxury.

Eventually train travel fell off, and Route 66 gave way to the Interstate, and not long after that everything was the same, and the Inter-

reminders in nearly every business, and there's even **Standin' on the Corner Park** along the town's main street, featuring a statue of a man doing just that. The primary reason to stop in Winslow is to see **La Posada,** Southwestern architect Mary Colter's masterpiece and a place where Fred Harvey–style outback elegance is kept alive.

The **Winslow Chamber of Commerce** (101 E. Second St., 928/289-2434) offers tourist information and advice on the region.

Accommodations and Food

There are several chain hotels and fast-food places off the Interstate at Winslow for those in a hurry.

The independently operated **☾ Turquoise Room** (928/289-2888, breakfast, lunch, and dinner, $9–20, reservations required for dinner) just off La Posada's main lobby serves "Fred Harvey–inspired" meals like prime rib and steak, and a wild blend of gourmet dishes under the heading "Native American–inspired

state Territory became the province of chain hotels and those restroom machines that blow hot air on your hands. La Posada closed in the 1950s, and sat disused until a few years ago when Affeldt and Mion saved it. Now the old hotel has been restored beyond even its original glory, and it's booked up often with guests from all over the world. The hotel is es- pecially popular these days with Europeans, many of whom rent motorcycles and ride the remainders of Route 66, searching for some lost version of the "America Road." Affeldt said recently that the irony of this phenom- enon was not lost on a modern-day celebrity visitor to La Posada: the "Easy Rider" himself, Peter Fonda.

© TIM HULL

Mary Jane Colter's masterpiece, La Posada Hotel in Winslow

© TIM HULL

A meteor fell to earth long ago, creating a big hole in the high desert plain.

nouvelle cuisine." Interesting, creative, and delicious is what that means. This is the best restaurant in the region and one of the best in the state.

METEOR CRATER

This sight (I-40 and Meteor Crater Rd., 928/289-4002, www.meteorcrater.com, 7 A.M.–7 P.M. in summer, 8 A.M.–5 P.M. the rest of the year, $15 adults, $13 seniors, $7 kids 6–17) though impressive, is perhaps best viewed prior to a visit to, say, Canyon de Chelly or the Grand Canyon. Compared to those nearby attractions, built over eons by wind and water, this pock-mark has trouble looking like more than the hole in the ground it is, isolated on the plain off I-40.

But an interesting hole nonetheless, being born from the collision of an asteroid with the high desert grasslands about 50,000 years ago. A small museum examines this and other meteor sites, and the role the crater and its owner played in the study of meteors and in the U.S. space program. There's a 10-minute film about the crater, and rangers offer short interpretive hikes, but insist that you have closed-toe shoes to tag along. A **Subway**

on-site sells sandwiches and drinks. Unlike most of the outdoor sights in Arizona, Meteor Crater is run by a private corporation. The $15 adult entrance price is, truthfully, a bit steep for what you get.

HOMOLOVI RUINS STATE PARK

Here in the grasslands south of the Hopi Mesas, along the banks of the Little Colorado River, the *Hisatsinom* (Anasazi) settled for a time in the 1200s and 1300s before moving on northward to Black Mesa. A few crumbling rock aggregations and beds of shattered pottery, what remains of decades of looting, sit on dry promontories. It's a beautiful place, windy and desolate, but the ruins aren't as impressive as others nearby. This is a good place to start a trip to Indian Country and its ancient castles; afterward, it pales in comparison to what you've already seen. The visitors center (I-40 to U.S. 87 North at Winslow, 928/289-4106, 8 A.M.–5 P.M. daily, $5 per car) has one of the best selections of books on Southwestern archaeology in the region and offers a chance to converse with Hopi artists. There are picnic tables and trails on the park, and a 53-site campground ($10–20) with hookups and showers.

THE GRAND CANYON AND THE ARIZONA STRIP

There's a reason why Arizona's official nickname is "The Grand Canyon State." Any state with one of the true wonders of the world would be keen to advertise its good luck.

The canyon must simply be seen to be believed. If you stand for the first time on one of the South Rim's easily accessible lookouts and don't have to catch your breath for the surprise and wonder, you might need to check your pulse. Staring into the canyon brings up all kinds of existential questions; its brash vastness can't be taken in without conjuring some big ideas and questions about life, humanity, God. Take your time here—you'll need it.

The more adventurous can make reservations, obtain a permit, and enter the desert depths of the canyon, taking a hike, or even a mule ride, to the Colorado River, or spending a weekend trekking rim-to-rim with an overnight at the famous Phantom Ranch, deep in the canyon's inner gorge. The really brave can hire a guide and take a once-in-a-lifetime trip down the great river, riding the roiling rapids and camping on its serene beaches.

There are plenty of places to stay and eat, many of them charming and historic, on the canyon's South Rim. If you decide to go to the high, forested, and often snowy North Rim, you'll drive through a corner of the desolate Arizona Strip, which has a beauty and a history all its own.

Water-sports enthusiasts will want to make it up to the far northern reaches of the state to the Glen Canyon Recreation Area to do some water skiing or maybe rent a houseboat, and anyone interested in the far end of America's engineering prowess will want to see Glen Canyon Dam, holding back the once-wild Colorado.

© TIM HULL

THE GRAND CANYON AND THE ARIZONA STRIP

UTAH

Santa Clara
St. George
Washington
Beaver Dam Mountains
Beaver Dam Mountains Wilderness
59
Cottonwood Point Wilderness
15
Hildale
Colorado City
Cane Beds
Kaibab
Littlefield
VIRGIN RIVER CANYON RECREATION AREA
Paiute Wilderness
389
Vermilion
Mesquite
15
▲ Mt Bangs 8,012ft
ARIZONA
Pipe Spring National Monument
Virgin River
Virgin Mountains
Hurricane Cliffs
Kanab
Grand Canyon-Parashant National Monument
Hidden Canyon
Plateau
Grand Wash Cliffs Wilderness
Poverty Mountain 6,791ft ▲
Mount Trumbull
Mt Trumbull 8,028ft ▲
NEVADA
Shivwits
▲ *Mt Trumbull Wilderness*
Grand Canyon National Park
Mt Logan Wilderness
Supai
Parashant Canyon
Lake Mead National Recreation Area
★ TOROWEAP
HUALAPAI HILLTOP ■
Lake Mead
Mt Dellenbaugh 7,072ft
River
Aubrey Cliffs
Coconino
Lake Mead National Recreation Area
GRAND CANYON WEST ★
Sanup Plateau
Grand Canyon
Colorado
☾ **NORTH RIM**
18
★ **DIAMOND CREEK**
White Hills
Dolan Springs
Red Lake
Grand Wash Cliffs
Music Mountains
HUALAPAI INDIAN RESERVATION
Peach Springs Canyon
Mt Tipton Wilderness
▲ Mt Tipton 7,148ft
Peach Springs
Chloride
Truxton
✛ **GRAND CANYON CAVERNS**
66
93
Cerbat Mountains
Hackberry
Valentine
66
Peacock Mountains
Cottonwood Mountains
40
Seligman
Golden Valley
40
Kingman

© AVALON TRAVEL

0   10 mi

0   10 km

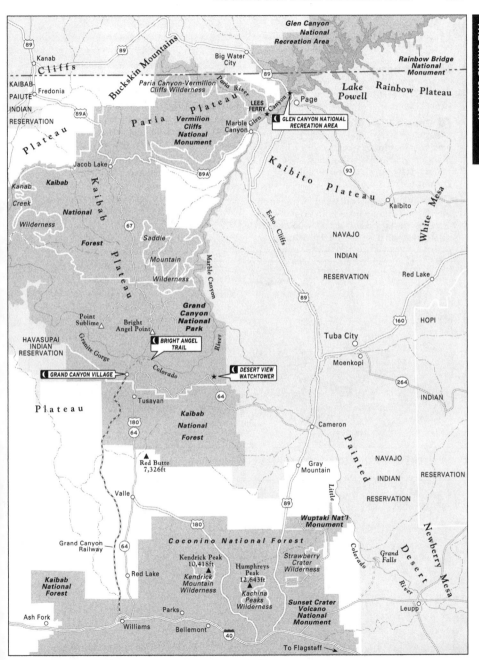

HIGHLIGHTS

◖ Grand Canyon Village: Stroll along an easy path with the vast canyon on one side and rustic, romantic architecture on the other (page 215).

◖ Desert View Watchtower: See one of architect Mary Colter's finest accomplishments – a rock tower standing tall on the edge of the canyon, its design based on mysterious Anasazi structures still standing in the Four Corners region (page 224).

◖ Bright Angel Trail: Don't just stand on the rim and stare – hike down Bright Angel Trail, the most popular trail on the South Rim, its construction based on old Native American routes. Or choose one of several additional trails to see the arid grandeur of the inner canyon (page 224).

◖ North Rim: Be one of the few visitors to drive through the Arizona Strip, climb to the forested Kaibab Plateau, and stand on the spectacular North Rim (page 231).

◖ Glen Canyon National Recreation Area: Rent a houseboat or fish the waters of Lake Powell, a man-made lake formed by the Glen Canyon Dam, a grand engineering feat that has drawn the unending ire of environmentalists (page 251).

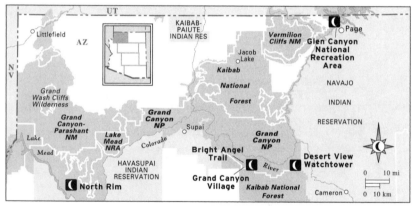

LOOK FOR ◖ TO FIND RECOMMENDED SIGHTS, ACTIVITIES, DINING, AND LODGING.

© TIM HULL

Gateways to the Canyon

Grand Canyon National Park, especially its South Rim, has some of the best accommodations in the entire national park system, but it's not always possible to get reservations. What's more, while the park's lodging rates are audited annually and generally compare favorably to those offered outside the park, it's possible to find excellent deals at one of several gateway towns around canyon country. Using one of these places as a base for a visit to the canyon makes sense if you're planning on touring the whole of the canyon lands and not just the park. Besides offering affordable and even a few luxurious places to stay and eat, these gateways are often interesting in their own right and deserving of some attention from the traveler, especially those interested in the history of this hard and spacious land.

CAMERON

About 50 miles north of Flagstaff along Highway 89, near the junction with Route 64 (the route to the park's east gate), the nearly 100-year-old **(Historic Cameron Trading Post and Lodge** (800/338-7385, www.cameron tradingpost.com, $99–179 d) is only about a 30-minute drive from the Desert View area of the park, a good place to start your tour. Starting from the east entrance you'll see the canyon gradually becoming grand. Before you reach the park, the Little Colorado drops some 2,000 feet through the arid, scrubby land, cutting through gray rock on the way to its marriage with the big river to create the **Little Colorado Gorge.** Stop here and get a barrier-free glimpse at this lesser chasm to prime yourself for what is to come, and there are usually plenty of booths set up selling Navajo arts and crafts and a lot of touristy souvenirs at two developed pull-offs along the road.

The Cameron Lodge is a charming and affordable place to stay, and is a perfect base for a visit to the Grand Canyon, Indian Country, and the Arizona Strip. It has a good restaurant, a Native American art gallery, a visitors center,

a huge trading post/gift shop, and an RV park. A small grocery store sells food and other staples if you don't want to eat at the restaurant, which serves American and Mexican favorites and, of course, huge heaping Navajo tacos. The rooms are decorated with a southwestern Native American style and are very clean and comfortable, some with views of the Little Colorado River and the old 1911 suspension bridge that spans the stream just outside the lodge. There are single-bed rooms, rooms with two beds, and a few suites that are perfect for families. The stone-and-wood buildings and the garden-patio, laid out with stacked sandstone bricks below the open-corridor rooms, create a cozy, historic setting and make the lodge a memorable place to stay. The vast, empty red plains of the Navajo Reservation spread out all around and create a lonely, isolated atmosphere, especially at night, but the rooms have TVs and cable and free wireless Internet, so you can be connected and entertained even way out here.

If you're visiting in the winter, the lodge drops its prices significantly during this less crowded touring season. In January and February, you can get one of the single-bed rooms for about $59 d.

WILLIAMS

This small historic town along I-40 (what used to be Route 66) is the closest Interstate town to Route 64, and thus has branded itself "The Gateway to the Grand Canyon." It has been around since 1874 and was the last Route 66 town to be bypassed by the Interstate (not until 1984). As a result, and because of a small resurgence over the last few decades owing to the rebirth of the Grand Canyon Railroad, Williams has a good bit of charm—the entire downtown area is on the National Register of Historic Places. It's worth a stop and an hour or two of strolling about, and there are a few good restaurants. It's only about an hour drive to the South Rim from Williams, so many consider it a convenient base for exploring the region.

© ELIZABETH JANG

Williams, on Route 66

Shopping

The **Turquoise Tepee** (114 W. Route 66, 928/635-4709, 10 A.M.–5 P.M. daily) has been selling top-shelf Native American arts and crafts, Western wear, and regional souvenirs for four generations. There's a lot to see in this store. The same goes for **Native America** (117 E. Route 66, 928/635-4600, 8 A.M.–10 P.M. in summer, 8 A.M.–6 P.M. winter), a Native American–owned shop with Hopi and Navajo arts and crafts.

Accommodations and Food

Williams has some of the most affordable independent accommodations in the Grand Canyon region, as well as several chain hotels.

It's difficult to find a better deal than the clean and basic **El Rancho Motel** (617 E. Route 66, 928/635-2552 or 800/228-2370, $35–73 d), an independently owned motel on Route 66 with few frills save comfort, friendliness, and a heated pool open in season. The **Canyon Country Inn** (442 W. Route 66, 928/635-2349, $39–85 d) is a basic and affordable place to

stay, offering free continental breakfast and high-speed Internet. The **Grand Canyon Railway Hotel** (235 N. Grand Canyon Blvd., 928/635-4010, $89–179 d) stands now where Williams' old Harvey House once stood. It has a heated indoor pool, two restaurants, a lounge, a hot tub, a workout room, and all sorts of other amenities.

A northland institution with some of the best steaks in the region, **⟨ Rod's Steak House** (301 E. Route 66, 928/635-2671, www.rods-steakhouse.com, 11 A.M.–9:30 P.M. Mon.–Sat., closed Sun., $11.50–35) has been operating at the same site for more than 50 years. The food is excellent, the staff is friendly and professional, and the menus are shaped like steers. The **Pine Country Restaurant** (107 N. Grand Canyon Blvd., 928/635-9718, 5:30 A.M.–9:30 P.M. daily, $5–10) is a family-style place that serves good food and home-made pies. Check out the beautiful paintings of the Grand Canyon on the walls. **Twisters '50s Soda Fountain and Route 66 Café** (417 E. Route 66, 928/635-0266, 8 A.M.–close daily, $5–10) has 1950s music and decor and delicious diner-style food, including memorable root-beer floats. Even if you're not hungry, check out the gift shop selling all kinds of road-culture memorabilia.

Information and Services

Stop at the **Williams-Kaibab National Forest Visitor Center** (200 W. Railway Ave., 928/635-1418 or 800/863-0546, 8 A.M.–6:30 P.M. daily in summer, 8 A.M.–5 P.M. daily fall and winter) for information about Williams, Grand Canyon, and camping and hiking on the Kaibab National Forest.

TUSAYAN

Just outside Grand Canyon National Park's south gate, along Route 64, Tusayan is a collection of hotels, restaurants, and gift shops that has grown side-by-side with the park for nearly a century. The village makes a good base for a visit to the park, especially if you can't get reservations at any of the in-park lodges. While there are a few inexpensive chain hotels here, a stay in Tusayan isn't on the whole cheaper than lodging in the park, but there are many more places to eat here than there are inside the park.

Sights

Tusayan is perhaps best known as the home of the **National Geographic Grand Canyon Visitors Center** (Rte. 64, 928/638-2468, www.explorethecanyon.com, 8:30 A.M.–8:30 P.M. Mar.–Oct., 10:30 A.M.–6:30 P.M. Nov.–Feb., $12.75 over age 11, $9.59 ages 5–10, under 5 free), which has been a popular first stop for park visitors since the 1980s. Truth be told, even with the recent addition of the corporate logo–clad **Grand Canyon Base Camp #1,** an interactive display of canyon history, lore, and science, the center wouldn't be worth a stop if not for its **IMAX Theater.** The colossal screen shows the 35-minute movie, *Grand Canyon— The Hidden Secrets,* every hour. The most popular IMAX film ever (some 40,000,000 people have reportedly seen it), the movie is quite thrilling, affording glimpses of the canyon's

more remote corners that feel like real time, if not reality. If you can afford the admission price, this is a fun way to learn about what you're about to see in the park. If you're going budget, skip it and drive a few miles north, where you're likely to forget about both movies and money while staring dumbfounded into that gorge.

Shopping

Approaching the South Rim along Route 64, stop for a bit at The **Double Eagle Trading Company** (Rte. 64, 877/635-5393, www.double eagletrading.com), in Valle. Double Eagle is a real trading post, in that the proprietors still trade directly with some Native American artisans. There is an excellent selection of Native American arts and crafts here, and all kinds of other curiosities, mostly of the Old West variety, to keep you browsing for a while.

Accommodations

Before you reach Tusayan you'll pass through Valle, a tiny spot along Route 64, where you'll find one of the better deals in the whole canyon region. The **Red Lake Campground and Hostel** (8850 N. Rte. 64, 800/581-4753, $15 per person, per night), where you can rent a bed in a shared room, is a basic but reasonably comfortable place sitting lonely on the grasslands; it has shared bathrooms with showers, a common room with a kitchen and a TV, and an RV park ($20) with hookups. If you're going super-budget, you can't beat this place, and it's only about 45 minutes from the park's south gate. The **Red Feather Lodge** (Rte. 64, 928/638-2414, www.redfeatherlodge.com, $69–159), though more basic than some of the other places in Tusayan, is a comfortable, affordable place to stay with a pool, hot tub, and clean rooms.

The **Grand Hotel** (Rte. 64, 928/638-3333, www.grandcanyongrandhotel.com, $99–199 d), resembling a kind of Western-themed ski lodge, has very clean and comfortable rooms, a pool, hot tub, fitness center, and a beautiful lobby featuring a Starbucks coffee kiosk. The **Best Western Grand Canyon Squire**

Inn (Rte. 64, 928/638-2681, www.grand canyonsquire.com, $75–195 d) has a fitness center, pool and spa, salon, game room, and myriad other amenities, so many that it may be difficult to get out of the hotel to enjoy the natural sights.

Food

Try **Canyon Star Restaurant** (928/638-3333, 7–10 A.M. and 11:30 A.M.–10 P.M., $10–25) inside the Grand Hotel, which serves Southwestern food, steaks, and ribs, and features a saloon in which you can belly up to the bar on top of an old mule saddle (it's not that comfortable). **The Coronado Room** (928/638-2681, 5–10 P.M. $15–28) inside the Grand Canyon Squire Inn serves tasty steaks, seafood, Mexican-inspired dishes, and pasta. If you're craving pizza after a long day exploring the canyon, try **We Cook Pizza & Pasta** (Rte. 64, 928/638-2278, $7–15) for an excellent, high-piled pizza pie.

The Grand Canyon

The reality of the Grand Canyon is often suspect even to those standing on its rim. "For a time it is too much like a scale model or an optical illusion," wrote Joseph Wood Krutch, a great observer and writer of the Southwest. The canyon appears at first, Krutch added, "a man-made diorama trying to fool the eye." It is *too big* to be immediately comprehended, especially to those visitors used to the gaudy, lesser wonders of the human-made world.

Once you accept its size and you understand that a river, stuffed with the dry rocks

© ELIZABETH JANG

the canyon's South Rim

and sand of this arid country, bore this mile-deep, multicolored notch in the Colorado Plateau, the awesome power of just this one natural force—its greatest work here spread before you—is bound to leave you breathless and wondering what you've been doing with your life heretofore. If there is any sacred place in the natural world, this is surely one. The canyon is a water-wrought cathedral, and no matter what beliefs or preconceptions you approach the rim with, they are likely to be challenged, molded, cut away, and revealed like the layers of primordial earth that compose this deep rock labyrinth, telling the history of the planet as if they were a geology textbook for new gods. And it is a story in which humans appear only briefly, if at all.

Visitors without a spiritual connection to nature have always been challenged by the Grand Canyon's size. It takes mythology, magical thinking, and storytelling to see it for what it really is. The first Europeans to see the canyon, a detachment of Spanish conquistadores sent by Coronado in 1540 after hearing rumors of the great gorge from the Hopi, at first thought the spires and buttes rising from the bottom were about the size of a man; they were shocked, upon gaining a different perspective below the rim, that they were as high or higher than the greatest structures of Seville. Human comparisons do not work here. Preparation is not possible.

Never hospitable, the canyon has nonetheless had a history of human occupation for around 5,000 years, though the settlements have been small and usually seasonal. It was one of the last regions of North America to be explored and mapped. The first expedition through, led by the one-armed genius John Wesley Powell, was completed at the comparatively late date of 1869. John Hance, the first Anglo to reside at the canyon, in the 1880s explored its depths and built trails based on ancient native routes. A few other tough loners tried to develop mining operations here, but soon found out that guiding avant-garde canyon tourists was the only sure financial bet in the canyon lands. It took another 20 years or so and the coming of

the railroad before it became possible for the average American tourist to see the gorge.

The black and white statistics, though impressive, do little to conjure an image that would do the canyon justice. It is some 277 river miles long, beginning just below Lee's Ferry on the north and ending somewhere around the Grand Wash Cliffs in northwestern Arizona. It is 18 miles across at its widest point, and an average of 10 miles across from the south to the north rim. It is a mile deep on average; the highest point on the rim, the north's Point Imperial, rises nearly 9,000 feet above the river. Its towers, buttes, and mesas, formed by the falling away of layers undercut by the river's incessant carving, are red and pink, dull green and green-tipped, though these basic hues are altered and enhanced by the setting and rising of the sun, changed by changes in the light, becoming throwaway works of art that astound and then disappear.

It is folly, though, to try too hard to describe and boost the Grand Canyon. The consensus, from the first person to see it to yesterday's gazer, has generally amounted to "You just have to see it for yourself." Perhaps the most poetic words ever spoken about the Grand Canyon, profound for their obvious simplicity, came from Teddy Roosevelt, speaking on the South Rim in 1903. "Leave it as it is," he said. "You cannot improve on it; not a bit."

PLANNING YOUR TIME

The ideal South Rim–only trip lasts three days and two nights (with the first and last days including the trip to and from the rim). This amount of time will allow you to see all the sights on the rim, to take in a sunset and sunrise over the canyon, and even do a day hike or a mule trip below the rim. If you just have a day, about five hours or so will allow you to see all the sights on the rim and take a very short hike down one of the major trails. If you include a North or West Rim excursion, add at least one or two more days and nights. It takes at least five hours to reach the North Rim from the South, perhaps longer if you take the daily

Fortunately, there are guard rails at the South Rim viewing points.

shuttle from the south instead of your own vehicle. The West Rim and the Hualapai and Havasupai Indian Reservations are some 250 miles from the South Rim over slow roads, and a trip to these remote places should be planned separately from one to the popular South Rim. The most important thing to remember when planning a trip to the canyon is to plan far ahead, even if you're just, like the vast majority of visitors, planning to spend time on the South Rim. Six months' advance planning is the norm, longer if you are going to ride a mule down or stay overnight at Phantom Ranch in the inner canyon.

Seasons

At about 7,000 feet, the South Rim has a temperate climate, warm in the summer months, cool in fall, and cold in the winter. It snows in the deep winter and often rains in the late afternoon in late summer. Summer is the park's busiest season—and it is *very* busy—four or five million visitors from all over the world will be your companions, which isn't as bad as

some make it out to be. People-watching and hobnobbing with fellow tourists from the far corners of the globe become legitimate enterprises if you're so inclined. During the summer months (May–September) temperatures often exceed 110°F in the inner canyon, which has a desert climate, but cool by 20–30°F up on the forested rims. There's no reason for anybody to hike deep into the canyon in summer. It's not fun, and it is potentially deadly. It is better to plan a marathon trek in the fall.

Fall is a perfect time to visit the park: it's light-jacket cool on the South Rim and warm but not hot in the inner canyon, where high temperatures during October range 80–90°F, making hiking much more pleasant than it is during the infernal summer months. October or November are the last months of the year during which a rim-to-rim hike from the North Rim is possible, as rim services shut down by the end of October and the only road to the rim is closed by late November, and often before that, from winter snowstorms. It's quite cold on the North Rim during October, but on the

South Rim it's usually clear, cool, and pleasant during the day and snuggle-up chilly at night. Fall is a wonderful time to be just about anywhere in Arizona. A winter visit to the South Rim has its own charms. There is usually snow on the rim January–March, contrasting beautifully with the red, pink, and dusty green canyon colors. The crowds are thin and more laid-back than in the busy summer months. It is, however, quite cold, even during the day, and you may not want to stand and stare too long at the windy, bone-chilling viewpoints.

SOUTH RIM

The South Rim is by far the most developed portion of Grand Canyon National Park (928/638-7888, www.nps.gov/grca, open 24 hours a day, seven days a week, $25 per car for seven-day pass) and should be seen by every American, as Teddy Roosevelt once recommended. Here you'll stand side by side with people from all over the globe, each one breathless on their initial stare into the canyon and more often than not hit suddenly with an altered perception of time, human history, even God. Don't let the rustic look of the buildings fool you into thinking you're roughing it. The park's easy, free shuttle service will take you all over if you don't feel like walking the level rimside trails. The food here is far above average for a national park. The restaurant at El Tovar offers some of the finest, most romantic dining in the state, and all with one of the great wonders of the world just 25 feet away.

◖ Grand Canyon Village

Though you wouldn't want to make a habit of it, you could spend a few happy hours at

---

THE CANYON AND THE RAILROAD

Musing on the Grand Canyon in 1902, John Muir lamented that, thanks to the railroad, "children and tender, pulpy people as well as storm-seasoned travelers" could now see the wonders of the West, including the Grand Canyon, with relative ease. It has always been for storm-seasoned travelers to begrudge us tender, pulpy types a good view. As if all the people who visit the canyon every year couldn't fit in its deep mazes and be fairly out of sight. Muir came to a similar conclusion after actually seeing the railway approach the chasm: "I was glad to discover that in the presence of such stupendous scenery they are nothing," he wrote. "The locomotives and trains are mere beetles and caterpillars, and the noise they make is as little disturbing as the hooting of an owl in the lonely woods."

It wasn't until the Sante Fe Railroad reached the South Rim of the Grand Canyon in 1901 that the great chasm's now famous tourist trade really got going. Prior to that travelers faced an all-day stagecoach ride from Flagstaff at a cost of $20, a high price to pay for sore bones and cramped quarters.

For half a century or more the Santa Fe line from Williams took millions of tourists to the edge of the canyon. The railroad's main concessionaire, the Fred Harvey Company, enlisted the considerable talents of Arts and Crafts designer and architect Mary Jane Colter to build lodges, lookouts, galleries and stores on the South Rim that still stand today, now considered to be some of the finest architectural accomplishments in the entire national parks system. Harvey's dedication to simple, high-style elegance and Colter's interest in and understanding of Pueblo Indian architecture and life ways created an artful human stamp on the rim that nearly lives up to the breathtaking canyon it serves.

The American love affair with the automobile, the rising mythology of the go-west road trip, and finally the Interstate Highway killed train travel to Grand Canyon National Park by the late 1960s. In the 1990s, however, entrepreneurs revived the railroad as an excursion and tourist line. Today, the Grand Canyon Railroad carries more than 250,000 passengers to the South Rim every year, a phenomenon that has reduced polluting automobile traffic in the cramped park by some 10 percent.

THE GRAND CANYON

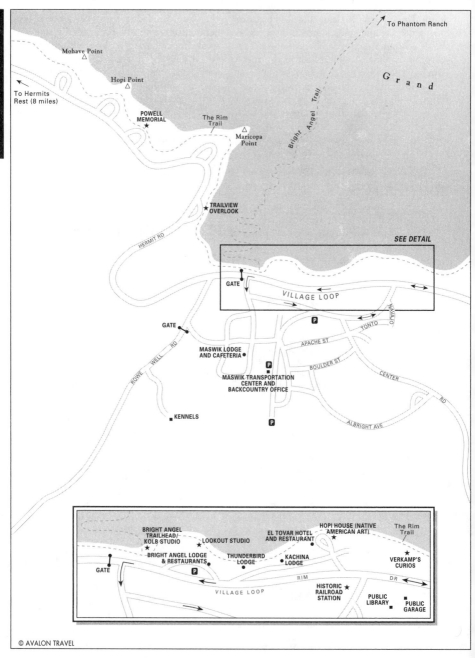

To Phantom Ranch

Mohave Point
△

Hopi Point
△

To Hermits
Rest (8 miles)

POWELL
MEMORIAL
★

The Rim
Trail

Maricopa
Point
△

Grand

Bright Angel Trail

★ TRAILVIEW
OVERLOOK

HERMIT RD

SEE DETAIL

GATE

VILLAGE LOOP

NAVAJO

GATE

P

TONTO

APACHE ST

ROWE WELL RD

MASWIK LODGE
AND CAFETERIA ■

BOULDER ST

CENTER

P

MASWIK TRANSPORTATION
CENTER AND
BACKCOUNTRY OFFICE ■

RD

■ KENNELS

ALBRIGHT AVE

P

BRIGHT ANGEL
TRAILHEAD/
KOLB STUDIO
★

LOOKOUT STUDIO
★

EL TOVAR HOTEL
AND RESTAURANT
★

HOPI HOUSE (NATIVE
AMERICAN ART)
★

The Rim
Trail

BRIGHT ANGEL LODGE
& RESTAURANTS ●

THUNDERBIRD
LODGE ●

KACHINA
LODGE ●

VERKAMP'S
CURIOS ★

GATE

P

RIM

DR

VILLAGE LOOP

HISTORIC ★
RAILROAD
STATION

PUBLIC
LIBRARY ■

■ PUBLIC
GARAGE

© AVALON TRAVEL

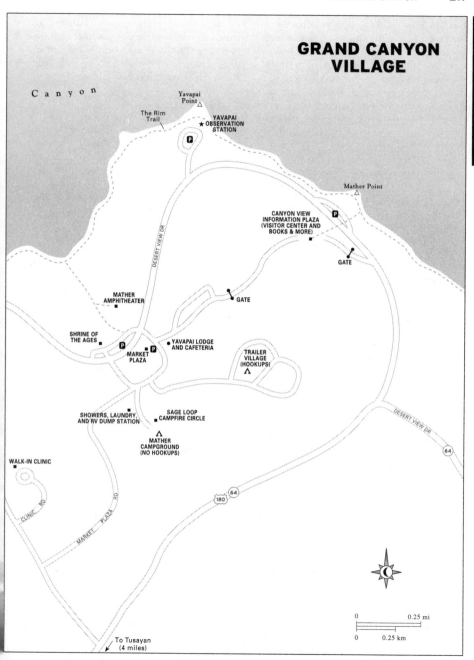

GRAND CANYON VILLAGE

Canyon

Yavapai Point △

The Rim Trail

★ YAVAPAI OBSERVATION STATION

🅿

Mather Point △

CANYON VIEW INFORMATION PLAZA (VISITOR CENTER AND BOOKS & MORE)

🅿

GATE

DESERT VIEW DR

MATHER AMPHITHEATER

GATE

SHRINE OF THE AGES

🅿 🅿

MARKET PLAZA

YAVAPAI LODGE AND CAFETERIA

TRAILER VILLAGE (HOOKUPS) ⋀

DESERT VIEW DR

SHOWERS, LAUNDRY, AND RV DUMP STATION

SAGE LOOP CAMPFIRE CIRCLE

⋀ MATHER CAMPGROUND (NO HOOKUPS)

64

WALK-IN CLINIC

CLINIC RD

MARKET PLAZA RD

{180} 64

0   0.25 mi

0   0.25 km

To Tusayan (4 miles)

Grand Canyon Village with your back to the canyon. Then again, this small assemblage of hotels, restaurants, gift shops, and lookouts offers some of the best view points from which to gaze comfortably at all that multicolored splendor. Here is a perfect vantage from which to spot the strip of greenery just below the rim called **Indian Gardens,** and follow with your eyes—or even your feet—the famous **Bright Angel Trail** as it twists improbably down the rim's rock face. Here you can also see some of the most interesting and evocative buildings in the state, all of them registered National Historic Landmarks. If you're just visiting for the day, you can drive into the village and park your car in the El Tovar parking lot or at a rather large, mostly dirt lot near the train depot. More often than not, especially in the summer, the El Tovar lot will be full. You can also park at the large lot at Market Plaza and then take the shuttle bus around the park. The Backcountry Information Office also has a rather large parking lot, the southern portion of which can accommodate RVs and trailers.

The Bright Angel Lodge

The village's central hub of activity, this rustic lodge was designed in 1935 by Mary Jane Colter to replace the old Bright Angel Hotel, built by John Hance in the 1890s, and the tent-city Bright Angel Camp which sat near the trail of the same name. The lodge resembles a rough-hewn hunting lodge constructed of materials found nearby and was meant to welcome not the high-toned traveler, but the middle-class tourist. In the lobby you'll see Colter's "geologic fireplace," a 10-foot-high re-creation of the canyon's varied strata. The stones were collected from the inner canyon by a geologist and then loaded on the backs of mules for the journey out. The fireplace's strata appear exactly the same as those stacked throughout the canyon walls, equaling a couple billion years of earth-building from bottom to rim.

In a room off the lobby there's a small museum with fascinating exhibits about Fred Harvey, Colter, and the early years of Southwestern tourism. The lodge includes a collection of small

cabins just to the west of the main building, and the cabin closest to the rim was once the home of **Bucky O'Neill,** an early canyon resident and prospector who died while fighting with Teddy Roosevelt's Rough Riders in Cuba.

El Tovar

Just east of the lodge is the South Rim's first great hotel and the picture of haute-wilderness style. Designed in 1905 by Charles Whittlesey for the Santa Fe Railroad, El Tovar has the look of a Swiss chalet and a log-house interior, watched over by the wall-hung heads of elk and buffalo; it is at once cozy and elegant. This Harvey Company jewel has hosted dozens of rich and famous canyon visitors over the last century, including George Bernard Shaw and presidents Teddy Roosevelt and William Howard Taft. On the rim side, a gazebo stands near the edge. While it is a wonderfully romantic building up close, EL Tovar looks even more picturesque from a few of the viewpoints along the Hermit Road, and you can really get a good idea of just how close the lodge is to the gorge seeing it from far away. Inside you'll find two gift shops and a cozy lounge where you can have a drink or two while looking at the canyon. The El Tovar's restaurant is the best in the park; it's quite pleasant to sink into one of the arts-and-crafts leather chairs in the rustic, dark-wood lobby.

Hopi House

A few steps from the El Tovar's front porch is Colter's Hopi House, designed and built as if it sat not at the edge of Grand Canyon but on the edge of Hopiland's Third Mesa. Hopi workers used native materials to build this unique gift shop and Native arts museum. The Harvey Company even hired the famous Hopi-Tewa potter Nampeyo to live here with her family while demonstrating her artistic talents, and by extension Hopi life ways, to tourists. This is one of the best places in the region for viewing and buying Hopi, Navajo, and Pueblo art (though most art is quite expensive), and there are even items on view and for sale made by Nampeyo's descendants.

© ELIZABETH JANG

Hopi House, a gift shop and arts museum, was built with native materials.

Lookout Studio

Mary Colter also designed the Lookout Studio west of the Bright Angel Lodge, a little stacked-stone watch house that seems to be a mysterious extension of the rim itself. The stone patio juts out over the canyon and is a popular place for picture taking. The Lookout was built in 1914 exactly for that purpose—to provide a comfortable but "indigenous" building and deck from which visitors could gaze at and photograph the canyon. It was fitted with high-powered telescopes and soon became one of the most popular snapshot scenes on the rim. It still is today, and on many days you'll be standing elbow to elbow with camera-carrying tourists clicking away. As she did with her other buildings on the rim, Colter designed the Lookout to be a kind of amalgam of Native American ruins and backcountry pioneer utilitarianism. Her formula of using found and native materials stacked haphazardly works wonderfully. When it was first built, the little stone hovel was so "authentic" that it even had weeds growing out of the roof. Inside, where you'll find books and canyon souvenirs, the studio looks much as it did when it first opened. The jutting stone patio is still one of the best places from which to view the gorge.

Kolb Studio

This 100-year-old wood house nearly hanging from the rim is significant not so much for its design but for the human story that went on inside. It was the home and studio of the famous Kolb Brothers, pioneer canyon photographers, moviemakers, river-rafters, and entrepreneurs. Inside there's a gift shop, a gallery, and a display about the brothers, who, in 1912, rode the length of the Colorado in a boat with a movie camera rolling. The journey resulted in a classic book of exploration and river-running, Emery Kolb's 1914 *Through the Grand Canyon From Wyoming to Mexico*. The Kolb Brothers were some of the first entrepreneurs at the canyon, setting up a photography studio, at first in a cave near the rim and then in this house, to sell pictures of tourists atop their mules as early as 1902. After a falling out, the younger Emery Kolb stayed on at the canyon until his death in 1976, showing daily the film of the brothers' river trip to several generations of canyon visitors.

THE GRAND CANYON

The Viewpoints

While the canyon's unrelenting vastness tends to blur the eyes into forgetting the details, viewing the gorge from many different points seems to cure this; however, there are some 19 named viewpoints along the South Rim Road, from the easternmost Desert View to the westernmost Hermit's Rest. Is it necessary, or even a good idea, to see them all? No, not really. For many it's difficult to pick out the various named buttes, mesas, side-canyons, drainages and other features that rise and fall and undulate throughout the gorge, and one viewpoint ends up looking not that different from the next. To really get the full experience, the best way to see the canyon viewpoints is to park your car and walk along the Rim Trail for a few miles, if not its whole length (if you get tired you can always hop on the free shuttle at any of its many stops), seeing the gorge from developed points all along, as well as from the trail itself. Driving to each and every viewpoint is not that rewarding and tends to speed up your visit and make you miss the subtleties of the different views. Consider really getting to know a few select viewpoints rather than trying to quickly and superficially hit each one. Any of the viewpoints along the Hermit Road and Desert View Drive are ideal candidates for a long love affair. That being said, the views from just outside El Tovar or the Bright Angel Lodge, right smack in the middle of all the bustling village action, are as gorgeous as any others, and it can be fun and illuminating to watch people's reactions to what they're seeing. In reality, there isn't a bad view of the canyon, but if you only have so much time, it's never a bad idea to ask a ranger at Canyon View Information Plaza or Yavapai Observation Station what their favorite viewpoint is and why. Everybody is going to have a different answer, but it stands to reason that those who actually *live* at the canyon are going to have a more studied opinion. The shuttle bus drivers are also great sources of information and opinions. Whatever you do, try to get to at least one sunset and one sunrise at one or more of the developed viewpoints; the canyon's

Teddy Roosevelt once recommended that the Grand Canyon should be seen by every American.

© ELIZABETH JANG

colors and details can get a bit monotonous after the initial thrill wears off (if it ever does), but the sun splashing and dancing at different strengths and angles against the multihued buttes, monuments, and sheer, shadowy walls cures that rather quickly.

As most South Rim visitors enter through the park's south entrance, it's no surprise that the most visited viewpoint in the park is the first one arrived at along that route—**Mather Point,** named for the first National Park Service Director, Stephen T. Mather. Mather Point, while crowded, offers a typically astounding view of the canyon and is probably the mind's-eye view that most casual visitors take away. It can get very busy here, especially in the summer. If you're going to the park's main visitors center, **Canyon View Information Plaza** (and you should), you'll park near here and walk a short paved path to the information plaza. At the viewpoint, you can walk out onto two railed-off jutting rocks to feel like you're hovering on the edge of an abyss, but you may have to stand in line to get right up to the edge. A good way to see this part of the park is to leave your car at the large parking area at Mather (which is often full, of course) and then walk a short way along the Rim Trail west to **Yavapai Point** and the excellent, newly refurbished **Yavapai Observation Station,** the best place to learn about the canyon's geology and get more than a passing understanding of what you're gazing at. It's a good idea to visit the Yavapai Observation Station before you hit any of the other viewpoints (unless you are coming in from the east entrance).

Yavapai Observation Station

First opened in 1928, this limestone-and-pine museum and bookstore (8 A.M.–6 P.M. in the winter and 8 A.M.–7 P.M. starting April 15 daily, free) hanging off the rim is the best place in the park to learn about the canyon's geology—it is a must-see for visitors interested in learning about what they are seeing. The building itself is of interest; designed by architect Herbert Maier, the stacked-stone structure, like Colter's buildings, merges with the rim itself to appear a forgone

and inevitable part of the landscape. The site for the station, which was originally called the Yavapai Trailside Museum, was handpicked by canyon geologists as the very best for viewing the various strata and receiving a rimside lesson on the region's geologic history and present. Inside the building, you'll find in-depth explanations and displays about canyon geology that are fascinating and easily understood. Too much of the introductory geology found in guidebooks and elsewhere is jargon-laden, confused and confusing and not very useful to the uninitiated. Not here: many of the displays are new and use several different approaches, including maps, photographs, and three-dimensional models—coupled with the very rocks and cliffs and canyons and gorges they're talking about right outside the windows—to create fascinating and easy-to-grasp lessons. Particularly helpful is the huge topographic relief map of the canyon inside the observation center. Spend some time looking over the map in detail and you'll get a giant's-eye view of the canyon that really helps you discern what you're seeing once you turn into an ant again outside on the ledge.

Hermit Road

March through November the park's free shuttle goes all the way to Mary Colter's **Hermit's Rest,** about seven miles from the village, along the park's western scenic drive, called the Hermit Road. It takes approximately two hours to complete the loop, as the bus stops at eight viewpoints along the way. On the return route, buses stop only at Mohave and Hopi Points. A few of the Hermit Road viewpoints are some of the best in the park for viewing the sunsets. To make it in time for such dramatic solar performances, get on the bus at least an hour before sunset. There is often a long wait at the Hermit's Rest Transfer Stop just west of the Bright Angel Lodge. The bus drivers will always be able to tell you when sunset is expected and the times are also listed in *The Guide* newspaper handed out as you enter the park.

Throughout 2008 and perhaps into 2009 the Hermit Road is set to undergo much-needed repairs and repaving, and it is scheduled to

THE GRAND CANYON

© TIM HULL

Mary Colter's Hermit's Rest gift shop and snack bar

be closed intermittently to all traffic. Before you visit the park you should call or check the park's website (www.nps.gov/grca/parkmgmt/hermit.htm) for updates about this project, which could potentially keep visitors from seeing the spectacular western section of the South Rim during construction.

Each of the Hermit Road lookouts provides a slightly different perspective on the canyon, whether it be a strange unnoticed outcropping or a brief view of the white-tipped river rapids far, far below. The first stop along the route is the **Trailview Overlook,** from which you can see the Bright Angel Trail twisting down to and across the plateau to overlook the Colorado River. The next major stop along the route is **Maricopa Point,** which provides a vast, mostly unobstructed view of the canyon all the way to the river. The point is on a promontory that juts out into the canyon over 100 feet. To the west you can see the rusted remains of the Orphan Mine, first opened in 1893 as a source of copper and silver—and, for a few busy years during the height of the Cold War, uranium. Consider

taking the 10- to 15-minute hike along the Rim Trail west past the fenced-off Orphan Mine and through the piney rim world to the next point, **Powell Point.** Here stands a memorial to the one-armed explorer and writer, John Wesley Powell, who led the first and second river expeditions through the canyon in 1869 and 1871. The memorial is a flat-topped pyramid, which you can ascend and stand tall over the canyon. You can't see the river from here but the views of the western reaches of the gorge are pretty good, and this is a strong candidate for a sunset-viewing vantage point. About a quarter of a mile along the rim trail from Powell Point is **Hopi Point,** which offers sweeping and unobstructed views of the western canyon. As a result, it is the most popular west-end spot for viewing the sun dropping red and orange in the west. North from here, across the canyon, look for the famous mesas named after Egyptian gods—Isis Temple, Horus Temple, and Osiris Temple. The next viewpoint heading west is **Mohave Point,** from which you can see the Colorado River and a few white-tipped rapids. Also visible from here are the 3,000-foot red-and-green cliffs that surround the deep side-canyon, appropriately named **The Abyss.-** Right below the viewpoint you can see the red-rock mesa called the Alligator. The last viewpoint before Hermit's Rest is **Pima Point,** a wide-open view to the west and the east, from which you can see the winding Colorado River and the Hermit Trail twisting down into the depths of the canyon.

Hermit's Rest

The final stop on the Hermit Road is the enchanting gift shop and resthouse called Hermit's Rest. As you walk up a path through a stacked-boulder entranceway, from which hangs an old mission bell, the little stone cabin comes into view. It looks as if some lonely hermit came out here and stacked rock upon rock until something haphazard but cozy rose off the rim; it is a structure familiar more to the world of fairy tales than to the contemporary world. Inside, the huge yawning fireplace, tall and deep enough to be a room itself, dominates the warm, rustic front room, where there are a few seats chopped out of stumps, a Navajo blanket or two splashing color against the gray stone, and elegant lantern-lamps hanging from the stones. Outside, the views of the canyon and down the Hermit's Trail are spectacular, but something about that little rock shelter makes it hard to leave.

Desert View Drive

One more Mary Colter construction—arguably her greatest—and a Puebloan ruin are located along Desert View Drive, the 25-mile eastern drive from the village. The viewpoints along this drive, which one ranger called the "quiet side of the South Rim," gradually become more desert-like and are typically less crowded. The free shuttle goes only as far as **Yaki Point,** a great place to watch the sunrise and near the popular South Kaibab Trailhead. Yaki Point is at the end of a 1.5-mile side road two miles east of Highway 180. The area is closed to private vehicles. Along Desert View Drive, make sure not to miss the essential **Grandview Point,**

where the original canyon lodge once stood long ago. From here the Grandview Trail leads below the rim. The viewpoint sits at 7,400 feet, about 12 miles east of the village and then a mile on a side road. It's considered one of the grandest views of them all, hence the name; the canyon spreads out willingly from here and the sunrise in the east hits it all strong and happy. To the east, look for the 7,844-foot monument called the Sinking Ship and to the north below look for Horseshoe Mesa. This is a heavily wooded area, so for the best view hike a bit down the Grandview Trail. The steep and narrow trail is tough, but if you're prepared to hike you can descend three miles to Horseshoe Mesa.

Moran Point, east of Grandview, is just eight miles south of Cape Royal (as the Condor flies) on the North Rim and offers some impressive views of the canyon and the river. The point is named for the great painter of the canyon, Thomas Moran, whose brave attempts to capture the uncapturable on canvas helped create the buzz that led to the canyon's federal protection. Directly below the left side of the point you'll see Hance Rapid, one of the largest on the Colorado. It's three miles away, but if you're quiet you might be able to hear the rushing and roaring. Farther on the Desert View Drive you'll come to **Lipan Point,** with its wide-open vistas and the best view of the river in the park. At Desert View, from the top of the watchtower, you'll be able to catch a faraway glimpse of sacred Navajo Mountain near the Utah-Arizona border, the most distant point visible from within the park.

Tusayan Museum and Ruin

The Tusayan Museum (9 A.M.–5 P.M. daily, free) has a small but interesting exhibit on the canyon's early human settlers. The museum is located near an array of 800-year-old Ancestral Puebloan ruins with a self-guided trail and regularly scheduled ranger walks. Since the free shuttle doesn't extend this far east, you have to drive to the museum and ruin; it's about 3 miles west of Desert View and 22 miles east of the village. It's worth the drive, though, especially if you're going to be heading to the Desert View section anyway (which you should). Though it hasn't been overly hospitable to humans over the eons, the oldest human-made artifacts found in the canyon date back about 12,000 years—little stick-built animal fetishes and other mysterious items. The displays in this museum help put human life on the rim and in the gorge in context, and the little ruin is fascinating. Imagine living here along the rim, walking everyday to the great gorge, tossing an offering of cornmeal into the abyss, and wondering what your hidden canyon gods were going to provide you with next.

(Desert View Watchtower

What is perhaps the most mysterious and thrilling of Colter's canyon creations, the Desert View Watchtower is an artful homage to smaller Anasazi-built towers found at Hovenweep National Monument and elsewhere in the Four Corners region, the exact purpose of which is still unknown.

The tower's high windy deck is reached by climbing the twisting steep steps winding around the open middle, the walls painted

with visions of Hopi lore and religion by Hopi artist Fred Kabotie. Pick up *The Watchtower Guide* free in the gift shop on the bottom floor for explanations on the meanings of the paintings and symbols. From the top of the watchtower, the South Rim's highest viewpoint, the whole arid expanse opens up, and you feel something like a lucky survivor at the very edge of existence, even among the crowds. Such is the evocative power, the rough-edged Romanticism, of Colter's vision.

(Bright Angel Trail

Hiking down the Bright Angel, you quickly leave behind the twisted greenery of the rim and enter a sharp and arid landscape, twisting down and around switchbacks on a trail that is sometimes all rock. Step aside for the many mule trains that go down this route, and watch for the droppings, which are everywhere. Because this trail is so steep, it doesn't take long for the rim to look very far away, and you soon feel like you are deep within a chasm and those rim-top people are mere ants scurrying about.

© TIM HULL

Colter's Desert View Watchtower at the Grand Canyon's South Rim

The most popular trail in the canyon owing to its starting just to the west of the Bright Angel Lodge in the village center, the Bright Angel Trail was once the only easily accessible corridor trail from the South Rim, and a $1 hikers' toll was charged by Ralph Cameron, who constructed the trail based on old Native routes. The trail's general route has always been a kind of inner canyon highway, as it is blessed with a few springs. The most verdant of these is Indian Gardens (for centuries exactly that), a welcome slip of green on an otherwise red and rocky land, about 4.5 miles down from the trailhead. Many South Rim visitors choose to walk down Bright Angel a bit just to get a feeling of what it's like to be below the rim.

If you want to do something a little more structured, the three-mile round-trip hike to the **Mile-and-a-Half Resthouse** makes for a good introduction to the steep, twisting trail. A little farther on is **Three-Mile Resthouse,** a six-mile round-trip hike. Both resthouses have water seasonally. One of the best day hikes from the South Rim is the nine-mile round-trip to beautiful **Indian Gardens,** a cool and green oasis in the arid inner canyon. This is a rather punishing day hike, and not recommended in the summer. Same goes for the just-over-12-mile round-trip trudge down to **Plateau Point,** from which you can see the Colorado River winding through the inner gorge. Unless you have somewhere you absolutely have to be, you'll want to consider getting a backcountry permit and camping below the rim rather than trying to do Plateau Point or even Indian Gardens in one day.

Hiking and Biking

Something about a well-built trail twisting deep into an unknown territory can spur even the most habitually sedentary canyon visitor to begin an epic trudge. This phenomenon is responsible for both the best and worst of the South Rim's busy recreation life. It is not uncommon to see hikers a mile or more below the rim picking along in high heels and sauntering blithely in flip-flops, not a drop of water between them.

It's best to go to the canyon prepared to hike, with the proper footwear and plenty of snacks and water. Just figure that you are, in all probability, going to want to hike a little. And since there's no such thing as an easy hike in Grand Canyon, going in prepared, even if it's just for a few miles, will make your hike infinitely more pleasurable. Also, remember that there aren't any loop hikes here: If you hike in a mile—and that can happen surprisingly quickly—you also must hike out (up) a mile.

RIM TRAIL

If you can manage a 13-mile, relatively easy walk at an altitude of around 7,000 feet, the Rim Trail provides the single best way to see all of the South Rim. The trail, paved for more than half its length, runs from Desert Drive's Pipe Creek Vista through the village and all the way to Hermit's Rest, hitting every major point of interest and beauty along the way. The trail gets a little tough as it rises a bit past the Bright Angel Trail Head just west of the village, and it turns to dirt west of Maricopa Point. It never gets too difficult, though, and would be considered an easy, scenic walk by just about anybody, kids included. But perhaps the best thing about the Rim Trail is that you don't have to hike the whole 13 miles—far from it. There are at least 16 shuttle stops along way, and you can hop on and off the trail at your pleasure.

SOUTH KAIBAB TRAIL

Steep but short, the 6.4-mile South Kaibab Trail provides the quickest, most direct South Rim route to and from the river. It's popular with day hikers and those looking for the quickest way into the gorge, and many consider it superior to the often-crowded Bright Angel Trail. The trailhead is located a few miles east of the village near Yaki Point, but it can be easily reached by shuttle bus on the Kaibab Trail Route. The 1.8-mile round-trip hike to **Ooh Aah Point** provides a great view of the canyon and a relatively easy hike along the steep switchbacks. **Cedar Ridge** is a three-mile round-trip hike down the trail, well worth it for the views of O'Neill Butte and Vishnu Temple. There is no water provided anywhere

HIKING GRAND CANYON – THE EASY WAY

One of the first things you notice while journeying through the inner canyon is the advanced age of many of your fellow hikers. It is not uncommon to see men and women in their 70s and 80s hiking along at a good clip, packs on their backs and big smiles on their faces.

At the same time, all over the South Rim you'll see warning signs about overexertion, each featuring a buff young man in incredible shape suffering from heat stroke or exhaustion, with the warning that most of the people who die in the canyon – and people die every year – are people like him. The point here is this: You need not be a wilderness expert or marathon runner to enjoy even a long, 27-mile, rim-to-rim hike through the inner canyon. Don't let your fears hold you back from what is often a life-changing trip.

There are several strategies that can make a canyon hike much easier than a forced march with a 30-pound pack of gear on your back. First of all, don't go in the summer; wait until September or October, when it's cooler, though still quite warm, in the inner canyon. Second, try your best to book a cabin or a dorm room at Phantom Ranch rather than camping. That way, you'll need less equipment, you'll have all or most of your food taken care of, and there will be a shower and a beer waiting for you upon your arrival. Also, for about $50 you can hire a mule to carry up to 30 pounds of gear for you, so all you have to bring is a day pack, some water, and a few snacks. This way, instead of suffering while you descend and ascend the trail, you'll be able to better enjoy the magnificence of this wonder of the world.

along the trail. If you are interested in a longer haul, the six-mile round-trip hike to **Skeleton Point,** from which you can see the Colorado, is probably as far along this trail as you'll want to go in one day, though in summer you might want to reconsider descending so far. Deer, bighorn sheep, and California condors are regularly seen along the South Kaibab Trail.

HERMIT TRAIL
Built by the Santa Fe Railroad as an antidote to the fee-charging keeper of the Bright Angel Trail, The Hermit Trail just past Hermit's Rest leads to some less visited areas of the canyon. This trail isn't maintained with the same energy as the well-traveled corridor trails are, and there is no potable water to be found. A good introduction to the trail is a jaunt down to the **Waldron Trail Junction,** just under three miles round-trip, where you'll see the remains of an old camp and a mescal pit used by long-ago canyon inhabitants. A popular destination along this trail is beautiful **Santa Maria Spring,** a hike of just over four miles round-trip, where there's a little rock shelter, a seeping spring, and a view of Hermit's Creek below.

MOUNTAIN BIKING ON THE RIM
The **Tusayan Bike Trails** are a series of single-track trails and old mining and logging roads organized into several easy to moderate loop trails for mountain bikers near the park's south entrance. The trails wind through a forest of pine, juniper, and piñon, and there are usually plenty of opportunities to see wildlife. The longest loop is just over 11 miles, and the shortest is just under four miles. At the beginning of the trails there's a map of the area showing the various loops. Pick up the trails on the west side of Route 64 north of Tusayan, about a mile south of the park entrance.

Accommodations
There are six lodges within Grand Canyon National Park's South Rim confines. Over the last decade or so most of the rooms have been remodeled and upgraded, and you won't find any of them too much more expensive than those outside the park, as the rates are set and controlled by an annual review comparing the park's offerings to similar accommodations elsewhere.

A stay at ◖ **El Tovar** (303/297-2757,

$140–325 d), more than 100 years old and one of the most distinctive and memorable hotels in the state, would be the secondary highlight—after the gorge itself—of any trip to the South Rim. The log-and-stone National Historic Landmark standing about 20 feet from the rim has 78 rooms and suites, each with cable TV. The hotel's restaurant serves some of the best food in Arizona for breakfast, lunch, and dinner, and there's a comfortable cocktail lounge off the lobby with a window on the canyon. A mezzanine sitting area overlooks the log-cabin lobby, and a gift shop sells Native American art and crafts and canyon souvenirs. If you're looking to splurge on something truly exceptional, a honeymoon suite overlooking the canyon is available for about $325 per night.

When first built in the 1930s, the **Bright Angel Lodge** (303/297-2757, $52–143 d) was meant to serve the middle-class travelers then being lured by the Santa Fe Railroad, and it is still affordable and comfortable, while retaining a rustic character that fits perfectly with the wild canyon just outside. Lodge rooms don't have televisions, and there is generally only one bed in each room. Some of the lodge rooms have shared bathrooms, so if that bothers you make sure to ask for a room with a private bath. The lodge's cabins just west of the main building are a little better equipped, with private baths, TVs, and sitting rooms. There's a gift shop; drinking and dining options include a small bar; a family-style restaurant serving breakfast, lunch, and dinner; and a more upscale eatery that serves lunch and dinner.

Standing along the rim between El Tovar and Bright Angel, the **Kachina Lodge** (303/297-2757, $125–142 d), a more recent addition to the canyon's accommodations list, offers basic, comfortable rooms with TVs, safes, private baths, and refrigerators. There's not a lot of character here, but its location and modern comforts make the Kachina an ideal place for families to stay. The **Thunderbird Lodge** (303/297-2757, $125–142 d) is located in the same area and has very similar offerings.

Maswick Lodge (303/297-2757, $79–130 d) is another non-historical lodging option,

located just west of the village about a quarter mile from the rim. The hotel has a cafeteria-style restaurant that serves just about everything you'd want and a sports bar with a large-screen television. The rooms are basic and comfortable, with TVs, private baths, and refrigerators. **Yavapai Lodge** (303/297-2757, $100–118 d) is east of the village and is another of the non-historic facilities that offers nice rooms with all the comforts but little character or artistic value, though you don't really need any of that when you've got the greatest sculpture garden in the world just half a mile away.

CAMPING

Mather Campground (877/444-6777, www.recreation.gov, $18 per night though Nov. 24, $15 thereafter, first-come, first served, reservations up to six months ahead) is located in the village and offers basic campsites with grills. It has bathroom facilities with showers, and laundry facilities are offered for a fee. The campground is open to tents and trailers but has no hookups and is closed to RVs longer than 30 feet. If you're in a rolling mansion, try next door at **Trailer Village** (888/297-2757, www.xanterra.com, $28 per night), where you'll find hookups. About 25 miles east of the village, near the park's east entrance, is **Desert View Campground** ($12 per night, first-come, first served, closes mid-Oct. depending on weather), with 50 sites for tents and small trailers only, no hookups. There's a bathroom with no showers, and only two faucets with running water. Each site has a grill but little else.

Food

◖ **El Tovar Dining Room** (928/638-2631 ext. 6432, 6:30–11 A.M. breakfast, 11:30 A.M.–2 P.M. lunch , 5–10 P.M. dinner daily, $9–16 lunch, $7–28 dinner, reservations are required) is truly carrying on the Fred Harvey Company traditions on which it was founded more than 100 years ago. A serious, competent staff serves fresh, creative, locally inspired dishes in a cozy, mural-clad dining room that has not been significantly altered from the way it looked back when Teddy Roosevelt and Zane Gray ate here.

The wine, entrées, and desserts are all top-notch and would be mightily enjoyed anywhere in the world—but they always seem to be that much more tasty with the sun going down over the canyon. Pay attention to the specials, which usually feature some in-season native edible and are always the best thing to eat within several hundred miles in any direction.

The Arizona Room (928/638-2631, 11:15 A.M.–10 P.M. daily mid-Feb.–Oct., 4:30–10 P.M. daily Nov.–Dec., 11:15 A.M.–3 P.M. daily Jan.–mid-Feb., $7–12 lunch, $12–25 dinner) serves Southwestern-inspired steak, prime rib, fish, and chicken dishes amidst a stylish, but still casual, atmosphere. There's a full bar, and the steaks are excellent—hand-cut and cooked just right with unexpected sauces and marinades. The Arizona Room is closed for dinner in January and February, and closes to the lunch crowd November–February.

If you only have one nice dinner planned for your trip, think about choosing El Tovar over the Arizona Room (but make sure to make a reservation in advance). The food is great at both places, but El Tovar has so much atmosphere and is not that much more expensive than the Arizona Room, which doesn't have the historical and aesthetic interest that's all over El Tovar. Although, thinking about the Arizona Room's baby-back ribs with prickly pear barbecue sauce makes one question such a recommendation.

Bright Angel Restaurant (928/638-2631, breakfast, lunch, and dinner daily, $3–9) just off the Bright Angel Lodge's lobby is a perfect place for a big, hearty breakfast before a day hike below the rim, serving all the standard, rib-sticking dishes amidst decorations and ephemera recalling the Fred Harvey heyday. At lunch there's stew, chili, salads, sandwiches, and burgers, and for dinner there's steak, pasta, and fish dishes called "Bright Angel Traditions," along with a few offerings from the Arizona Room's menu as well. Nearby is the **Bright Angel Fountain,** which serves hot dogs, ice cream, and other quick treats.

Maswik Cafeteria (928/638-2631, breakfast, lunch, and dinner daily, $3–9) is an ideal place for a quick, filling, and delicious meal. You can find just about everything here—burgers, salads, country-style mashed potatoes, french fries, sandwiches, prime rib, chili, and soft-serve ice cream, to name just a few of the dozens of offerings. Just grab a tray, pick your favorite dish, and you'll be eating in a matter of a few minutes. There's a similar cafeteria-style restaurant at the Yavapai Lodge to the east of village.

Shopping

There are more than 16 places to buy gifts, books, souvenirs, supplies, and Native American arts and crafts at the South Rim. Nearly every lodge has a substantial gift shop in its lobby, as do Hermit's Rest, Kolb Studio, Lookout Studio, and the Desert View Watchtower.

For books, the best place to go is **Books & More** at the Canyon View Information Plaza, operated by the nonprofit Grand Canyon Association. Here you'll find all manner of tomes about canyon science and history for both adults and children. All of the gift shops have a small book section, most of them selling the same general selection of popular canyon-related titles. If you're in need of camping and hiking supplies to buy or rent—including top-of-the-line footwear, clothes, and backpacks—try the general store at the **Canyon Village Market Place.** Here you'll also find groceries, toiletries, produce, alcohol and myriad other necessities, like "I hiked the Grand Canyon" T-shirts and warm jackets in case you forgot yours.

Whether you're a semi-serious collector or a first-time dabbler, the best place on the South Rim to find high-quality Native arts and crafts is inside Mary Colter's **Hopi House,** where pottery, baskets, overlay jewelry, sand paintings, kachina dolls, and other treasures are for sale. Don't expect to find too many great deals here though—most of the best pieces are priced accordingly.

Information and Services

Canyon View Information Plaza (9 A.M.–5 P.M. daily) near Mather Point is the perfect place to begin your visit to the park. You get there by

SO LONG TO A GRAND CANYON INSTITUTION: VERKAMP'S CURIOS

It's not often that the mere closing of a small, family-run curio shop makes the newspapers all over the world, but most such shops haven't been operating for more than 100 years on the edge of one of the great wonders of the world.

In September 2008, **Verkamp's Curios** at Grand Canyon National Park closed its doors for good. The news inspired dozens of feature stories in the media, and canyon visitors from around the world likely remembered the Kachina Doll, T-shirt, Zuni Fetish, or refrigerator magnet they'd bought at the small shop across the parking lot from El Tovar Hotel when they read the news.

Visitors to Arizona's most popular tourist destination had been purchasing mementos of their trips from the Verkmamp's since before the park was a park: the store began in a white canvas tent on the edge of the gorge way back in 1898. So why close now? The current Verkamp's told the Associated Press (AP) that they had "bureaucratic process fatigue."

In 1998, Congress passed a law directing the National Parks Service to no longer give preference to existing permit holders when renewing permits to operate businesses within the parks. This made the process much more expensive and time-consuming than it had ever been for the Verkamp's. Also, "family dynamics" played a role, according to one store employee. Family matriarch Susie Verkamp said as much when she told the AP that there was really nobody left in the family who wanted to be involved in the business. A non-Verkamp manager had been in charge of day-to-day operations at the shop since 1995, though the Verkamp's had remained actively involved, the AP reported.

While there are still plenty of gift shops at the Grand Canyon in which to buy your souvenirs, the closing of Verkamp's represents the end of era. There are few non-corporate permit holders left in the National Parks anymore, and now there is one less.

walking the short path from the Mather Point parking lot or by hopping off the free shuttle, for which plaza serves as a kind of central hub. Inside the information center there are displays on canyon history and science, and rangers are always around to answer questions, give advice, and help you plan your visit.

As you enter the park you'll get a copy of the ***The Guide,*** a newsprint guide to the South Rim that is indispensable. Make sure you read through it; it's pretty comprehensive and will likely answer most of your questions.

LECTURES AND PROGRAMS

The staff at the South Rim does an above-average job keeping guests comfortable, informed, and entertained. Rangers seem to be always giving lectures, leading walks, and pointing out some little-known canyon fact—and such activities at Grand Canyon are typically far more interesting than they are at other, less spectacular places. It

will be worth your time to attend at least one of the regularly illuminating lectures held most nights at the **Shrine of the Ages** during your visit to the South Rim. Check *The Guide* for specific times and topics. Every day prior to late October there are at least 10 ranger programs offered at various sites around the rim. Typically these programs last between fifteen minutes and an hour and are always interesting.

Getting There

The majority of Grand Canyon visitors drive here, reaching the South Rim from either **Flagstaff** or **Williams** and entering the park through the south or east gates. The south entrance is usually the busiest, and during the summer traffic is likely to be backed up somewhat. The quickest way to get to the south gate by car is to take Route 64 from Williams. It's about a 60-mile drive across a barren plain; there are a few kitschy places to stop along the way, including Bedrock City, a rather dilapidated model of the Flinstones' hometown with an RV park and a gift shop.

From Flagstaff take U.S. 180 through the forest past the San Francisco Peaks for about 80 miles. The road merges with Route 64 at Valle. To reach the east entrance, take U.S. 89 north from Flagstaff to Cameron, then take Route 64 west to the entrance. This longer route is recommended if you want to see portions of Navajo country on your way to the canyon, and entering through the east entrance will put you right at Desert View, the Desert View Watchtower, and Tusayan Museum and Ruin—sights that otherwise you'll have to travel 25 or so miles east from Grand Canyon Village to see.

BY AIR

The Grand Canyon Airport at Tusayan, just outside the park's south entrance, has flights from Las Vegas, Nevada, daily and from other major Southwestern ports as well. Both Flagstaff and Williams have small airports, but most visitors fly into Sky Harbor in Phoenix,

rent a car, and drive about three hours north to the South Rim. You can rent a car at Tusayan, and there are rental places in Flagstaff and Williams as well. A shuttle runs hourly between Tusayan and Grand Canyon Village.

BY BUS
Open Road Tours and Transportation
(877/226-8060, www.openroadtours.com) offers twice-daily shuttles from Flagstaff to the Grand Canyon for $54 round-trip for adults. The company also offers shuttles to the Grand Canyon Railroad depot in Williams and to Tusayan. An Open Road Tours shuttle departs Phoenix twice a day and arrives in Flagstaff in time to meet the Grand Canyon shuttle ($76 round-trip for an adult).

GRAND CANYON RAILROAD
A fun, retro, and environmentally conscious way to reach the park, the **Grand Canyon Railroad** (800/843-8724, www.thetrain .com, $65–170 for single adult, depending on accommodations) re-creates what it was like to

GRAND CANYON RAILWAY

On some Grand Canyon Railroad trips, there's even a mock train robbery – complete with bandits on horseback with blazing six-shooters.

visit the great gorge in the early 20th century. It takes about 2.5 hours to get to the South Rim depot from the station in Williams, where the **Grand Canyon Railroad Hotel** (928/635-4010, www.thetrain.com, $89–179 d) and restaurant just beyond the train station makes a good base, attempting as it does to match the atmosphere of the old Santa Fe Railroad Harvey House that once stood on the same ground.

During the trip, one is always wondering when the train is going to speed up, but it never really does, rocking at about 60 mph through pine forests and across a scrubby grassland shared by cattle, elk, pronghorn, coyotes, and red-tailed hawks, all of which can be viewed from a comfortable seat in one of the old refurbished cars. Along the way, there are ruins of the great railroad days, including ancient telegraph posts still lined up along the tracks.

A trip to and from the Grand Canyon on the old train is recommended for anyone who is interested in the heyday of train travel, the Old West, or the golden age of southwestern tourism—or for anyone desiring a slower-paced journey across the northland. Besides, the fewer visitors who drive their vehicles to the rim, the better. Kids seem to especially enjoy the train trip, as comedian-fiddlers often stroll through the cars, and on some trips there's even a mock train robbery complete with bandits on horseback with blazing six-shooters.

Getting Around
SHUTTLES
The park operates an excellent free shuttle service with comfortable buses fueled by compressed natural gas. It's a good idea to park your car for the duration of your visit and use the shuttle. It's nearly impossible to find parking at the various sights, and the traffic through the park is not always easy to navigate—there are a lot of one-way routes and oblivious pedestrians that can lead to needless frustration. Make sure you pick up a copy of the free park newspaper, **The Guide,** which has a map of the various shuttle routes and stops.

Pretty much anywhere you want to go in the park a shuttle will get you there, and you rarely have to wait more than 10 minutes at any stop. That being said, there is no shuttle that goes all the way to the Tusayan Museum and Ruin or the Watchtower near the east entrance. Shuttle drivers are a good source of information about the park, and they are generally very friendly and knowledgeable, and a few of them are genuinely entertaining. The shuttle conveniently runs from around sunup until about 9 P.M., and drivers always know the expected sunrise and sundown times and seem to be intent on getting people to the best overlooks to view these two popular daily park events.

TOURS
Xanterra, the park's main concessionaire, offers in-park bus tours through its **Fred Harvey Transportation Co.** (888/297-2757, $14–40 adults, kids under 16 free with paying adult). Sunrise tours are available, and longer drives to the eastern and western reaches of the park are offered. This is a comfortable, educational and entertaining way to see the park, and odds are you will come away with a few new friends— possibly even a new email pal from abroad. Only pay for a tour if you like being around a lot of other people and listening to mildly entertaining banter from the tour guides for hours at a time. It's easy to see and learn about everything the park has to offer without spending extra money on a tour. If you like being on your own and getting out away from the crowds, this is not for you.

Several companies offer helicopter tours of the canyon of varying lengths. One of the better operators is **Maverick Helicopters** (888/261-4414, www.maverickhelicopter .com, $175 for 25 minutes, $235 for 45 minutes). Though not ideal from the back-to-nature point of view, a helicopter flight over the canyon is an exciting, rare experience, and by most accounts is well worth the rather expensive price.

◖ NORTH RIM
Standing at Bright Angel Point on the Grand Canyon's North Rim, crowded together with

several other gazers as if stranded on a jetty over a wide hazy sea, blurred evergreens growing atop great jagged rock spines banded with white and red, someone whispers, "It looks pretty much the same as the other rim."

It's not true—far from it—but the comment brings up the main point about the North Rim: Should you go? Only about 10 percent of canyon visitors make the trip to the North Rim, which is significantly less developed than the South; there aren't as many activities, other than gazing, unless you are a hiker and a backcountry wilderness lover. The coniferous mountain forests of the Kaibab Plateau, broken by grassy meadows painted with summer wildflowers, populated by often-seen elk and mule deer, dappled with aspens that turn yellow and red in the fall and burst out of the otherwise uniform dark green like solitary flames, are themselves worth the trip. But it is a long trip, and you need to be prepared for a land of scanty services and the simple, contemplative pleasures of nature in the raw.

Sights

Even if you aren't staying at the 80-year-old **Grand Canyon Lodge,** a rustic log-and-stone structure perched on the edge of the rim at the very end of the highway, don't make the trip to the North Rim without going into its warm Sun Room to view the gorge through the huge picture windows. You may want to sink into one of the comfortable couches and stare for hours. At sunset, head out to the Adirondack chairs on the lodge's back patio and watch the sun sink over the canyon; everybody's quiet, hushed in reverence, bundled up in jackets and sweaters and wondering how they came to such a rare place as this. Right near the door leading out to the patio, check out sculptor Peter Jepson's charming life-size bronze of **Brighty,** a famous canyon burro whose story was told in the 1953 children's book *Brighty of the Grand Canyon* by Marguerite Henry. A display nearby tells the true-life aspects of Brighty's story, and they say if you rub his bronze nose you'll have good luck. The book, along with a movie based on the story, is available at gift shops

and bookstores on both the North and South Rims.

There are three developed viewpoints at the North Rim, each of them offering a distinctive look at the canyon. **Bright Angel Point,** just outside the lodge's back door, looks over Bright Angel Canyon and provides a view of Roaring Springs, the source of Bright Angel Creek and the freshwater source for the North Rim and the inner canyon. **Point Imperial,** at 8,803 feet, is the highest point on the North Rim and probably has the single best view from the rim.

Cape Royal Drive

You can reach Point Imperial and several other lookout spots on the Cape Royal Scenic Drive, one of the most scenic, dramatic roads in the state. From the lodge to Cape Royal it's about 23 miles one-way on a paved road that wends through the mixed conifer and aspen forests of the Walhalla Plateau. There are plenty of chances for wildlife-spotting and lots of stops and short trails to viewpoints offering breathtaking views of the canyon off to the east and even as far as Navajoland. Plan to spend at least half a day and take food and water. Go to Point Imperial first, reached by a three-mile side-road at the beginning of the Cape Royal Road. The best way to do it would be to leave the lodge just before sunrise and watch the show from Point Imperial, and then hit the scenic drive for the rest of the day, stopping often along the way. Binoculars would be of use on this drive, as would, of course, a camera. Along the way, Vista Encantadora (Charming View) provides just that, rising above Nanokoweap Creek. Just beyond that is Roosevelt Point. When you finally reach the point of the drive, Cape Royal at 7,865 feet, you'll walk out on a short paved trail for an expansive and unbounded view of the canyon—one of the very best, from which, on a clear day, you can spot the South Rim's Desert Watchtower way across the gorge and the river far below. Along the short trail you'll pass **Angel's Window,** an unlikely rock arch that seems designed by some overly ambitious god trying to make an already intensely rare and wonderful view even more so.

Accommodations and Food

Built in the late 1930s after the original lodge burned down, 🄲 **Grand Canyon Lodge** (888/297-2757 or 928/638-2611, $102–147) has the only in-park accommodations on the North Rim. The rustic but very comfortable log-and-stone lodge has a large central lobby, a high-ceilinged dining room, a deli, a saloon ($6 for a beer), a gift shop, a general store, and a gas station. The rooms are cabins scattered around the property, each with a bathroom and most with a gas-powered fireplace that makes things very cozy on a cold night. The lodge is open from mid-May through mid-October. You must book far in advance, though there are sometimes cancellations that could allow for a last-minute booking. The **Grand Canyon Lodge Dining Room** (928/638-2611, breakfast, lunch, and dinner daily, $8–25, reservations are required for dinner) is the only restaurant in the park, serving fish, pasta, and steaks for dinner, and soups, sandwiches, and salads for lunch. It's not great and is even less so toward the end of the season (late October), but it is the only thing going for several miles around.

The **Kaibab Lodge** (928/638-2389, $85–155) is a small gathering of basic cabins behind the tree line at the edge of a meadow along Route 67, about five miles north of the park boundary. You can rent cabins of varying sizes and enjoy the lounge, gift shop, and warm fireplace in the lobby. The lodge closes in early November. **Kaibab Lodge Restaurant** (breakfast, lunch, and dinner daily, $6.25–18.95) serves well-made, hearty fare perfect for the high, cool country—much better than the in-park eatery.

CAMPING

The in-park **North Rim Campground** (877/444-6777, www.recreation.gov, $18 per night, no hookups) has basic camping spots near the rim, with showers and coin-operated laundry. South of Jacob Lake about 25 miles on Route 67 is the **DeMotte Campground,** operated by the U.S. Forest Service ($16 per night, May–Oct., no reservations), about seven miles north of the park entrance. It has 38 sites with tables and cooking grills, toilets and drinking water. Tents, trailers, and motor homes are allowed, but there are no utility hookups or dump stations available. **Kaibab Camper Village** (Rte. 67, just south of Jacob Lake, 928/643-7804 or 800/525-0924) has full hookup sites for $31 per night, and basic tent sites for $15 per night. The village also has cabins for $75 per night and offers fire pits, tables, toilets, and coin-operated showers.

Recreation

It's significantly cooler on the high, forested North Rim than it is on the South, making hiking, especially summer hiking, and even more so summertime hiking below the rim, much less of a chore. There are a few easy rim trails to choose from, and several tough but unforgettable day hikes into the canyon along the North Kaibab Trail.

Easy trails lead to and from all the developed scenic overlooks on the rim, their trailheads accessible and well-marked. **The Guide** has a comprehensive listing of the area's trails and where to pick them up. The three-mile round-trip **Transept Trail** is an easy, short hike along the forested, green rim from the Grand Canyon Lodge to the campground that provides a good overview of the park. Hiking along the rim is an excellent way to see the canyon from many different points of view. A highly recommended, longer hike is along the five-mile round-trip **Uncle Jim Trail** through the pine forest and out to an overlook from which you can watch backpackers winding their way down the North Kaibab Trail's twisting switchbacks, and maybe see a mule train or two along the way. If you have most of a day, both the **Widforss Trail** and the **Ken Patrick Trail** lead through the forest and along the rim for up to 10 miles. You can take the Ken Patrick all the way through the thick pine and mixed conifer forest to Point Imperial, the rim's highest point at 8,803 feet and one of the most spectacular sunrise spots in the park.

NORTH KAIBAB TRAIL

The North Kaibab starts out among the co-niferous heights of the North Rim, a forest trail that soon dries out and becomes a red rock desert, the trail cut into the rock face of the cliffs and twisting down improbable routes hard against the cliffs, with nothing but your sanity keeping you away from the gorge. Sooner than you realize the walls close in and you are deep in the canyon, the trees on the rim just green blurs now. A good intro-duction to this corridor trail and ancient na-tive route is the short, 1.5-mile round-trip jog down to the **Coconino Overlook,** from which, on a clear day, you can see the San Francisco Peaks and the South Rim. A four-mile round-trip hike down will get you to **Supai Tunnel,** blasted out of the red rock in the 1930s by the Civilian Conservation Corps. A little more than a mile on and you'll reach the **The Bridge in the Redwall** (5.5 miles round-trip), built in 1966 after a flood ruined this por-tion of the trail. For a tough, all-day hike that

The hike down the North Kaibab Trail to Roaring Springs is one of the most popular North Rim day hikes.

© TIM HULL

will likely have you sore but smiling the next morning, take the North Kaibab five miles in to **Roaring Springs,** the source of life-giving Bright Angel Creek. The springs fall headlong out of the cliffside and spray mist and rain-bows into the hot air. Just remember, you have to go five miles up and out, too. Start hiking early and take plenty of water.

NORTH RIM MULE RIDES

The mules at the North Rim all work for **Canyon Trail Rides** 435/679-8665, www .canyonrides.com, May 15–Oct. 15), the park's northside trail-riding concessionaire. Guides will take you and your friendly mule on a one-hour rimside ride for $30, or a half-day ride down the North Kaibab to the Supai tunnel for $65. A full-day ride to Roaring Springs includes a box lunch and, likely, a sore behind ($125 per person). Kids have to be at least seven years old to take part in a one-hour ride, at least 10 for the half-day and 12 for the full-day rides. There's a 200-pound weight limit. Call ahead for a reservation if this is something you're set on doing; if you're not sure, you might be able to hop on last-minute, though probably not in June, which is the busiest time at the North Rim.

Information and Services

The **North Rim Visitor Center and Bookstore** (8 A.M.–6 P.M. daily May–Oct.) near the Grand Canyon Lodge has informa-tion, maps, and exhibits on North Rim sci-ence and history. The nonprofit Grand Canyon Association operates the bookstore.

Getting There and Around

While it's only an average of about 10 miles across the canyon from points on the South Rim to points on the North Rim—but only if you're a hawk or a raven or a condor—it's a 215-mile, five-hour drive for those of us who are primarily earthbound. The long route north is something to behold, moving through a corner of Navajoland, past the towering Vermillion Cliffs, and deep into the high conifer forests of the Kaibab Plateau. On the plateau, which at its highest reaches above 9,000 feet, Route 67 from Jacob Lake to the North Rim typically closes to vehicles by late November until May. In the winter, it's not uncommon for cross-country skiers and snowshoe hikers to take to the closed and snow-covered highway, heading with their own power toward the canyon and the North Kaibab Trail.

The **Trans Canyon Shuttle** (928/638-2820, $70 one-way, $130 round-trip, reservations are required) makes a daily round-trip excursion between the North and South Rims, departing the North at 7 A.M. and arriving at the South Rim at 11:30 A.M. The shuttle then leaves the South at 1:30 P.M. and arrives back at the North Rim at 6:30 P.M.

To get from the Grand Canyon Lodge—the park's only accommodations on the North Rim—to the North Kaibab Trailhead, take the **Hikers Shuttle** ($7 for first person, $4 for each additional person), which leaves the lodge twice daily first thing in the morning. Tickets must be purchased the day before at the lodge.

If you paid your $25 park entrance fee at the South Rim, this will be honored at the North as long as you go within seven days. If not, you'll have to pay an additional $25. A North Rim edition of the park's helpful newspaper *The Guide* is passed out at the North Rim entrance.

THE INNER CANYON

Inside the canyon is a desert, red and pink and rocky, its trails lined with cactus and scrub. It's not down at the ground that you're usually looking, though. It's those walls, tight and claustrophobic in the interior's narrowest slots, that make this place a different world altogether. A large part of a canyon-crossing trudge takes place in Bright Angel Canyon along Bright Angel Creek. As you hike along the trail beside the creek, greenery and the cool rushing of creek clash with the silent heat washing off the cliffs on your other flank.

On any given night there are only a few hundred visitors sleeping below the rim—at either Phantom Ranch, a Mary Colter–designed

© TIM HULL

The deer in the Grand Cayon seem to be posing for pictures.

lodge near the mouth of Bright Angel Canyon, or at three campgrounds along the corridor trails. While until a few decades ago visiting the inner canyon was something of a free-for-all, these days access to the interior is strictly controlled; you have to purchase a permit ($10 plus $5 per night per person) to spend the night, and it's not always easy to get a permit—each year the park receives 30,000 requests for a backcountry permit and issues only 13,000.

No matter which trail you use, there's no avoiding an arduous, leg- and spirit-punishing hike there and back if you really want to see the inner canyon. It's not easy, no matter who you are, but it is worth it; it's a true accomplishment, a hard walk you'll never forget.

Planning Your Time

If you want to be one of the small minority of canyon visitors to spend some quality time below the rim, consider staying at least one full day and night in the inner canyon. Even hikers in excellent shape find that they are sore after trekking down to the river, Phantom Ranch, and beyond. A rim-to-rim hike, either from the south or from the north, pretty much requires at least a day of rest below the rim. The ideal inner canyon trip lasts three days and two nights: one day hiking in, one day of rest, and one day to hike out.

River trips generally last a minimum of three days to up to three weeks and often include a hike down one of the corridor trails to the river. Depending on how long you want to spend on the river, plan far, far in advance and consider making the river trip your only activity on that particular canyon visit. Combining too much strenuous, mind-blowing, and life-changing activity into one trip tends to water down the entire experience.

Permits and Reservations

The earlier you apply for a permit the better, but you can't apply for one prior to the first of the month four months before your proposed trip date. The easiest way to get a permit is to go to the park's website (www.nps.gov/grca/planyourvisit/overnight-hiking.htm), print out a backcountry permit request form, fill it

out, and then fax it first thing in the morning on the date in question—for example, if you want to hike in October, you would fax (928/638-2125) your request on June 1. Have patience; on the first day of the month the fax number is usually busy throughout the day—keep trying. On the permit request form you'll indicate where you plan to stay. If you are camping, the permit is your reservation, but if you want to stay at Phantom Ranch, you must get separate reservations, and that is often a close-to-impossible task. For more information on obtaining a backcountry permit, call the South Rim Backcountry Information Center (928/638-7875, 8 A.M.–5 P.M. daily).

Hiking

There are many lesser-known routes into the canyon, but most hikers stick to the corridor trails—Bright Angel, South Kaibab, and North Kaibab. The Bright Angel Trail from the South Rim is the most popular, but the South Kaibab is significantly shorter, though much steeper. The **North Kaibab,** from the North Rim, is the only trail to the river and Phantom Ranch

Bright Angel Creek runs through Bright Angel Canyon.

© TIM HULL

© TIM HULL

The Bright Angel and the South Kaibab are the two most popular trails for reaching the inner gorge from the South Rim.

from the North. The rim-to-rim hike is popular, and you can choose, as long as the season permits, to either start on the north or south. Starting from the South Rim, you may want to go down the Bright Angel to see beautiful Indian Gardens; then again, the South Kaibab provides a faster, more direct route to the river. If you start from the north, you may want to come out of the canyon via the South Kaibab, as it is shorter and faster, and at that point you are probably going to want to take the path of least resistance. Remember though, while it's shorter, the South Kaibab is a good deal steeper than the Bright Angel, and there is no water available.

DAY HIKES AROUND PHANTOM RANCH

Some people prefer to spend their time in the canyon recovering from the hard walk or mule ride that brought them here, and a day spent cooling your feet in Bright Angel Creek or drinking beer in the cantina is not a day wasted. However, if you want to do some exploring around Phantom Ranch, there are a few popular day hikes from which to choose.

When you arrive, the friendly rangers will usually tell you, unsolicited, all about these hikes and provide detailed directions. If you want to get deeper out in the bush and far from the other hikers, ask one of the rangers to recommend a lesser-known route.

A highly recommended and rather short hike is along the precipitous **River Trail,** high above the Colorado just south of Phantom Ranch. The Civilian Conservation Corps (CCC) blasted this skinny cliffside trail out of the rock walls in the 1930s to provide a link between the Bright Angel and the South Kaibab Trail. Heading out from Phantom it's about a 1.5-mile loop that takes you across both suspension bridges and high above the river. It's an easy walk with fantastic views and is a good way to get your sore legs stretched and moving again.

Another popular, CCC-built trail near Phantom is the **Clear Creek Loop,** which takes you high above the river and provides some excellent views up and down the inner gorge. The rangers seem to recommend this hike the most, but, while it's not tough, it can be a little steep and

one of two bridges spanning the Colorado River in the Grand Canyon's inner gorge near Phantom Ranch

© TIM HULL

rugged, especially if you're exhausted and sore. The views are, ultimately, well worth the pain. If you hiked in from the South Rim and you have a long, approximately 11-mile round-trip day hike in you, head north on the North Kaibab from Phantom Ranch to beautiful **Ribbon Falls,** a mossy, cool-water oasis just off the hot dusty trail. The falls are indeed a ribbon of cold water falling hard off the rock cliffs, and you can scramble up the slickrock and through the green creekside jungle and stand beneath the shower. This hike will also give you a chance to see the eerie, claustrophobic "Box," one of the strangest and most exhilarating stretches of the North Kaibab.

Mule Rides

For generations the famous Grand Canyon mules have been dexterously picking along the skinny trails, loaded with packs and people. Even the Brady Bunch rode them, so they come highly recommended. A descent into the canyon on the back of a friendly mule—with an often taciturn cowboy-type leading the train—can be an unforgettable experience, but don't assume that because you're riding and not walking that you

won't be sore in the morning. A day trip down the Bright Angel to Plateau Point, from which you can see the Colorado, costs $139 per person and includes lunch. One night at Phantom Ranch, meals included, and a ride down on a mule costs $376.50 per person or $666 for two. Two nights at Phantom, meals, and a mule ride costs $530.90 per person or $887.50 for two. For reservations call 888/297-2757 or visit www .grandcanyonlodges.com. Call six months or more in advance.

River Trips

People who have been inside the Grand Canyon often have one of two reactions—they either can't wait to get back or else they swear never to return. This is doubly true of those intrepid souls who ride the great river, braving whitewater roller coasters while looking forward to a star-filled evening camped, dry, and full of gourmet camp food, on a white beach deep in the gorge. To boat the Colorado, one of the last explored regions of North America, is quite simply one of the most exciting and potentially life-changing trips the West has to offer.

Because of this well-known truth, trips are not cheap and not exactly easy to book. Rafting season in the canyon runs from April to October, and there are myriad trips to choose from—from a three-day long-weekend ride to a 21-day full-canyon epic. An Upper Canyon trip will take you from River Mile 0 at Lee's Ferry through the canyon to Phantom Ranch, while a Lower Canyon trip begins at Phantom, requiring a hike down the Bright Angel with your gear on your back. Furthermore, you can choose a motorized pontoon boat, as some three-fourths of rafters do, a paddleboat, a kayak, or some other combination. It all depends on what you want and what you can afford. If you are considering taking a river trip, the best place to start is the website of the **Grand Canyon River Outfitters Association** (www.gcroa .org), a nonprofit group of about 16 licensed river outfitters, all of them monitored and approved by the National Parks Service, each with a good safety record and relatively similar rates. After you decide what kind of trip you want, the website links to the individual outfitters for booking. If you are one of the majority of river explorers who can't wait to get back on the water once you've landed at the final port, remember that there's a strict one trip per year per person rule enforced by the Park Service.

Accomodations and Food

Designed by Mary Colter for the Fred Harvey Co. in 1922, **Phantom Ranch** (888/297-2757, www.grandcanyonlodges.com, $32 per person for dormitory, $87 for cabin up to two people, $12 for each additional person), the only non-camping accommodation inside the canyon, is a shady, peaceful place that you're likely to miss and yearn for once you've visited and left it behind. Perhaps Phantom's strong draw, like a Siren wailing from the inner gorge, is less about its intrinsic pleasures and more about it being the only sign of civilization in a deep wilderness that can feel like the end of the world, especially after a 17-mile hike in from the North Rim. But it would probably be an inviting place even if it were easier to get at, and it's all the better because it's not.

As such, it is very difficult to make a reservation. Some people begin calling a year out and still can't get a room, while others show up at the South Rim, ask at the Bright Angel Lodge, and find that a cancellation that very day has left a cabin or bed open. This strategy is not recommended, but it has been known to work. Phantom has several cabins and two dormitories, one for men and one for women, both offering bathrooms with showers. The lodge's center point is its cantina, a welcoming, air-conditioned, beer- and lemonade-selling sight for anyone who has just descended one of the trails. Two meals a day are served in the cantina—breakfast, made up of eggs, pancakes, and thick slices of bacon ($16.50), and dinner, with a choice of steak ($33.55) or stew ($21.30). The cantina also offers a box lunch with a bagel, fruit, and salty snacks for $9.50. Reservations for meals are also difficult to come by.

Most nights and afternoons, a ranger based at Phantom Ranch will give a talk on some aspect of canyon lore, history, or science. These events are always interesting and always well attended, even in the 110°F heat of the summer.

Phantom is located near the mouth of Bright Angel Canyon, within a few yards of clear, babbling Bright Angel Creek, and is shaded by large cottonwoods planted in the 1930s by the Civilian Conservation Corps. There are several day hikes within easy reach, and the Colorado River and the two awesome suspension bridges that link one bank to the other are only about a quarter mile from the lodge.

CAMPING

There are three developed campgrounds in the inner canyon: **Cottonwood Campground,** about seven miles from the North Rim along the North Kaibab Trail; **Bright Angel Campground,** along the creek of the same name near Phantom Ranch; and **Indian Garden,** about 4.5 miles from the South Rim along the Bright Angel Trail. To stay overnight at any of these campgrounds you must obtain a permit from the Backcountry Office on the South Rim (928/638-7875, $10 for permit plus $5 per person per night). All three campgrounds offer bathrooms and a freshwater spigot, picnic tables and food storage bins to keep the critters out. There are no showers or any other amenities.

The best campground in the inner canyon is Bright Angel, a shady, cottonwood-lined setting along cool Bright Angel Creek. Because of its easy proximity to Phantom Ranch, campers can make use of the cantina, even eating meals there if they can get a reservation, and can attend the ranger talks offered at the lodge. There's nothing quite like sitting on the grassy banks beside your campsite and cooling your worn feet in the creek.

GRAND CANYON WEST

Since the Hualapai (WALL-uh-pie) Tribe's Skywalk opened to much international press coverage a few years ago, the remote western reaches of Grand Canyon have certainly gotten more attention than in the past. Though no less remote, there has been an uptick in tourism to the Hualapai's portion of the rim, which is about two hours of dirt-road driving from the Hualapai Reservation's capital, Peach Springs, located along Route 66 east of Kingman. All that press has at the same time led to a little confusion. At the South Rim visitor center, one can usually hear the question, "How do we get to the Skywalk?" a few times an hour, followed by moans of disbelief and the cancellation of plans when the answer comes that it's about 250 miles away. If you want to experience Grand Canyon West, it's a good idea to plan a separate trip, or else carve out at least two extra days to do so. Along the way, you can drive on the longest remaining portion of the Mother Road, and, if you have a few days on top of that, hike down into Havasupai Canyon and see its famous, fantastical waterfalls.

Havasupai Indian Reservation

The Havasu 'Baaja (People of the Blue-Green Water) have been living in their lush, isolated corner of Grand Canyon for hundreds of years, a hidden riparian Eden of cottonwoods, waterfalls, and deep pools of 70°F water. There are

four amazing waterfalls that attract thousands of tourists to this out-of-the-way place every year—Navajo Falls, Havasu Falls, Mooney Falls (a ribbon of white water falling 200 feet from the sheer red-rock cliffs), and Beaver Falls—all of them a short hike from the small village of Supai or a rustic campground nearby, and each tumbling into a pool of enticing water in which you can swim and float as you consider the red and pink cliffs all around you. The best time to go is April through October, and it's a good idea to plan far ahead. Check out the tribe's website (www.havasupaitribe .com) for more information. There's a $35 per person entrance fee.

The tribe runs a small lodge in the village of Supai, **Havasupai Lodge** (928/448-2111 or 928/448-2201, www.havasupaitribe.com, $145 per night up to four people, $40 per room per night, deposit required), with 24 rooms, each with two double beds, air-conditioning, and a private bathroom. The village also has a café that serves breakfast, lunch, and dinner, and a general store.

The tribe's cottonwood-covered **campground,** a few miles from the village, offers primitive sites on a first-come, first-served basis with composting toilets, picnic tables, and water that must be treated. There are no fires allowed, and you must pack out all your trash.

Hualapai Indian Reservation

While Peach Springs is the capital of the Hualapai Reservation, there's not much there but a lodge and scattered housing. The real attractions are up on the West Rim about 50 miles and two hours away. Peach Springs makes for an obvious base for a visit to the West Rim, which has several lookout points, the famous new Skywalk, and a kitschy Old West–style tourist attraction called Hualapai Ranch. The tribe's **Hualapai River Runners** will take you on a day trip on the river (928/769-2219), and there are several all-inclusive package tours to choose from. Check out the tribe's website (www.destinationgradcanyon.com) for more information.

The **Hualapai Lodge** (900 Route 66,

928/769-2230, www.destinationgrandcayon .com, $75–105 d) in Peach Springs has a heated, saltwater pool, an exercise room, gift shop, and 57 rooms. The lodge's restaurant, **Diamond Creek** ($6–12), serves American and Native American dishes for lunch and dinner.

SKYWALK

The Skywalk (877/716-9378, www.grand canyonskywalk.com, prices start at $81.20 for adults and $60 for kids 4–11) is as much an art installation as it is a tourist attraction. A horseshoe-shaped glass and steel platform jutting out 70 feet from the canyon rim, it appears futuristic surrounded by the rugged, remote western canyon. It's something to see for sure, but is it worth the long drive and the high price-tag? Not really. If you have time for an off-the-beaten-path portion of your canyon trip, it's better to go to the North Rim and stand out on Bright Angel Point—you'll get a similar impression, and it's free.

Getting There and Around

The best way to get to Grand Canyon West is to take I-40 to the Ashfork exit and then drive west on Route 66. Starting at Ashfork and heading west to Peach Springs, the longest remaining portion of Route 66 moves through **Seligman,** a small roadside town that is a reminder of the heyday of the Mother Road. The route through Seligman, which stands up to a stop and a walk around if you have the time (see *The Lower Colorado River* chapter), is popular with nostalgic motorcyclists, and there are a few eateries and tourist-style stores in town. Just west of Seligman is **Grand Canyon Caverns** (928/422-3223, www.gccaverns.com, 9 A.M.–6 P.M. daily, $12.95), a sight that continues the retro feel of the route. An elevator drops you 21 stories into the largest dry cavern in the United States, where the temperature remains 56°F year-round. You can walk along lighted trails that wind through the cavern, then shop, eat, and even stay the night at this 80-year-old attraction, in which, during the Cold War, tons of provisions were stored in case of nuclear war. Once you reach Peach Springs, take Antares Road 25 miles, then turn right on Pierce Ferry Road for 3 miles, then turn east onto Diamond Bar Road for 21 miles, 14 of it on dirt. Diamond Bar Road ends at the only entrance to Grand Canyon West. The 49-mile trip takes about two hours. For park-and-ride reservations, call 702/260-6506.

To reach Havasupai Canyon, turn north on Indian Route 18 just before Peach Springs and drive 68 miles north to a parking area at Hualapai Hilltop. From there it's an eight-mile hike in to Supai Village and the lodge, 10 miles to the campground. The trail is moderate but quite rocky and a bit steep in some parts. If you don't want to hike in, you can arrange to rent a horse (928/448-2121, 928/448-2174, or 928/448-2180, www.havasupaitribe.com, $120 round-trip to lodge, $150 round-trip to campground), or even hire a helicopter (623/516-2790, $85 per person one-way).

The Arizona Strip

If there is any wild loneliness left in America, it is holed up on the Arizona Strip. This five-million-acre wilderness of crumbling red-rock walls, fallen boulders, and long sagebrush sweeps, humpbacked by the evergreen Kaibab Plateau, has only been accessible by highway from within Arizona since 1929 and the opening of the old Navajo Bridge across the Colorado River. Before that, only Latter-day Saints and Paiutes made a go of it here on any serious scale. The region is still inhabited primarily by polygamists and hermits, river guides and a few residents of the Kaibab Paiute Indian Reservation.

Think of the "strip" as exactly that: A narrow band of Arizona territory hemmed on the north by Utah's southern border, the south by the Grand Canyon, on the east by the

Colorado River and on the west by Nevada's eastern border. Within that band are several semi-desert grassland valleys; the long red-rock southern escarpment of the Paria Plateau, a vast tableland protected as the Vermillion Cliffs National Monument; a green and meadowy forest, smothered by deep snow come winter; and an historic human crossing-point where the Paria River washes into the Colorado, the only rest in the great river's canyon-cutting ways for hundreds of miles.

The first Europeans to enter the strip were the path-finding priests of the Dominguez-Escalante expedition in 1776, looking for a northern route from New Mexico to California. In the later 1800s Mormon pioneers from Utah were encouraged by their church leaders to settle in the region; some found the isolation of the strip to their advantage after the official LDS church outlawed polygamy in the 1890s; others raised cattle and cut wood and fought with the Navajo and Paiute over the land's scant resources. When construction on a Mormon temple began in St. George, Utah, to the west, the fruits of the Mormon ranch at Pipe Spring, now a national monument, and the conifers growing atop Mt. Trumbull were used to feed the workers and build the temple. In the years before the railroad, the red-dust wagon road across this territory was known as the "Honeymoon Trail," as it was beaten and smoothed by a stream of LDS making the long journey from settlements along the Little Colorado River to St. George, where their unions would be officially sealed in the temple.

These days the strip isn't that different from the way it was before the bridge put Lee's Ferry out of business and any Arizonan with a sedan and a canteen could explore it. It remains lonely, isolated, and unpaved, for the most part. There are a few exceptions, of course; about 15 miles upstream from the Lee's Ferry crossing, Glen Canyon Dam has stopped the old warm and muddy Colorado and impounded its water in a 186-mile, canyon-flooding reservoir, where millions of boaters, anglers, and water lovers play year-round. The river that trickles out the other side of the dam is far from what it was in the old days, now running mostly clear and cold and predicable through its great, sculpted canyons.

A place of outlander history, desolate beauty, and long, quiet spaces, the Arizona Strip isn't for everyone. But for those who take the time and effort to explore it, it can become a haunting landscape, magnetized and well remembered in both dream and waking life.

PLANNING YOUR TIME

This is classic road-trip territory, and if you're already in-state with a rental car or your own vehicle, consider taking time to at least drive the **Vermillion Cliffs Highway,** a paved two-lane route that runs, more or less, from St. George, Utah, to Lee's Ferry and Marble Canyon, using Route 59 in Utah, Arizona Highway 389, and U.S. 89A. Along the way you'll pass through the entire strip, ascending and coming back down the Kaibab Plateau and crossing the Colorado River. This can be done in one long day from either the west or the east, but if you want to stop and really see the landscape take at least two days. If you're heading west to east, you might want to stay the night in Fredonia, Kanab, Utah; St. George, Utah; or even Mesquite, Nevada, near the Virgin River Gorge. If you're heading east to west, the Cameron Trading Post and hotel on U.S. 89, near the Little Colorado River and the eastern entrance to Grand Canyon National Park's South Rim, makes a good stopping destination. The most logical way to see the strip is to fold it into an excursion from the South Rim to the North Rim. Leave the South Rim early in the morning, cross the eastern strip, spend the night and the next day at the North Rim, then keep heading west down the Kaibab Plateau to Pipe Springs National Monument and on to St. George. From there it's easy to go on and explore Western Arizona and the Lower Colorado.

If you plan on doing more than road-tripping, such as hiking the empty spaces of the Vermillion Cliffs or standing on the unfenced edge of the Grand Canyon at Toroweap, it's

Barbed wire marks the Arizona Strip rangeland at the base of the Vermillion Cliffs.

© TIM HULL

best to plan ahead and to have at least a high and tough SUV, if not a four-wheel-drive.

THE VERMILLION CLIFFS HIGHWAY

Don't think of this scenic journey in terms of political boundaries, for it clips two other states. Rather, it is a journey over a landscape, through a region with a history that cannot be understood without seeing the formidable barriers thrown up by nature. If you begin your drive of the highway from the west, the best place to start is Mesquite, Nevada, along I-15. (From the east start at Cameron; see *Gateways to the Canyon* in this chapter). Mesquite is a small but accommodations-packed town full of gambling senior citizens and cheap but nice casino-hotels on the order of Laughlin. It's common to find a comfortable room in the **Virgin River Casino** (100 Pioneer Blvd. Mesquite, Nev., 877/438-2929, www .virginriver.com) for $25–50, especially on a weekday, and there is a good buffet, a pool, a movie theater, and a lot more. From Mesquite,

head north on I-15 toward St. George, Utah. Just outside of town, you'll enter a corner of Arizona through which the Virgin River flows, cutting through the rocks to create the spectacular Virgin River Gorge.

Virgin River Gorge

The Virgin River, the strip's only perennial stream other than the Colorado River, cuts a dramatic rock maze through the Virgin and Beaver Dam Mountains in the far northwest corner of Arizona on its way toward Lake Mead and the lower Colorado. For several miles along I-15 between Mesquite and St. George, the views are towering and car crash–inducing: high and dry rock mountains, rough and jagged and molded haphazardly by the river, covered with hold-out Mojave Desert vegetation, tripped over by desert bighorn and mountain lions. Few sections of the speedy Interstate move through such precipitous, wild scenery, and it's best to stop and look around at one of the several pull-outs along the slipstream rather than craning your neck

© TIM HULL

Trails in the Virgin River Canyon Recreation Area provide easy access to the Virgin River.

while trying to keep your eyes on the road. A good place to stop is Exit 18 (the Cedar Pocket Interchange), at the **Virgin River Canyon Recreation Area** (435/688-3200, www.blm.gov/az/outrec/camping/vrcg.htm), about 20 miles south of St. George and halfway through the gorge. This Mojave Desert riparian scene has a few easy and sandy trails that lead down to the river—its flows highly susceptible to the season—and great views of the cliffs and mountains. It is snugged in between two of the wildest wildernesses anywhere—The 19,600-acre **Beaver Dam Wilderness Area** and 84,700-acre **Paiute Wilderness Area**—and has about 75 campsites for $8 per night.

St. George to Pipe Springs

Interstate travel ends at St. George, the capital of Mormon expansion into southern Utah and Northern Arizona. Here you can visit the beautiful white LDS temple (490 S. 300 E., 435/673-5181, 9 A.M.–9 P.M. daily, free), dedicated in 1877 and built using supplies and wood gathered on the strip. Continuing

east out of St. George, you can either take the northeast route along Route 9 to swing by the otherworldly **Zion National Park** (435/772-3256, www.nps.gov/zion, $25 per car), or head straight to the heart of the strip southeast on Route 59, past the tiny polygamist town of Colorado City-Hilldale on the Arizona-Utah border, and on to Highway 389 and **Pipe Spring National Monument.**

Pipe Spring National Monument

This shady, watered spot (928/643-7105, www.nps.gov/pisp, $5) on an otherwise dry and windy, red-dirt and sagebrush plain, is the strip's best historic site. A museum and visitors center fronts a well-preserved fortified ranch house and a few historic outbuildings, a compound built in the 1860s and 1870s by Mormon pioneers intent on keeping the titular spring—a rare predicable water source in an otherwise arid landscape—to themselves and out of the hands of the Kaibab Paiute (on whose reservation the monument now sits) and Navajo, who had used it for centuries prior to the Anglo arrival. This and other conflicts lead

© TIM HULL

the Arizona Strip patched with snow near Pipe Springs

to a short war and regular scuffles between the natives and the Mormons, who raised cattle for meat and cheese here, much of which was taken west weekly to feed temple workers in St. George.

An excellent museum inside the visitors center has several displays that tell the history of both Native American and Mormon settlement on the strip and shows artifacts of both cultures. For an in-depth introduction to the history and politics of the strip, this museum can't be beat. After looking over the displays and the bookstore and gift shop, you can head out to the fort for a personal tour by a volunteer (about every half-hour in the busy season). The guide will take you through each room in the fortified home, called **Windsor Castle,** each furnished with period furniture and still displaying the open notches in the walls through which a rifle could be pointed to stop any outside attack. The tour also takes you into the factory-like rooms where cheese and other provisions were prepared and recalls the hardscrabble life on the 19th century strip. The fort had the first telegraph in Arizona, part of which

is still here. There is also a trail that extends about half a mile up a rise behind the fort that provides an expansive view of the vast plain stretching out toward the lonely Mt. Trumbull to the south. A beautiful, isolating view, quiet except for the wind and the crunch of your feet on the rocky red ground. The rangers at Pipe Spring are excellent sources of information about touring the strip.

Grand Canyon-Parashant National Monument and Toroweap

Way off to the south and west of Pipe Spring rises the Shivwits Plateau and the huge, inaccessible **Grand Canyon-Parashant National Monument** (BLM Arizona Strip District, 345 East Riverside Dr., St. George, Utah, 435/688-3200, www.blm.gov/az/st/en/fo/arizona_strip_field.html, www.nps.gov/archive/para/visit.html, 7:45 A.M.–5 P.M. Mon.–Fri., 10 A.M.–3 P.M. Sat.) There are no paved roads within this million-acre wilderness, no visitors centers, well-stocked campgrounds or concessionaires—truthfully, no services of any kind. There are, however, opportunities for the intrepid and well-prepared visitor to see nature in its rawest state.

The plateau, rising to heights between 6,000 and 7,000 feet and covered by semidesert sweeps, short piñon forests and stands of ponderosa pine on its mountains, marks the transition from the Mojave Desert basin and range province to the Colorado Plateau and is home to one of the loneliest and most inspiring Grand Canyon views anyone with a tough vehicle and several hours of hard travel in them can see. In the monument's western reaches, southwest of Pipe Spring, the Toroweap Valley stretches out toward the rim and **Toroweap Point** (sometimes both are called Tuweap, after an abandoned town nearby), a hard-won but amazing viewpoint, without fence or crowd, from which to see the canyon and the Colorado rushing by about 3,000 feet below. There are a few campsites right on the unhemmed rim, and more at a campground nearby, which are free but have no water or much of anything else. The mighty Lava Flow Rapids stir up the river just below the point, and nearby Vulcan's Throne, a volcanic remnant, rises 50 feet or more from the plain. There is a ranger station nearby the viewpoint, and a few short trails run along the rim. While this is a truly wondrous place to visit, it's not easy getting here.

There are a few different ways to get to Toroweap Point (which is technically within Grand Canyon National Park), all of them rough, washboarded, and possibly impassable during inclement weather. Make sure you take supplies and tools with you, and a map as well. The most popular route to the viewpoint is nine miles west of Fredonia off Highway 389, road 109. It's about 60 miles of rough, slow travel from there following signs. This is an all-day, if not multi-day trip that should not be taken lightly or on a whim.

Also within the monument are the conifer-topped mountains, Trumbull and Logan, both reaching around 8,000 feet and in the old days supplying the only source of lumber on the strip. Both rise within federal Wilderness Areas in the scrub south of Pipe Spring; you'll pass by them on the way to Toroweap, and you can

take a side trip to hike the short trails to both mountaintops or to walk to the half-mile trail to **Nampaweap,** a petroglyph site. For advice on visiting these areas, talk to a ranger at the **North Kaibab Ranger District** (430 S. Main Street, Fredonia, 928/643-7395), one of the rangers at Pipe Spring National Monument, or the folks at the BLM office in St. George.

Fredonia

This small settlement of about 1,000 persons at the junction of Highway 389 and U.S. 89A is a green and tidy village, a former polygamist holdout and now a place of brief respite and gear-storage for river guides and canyonland explorers. The name means "free woman" in Spanish. It is Arizona's northernmost town, just four miles south of the border with Utah, originally settled by residents of Kanab just across the line to the north. It's the strip's only town of any size, and a good base for whatever you're doing in the region. You'll find more varied accommodations, including several chain hotels and restaurants, about seven miles north on 89A in Kanab, Utah.

The best place to stop in Fredonia is the **Juniper Lodge** (465 South Main, 928/643-7752, www.juniperlodge.info, $60 d), a clean and affordable place that was remodeled in 2007 (it was formerly called the Crazy Jug Motel). The lodge's **Sage House Grill** has a river-runner theme and serves excellent breakfasts, lunches, and dinners, all of them hearty and rib-sticking and thoughtfully prepared. There's also an RV park on-site ($18.50). Note: The Juniper Lodge was sold as this book was going to press. Chances are the lodge and Sage House Grill restaurant will reopen under a different name and be just as good, if not better. It is worth checking out if you are in the area.

The Kaibab Plateau

After Fredonia, U.S. 89A begins to rise into a piñon-juniper woodland that quickly becomes a Ponderosa Pine forest as the highway climbs the massive upsweep in the land known as the Kaibab Plateau. This island-like highland, surrounded by arid valleys and giving way on its southern edge to the Grand Canyon, measures about 60 miles from north to south and roughly 45 miles east to west, ranging in height, and so climate and flora, from 3,000 and 9,200 feet. In the plateau's highest ranges, viewed easily by driving Route 67 from Jacob Lake to the North Rim, lush mixed conifer forests with intermittent aspens crowd the edges of green subalpine meadows. One of the state's best forest landscapes, the Kaibab has long been logged and hunted; there are old logging and Jeep trails crisscrossing the tableland which make backcountry exploring relatively easy, though only in a four-wheel drive and not in the winter. After November you are likely to find Route 67 to the North Rim closed, but U.S. 89A usually stays open year-round, even when the plateau is covered in a thick blanket of white.

While negotiating the steep and twisty highway on the west side of the plateau—or descending it if you're coming from the east—look for the sign for the **Le Fevre Overlook** and stop at the pull-out for a great view.

ACCOMMODATIONS AND FOOD

The primary services area for the Kaibab Plateau is the **Jacob Lake Inn** (Junction of U.S. 89A and Rte. 67, 928/643-7232, www .jacoblake.com, $94–133 for rooms, $75–122 for cabins, 6:30 A.M.–10 P.M.), about 40 miles from the North Rim at the junction of U.S. 89 A and Route 67. The complex has a small, relatively new hotel building with television and Internet available in some rooms, several rustic (though not necessarily in a good way) cabins, a restaurant, gift shop, small general store, bakery, and a gas station. They may have variable hours in winter; call ahead before planning on a stop. The restaurant serves good comfort food, warm and filling.

INFORMATION

Next to the Jacob Lake Inn, the rangers at the **Kaibab Plateau Visitors Center** (Rte. 67 and U.S. 89A, Jacob Lake, 928/643-7298, open summer only) can give you advice on hiking and exploring the plateau, and there's a good selection of books for sale and a few displays on the area's flora and fauna.

Vermillion Cliffs National Monument

Most Arizona Strip visitors see only the southern escarpment of the Paria Plateau as they cut through the valley along 89A. It is that edge's high crumbling sandstone cliffs that give this national monument of swirling slickrock and narrow, high-walled river canyons its name. The cliffs are best viewed from an established viewpoint about 10 miles east of Jacob Lake, as the highway begins to descend to the House Rock Valley.

The Paria River cuts through the northeast portion of the 294,000-acre monument, creating Paria Canyon, one of most popular canyonland backpacking trips (38 miles, about five days, reserved $5 permit required), with high, red and purple and black sandstone cliffs rising above narrow slots of sand and water. There aren't any services or visitors centers on the remote monument, and much of it is within the **Paria Canyon-Vermillion Cliffs Wilderness Area** and so can't be accessed by car. The area is best explored from the north, along Highway 89 in Utah between Kanab and Page, Arizona. From Page, head west on U.S. 89 for about 30 miles to reach the BLM's **Paria Canyon-Vermillion Cliffs Wilderness Ranger Station,** where you can get advice on visiting the area; it serves as a kind of visitors center and crossroads for backpackers and day hikers. This is really the kind of place you have to plan ahead for; most of the best areas require a permit, and those are given out on a lottery system for some of the most popular attractions. You can also access the monument from the west on the compacted-dirt House Rock/Coyote Valley Road (BLM Road 1065), off the south side of U.S. 89A at House Rock, which leads to the **Coyote Buttes Permit Area.** Coyote Buttes has a north and south section—the north is best gained via U.S. 89 in Utah. This is a world-famous trekking area where there are several trails that lead through a strange rock world of twisted, undulating, multicolored sandstone formations, often appearing as if rough, red, yellow, and pink water was held up and petrified. Along these trails you'll see all the sandstone arches, alcoves, spires, domes, amphitheaters, and buttes that make the canyonlands so exotic and enticing. A limited number of people are allowed in each day, even for day hiking, so make sure to get a permit ($5, www.blm.gov/az/asfo/paria/coyote_buttes/permits.htm) before traveling. For more information on the monument, talk to the folks at the BLM's **Arizona Strip Field Office** (345 E. Riverside Dr., St. George, UT, 435/688-3200) or the **Kanab Field Office** (435/644-4600).

Cliff Dwellers and House Rock Valley

U.S. 89A continues on through the red-dirt and sagebrush House Rock Valley at the base of the Kaibab Plateau, looked over by the Vermillion Cliffs. Just after passing the lodge in the wide spot in the road known as Cliff Dwellers—so named not for some mysterious Pueblo ruins nearby but simply because those who dwell here dwell near cliffs—you'll see a little sandstone-brick structure tucked beneath a fallen boulder, like some kind of canyon-country Hobbit house, the red-rock slabs and the sculpted boulder as indistinguishable from the cliffs as the chipped light-blue trim paint is from the ever-empty sky. This little rock house, nearly melding into the vermillion scenery, is one of the most enchanting structures in all of Arizona. There's usually a Navajo or two selling jewelry here, and you can walk around and duck in and out of the strange rock hovels, as long as you realize that this is private property and should be treated as such. The house and the other little shelters were built by Blanche and Bill Russell, the area's original homesteaders, who operated a trading post out of the rock house. The Russells also catered to the needs of Mormon travelers moving through the valley on their way to the St. George temple.

For food and accommodation, try the small **Cliff Dweller's Lodge** (928/355-2261 or 800/962-9755, www.cliffdwellerslodge.com, $75–85 d). The lodge is nearly drowned by the scenery around it, tucked beneath the base of the red cliffs. This lodge offers nice rooms with satellite television, and the restaurant serves good breakfasts, lunches, and dinners ($10–25)—everything from fajitas and ribs, to falafel and halibut.

Lee's Ferry

One of the strip's signature stops is Lee's Ferry, within the Glen Canyon National Recreation Area (www.nps.gov/glca/planyourvisit/lees-ferry.htm). Reached via paved road past high red buttes just east of Cliff Dwellers (look for the sign), Lee's Ferry is the only spot in hundreds of miles of canyonland where you can drive down to the Colorado River. It's named for a man who occupied the area rather briefly in the early 1870s, Mormon outlaw John D. Lee, one of the leaders of the infamous Mountain Meadows Massacre in Utah. Lee was exiled to this lonely spot after he and others attacked and murdered more than 100 westbound Arkansas emigrants moving through Utah Territory during a period when relations between the Utah Mormons and the U.S. government were strained, to say the least. One of Lee's wives, Emma Lee, ended up running the ferry more than Lee ever did; he soon lit out and lived as a kind of fugitive until he was finally, in 1877, recalled home and sentenced to death. The proclamation was carried out by firing squad on the very ground where the massacre had taken place. To the end and in a published memoir, Lee insisted that he was a scapegoat for the higher-ups, and many believe the massacre occurred on the orders of the Prophet Brigham Young.

The Lee family operated a small ranch and orchard near the crossing, the remnants of which can still be seen on a self-guided tour of the **Lonely Dell Ranch Historic Site,** which includes the rusting remains of a mining operation, several old boat ruins, and a graveyard. There are a few rocky hiking trails around the area, but one of the best things to do here is to simply sit on a soggy beach and watch the river flow by the sun-spattered cliffs. There's a nice campground ($12, no hookups) if you feel like staying, and a ranger station and launch ramp as well.

For long before and after Lee lent his name to the crossing, this two-mile break in the Colorado River's canyon-digging, near the mouth of the Paria River, was one of the very few places to cross the river in southern Utah and northern Arizona; in fact, it remained so until the bridging of the Colorado at Marble Canyon in 1929. Today, the area is the starting block for thousands of brave river-trippers who venture into the Grand Canyon atop the Colorado every year. It's also a popular fishing spot, though the trout here have been introduced and were not native to the warm muddy flow before the dam at Glen Canyon changed the Colorado's character. For guides, gear, and any other information about the area, try **Lee's Ferry Anglers** (928/355-2261 or 800/962-9755, www.leesferry.com) located at the Cliff Dweller's Lodge.

Lee's Ferry is also significant because it provides the dividing line between the upper and lower states of the Colorado River's watershed, inasmuch as they were divided by the compact that divvied up the river's water for human use. This has made Lee's Ferry "river mile 0," the gateway and crossroads to both the upper and lower Colorado, and the place where its annual flows are measured and recorded.

Lee's Ferry Lodge at Vermillion Cliffs (U.S. 89A near Marble Canyon, 928/355-2231 or 800/451-2231, www.leesferrylodge.com, $63 d) has comfortable rooms and a delicious restaurant serving hearty fare perfect after a long day of outdoor play, and its beer selection (more than one hundred different bottles) is outrageously diverse for such an out-of-the-way place. The steaks are hand-cut, and the ribs are outstanding, smothered in the lodge's special homemade sauce. The lodge serves breakfast, lunch, and dinner daily ($10–20).

Navajo Bridge and Marble Canyon

A few miles before 89A runs into U.S. 89 south toward Navajoland and the Grand Canyon, two bridges span Marble Canyon, where the

© TIM HULL

The first Navajo Bridge over Marble Canyon was replaced in the 1990s.

WARREN JEFFS AND COLORADO CITY

Just west of Pipe Spring National Monument, the polygamist community of Colorado City-Hilldale, with a population of about 6,000 persons, sits in the jagged shadow of the Vermillion Cliffs. These sister towns, stretching across the Utah border, are little more than a collection of large homes that appear to have been built in stages and never quite finished, tri- and quad-plexes with little attention paid to finish carpentry, as if new wings had to go up quickly and cheaply all the time.

These isolated towns have been the subject of a lot of lurid media interest over the last several years thanks to the arrest and conviction of Warren Jeffs, erstwhile leader of the Fundamentalist Church of Jesus Christ of Latter-day Saints. Nearly all the property here, and all those sprawling homes, used to be owned by the church's financial arm, the United Effort Plan, which was controlled by Jeffs. Most FLDS members were born into the sect, the descendants of a splinter group of Mormons who never accepted the mainstream LDS church's giving up of polygamy in 1890, and who migrated to this dry and windy, off-track place in the 1920s and 1930s.

Jeffs became the hereditary leader of the FLDS, Colorado City, and all the people in it in 2001. Jeffs was by many accounts a fickle and cruel leader, expelling community members for perceived lapses in morality while forcing underage girls into sexual relationships and into marriage with much older men. After several complaints were filed in Utah and Arizona, in 2005 a grand jury indicted Jeffs on two counts of sexual conduct with a minor and conspiracy. Jeffs left Colorado City and became a fugitive. A yearlong manhunt ensued, which saw Jeffs named to the FBI's Ten Most Wanted List. In 2006 he was captured near Las Vegas. He was tried and sentenced in Utah to five years to life for rape as an accomplice. At this writing Jeffs faced similar charges in Arizona and was due to be extradited to Kingman.

Things are getting better, it seems, for Colorado City's residents. In early 2008, the Associated Press reported that the United Effort Plan had been dissolved, and now those who built the sprawling, multi-family homes have a chance to actually own them.

To learn more about the history of the FLDS, check out Jon Krakauer's excellent *Under the Banner of Heaven*, and Carolyn Jessop's *Escape*, which tells the harrowing story of an FLDS woman who chose to flee in the night from Colorado City with her children rather than live under Jeffs' erratic regime.

Colorado River digs deep again after its surfacing at Lee's Ferry. This is the exit from or the entrance to the heart of the strip, depending on which way you're headed. The original Navajo Bridge was opened in 1929, the first bridge to cross this part of the Colorado, putting Lee's Ferry out of business for good. By 1995, a new bridge had opened, as the original was not up to the increased traffic along 89A. The original bridge is now kept open for sightseers, and you can walk over it and look down at the river flowing through magnificent Marble Canyon, here at the very start of the Grand Canyon. The **Navajo Bridge Interpretive Center** (928/355-2319, www.nps.gov/glca/historyculture/navajobridge .htm, 9 A.M.–5 P.M., Apr.–Oct.) has a book shop and displays about the bridge, and there are usually several booths selling Native American arts and crafts.

PAGE AND LAKE POWELL

The town would not exist without the lake, and the lake would not exist without the dam: such is the symbiotic chain of existence here in the slickrock lands around sunken Glen Canyon, where water-lovers come to play among the red and pink sandstone labyrinths.

Page is a small, tidy town with a higher-than-normal number of churches for its size; they are all lined up along one long block at the beginning of this resort burg's main drag. The population here was once composed primarily of dam builders and their families, for the town was founded in 1957 as a government-run camp for Glen Canyon Dam workers, built on land formerly owned by the Navajo but traded for a slice of property in Utah. These days Page has sizable Latter-day Saint and Navajo communities, and the population swells with boaters, water skiers, swimmers, and houseboat loungers in the spring and summer. The business life of Page is now dedicated to that influx, so there are plenty of chain hotels and restaurants here if you don't want to stay and eat at Wahweap Marina, the lake's largest marina and the center of most Arizona visits to the lake, most of which is in Utah.

Sights

Just off Page's main drag is the **John Wesley Powell Museum and Visitor Information Center** (6 N. Lake Powell Blvd., 928/645-9496 or 888/597-6873, www.powell museum.org, 9 A.M.–5 P.M. Mon.–Fri., $5 adults over 12, $1 kids under 12), named, as is the nearby man-made lake, for the one-armed Civil War veteran, scientist, writer, and explorer who led the first two river expeditions through the Grand Canyon. The center has an excellent bookstore, and the friendly staff can help you book boat and air tours, but the museum itself takes a little more effort to enjoy. While there is a lot of information on Powell and the river-runners who followed in his path, most of the displays are made up of long articles that you have to stand there and read. Children will likely be impatient, though there's a small interactive display on the natural science of the area.

A color-swirled, weather-worn slot in a mesa on Navajoland, **Antelope Canyon Navajo Tribal Park** (928/698-2808, 8 A.M.–5 P.M. daily Apr.–Oct., $6 admission, guided tours extra) is a few miles outside Page on Highway 98. This popular crevice of twisting and twirling smooth-rock has two sections—an upper, into which you must climb down a ladder bolted to the rock wall, and a lower, reached by an easy walk along a sandy bottomland. A

visit to either requires the presence of a Navajo guide—no exceptions. **Antelope Canyon Tours** (928/645-9102 or 928/660-0739, www .antelopecanyon.com) in Page will take you out in one of its big four-wheelers for a 1.5-hour general tour or a 2.5-hour photographer's tour. You can also usually hire a guide at the site.

◖ Glen Canyon National Recreation Area

Sprawling over the Arizona-Utah border and some 1.25 million acres, Glen Canyon National Recreation Area (928/608-6200, www.nps.gov/glca, $15 per car for seven-day pass) is a popular boating, fishing, and hiking area centered on **Lake Powell,** the continent's second largest man-made lake. Created by the damming of the Colorado River and the destruction of the river-sculpted Glen Canyon, the lake is 186 miles long and has more than a thousand miles of meandering desert shoreline. Its waters run through a red-rock maze of skinny side canyons, like canals around an ornate, abandoned city sculpted out of sandstone. During the spring and summer months the lake is crowded with sometimes rowdy Jet Skiers, water-skiers, and houseboat residents, but one could visit the area and never get wet—the canyon-country scenery is enough to draw and keep even the most water-averse visitors. The whole area resembles one vast, salmon-pink sand dune frozen and petrified at once—it is a desolate, lonely place sometimes, beautiful and sacred, but also a reminder of how humans can change a seemingly unalterable landscape at their will.

Probably the most popular activity on Lake Powell is houseboating. The floating mansions chug among the buttes and spires, while their residents shoot water cannons at each other and stop at night for bonfires and parties on the few beaches around the lake. It's expensive to rent one of the boats, most of which sleep up to 12 people and have all the comforts of a land-loving home and then some. On average, expect to pay about $100–150 per person per day for a houseboat, which you can rent from three days up to seven days. You can rent a boat

THE DAM AND THE RIVER

Looking out at the dam through large picture windows in Glen Canyon's **Carl Hayden Visitor Center** (928/648-6404 or 928/608-6072, www.nps.gov/glca, 8 A.M.–5 P.M. daily, free tours offered), it's difficult not to be impressed. The great concrete slab shimmed into the narrow Navajo-sandstone channel allows for the storage of some 27,000,000 acre-feet of water (an acre-foot of water is roughly the amount that a family of four uses in a year); it's a brash reclamation feat if there ever was one. But it is also difficult to see Lake Powell, the man-made reservoir turned water playground created by the dam, and not feel that something was lost in the flooding of once-spectacular Glen Canyon and the irrevocable alteration of the Colorado River's ecosystem.

The writer and desert-country anarchist Edward Abbey, whose famous 1975 trickster-novel *The Monkey Wrench Gang* envisions the destruction of Glen Canyon Dam by a group of eco-warriors, described the long lost canyon, waiting silent about three hundred feet below Lake Powell's glassy surface, as a "once lovely wonderland of grottoes, alcoves, Indian ruins, natural stone arches, cottonwood groves, springs and seeps and hanging gardens of ivy, columbine, and maidenhair fern – and many other rare things."

Along with the sinking of this natural wonderland, the dam severely altered the character of the Colorado River downstream. A sediment-laden river – a characteristic of the mighty flow that allowed it to carve those famous canyons – the Colorado River once ran warm and muddy, filled with native fish and lined by beaches and groves of cottonwood and willow. Now that the flow is stopped at the dam and impounded, the once sediment-heavy river runs cool and clear coming out of the other side, which has encouraged exotic, invasive plant and fish species to thrive to the detriment of the native flora and fauna. Beaches that are eroded don't come back so easily because of the lack of sediment in the river flow, and a controlled flow has replaced the natural flood cycle of the river, leading to the disappearance of an entire ecosystem.

Many people, including some who once supported the dam's construction, now believe that too much was lost for what was gained. The dam is surely an awesome sight, and it will either draw your admiration for the brave and tough men who built it from 1957 to 1964, or your disgust for the once-wild river that it changed forever. More likely, you'll feel a little bit of both, and you will agree with Abbey, who conceded that "though much has been lost, much remains."

Since the 1990s the river below the dam has been purposely flooded several times with timed releases of flows from the reservoir. An army of scientists then moves into the canyon along the river to determine the flood's effects on the ecosystem. While these experiments have been helpful, many scientists believe they happen too infrequently to make much of a difference in combating the dam's negative influence downriver.

© TIM HULL

Glen Canyon Dam

at Wahweap Marina (www.lakepowell.com/ houseboats/), and it's best to plan far ahead and make a reservation (888/896-3829).

WAHWEAP MARINA

The largest marina in the recreation area and the center of Arizona-side visits to Lake Powell, the **Wahweap Marina** (928/645-2433, www .lakepowell.com) offers lodging, food, boat and other watercraft rentals, camping, RV parking, tours, and shopping all within one area. Aramark is the main concessionaire at the marina, running the **Lake Powell Resort and Marina** (100 Lakeshore Dr., 928/645-2433, $94–198 d), where you can rent the equipment to do just about anything on the lake. The hotel has two heated pools, a sauna, a hot tub, and a workout room. The marina's **Rainbow Room** (100 Lakeshore Dr., 928/645-2433, 6 A.M.–2 P.M. and 5–10 P.M. daily in season, 7 A.M.–1:30 P.M. and 5–9 P.M. daily in winter, $6–16) at the Lake Powell Resort has lakeview tables and serves delicious fish, steak, pork chops, and pasta for dinner and a buffet at lunch.

Between April and October, the marina offers several boat tours of the lake, including dinner and breakfast cruises and day trips to Rainbow Bridge and elsewhere. The red rocks grow warm and flash their deep hidden colors during sunrise and sunset, and a boat tour is a great way to experience this. There are nighttime tours of the lake for a view of the city of stars that emerges from the huge, clear sky. Depending on their length, boat tours from Wahweap run $31–124. The marina has a sandy beach with chairs, cabanas, and kayaks for rent, and it offers guided fishing tours and water skiing instructions, among myriad other activities.

RAINBOW BRIDGE NATIONAL MONUMENT

Rainbow Bridge, the world's largest arched rock span and one of the true wonders of the natural world, is a sacred site to the Navajo, who call it *Nonnezoshi* (rainbow turned to stone). An improbable arch of reddish-orange sandstone 290 feet high, the "bridge" is one of the most popular sites within the recreation area, even with the difficulty in getting there and the admonitions against walking under the arch in deference to Navajo beliefs. While you can gear up for a multi-day backpack trip across the hot, rugged land to reach the wonder on foot, most visitors take a 50-mile, all-day boat tour from Wahweap Marina or take their own boat to the well-signed port of call. Aramark (800/528-6154, www.lakepowell .com) is in charge of tours. The trip includes an easy two-mile round-trip hike from the dock to the arch.

Accommodations and Food

Millions of tourists drive through Page every season to see Lake Powell and the canyonlands, and as a result the area has all the usual chain hotels and several chain restaurants. Most of the accommodations are mid-range. There's a very affordable and clean **Motel 6** (637 S. Lake Powell Blvd., 928/645-5888, $55–81 d) with a pool and interior corridors, and the **Best Western at Lake Powell** (208 N. Lake Powell Blvd., 928/645-5988, $99–159 d) serves a good continental breakfast and offers wireless Internet. For dinner try **Strombolli's Italian Restaurant & Pizzeria** (711 N. Navajo Dr., 928/645-2605, 11 A.M.–close Mon.–Sat., noon–close Sun., $8–10) for delicious Italian entrées like baked ravioli with meat sauce.

Information and Services

The **Page Lake Powell Tourism Bureau** (647-A Elm St., 928/660-3405, www.page lakepowelltourism.com) has all kinds of information on Page, Glen Canyon, and the rest of the region, and the staff there can help you book tours.

THE LOWER COLORADO RIVER

The great river is the chief draw of this region, and there's always much to see and do in the small resort communities along its banks, especially if you like getting wet.

Here you can marvel at the engineering audacity of Hoover Dam, which sought to tame the Colorado and bring hydroelectricity, irrigation, and predictable flows to the desert. Spend hot, lazy days by the water at Lake Havasu City, and stroll across London Bridge, rebuilt here in the desert in the 1970s. Discover the Old West in Yuma, and the history of American road culture in Kingman and along the lonely remains of old Route 66.

Several river-and-desert wildlife refuges and the red-rock stretches of Lake Mead National Recreation Area offer a glimpse at the power nature still wields over us, no matter how much we try to control it. And the shifting sand dunes outside of Yuma will make you wonder if you wandered into the Sahara.

This region is often the hottest in the state, if not the country, but the cool waters of the Colorado make it a resort destination for thousands of water-loving visitors every year.

PLANNING YOUR TIME

A week is sufficient to tour the west coast in depth, but a scenic drive-through with a stop for a dip in the river, or a boat tour, and a visit to all the essentials can be done in a long weekend. It's best to start at one end and drive south or north, hitting towns and sights along the river. From the north, start at Lake Mead National Recreation Area (or in Las Vegas, just an hour or so to the northwest) and move

HIGHLIGHTS

◖ **Hoover Dam:** Tour one of the largest concrete dams in the world, holding back the Colorado River in a barren desert canyon (page 258).

◖ **Driving Historic Route 66:** Sink back into a simpler time when road travel was slower and a good deal more interesting by driving the longest remaining stretch of the old Mother Road, where nostalgia for a long-gone American road culture rules and there's something fascinating and forgotten around every bend (page 266).

◖ **London Bridge:** Discover a picturesque bridge that once spanned the Thames in London, now reaching across the Lake Havasu channel (page 270).

◖ **Yuma Territorial Prison State Historic Park:** Witness how the rapscallions and outlaws of Arizona's wild Territorial days lived in this legendary Old West prison (page 278).

LOOK FOR ◖ TO FIND RECOMMENDED SIGHTS, ACTIVITIES, DINING, AND LODGING.

LOWER COLORADO RIVER

south on Highway 93 to Kingman. Along the way, visit the recreation area and Hoover Dam, an absolutely essential stop in this region. From Kingman, take Historic Route 66 over Sitgreaves Pass and through the little Old West re-enactment town of Oatman, with its friendly semi-wild burros. If you want to gamble or splash in the Colorado, from Oatman head west to Highway 95 and Bullhead City-Laughlin; if you want to skip Route 66 altogether and head straight back to the river, take Highway 68 west from Kingman. If you're more interested in desolate stretches than riverplay, you can keep south on Route 66 from Oatman to Topok and the Havasu National Wildlife Refuge. A brief tug east on I-40 and then south through the seemingly empty land along Highway 95 will take you right into Lake Havasu City, where you can stroll beneath

The Oatman Hotel once welcomed Route 66 drivers.

© TIM HULL

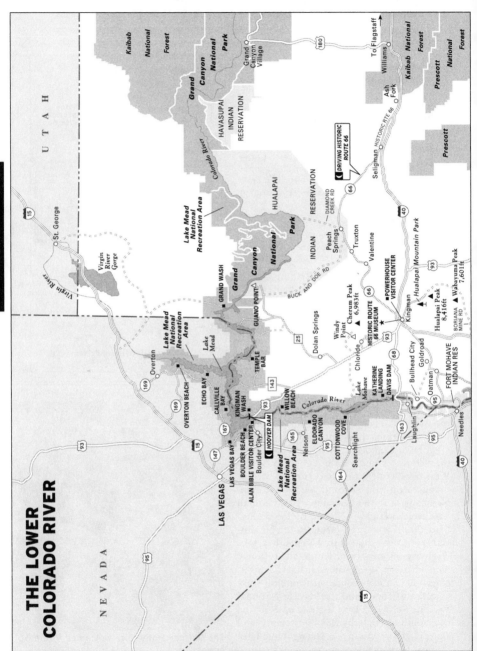

THE LOWER COLORADO RIVER

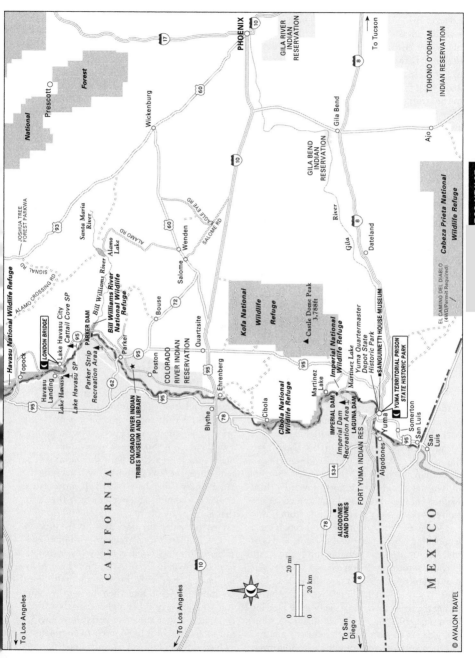

LOWER COL

London Bridge and maybe rent a boat or book a cruise up to wild Topok Gorge. Keep heading south through the sparse, jagged desert through Parker and Quartzsite and then on to Yuma, the southern end of the tour. A short drive west into California on I-8 will take you to the strange and thrilling Algodones Dunes, where you can imagine that you're floating above the Dune Sea in *Return of the Jedi*. Just west of Highway 95 north of Yuma you'll find Martinez Lake, where you can book a boat tour into the Imperial National Wildlife Refuge. To reach the refuge on your own, take I-10 from Quartzsite to Blythe, California, then Highway 78 south. Also just a bit north of Yuma along Highway 95 you'll pass the huge Kofa National Wildlife Refuge, where you can take a short hike into Palm Canyon to see the state's only native palm trees. If you're starting from Yuma in the south, which makes sense if you're coming from either Tucson or Phoenix, reverse the route, taking Highway 95 north across the desert, then Route 66 northeast, then Highway 93 northwest to Hoover Dam.

Lake Mead National Recreation Area

Water spreads like exploring fingers over the dry, scrubby land, molding a wet playground out of the necessities of industry and progress. It wasn't enough for those reclaimers of the 1930s to stop the Colorado River dead in its tracks and impound all the water the imagined Southwestern empire would need. Why not create a boating and fishing empire while we're at it? And so we have this 290-square-mile, 2.5-million-acre national recreation area, the nation's first.

There are two desert lakes here: Mead, at 115 miles long the continent's largest manmade body of water, and the smaller Mojave, 67 miles downriver. Two dams hold the waters back: Hoover, some 70 stories high, keeps Lake Mead in check, while the smaller Davis Dam has its back to Mojave. The placid waters lap at more than 700 miles of Mojave Desert shoreline in two states and stretch north toward a third. Millions of waterborne and sun-stained revelers find this place every year, flocking from nearby Las Vegas and the Arizona cities. There is excellent fishing here, no matter the season, and boating, swimming, scuba diving, sun bathing, and houseboat touring. If you're not a water type, a tour of Hoover Dam or a slow drive along Lake Mead's scenic North Shore Road—the sun igniting the red-rock cliffs of the Bowl of Fire, bighorn sheep picking along the rough rock spines along the road—are enough to justify a visit.

Due to prolonged drought in the Southwest, the recreation area has been plagued in recent years by low water levels—in some places it is 60 feet below normal levels—causing the closure of a few areas. It's a good idea to call the recreation area's headquarters (601 Nevada Way, Boulder City, NV, 702/293-8907, www .nps.gov/lame) or check the website before making your travel plans.

◖ HOOVER DAM

Once the largest dam of its kind just about anywhere, the Hoover Dam is still one of the nation's greatest engineering and construction feats and stands today as a testament to the brawn and ambition of a people set on taming a wild river. The Southwest as we know it simply would not exist without this dam. At the same time, the Colorado River will never be the same, and we may have traded an entire native river ecosystem for a more predictable flow than that allowed by the natural flood and drought cycles that ruled the wild river. In the process, an epic human story played out, with thousands of men climbing the sheer rock walls of an overheated canyon in the middle of nowhere, holding back a river with concrete and will. Some say more than 700 men died during the dam's construction (a number higher than the official estimates), which took five years and about 3.2 million cubic yards of concrete to complete.

Not only is Hoover Dam an engineering

© TIM HULL

A tour of Hoover Dam takes you deep into the structure to see the Colorado River from a different perspective.

audacity of the highest order, it's a rather stylish one at that. Heading west out of Kingman along U.S. 93, suddenly the walls of Black Canyon close in and the huge concrete slab of the dam comes into view. You have to drive over the dam to reach Nevada and the **Parking Garage** (8 A.M.–6 P.M. daily, $7 cash only), passing sculptor Oskar J. W. Hansen's soaring *Winged Figures of the Republic,* two 30-foot-high bronze man-angels with arms bearing the strained and hard muscles of the long-gone dam builders attached to upstretched wings, meant to symbolize, according to the artist, "the enormous power of trained physical strength, equally enthroned in placid triumph of scientific accomplishment."

The **Hoover Dam Visitor Center** (702/494-2517 or 866/730-90979, www.usbr.gov/lc/hooverdam/service/index.html, 9:30 A.M.–5 P.M. daily, $8 without tour) has numerous exhibits on the building of the dam and the scientific and social justifications behind the enormous undertaking.

There's a short movie, and an elevator to the roof and the best overview of the dam complex and the river flowing beyond it on down to Lake Mojave. If you're here already, it's worth it to take one of two tours offered. The **Powerplant Tour** ($11, $9 kids 4–16) lasts about two hours and gives a comprehensive view of the dam and an explanation of how it works. The **Hoover Dam Tour** ($25, no kids under 8 allowed) lasts about 1.5 hours and goes deep into the dam and reveals the inner workings of the huge complex. This tour is highly recommended and is worth the extra money; it includes a booklet about the dam for each participant. You get to walk the rounded and brightly lit, low-ceiling corridors inside the damworks, and view the lazy band of river from high up in the dam. This tour also provides a chance to see all the beautiful Art Nouveau touches folded into the design of the dam complex in the 1930s, an arguably more stylish era than our own. The entire inner complex is floored with a gray Italian marble flecked with reds and yellows, and there are stylized Native American–inspired designs etched into the floor in even the most out-of-the-way corners. In summer, the first tour begins at 9:15 A.M. and the last tour begins at 5:15 P.M. In winter, the last tour begins at 4:15 P.M. The last tickets are sold an hour before the last tour. There's a standard gift shop near the parking garage, and a little café that serves good hamburgers, sandwiches, hot dogs and other tasty eats.

LAKE MEAD

The largest of the two lakes in the recreation area, Lake Mead has 247 square miles of surface area and extends about 115 miles up the Colorado and another 35 up the Virgin River. It is very hot here in the summer, despite all the splashing and frolicking going on in the water. There is little shade in the Mojave, and the sun is incessant and unforgiving. The vegetation is sparse—nothing but rocks, scrub, and barren red, pink, and blue hills, sharp and jagged. The native terrain seems out of touch with the man-made oases around the lake, with their imported palm trees and other assorted lush touches, creating a contradictory atmosphere that is strange and thrilling. Throngs flood the lake country, with speedboats, sailboats, and fishing boats in tow, on any given spring or summer weekend. From April through October the high temperatures are generally in the 80s, then the 90s, then up to the triple digits in deep summer, then back down to the 90s and then 80s. By November and through March the weather is cooler, though certainly not cold. Water temperatures range from 45°F in winter to 85°F in the summer. One of the least crowded times of year to visit is January and February, though you might not want to get in the water during this time. The best place to start is the **Alan Bible Visitor Center** (U.S. 93 and Lakeshore Scenic Dr., four miles southeast of Boulder City, Nev., 702/293-8990, www .nps.gov/lame/, 8:30 A.M.–4:30 P.M. daily $5 per vehicle, good for five days) just west of Hoover Dam along U.S. 93. Here you'll find helpful rangers and volunteers with all the information and maps you'll need for your visit.

NORTHSHORE ROAD

If you're only going to be in the area for a day or so, or if you're not the water-sports type, the best way to see the recreation area's natural wonders is to take a slow, scenic drive along Lake Mead's **Northshore Road.** From the entrance station near the Alan Bible Visitor Center, head north on Lakeshore Scenic Drive, which turns into North Shore Road. You'll pass all the major west- and north-end bays and beaches, and you can turn off at any point and stop. The road extends more than 50 miles along the shore and eventually becomes Route 169 near Overton, Nevada. Try to make it as far as the spectacular **Bowl of Fire** at the base of the Muddy Mountains, about 25 miles from the entrance. The Bowl of Fire is so named for the deep red rocks jutting up off the desert, which light up as if ablaze, especially as the sun is dropping in the west. Climb up about half a mile to the overlook on the **Northshore Summit Trail** (it's well signed at the trailhead) for one of the best views in the region. Keep

your eyes open along the rocky spines of the mountains on both sides of the road, for you're likely to see a few bighorn sheep negotiating the rugged terrain.

RECREATION
Hiking and Biking

One of the longer hikes in the recreation area will take you to natural hot springs in a slot canyon below Hoover Dam. The hike to **Arizona Hot Springs,** in White Rock Canyon, is a six-mile round-trip, moderately rough trek to the Colorado River and into a side canyon with nearly vertical walls and the spare and rocky landscape typical of this inhospitable but strangely beautiful land. This isn't for the weak, though—you have to climb down a 20-foot ladder stuck in the rocks to reach the best pools, and the walk back to the car can be a tough trudge even for well-worn hikers. To reach the trailhead go east from the visitors center about eight miles, four miles past Hoover Dam on U.S. 95 to a dirt parking lot, which is at the head of White Rock Canyon (the trailhead is on the map you'll get when entering the recreation area). Just outside the visitors center is the trailhead for the **Railroad Tunnel Trail,** which leads along the disused right-of-way built during the construction of Hoover Dam and through five spooky old train tunnels. From the visitors center to the entrance to the fifth tunnel is just over two miles one-way. A hike from the visitors center through all five tunnels to the dam is just over three miles one-way. The recreation area's newspaper, *Desert Views,* has a comprehensive listing of the trails around Lake Mead, most of which are quite short and lead to some overlook or scenic feature. Be careful hiking here, especially in the summer, when you probably won't want to do much walking, let alone long hard desert trekking.

There are more than 800 miles of backcountry dirt roads through the Mojave Desert in the recreation area, perfect for touring on a mountain bike. Ask at the visitors center for a map of the backcountry roads. Also try the Railroad Tunnel Trail for biking.

Boating

You can rent boats for fishing, exploring, waterskiing, and living the easy laketop life at **Las Vegas Boat Harbor** (702/293-1191) and **Lake Mead Marina** (which, due to low water levels in early 2008 moved permanently from its original location at Boulder Harbor two miles south to become part of Las Vegas Boat Harbor and Marina in Hemenway Harbor) and **Callville Bay Resort** (702/565-8958)—everything from 16-foot fishing crafts to big patio cruisers, 18-foot speedsters to houseboats that are roomier and more decked-out than most landbound homes.

If you're more about floating and skimming by your own power, look into **Black Canyon/Willow Beach River Adventures** (in Hacienda Hotel on Hwy. 93, 702/494-2204, 10:30 A.M.–5 P.M., Mon.–Fri., or call 702/293-8204, www.blackcanyonadventures.com/, $83–119), which offers all-day trips through the starkly beautiful Black Canyon at the base of Hoover Dam to Willow Beach, with several stops at beaches for swimming and frolicking and a waterside box lunch. **Boulder City Outfitters** (1631 Industrial Rd., Boulder City, Nev., 702/293-1190, www.bouldercityoutfitters.com, $163) also provides all-day guided tours of the same area with lunch.

Those with their own paddle craft need to get a permit ($10, plus $3 entrance fee) to launch at Black Canyon; you can get one through Black Canyon/Willow Beach Adventures in its office at the Hacienda Hotel just west of Hoover Dam.

A leisurely sightseeing cruise around Lake Mead, with some trips attended by either breakfast or dinner, is a popular way to take in the scenery. **Lake Mead Cruises** (702/293-6180, www.lakemeadcruises.com, $22–58) offers several different options.

You can rent a **houseboat** for three days or up to a week ($750–4,000); most sleep between 6 and 14 people and come with all kinds of extras depending on how much you want to pay. Contact **Seven Crown Resorts** (800/752-9669, www.sevencrown.com) or **Forever Houseboats** (800/255-5561, www.foreverhouseboats.com).

Swimming and Scuba Diving

The best place to swim and scuba dive is around **Boulder Beach,** not far from the visitors center, which has a cordoned swimming area that's popular with families. The area has been lately adversely affected by low water levels, but swimming there remains viable. There's a **Dive Park** at North Boulder Beach that's a great place for beginners and experts alike, and a few watercraft have been deliberately submerged here for exploring and pretending. **Boulder Islands,** large concrete tanks used to store water during the construction of the dam, is also a popular area for scuba enthusiasts. More experienced and adventuresome scuba divers have many options around the two lakes. Check out the website (www.nps.gov/lame/planyourvisit/scuba.htm#CP_JUMP_37496).

Fishing

Sport anglers launch on Lake Mead in search of striped and largemouth bass, rainbow trout, channel catfish and others. The biggest striped bass in Lake Mead have been known to weigh up to 50 pounds. Each of the marinas has fishing gear for sale and rent, boats for rent, fishing guides and information. The recreation area's website has an up-to-date fishing report at www.nps.gov/lame/fishrpt.html.

ACCOMMODATIONS AND FOOD

There are three lakeside lodges within the Lake Mead portion of the recreation area, each with a restaurant and bar. The **Echo Bay Resort** (702/394-4000, www.sevencrown.com, $70–125 d) has standard rooms, many with gorgeous lake views, and the **Temple Bar Resort and Marina** (928/767-3211, www.foreverhouseboats.com, $85–125) in the eastern part of the lake offers standard rooms, fishing cabins, and suites with kitchens, some with lake views and some with desert views. **Lake Mead Lodge,** near Boulder Beach, as of early 2008 was only taking reservations for up to 30 days in advance because of low water levels there, which at the same time led to the removal of the marina to nearby Las Vegas Harbor.

There are hundreds of **camping** spots around Lake Mead, each offered at $10 per night and obtained on a first-come, first-served basis. The campgrounds—with showers and tables and grills and all the other amenities a camper needs—are at **Boulder Beach** (154 sites), **Callville Bay** (80 sites), **Echo Bay** (166 sites), **Temple Bar** (153 sites), and **Las Vegas Bay** (89 sites). Visitors with RVs will find sites with full hookups at **Callville Bay Resort** (702/565-8958), **Echo Bay Resort** (702/394-4000), and **Temple Bar** (928/767-3211).

LAKE MOHAVE

This lake doesn't really seem like a lake at all but more like the river it's filled with. Mohave is thin and runs long through Black Canyon as if it were the untamed Colorado, widening at Arizona Basin and Cottonwood Basin to seem more lake-like. The scenery around Mohave is similar to that around Mead, spare and rocky, ruled by creosote and other scrub, with sandy beaches and hidden coves. The recreation opportunities are similar as well—fishing and waterskiing, houseboating and floating in the calm, warm water. To rent a boat or to hire a guide to take you on a tour of Mohave, try **Desert River Outfitters** (2649

Hwy. 95, Bullhead City, 888/529-2533, www.desertriveroutfitters.com, $25–80 for kayak rental; $35 3–4-hour guided trip on Lake Mohave).

A boat launch and placid waters ringed by ragged rock cliffs make **Willow Beach** a fine place for an easy day on the water with your canoe, fishing near a fish hatchery, or just lounging and picnicking on the hot desert beach. Waterfowl and other birds abound. Take U.S. 93 west toward Hoover Dam and turn at the sign for Willow Beach.

Accommodations and Food

Lake Mohave has two major marinas, both with small hotels with basic and clean lakeside rooms, stores, restaurants, bars, and boat and watercraft rentals (including house boats)—everything you'll need for a perfect time on the water. **Cottonwood Cove Resort & Marina** (702/297-1464, www.cottonwoodcoveresort.com/, $65–115 d) is on the Nevada side and has a nice little lodge and campground, and a great swimming beach popular with kids. On the Arizona side just outside of Bullhead City is **Lake Mohave Resort at Katherine Landing** (2690 E. Katherine Spur Rd., Bullhead City, 928/754-3245, www.sevencrown.com, $60–125 d), close to Davis Dam.

Kingman and Vicinity

Spread across a dry desert basin below pine-topped mountains and cut through by I-40, Kingman and its environs have long been a stopover for those traveling the two famous American trails along the 35th Parallel: The Santa Fe Railroad and Route 66. Indeed, the town, mostly a transportation hub and county government center these days, has secured its place in Americana, along with a few other Arizona towns, by appearing in that song, certainly one of the most frequently covered tunes of all time, written in 1946 by Bobby Troup and first recorded by the great Nat King Cole:

. . . Flagstaff, Arizona.
Don't forget Winona, Kingman,
Barstow, San Bernardino.
Won't you get hip to this timely tip,
when you make that California trip.
Get your kicks on Route 66.

The area's identity, at least for the sake of tourism, is all wrapped up in being the "Heart of Route 66," and there are a few nostalgic sights here harkening back to a time when cross-country travel was slower and, in a sense, more meaningful than it is today. Here you can peruse museums and stores featuring the

LOWER COLORADO RIVER

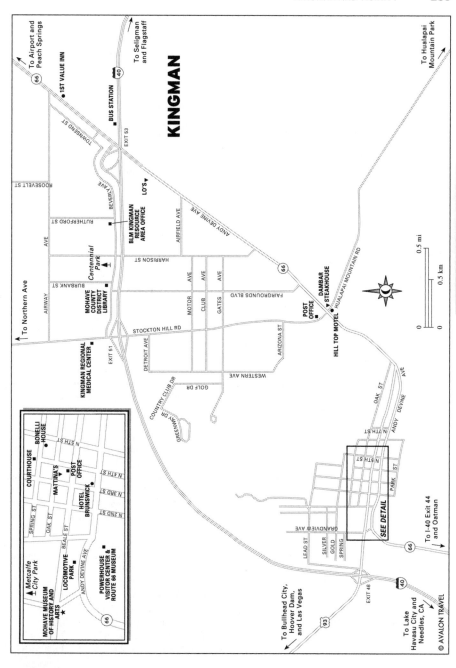

KINGMAN

To Airport and Peach Springs

To Seligman and Flagstaff

To Hualapai Mountain Park

1ST VALUE INN

BUS STATION

EXIT 53

TOWNSEND ST

ROOSEVELT ST

BEVERLY AVE

LO'S

RUTHERFORD ST

BLM KINGMAN RESOURCE AREA OFFICE

AIRFIELD AVE

ANDY DEVINE AVE

AVE

Centennial Park

HARRISON ST

To Northern Ave

AIRWAY AVE

BURBANK ST

MOHAVE COUNTY DISTRICT LIBRARY

MOTOR AVE

CLUB AVE

GATES AVE

FAIRGROUNDS BLVD

DAMBAR STEAKHOUSE

HUALAPAI MOUNTAIN RD

STOCKTON HILL RD

POST OFFICE

HILL TOP MOTEL

DETROIT AVE

KINGMAN REGIONAL MEDICAL CENTER

EXIT 51

ARIZONA ST

WESTERN AVE

GOLF DR

COUNTRY CLUB DR

GREENWAY DR

0.5 mi

0.5 km

OAK ST

ANDY DEVINE AVE

N 7TH ST

N 6TH ST

PARK ST

SEE DETAIL

To I-40 Exit 44 and Oatman

GRANDVIEW AVE

LEAD ST

SILVER ST

GOLD ST

SPRING ST

EXIT 48

To Bullhead City, Hoover Dam, and Las Vegas

To Lake Havasu City and Needles, CA

© AVALON TRAVEL

Inset map (detail):

Metcalfe City Park

MOHAVE MUSEUM OF HISTORY AND ARTS

BONELLI HOUSE

COURTHOUSE

N 5TH ST

MATTINA'S

POST OFFICE

N 4TH ST

HOTEL BRUNSWICK

N 3RD ST

N 2ND ST

SPRING ST

OAK ST

BEALE ST

LOCOMOTIVE PARK

ANDY DEVINE AVE

POWERHOUSE VISITOR CENTER & ROUTE 66 MUSEUM

artifacts and stories of the heyday of Route 66 travel, and then hop in your car and drive the rough and twisting remains of the Mother Road, through squat cactus forests and old lost towns still pining for the region's long-gone gold and silver mining days. The old route ends back at the river, where Bullhead City and Laughlin wait for you to get up on those water skis or shake the hand of the one-armed bandit.

SIGHTS

Much of what is worth seeing in Kingman is housed in one big stone building in the historic downtown (where there are some 60 registered historic buildings). Built in 1907 to supply power to the region's mines, the **Powerhouse Visitor Center** (120 W. Andy Devine Ave., 928/753-6106, 9 A.M.–6 P.M. daily in summer and spring, 9 A.M.–5 P.M. Dec.–Feb.) houses several locally themed stores, an old Route 66–style diner, a museum, and a visitors center with a wealth of information on the area. Across the street is **Locomotive Park,** where you can see a well-preserved steam engine and examine the area's history as an important railroad hub.

The highlight of the Powerhouse is the **Historic Route 66 Museum** (120 W. Andy Devine Ave., 928/753-9889, 9 A.M.–6 P.M. daily in summer and spring, 9 A.M.–5 P.M. Dec.–Feb., $4, kids under 13 free), where, through a series of detailed dioramas and displays, you'll learn everything you ever wanted to know about the movement of people through this dusty desert portion of the 35th Parallel, from the Native Americans to the Dust-Bowl refugees, to Route 66's heyday in the 1950s, through to today, when much of the road-romance found in those eras is dead and gone. But thanks to this excellent little museum, we can relive it all just a bit. Old American car and road culture enthusiasts should not miss this sight.

About a block away from the Powerhouse is the **Mohave Museum of History and Arts** (400 W. Beale St., 928/753-3195, 9 A.M.–5 P.M. Mon.–Fri., 1–5 P.M. Sat., $3, kids under 12 free), one of the state's better local history

museums. Here you'll learn all about Kingman's favorite son, actor Andy Devine, and there are some interesting Native American artifacts on display; there's also a gallery featuring the work of a rotating group of local artists. You can pick up a map for a self-guided tour of the historic downtown here or at the Powerhouse.

RECREATION AND EVENTS

If you missed North-Central Arizona's pine-belt, head to northwest Arizona's answer at **Hualapai Mountain Park** (www.mcparks.com), about 12 miles from Kingman. This sap-and-campfire–scented, 2,300-acre mountain park is high in the pines overlooking the scrub valley. The titular mountain range rises from the plain southeast of town to heights between 5,000 and nearly 8,500 feet, cloaked in the conifers typical of such elevations in Arizona. There are 18 cabins for rent through the **Mohave County Parks Division** (877/757-0915, www.mcparks.com/hmp/cabins.html, $60–110), built of stacked stone and wood by the Civilian Conservation Corps in the 1930s and sleeping 2–12 people, most with rustic old fireplaces—but also with kitchens and electricity. You can camp here, too, or park your RV among the pines ($12–20); most of the camping spots don't have zwater and are obtained on a first-come, first-served basis. The area has several miles of easy trails through the forest, all accessible from the **Hualapai Trailhead** in the park.

Early May brings thousands of Route 66 nostalgics and classic-car lovers to the old stretch of the Mother Road from Seligman to Kingman for the **Historic Route 66 Fun Run** (928/753-5001), several days filled with events like car shows and street fairs. In late September Kingman celebrates itself and its favorite son during **Andy Devine Days Parade & Community Fair** (928/757-7919).

SHOPPING

There are two shops in the **Powerhouse Visitor Center** (120 W. Andy Devine Ave., 928/753-6106, 9 A.M.–6 P.M. daily in summer and spring, 9 A.M.–5 P.M. Dec.–Feb.)

WHO IS ANDY DEVINE?

Kingman's favorite son was one of those great American character actors that most of us recognize but often can't name. His strained, gravelly but high voice, the result of a childhood accident that permanently damaged his vocal chords, and his size — a former football star, he was corpulent his entire adult life — make Andy Devine (1905-1977) stand out more than most.

While film buffs will remember Devine as the driver in John Ford's 1939 Western classic *Stage Coach,* John Wayne's break-out film, made partly in Monument Valley, or as one of the soldiers in John Huston's *The Red Badge of Courage* in 1951, his career was long and diverse, encompassing radio, both B- and A-grade movies, and television. He started out as a bit player in silent films during the 1920s and went on to entertain several generations.

Those of us who grew up in the 1970s and 1980s will likely remember Devine by his voice alone, which became that of the gentle and funny Friar Tuck in Disney's animated *Robin Hood* in 1973. Those who grew up in the 1950s and 1960s, on the other hand, remember Devine as "Jingle Jones" from the Western television series *Wild Bill Hickock,* or as the host of the Saturday morning show *Andy's Gang.* And, if you remember the 1930s and 1940s, you'll recognize that voice again as a regular on the Jack Benny radio show, where his greeting "Hiya, Buck!" made him famous, and of course you'll know Devine as the funny sidekick in many Roy Rogers Westerns.

Though Devine was born in Flagstaff a couple hours northeast of Kingman, where his father worked for the railroad, he moved to Kingman when he was just one year old. An on-the-job accident had taken the elder Devine's leg and a settlement with the railroad helped the family buy the Beale Hotel in Kingman, where Devine grew up and is celebrated in the local museum and during an annual festival and parade.

where you'll find items you might not be able to get too many other places. For Route 66 and American road-culture gifts and souvenirs check out the **Historic Route 66 Association of Arizona Gift Shop** inside the Powerhouse.

If you're into finding the treasures that other people have given up, there are a dozen or more antique and resale shops along East Beale Street in the historic old town area that are definitely worth wandering through.

ACCOMMODATIONS AND FOOD

There are several very affordable, basic hotels located on Andy Devine Avenue, Route 66, in Kingman's downtown area, some of them with retro-road trip neon signs and Route 66 themes. There are a good many chain hotels in town as well.

The **1st Value Inn** (3270 E. Andy Devine Ave., 928/757-7122, $50–80 d) has basic rooms and offers free high-speed internet and an outdoor pool, and the **Hill Top Motel** (1901 E. Andy Devine Ave., 928/753-2198, $46–92) offers free high-speed Internet and standard rooms.

The best place in town is the surprisingly affordable **Brunswick Hotel** (315 E. Andy Devine Ave., 928/718-1800, www.hotel-brunswick .com, $30–175), a historic boutique-style place with comfortable rooms and Western-eclectic interiors. Originally built in 1909, this little brick hotel downtown, with its Route 66–era neon sign and front-porch patios, has been remodeled a few times and has a nice balance of historic charm and contemporary comfort. It offers a free continental breakfast, and there's a great tavern on-site. The Brunswick is the most memorable place to stay in the whole region. The hotel's **Hubb's Bistro** (315 E. Andy Devine Ave., 928/718-1800, www.hotel-brunswick .com, 5–9 P.M. daily, $16–24) serves an ever-changing gourmet menu for dinner; there's a really good wine selection here as well.

The **Dambar & Steakhouse** (1960 E. Andy Devine Ave., 928/753-3523, 11 A.M.–10 P.M.

daily, $7–12) is popular with locals and serves great steaks and prime rib. The best restaurant for miles in any direction is **Mattina's Ristorante Italiano** (318 E. Oak St., 928/753-7504, 5–10 P.M. Tues.–Sat., $13–25), where you can get perfectly prepared Italian food and outstanding steaks and have a nice chat with the owner as he makes the rounds through the cozy dining room.

AROUND KINGMAN

Kingman is the service anchor for two historic and scenic drives, both of which take you through large swaths of left-alone desert and old mining ghost towns taken over by artisans and actors, up over mountain passes held together by strange cacti, across bridges swaying high above dry arroyos, and past abandoned outposts and tourists traps, the rusted shells of long-dead vehicles, and all those tiny white roadside crosses remembering road-weary tragedies. Finally, those drives will lead you to a few quirky and nostalgic sights that harken back to the golden age of the road trip.

(Driving Historic Route 66

The longest remaining stretch of Route 66 runs

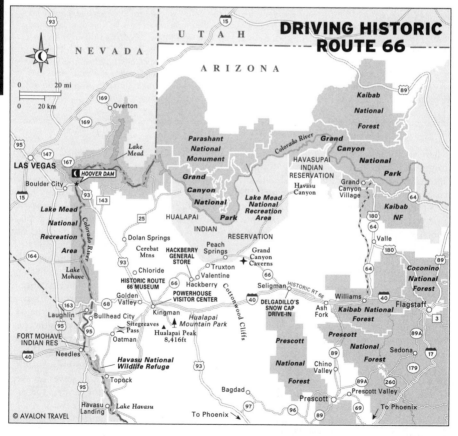

© TIM HULL

a lonely, forbidding stretch of Route 66

through the dry grasslands, cholla-choked deserts, and barren rocky mountains of north-western Arizona, about 165 miles between Ashfork on the east and Topok on the Colorado River to the west.

Ashfork sits just off I-40, 94 miles east of Kingman. From there head west to the Colorado River, following the Route 66 signs. Or, you can start from Topok, near the Havasu National Wildlife Refuge, and drive east, end-ing at Ashfork.

Heading from east to west, you'll pass through **Seligman** first, a tiny roadside set-tlement that still celebrates its Route 66 heri-tage every day. There are a few fun places to stop, and all the gift shops and food stands advertise with retro signs and a familiar 1950s style. This route is especially popular with motorcycle enthusiasts. Everybody stops at **Delgadillo's Snow Cap Drive-In** (Route 66, Seligman, 928/422-3291), a famous diner whose owners have been dedicated to enter-taining and teasing route travelers for gen-erations. The "cheeseburger with cheese" is legendary, as are the malts.

Then you'll pass through Peach Springs, capital of the Hualapai Indian Reservation (see *Grand Canyon West* in the *Grand Canyon* chapter), and then the nearly abandoned Truxton and Valentine, a few buildings dating from the 1930s to the 1950s moldering along the road. Then you'll pass Hackberry and the famous and much-photographed **Hackberry General Store.** Stop here and check out the clutter of memorabilia and Mother Road souvenirs. There are also some really cool road-map murals on the walls by artist Bob Waldmire. Then it's on through Kingman and the sweeping and lonely Sacramento Valley, a desert of creosote, and then up into the rocky **Black Mountains.** The road gets wash-boarded, and steep and curvy beyond reason, passing old ghost homes and mine shafts and a few sprawling, junkyard compounds before climbing up over Sitgreaves Pass and down the other side of the mountain to Oatman, home of the wild burros of Route 66, each de-scended from the beasts of burden that helped prospectors fight these desert hills more than a century ago.

© TIM HULL

The wild burros hang out in the streets of Oatman along historic Route 66.

OATMAN

Between 1904 and 1931 about $36 million in ore, mostly gold and silver, came out of these dry rocky hills. At its peak, the town of Oatman had some 10,000 residents. It went ghostly for a while after the mines shut down, but, as it was with so many mining towns in the southwest, Oatman was rediscovered in the 1960s and 1970s as a tourist stop along one of the roughest stretches of Historic Route 66. There are a few resale shops and gift boutiques here, a restaurant or two and a saloon. Some latter-day gunfighters will stage duels in the street on most days, and you can check out the old **Oatman Hotel,** where Clark Gable and Carol Lombard spent their honeymoon. But the real fun in Oatman, which is a touch kitschy and has few genuinely authentic buildings left anymore, is to feed and commune with wild burros. They're not really "wild" anymore—they'll walk right up and say hello, letting you pet their heads and feed them snacks sold by various vendors in town. There's usually a few baby burros milling around too.

Leaving Oatman and descending to the desert floor just east of the river, the foothills are covered with cholla, which blooms, along with a few dormant wildflowers, in the spring and adds a bit of bright shocking color to the landscape, making those warm and clear months the perfect time for this drive.

Driving U.S. Highway 93

Though not as popular as Route 66, U.S. 93 between Wickenburg, an hour north of Phoenix, and Hoover Dam, about an hour northwest of Yuma, has 200 miles of spectacular desert scenery. Just north of Route 71 before the town of Wikieup, U.S. 93 becomes the **Joshua Tree Forest Parkway.** Look out your window and you'll see why. A few miles outside of Kingman, Mohave County Road 125 leads to **Chloride** (four miles east from U.S. 93), an old mining town turned tourist town in the foothills of the Cerebat Mountains. Here you can browse through some shops and galleries, eat or stay at **Shep's Miners Inn** (928/565-4251/ www.shepsminersinn.com), where **Yesterdays**

Restaurant has some awesome murals; explore the ruins of mine shafts and brothels; watch gun fights (on the first and third Saturday July and August, every Saturday at high noon the rest of the year); and look at all the artwork and found-art in town, including famous rock-face murals by artist Roy Purcell.

BULLHEAD CITY AND LAUGHLIN

You pretty much have to be interested in either river games or games of chance to get anything out of a visit to Bullhead City and its cross-river Nevada neighbor Laughlin, often two of the hottest spots in the nation during the summer months. On August 11, 1983, at 2:21 P.M., the shade temperature in Bullhead City reached 132°F—the hottest on record. If neither gambling nor boating attracts you, skip it. However, if you'd like nothing more than to skim and spray around the river on a Jet Ski during the day and play poker and slots when the unforgiving sun finally dips away, this is the place for you. Bullhead City borders the Lake Mead National Recreation Area and is right near Lake Mohave, with its marinas and boat rental shops.

Entertainment and Events

Most of the gleaming desert casinos in Laughlin, Nevada, across the river from Bullhead City offer similar accommodations and extras, with basic, chilled rooms in glass towers, as well as pools, movie theaters, buffets, shops, and gambling all night and day—like Las Vegas, only smaller and riverside. The newer and less dusty and faded places are the **Aquarius Casino Resort** (1900 S. Casino Dr., 702/298-5111 or 800/662-5825, www.aquariuscasinoresort.com) and the **Avi Resort & Casino** (10000 Aha Macav Pkwy., 800/284-2946 or 702/535 5555, www.avi casino.com), while the **Riverside Resort Hotel & Casino** (1650 S. Casino Dr., 928/763-7070 or 800/227-3849, www.riversideresort.com) is the original, built by Don Laughlin himself.

In late April thousands of Harley-Davidson enthusiasts gather in the desert along the river for the **Laughlin River Run** (714/694-2800 or 800/357-8223), which includes concerts and festivals and all sorts of general revelry.

Accommodations and Food

There are several chain hotels in town, and there are casinos just across the river by way of two bridges. There are also resorts at Lake Mohave. Also check out the **Lodge on the River** (1717 Hwy. 95, 928/758-8080, www .lodgeonriver.com $40–145 d), a nice place with river-view rooms and suites.

The **Black Bear Diner** (1751 W. Hwy. 95, 928/763-2477, www.blackbeardiner.com, 6 A.M.–10 P.M. Sun.–Thurs., 6 A.M.–11 P.M. Fri.–Sat., $6–16) has good breakfasts, and **Colianno's Italian Restaurant** (1884 Hwy. 95, 928/758-7104, 11 A.M.–10 P.M. daily, $9–30) serves decent Italian favorites.

Lake Havasu City and Vicinity

This riverside haven for snowbird retirees and boat-cruising vacationers sprung up from the hot and sandy desert in 1963. A few years later, Havasu's developer, Robert McCulloch Sr., secured the master-planned community's place in history by bringing a bit of history to its brand-new shores. He purchased the London Bridge and shipped it to Arizona, where he installed it brick by brick across the channel at Pittsburgh Point, a peninsula now referred to locally as "the island." McCulloch also hired a former Disneyland designer to help create an "English Village" in the bridge's shadow, and the whole package has been a popular tourist draw ever since. These days, the state parks and riverside walkways and beaches along the reservoir are crowded most weekends in spring and even in summer—when the triple digits rule for three months or more—with boaters, anglers, and Jet Ski enthusiasts. During the college universe's annual spring break bacchanalia, hordes of bikini- and board short–clad coeds descend on the town, while at other times it seems as though everyone is over 60.

Lake Havasu City, like many other once-sleepy communities along the state's west coast, has grown immensely over the last decade or so, and there are more and more working families living here now and so more chain-stores and restaurants. For the visitor, however, it is still Lake Havasu, born from the building of Parker Dam and holding water that travels across the desert in canals to Phoenix and Tucson, that is the main draw. If you're not into water sports and if you wilt easily in the sun, consider spending no more than an afternoon here, strolling over and beneath the bridge and along the walkway next to the channel, watching the ducks dip and bob. If you want to get to know the reservoir, though, there are all manner of wet and cool things to do here, and there are several excellent restaurants as well.

SIGHTS AND RECREATION

If you're not boating or fishing or swimming or generally worshiping the sun here, you may find things a bit dull. The water is the place to be here, but you can easily get on it without getting wet. All along the main walkway under the bridge you'll find boat rentals, fishing guides, excursion cruises, and even a singing gondola ride. There are also unique shopping opportunities near the lake, and a few great places to eat. This is where you'll want to head first—just follow the signs to London Bridge, where the parking is generally free.

◖ London Bridge

This bridge (928/453-8883, free) began its long life in 1831, spanning the Thames River in London. First horses pulled carriages across it, and then the first cars chugged its length, and then, inevitably, the modern world caught up with it. By the early 1960s the old bridge no longer had what it takes to serve such a busy crossing, so the City of London sold it to Robert McCulloch, a chainsaw manufacturer just then

You can take a tour of Lake Havasu with a singing gondolier.

© TIM HULL

Lake Havasu City's founder shipped a dismantled London bridge to Arizona and then rebuilt it over the Colorado River.

entering the lucrative trade of master-planned retirement and resort communities. Now it spans a man-made channel of the Colorado River, walked and driven over by millions of sun-baked tourists every year. It's a strange sight, this old-world urban structure stuck out here the middle of the desert. The best views are from below, where the scene has a bit of a picturesque old London look to it—but not quite. The bridge's seeming incongruity isn't as strange as it appears, however. In the 19th century, the lower Colorado and The Arizona Strip, not too far north of this region, were settled by Mormon pioneers from Salt Lake City, many of whom were English. That has little to do with the bridge's travels, though. Take a half hour or so to walk across and under it, and read the plaques placed at either end that explain how these bricks from the north Atlantic wound up stacked here in the desert.

Lake Havasu State Park

This popular state park stretches along the river north and south of the bridge and includes **Windsor Beach** ($10 per car, camping $15), an excellent riverside campground and sunning spot (99 London Bridge Rd., 928/855-2784, www .pr.state.az.us/Parks/parkhtml/havasu.html, sunrise–10 P.M., $9 per car, camping $14–25). Jet Ski rentals are available at the park through **Windsor Beach Rentals** (928/453-4PWC, www.windsorbeachrentals.com, $55 per hour). If you're looking to laze around on the beach for a while and watch the people and the waterfowl, Windsor Beach is the place to do it.

Cattail Cove State Park

About 15 miles south of the bridge along Route 95 the tell-tale cattails that give this park its name rise up out of the water (Rte. 95, 928/855-1223, www.pr.state.az.us/Parks/parkhtml/cattail.html, sunrise–10 P.M. daily, $10 per car, camping $23). Here you'll find camping, boating, and fishing opportunities just a bit outside the main town area, including several primitive campsites along the shores accessible only by boat. There's a nice beach and good swimming here—a perfect place for a laid-back day or overnight riverine outing with the family. The nearby **Sand Point Marina** (7952 S. Sandpoint Rd., 928/855-0549, www.sand-pointresort.com) rents fishing boats ($40–90, 4–24 hours), pontoon boats ($200–375, 4–24 hours) and personal watercraft for up to three

people ($100–745, 2–72 hours); most require a $500 deposit. The marina also has a good restaurant and a general store in case you forgot your supplies.

EVENTS

Not surprisingly, most of Lake Havasu's annual events have something to do with the

---

WESTERN ARIZONA'S WILDLANDS

While the many dams built along the Colorado River during the era of reclamation in the 1930s and 1940s made it possible for the Southwest to grow and thrive as a habitat for humans, the loss of the river's natural and wild flow ruined much of the essential riparian habitat downstream. In an effort to restore what was lost and hold on to what remains, the U.S. Fish and Wildlife Service has established a number of wildlife refuges in western Arizona. These are wild and rugged places, not for the unprepared and the uninitiated. But for those looking for something far off the track, these protected lands provide some of the best bird-watching, wildlife-viewing, and nature-communing – especially of the desert and riverine kind – in the entire state.

Two of the refuges – Imperial and Havasu – feature well-established tour companies that will take you along the river and point out all there is to see. Traveling from south to north, first we cross the **Cabeza Prieta National Wildlife Refuge** (1611 N. Second St., Ajo, 520/387-6483, www.fws.gov/southwest/refuges/arizona/cabeza.html), east of Yuma in southwestern Arizona, a forbidding landscape hugging the U.S.-Mexico border. If you're looking for the Sonoran Desert in the raw, you'll find it here. The Cabeza Prieta (meaning "Dark Head" in Spanish, for the area's volcanic coloring) is a hot and sparse land, covered in cacti and creosote (and wildflowers and other blooming desert show-offs in the spring). The refuge provides 860,010 acres of habitat for desert creatures to roam, including bighorn sheep and cactus-pollinating lesser long-nosed bats. There's a small visitors center and short interpretive trail at the refuge office, where you have to stop first to pick up a per-

mit to explore the refuge. Most of the refuge is within the airspace of the Barry M. Goldwater Air Force Range, so there are often low-flying aircraft in the area, crossing the refuge on their way to the bombing ranges to the north. Somewhere out in that sublimely wild swath of Sonoran Desert, that great advocate of wild desert, the author Edward Abbey, is said to be buried in an unmarked grave.

Another unwatered refuge in this region is just north of Yuma along U.S. 95. The ruggedly beautiful **Kofa National Wildlife Refuge** (356 W. 1st Street, Yuma, 928/783-7861, www.fws.gov/southwest/refuges/arizona/kofa/) includes 665,400 acres of rough desert landscape, home to the dexterous bighorn and legions of reptiles who couldn't live anywhere else but this dry and sharp-rock land. Within the refuge is **Palm Canyon,** in the west end of the Kofa Mountains, where grow the only native palm trees in Arizona – a state that probably has more than its fair share of palms imported to its city streets. The half-mile hike into Palm Canyon to see the trees is one of the region's best. Along U.S. 95 north of Yuma, watch for the Palm Canyon sign, then follow the dirt road east for nine miles toward the mountains and the trailhead.

Heading west to the river, we find the 25,768-acre **Imperial National Wildlife Refuge** (Martinez Lake, 928/783-3317, www.fws.gov/southwest/refuges/arizona/imperial.html), a 30-mile desert-meets-wetland landscape teeming with water-loving birds and other wildlife. There's a visitors center here, a rough-and-tumble scenic drive that takes you through an unvarnished Sonoran Desert stretch, and a few awesome lookouts with views of the river valley. The 1.3-mile **Painted**

water. The biggest event of the year is probably Spring Break, which happens throughout March and April. The population skews young during this time of year, and if you're not looking for a party and crowds you might want to steer clear. In late February the **Mark Hahn Memorial Havasu 300 APBA National Team Endurance Race** (www.pwcfun.com/markhahn300.asp) brings together the nation's best Jet Ski pilots for a big race. Mid-march brings the **Lake Havasu Marine Associations Annual Boat Show** (928/453-8833), a three-day event featuring the best in watercraft, food, concerts, and all sorts of other fun. Later in March anglers come to town for the **U.S. Angler's Choice Fishing Tournament**

Desert Trail leads to a grand view as well. See *Recreation* in the *Yuma and Vicinity* section for information on boat tours into the refuge.

A few miles upriver and we come to the **Cibola National Wildlife Refuge** (66600 Cibola Lake Road, Cibola, 928/857-3253, www.fws.gov/southwest/refuges/CibolaNWR/), where you'll find some of the best birding in the region. Just outside the visitors center there's a short scenic drive (called Canada Goose Drive), along which you can stop and hike the one-mile loop nature trail, moving through a beautiful riparian habitat of cottonwood, willow, and mesquite forests. In winter, thousands of Canada geese, snow geese, ducks, and sandhill cranes are usually visible from an observation deck here.

Just north of Parker the Bill Williams River flows from the east into the Colorado River. A beautiful thin ribbon of water moving through a marshy forest of cattails announces the

Bill Williams River National Wildlife Refuge (60911 U.S. 95, Parker, 928/667-4144, www.fws.gov/southwest/refuges/arizona/billwill.html) along U.S. 95, which protects a thick cottonwood-willow forest and has excellent bird-watching and kayaking opportunities.

Farther north still, but still on the river, we come to the **Havasu National Wildlife Refuge** (317 Mesquite Ave., Needles, CA, 760/326-3853, www.fws.gov/southwest/refuges/arizona/havasu/), protecting 30 river miles of Colorado River habitat from Needles, California, to Lake Havasu City, Arizona, where one of the last remaining natural sections of the lower Colorado River flows through the 20-mile-long spectacle that is **Topock Gorge,** where you'll see bighorn sheep and other native animals. There are several concessionaires beneath the London Bridge in Lake Havasu City that offer guided tours of Topock Gorge.

© TIM HULL

The Bill Williams River flows into the Colorado at the Bill Williams Wildlife Refuge.

(800/360-7112, www.usanglerschoice
.net) and the **New Horizons' Pro-Am Bass
Tournament** (928/854-9378).

ACCOMMODATIONS

Though you could definitely do it, it is not
necessary to spend a lot of money to find a nice
place to stay on the lake.

The **Island Inn Hotel** (1300 McCulloch
Blvd., 928/680-0606 or 800/243-9955,
$49–275 d) has basic, affordable rooms
available near the water and right in middle of all the fun. The most popular place
in town is the **London Bridge Resort** Rte.
95, 928/855-0888, www.londonbridgeresort.
com, $99–519 d), right near the bridge and
overlooking the lake, which endeavors to look
"English" and offers several different room
choices with bridge and channel views, a good
restaurant, and a lot of extras. If you're camping or have an RV, the state parks are a good
bet, as is the **Sand Point Marina and RV
Park** (7952 S. Sandpoint Rd., 928/855-0549,
www.sandpointresort.com, $25–45).

FOOD

Juicy's River Café (25 N. Acoma,
928/855-8429, 7 A.M.–8 P.M. Mon.–Sat.,
7 A.M.–2 P.M. Sun., $8–15) serves delectable
breakfasts, sandwiches and homemade comfort fare for those who've worn themselves ex-
tra-hungry playing on the river. The cleverly
named **The Pour House** (2093 McCulloch
Blvd., 928/680-0063, 6 A.M.–9 P.M. daily,
$4–20) has been around forever and serves
great hamburgers and a probably the best
breakfast in town. A newer place, the **Barley
Brothers Brewery and Grill** (1425 McCulloch
Blvd, 928/505-7837, www.barleybrothers.com,
11 A.M.–1 A.M. daily, $8–20), makes the best
microbrew in the region and serves up tasty
desert pub–style meals. A bit more fancy
is **Krystal's Restaurant** (460 El Camino
Way, 928/453-2999, 4–10 P.M. daily, $11–40)
which has perfect prime rib and is a great
place for seafood and steaks, while **Shugrue's**
(1425 McCullock Blvd., 928/453-1400,

www.shugrues.com, 11 A.M.–9 P.M. Sun.–
Thurs., 11 A.M.–10 P.M. Fri.–Sat., $8–28) has
a great view, delicious seafood, and homemade
pastries and bread.

SHOPPING

Stick around the water to find distinctive
gifts and souvenirs at the **English Village**
(1477 Queens Bay, 928/855-0888, www
.amdest.com/az/lhc/ev/engv.html), under
bridge and across the channel you'll find the
Island Mall & Brewery (1425 McCulloch
Blvd., 928/855-6274, a two-story enclosed
mall. Away from the bridge and water area,
the **Main Street in the Uptown District**
(upper McCulloch, 1 mile east of London
Bridge) has more than 200 shops, including
Shambles Village, which has all kinds of antique galleries.

INFORMATION AND SERVICES

The **Lake Havasu City Convention and
Visitors Bureau** (314 London Bridge Rd.,
928/453-3444 or 800/242-8278, www.golake
havasu.com) can help you with all your questions and provide plenty of literature on sights
and events in Lake Havasu.

Watercraft Rentals

One of the better outfitters is **London
Bridge Watercraft Tours and Rentals**
(928/453-8883, www.havasuwatercraft
rentals.com), which operates out of **Crazyhorse
Campgrounds** (1534 Beachcomber Blvd.,
928/855-4033, www.crazyhorsecampgrounds
.com) on "the island" on the west side of the
bridge. There are any number of other rental
places along the walkway beneath the bridge,
offering all-day and dining excursions, fishing trips, expeditions into the Lake Havasu
Wildlife Refuge upriver, and paddleboats and
canoes for sticking closer to the shore. The rental
prices may change according to the season, with
Spring Break and other crowded times ushering
in higher fees. All of the rental places are going to
require some kind of deposit, typically taken care
of by handing over your credit card number.

PARKER AND
THE PARKER STRIP

The small resort town of Parker looks out on about 16 miles of swift-flowing Colorado River called the Parker Strip, where retirement and vacation homes line the banks between the town and Parker Dam to the north. Most of the land below and around Parker comprises the **Colorado River Indian Reservation,** 270,000 acres that include the beautiful, 16,400-acre **Swansea Wilderness Area,** about 25 miles northeast of town. This is one of the best stretches of the lower Colorado, and it's packed with boaters and other river-lovers most weekends in season. Again, though, if you're not a river-rat or trying to be one, there's not much of an incentive to stop.

Sights and Recreation

The small **Colorado River Indian Tribes Museum and Library** (Hwy. 95 at 2nd and Mohave, 928/669-9211, 8 A.M.–5 P.M. Mon.–Fri., 10 A.M.–3 P.M. Sat.) has some interesting exhibits and artifacts of this often overlooked tribe. **Buckskin Mountain State Park** (5476 Hwy. 95, 928/667-3231, www.pr.state.az.us/Parks/parkhtml/buckskin.html) and its **River Island Unit** (5200 Hwy. 95, 928/667-3386), about 12 miles north of Parker, has excellent camping, fishing, and boating opportunities. You can also drive over **Parker Dam** (760/663-3712) just north of the town; it's open to passenger vehicles only 5 A.M.–11 P.M. On the California side of the dam, there's a rough but scenic drive that will take you along the river and past a few historic sites and shoreline oases.

Accommodations and Food

The place to be in the Parker area is the Colorado Indian Tribe's **Blue Water Resort & Casino** (Rte. 95, 928/669-7000, www.bluewaterfun.com, $45–139), which has affordable, clean, chilly rooms that look out over the river and the marina, where you can rent boats and Jet Skis and park your own craft if

© TIM HULL

Boaters and Jet Skiers gather at Blue Water Marina near Parker.

you have one. Inside the hotel there's a buffet; slots, blackjack, and poker; and a multi-tiered pool and water slide that the kids won't want to leave behind. There's also a movie theater and a sports bar, among other amenities. The **Parker Strip Grill** (10230 Harbor Dr., 928/667-4054, 10 A.M.–9 P.M. Sun.–Thurs., 10 A.M.–10 P.M. Fri.–Sat.) has good burgers and other staples for hard-playing river types.

QUARTZSITE

This quiet desert spot on U.S. 95 between Parker and Yuma, right off I-10, is nearly deserted in the summer, when temperatures can and do reach 120°F fairly regularly. When the mercury dips, however, this wide spot in the road becomes crowded with itinerant retirees and roaming bands of gem and mineral dealers and other assorted swap-meet entrepreneurs. Throughout January and February, the streets in town are lined with booths and tables selling all manner of gems and jewelry and just about anything else you can think of, and on through the winter the RV tribe of retirees makes Quartzsite a temporary boomtown.

Even if it's summer and 110°F in the shade, if you happen to be passing through this settlement around lunch or dinnertime, make sure you stop at the ◖ **Grubstake** (725 North Central, I-95, 928/927-4485, 11 A.M.–2 A.M. Mon.–Sun., $7–16), where you can get the best plate of fish and chips in the state and a cool glass of Boddingtons' Ale (way out here in the middle of the desert!). The Grubstake also makes a great fried-shrimp po' boy and a plate of supposedly mini "slider" hamburgers that is actually three regular-size burgers on top of a huge pile of fries. The portions here are large to say the least, but you'll be happy you had to take some on the road with you.

THE NAKED BOOKSELLER OF QUARTZSITE

Paul Winer, the 64-year-old, nearly nude proprietor of the **Reader's Oasis** in Quartzsite (928/927-6551), has been selling books along the tiny desert town's main drag for nearly 20 years.

"I used to wear very brief shorts," he said. "I didn't drop them and feel free to be who I am until I had 180,000 books; then I thought I could do it."

Winer spent 25 years back east playing boogie-woogie piano, nude, under the name "Sweet Pie." He fought a protracted public indecency battle and eventually prevailed, he said. In lieu of recompense he chose to settle a rather large IRS bill free and clear, and then headed out to Arizona to see his parents. He started selling his mom's paperbacks at the big swap-meet gem-shows that give Quartzsite one of the largest populations in Arizona for a few weeks every winter, when the desert becomes a tent city and there are all manner of strange and interesting itinerant merchants around. Paul is here to stay, however; he's open year-round, he said, even when the heat reaches 120°F, which it is wont to do here in the summer. Arizona, he said, "is one of the few states that would tolerate someone like me on the main street of a town. It has a history of having the most obstinate, stubborn, off-the-wall people. There is still quite a tolerance for outsiders."

He has a lot of good books for sale, including an excellent selection of used books about the Southwest and children's books. Book-lovers who might otherwise be put off by Winer's lack of clothing – he usually wears a small thong-style loin-cloth and not much else on his thin and tanned frame – will want to think twice about missing this unique store. Winer is a smart, friendly fellow, and he won't hesitate to tell you his crazy story and recommend a book.

Yuma and Vicinity

Yuma has long been an important place to pass by. For centuries the area where the once wild Colorado and Gila Rivers found each other and merged was a natural crossing point for Native Americans, and during the great gold rush of 1849 the riverside desert became a crucial crossing and lifeline for all those prospectors and adventurers going to California. For a time steamboats chugged up and down the Colorado, docking at Yuma to load and unload supplies important to the settling of the Southwest. Some of the Wild West's most despicable characters found themselves sweltering in the hell of the Yuma Territorial Prison. In the era of reclamation Yuma became an important agricultural center, and it still is, producing winter lettuce and other crops. In 1915 Yuma became an important link in the nation's commercial scene with the opening of the famous Ocean-to-Ocean Highway Bridge over the Colorado. To most Arizonans who don't live on the state's west coast, Yuma is known mostly as a place to stop and get gas on the way to the cool ocean breezes of San Diego.

Today Yuma is a growing city of about 105,000 people with an economy based largely on agriculture and the service industry. From about November through March the city's population swells by some 90,000 people, many of them retirees and snowbirds seeking the easy life in one of Yuma's more than 80 RV and mobile home parks. While the town boasts sunny skies 95 percent of the year, and winter temperatures are often in the 70s and even the 80s, it is not a place that you want to visit during the height of summer. You'll find the temperature hovering many days around 110°F, cooling off very little at night. Consequently, some businesses and attractions have truncated hours or shut down all together when the heat reigns.

LOWER COLORADO RIVER

© TIM HULL

The Colorado River meanders through the Yuma Valley.

SIGHTS
◖ Yuma Territorial Prison State Historic Park

They say Yuma Prison wasn't as bad as its reputation suggests, that the more than 3,000 outlaws, polygamists, gunfighters, robbers, and murderers housed here between 1876 and 1909 were afforded three squares a day, health care, and education, conveniences many of their pioneer counterparts on the outside sorely lacked. But spend a little time exploring this popular state park (100 Prison Hill Rd., 928/783-4771, www.pr.state.az.us/Parks/parkhtml/yuma.html, 8 A.M.–5 P.M. daily, $4, kids 13 and under free) and you'll likely come to a different conclusion: This wasn't a place where you'd want to spend any time, especially in an era long before air-conditioning. If you think it's hot in Yuma today, just imagine being confined to a dark airless cell, the heat as incessant as the din from the cell block, full of half-mad prisoners and constant tubercular coughing.

There's not a lot left of the original buildings; Yuma citizens used the old prison as a

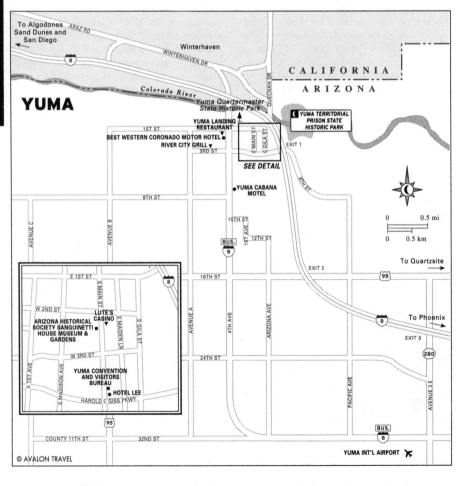

© AVALON TRAVEL

an example of a typical cell at Yuma Territorial Prison State Historic Park

kind of free lumber yard for years before it was made into a state park. During the Depression the cells served as temporary homes for hobos and destitute families. But the real interest here is the lore of the lawless territorial days, and there is much of it in the museum, where you'll learn all about the various characters who once called the dark cells home, as well as the colorful doctors and prison administrators who managed the place. You can climb up to the large guard tower and look over the slowly meandering Colorado as it snakes through wetlands below, and feel what it was like (sort of, anyway) to be confined to a prison cell way out here in the middle of the desert, far from home and grace. Plan on spending at least an hour or two here, as there is much to discover in the stories and artifacts of crime and punishment on the Southwestern frontier.

Yuma Quartermaster Depot State Historic Park

This small historic park (201 N. 4th Ave., 928/329-0471, www.pr.state.az.us/Parks/ parkhtml/yumacross.html, 9 A.M.–5 P.M. daily, $3, kids 13 and under free) on Yuma's main drag preserves the history of the U.S. Army's presence in Yuma from 1864 to 1883, when riverboat steamers brought supplies up from the mouth of the Colorado to serve Army outposts throughout the region. Before the railroad entered the Southwest, a six-month supply of food, clothing, ammunition and other staples was quartered here for distribution to forts in Arizona, Utah, Nevada, and New Mexico. At the park you can see the old commanding officer's quarters and a few other historic buildings and artifacts related to the Army's long occupation of the wild open West.

The most interesting story told at the park, which until the summer of 2007 was called Yuma Crossing Historic Park, is about the construction of the audacious Yuma Siphon, an engineering project that would sound ambitious even today. Using old Captain Nemo–style diving gear, workers built a concrete tunnel underneath the Colorado River in order to divert the river for use in agriculture,

LOWER COLORADO RIVER

© TIM HULL

A mid-day train crosses the Colorado River in Yuma.

changing the fate of Yuma forever and, really, securing the town's survival beyond being a way station for goods and people headed to California. At the park there are some excellent displays on the project, and a few of the old diving suits and other artifacts of this incredible reclamation feat.

Century House Museum

The history of Yuma is on display at this museum in the city's quiet historic downtown (40 S. Madison Ave., 928/782-1841, www.arizonahistoricalsociety.org, 10 a.m.–4 p.m. Tues.–Sat., $3, kids 12 and under free). Also called the **Sanguinetti House Museum** after the home's former owner, pioneer merchant E. F. Sanguinetti, the little adobe house has informative displays on the history of the lower Colorado region from prehistory through modern times, with period rooms and a shady garden patio and aviary with talking birds in cages. If you're really interested in the history of the region, make sure to converse with one

of the volunteer docents manning the main desk, who are usually longtime residents or natives of the area and can provide personal context to the historical displays. A separate adobe next door, formerly the residence of a riverboat captain, houses an excellent local- and regional-history bookshop.

Historic Downtown

Yuma's downtown has been going through a planned rebirth for a few decades now, and there are some cool old buildings from various eras still standing, including the art deco **Yuma Theatre** built in 1936. It has been resorted and now shows movies, and nearby the **Yuma Downtown Art Center** has four galleries showing the work of local and regional artists. Other buildings show the influence of Spanish Colonial Revival style and there are even a few old adobes still standing from the territorial days. It's easy to walk around the downtown, start at **Main Street Plaza** and just explore—there are a few shops, antique stores, galleries, and boutiques along the narrow streets, and on the edges of the downtown you'll see a few old historic homes. That being said, on most days the downtown is a bit quiet and deserted, especially in the summer. Still, it's a good place to get a feel for what Yuma used to be.

Algodones Dunes

Desert country neophytes might be a little disappointed with the relative lushness of the typical Arizona desert landscape, which defies with its diversity the daydream of Saharaesque dunes with nothing but white sand for miles and miles. If you were hoping for a "real desert," something on the order of Luke Skywalker's home planet of Tatooine, head across the bridge into California for a look at the southeastern end of the great shifting erg known as the Algodones Dunes, also called the Imperial Dunes. About 17 miles west on I-8 outside of Yuma take the Gray's Well exit to a parking lot on the edge of the dunes near the Midway campground, part of the **Imperial Dunes Recreation Area.** Here you can park your car and witness the 45-mile by 6-mile dunes—but don't go far. There is literally nothing out here but sand, and then more sand. If you think it looks like Tatooine that's because it is: George Lucas filmed portions of *Return of The Jedi* near here in the 1980s. These days the dunes are popular with motorcycle and ATV enthusiasts, who tear around nearby Glamis on holiday weekends in a great rumbling and rolling party. A few miles west on the frontage road from Gray's Well (follow the signs) you can see what remains of the old **Plank Road,** a movable highway of wooden planks once placed on top of the dunes so early car travelers could pass without sinking into the sand, this before highway technology advanced enough to build the interstate that now dissects the area. It's not recommended that you go here in the summer, nor should you take off across the dunes on foot. Just look, or maybe scamper

LOWER COLORADO RIVER

© TIM HULL

the shifting, empty dunes just across the California state line, west of Yuma

© TIM HULL

LOWER COLORADO RIVER

The remains of an old plank road that once crossed the Algodones Dunes.

up a tall dune near the parking lot and see what an expanse of nothing looks like—it's preternaturally beautiful, and a good place for meditating on, well . . . nothingness.

RECREATION

About 35 miles north of Yuma on Route 95 is **Martinez Lake,** where you can fish, boat, and view wildlife, among other activities. The 55,000-acre **Imperial National Wildlife Refuge** is just north of the lake and extends for 35 miles upriver, a renowned stop for various migratory bird species and full of desert-land mammals like bighorn sheep, mountain lions, bobcats, deer, wild horses, and burros.

A popular and fun way to see the refuge and the river is to take a boat tour with **Yuma River Tours** (1920 Arizona Ave., 928/783-4400, www.yumarivertours.com). Make sure to call ahead in summer as they have limited hours during the hot months. The best tour is the 4–5-hour, 32-mile boat trip to **Norton's Landing** ($69 per person, includes lunch), an old steamboat port and mining ghost town.

The tour takes you deep into the refuge, and the guides are expert at spotting and pointing out birds and mammals along the way. Reservations are required. Yuma River Tours also offers day and dining cruises on an old Sternwheeler boat ($45 per person), and overnight guided kayak and canoe trips.

At **Fisher's Landing** on Lake Martinez you can rent a boat for the day ($50); rent or buy fishing gear and book a guide to show you the best hideouts of bass, crappie, bluegill, stripers, and flathead catfish; and there's a restaurant serving burgers, sandwiches, fish, and steaks ($4.95–17.95), a motel and RV park (928/783-9589 or 800/876-7004, www.martinezlake.com, $20–87) and a general store.

ENTERTAINMENT AND EVENTS

For Vegas-style entertainment and games of chance, head over to **Quechan Paradise Casino** (I-8 to 4th Ave. exit, then north on S-24, 888/777-4946, www.paradise-casinos.com), where popular bands of yesteryear play often and there are slots, blackjack, poker, and lots of food and drinks.

In early January Yuma's historic downtown hosts the **Old Town Jubilee,** with artisans, entertainment and activities for the whole family. If you're in town in mid-February, when the weather in Yuma is perfect, don't miss **Yuma River Daze** and the **Yuma Crossing Days Festival,** three days celebrating local history and culture that includes river races, swimming, and a block party downtown.

ACCOMMODATIONS

Yuma has all the chain hotels and motels a town its size would ever want, and many of them are located just off I-8 or along 4th Avenue, the town's main commercial thoroughfare.

An affordable and clean place to stay is the **Yuma Cabana Motel** (2151 S. 4th Ave., 928/783-8311, www.yumacabana.com, $44–83), where amenities include free wireless Internet, a swimming pool, and a continental breakfast. The rooms are small and can seem a bit bleak with their concrete walls, but this is a fine place, especially for those on a budget. The best hotel in town is the **Best Western Coronado Motor Hotel** (233 4th Ave., 928/783-4453, $79–129 d), which has comfortable rooms and a friendly staff and is right in the center of everything. It has a pool and offers a free, full breakfast every morning.

The **Shilo Inn Hotel** (1550 S. Castle Dome Rd., 928/782-9511, www.shiloinns.com, $122–200 d) is a bit more upscale, offering a free breakfast buffet, free Internet, a nice pool area, and comfortable rooms. For something a little more historic and distinctive, head to Yuma's sleepy downtown to the **Hotel Lee** (390 S. Main St., 928/783-6336, www.hotel lee.com, $49–99), built in 1917 and renovated with a Victorian touch. The hotel is charming and the rooms are all individually decorated and have a historic ambience without sacrificing modern comforts.

FOOD

The must-visit restaurant in Yuma is **Lute's Casino** (221 S Main St., 928/782-2192, www .lutescasino.com, 9 A.M.–8 P.M. Mon.–Thurs., 9 A.M.–9 P.M. Fri.–Sat., 10 A.M.–6 P.M. Sun. $5–15) downtown, a place popular with locals and visitors alike. Even if you aren't hungry you'll enjoy sitting at one of the tall tables and drinking a brew, your neck craning to look at all the strange and hilarious—and even a bit bawdy—pictures covering the walls. The menu offers everything from burgers and hot dogs to burritos and tacos, all served up in huge portions. If you like hot dogs, don't miss Bob's Polish Kraut Dog ($4.50)—it's awesome. Lute's is also a good place to enjoy some nightlife with the locals.

The **Yuma Landing Restaurant** (195 4th Ave., 928/782-7427, www.yumalanding.com, 6 A.M.–9 P.M. Sun.–Thurs., 6 A.M.–midnight Fri.–Sat., $5–15) is on the site where the first airplane landed in Yuma, and it has all sorts of memorabilia about that and other town history on the walls. It serves an eclectic mix of salads, sandwiches, steaks, prime rib, and Mexican dishes and has a bar with a good happy hour. The **River City Grill** 600 W. 3rd St., 928/782-7988, www.rivercitygrill yuma.com 11:30 A.M.–2 P.M. Mon.–Fri. and 5–10 P.M. daily) serves top-notch seafood, sushi, lamb, beef, chicken, and vegetarian dishes in a cool contemporary setting, with a great patio for dining in the warmth of winter.

GETTING THERE AND AROUND

Yuma International Airport (2191 E. 32nd St., 928/726-5882, www.yumainternational airport.com) offers a few flights each day to L.A. and Phoenix, but you really need a car to explore this region and to get around Yuma. The main line in and out of the city is I-8, and if you're going north along the river use Route 95.

INFORMATION AND SERVICES

The **Yuma Convention and Visitors Bureau** (377 S. Main St., 928/783-0071, www .visityuma.com, 9 A.M.–5 P.M. Mon.–Fri., 9 A.M.–2 P.M. Sat., 9 A.M.–4 P.M. Sat. Nov.–Apr.) downtown has all kinds of pamphlets and advice for enjoying Yuma and the Lower Colorado River region.

BACKGROUND

The Land

The Arizona landscape is more varied than most, changing, with rises in elevation, from hot, cactus-choked **deserts** to scrubby bushlands to open **ponderosa pine forests** to coniferous, snowy highlands. Dry **grasslands** and long stretches of sagebrush plains spread across the higher deserts. Arizona is the only state where three major deserts converge: The Sonoran stretches across the southern portion of the state and includes the Phoenix and Tucson areas, while the Mojave dominates on the western reaches. The Chihuahuan Desert of Mexico stretches north into southeastern Arizona.

While it snows and rains much more in the high country than it does in the desert belt, the entire state is subject to what Lawrence Clark Powell called a "wrinkled dryness." Aridity is a constant no matter where you go. Spread thinly across the land, a few life-giving river ways and **riparian areas** are treasured as oases and predictably exploited. Arizona has 114,000 square miles, making it sixth in size among the states. Large tracts of wild, open land remain, and likely always will.

Few places have such extremes in elevation: You could travel from sea level along the

© ELIZABETH JANG

lower Colorado to the 12,600-foot peak of **Mount Humphrey,** part of the volcanic San Francisco Mountain range above Flagstaff, in a matter of a day or so. The White Mountains in the northeast part of the state tower above 10,000 feet and are often snow-capped. The Santa Catalinas, north of Tucson, rise to similar heights and feature the nation's southernmost ski run. A bit south of Tucson toward the U.S.-Mexico border, the Santa Rita Mountains tower above the Santa Cruz Valley, and just to the east the Huachuca Mountains do the same over the San Pedro Valley. Farther east the Pinaleño Range rises above 10,000 feet, with towering Mount Graham watching over the Gila Valley. Many of these high Southern Arizona mountain ranges have important international observatories on their high reaches, and the cities and towns around them, Tucson included, are encouraged to keep their street lights and other "light noise" to a minimum so as to keep the sky dark and clear. These southern ranges are often referred to as sky islands because they are exactly that: islands of biological diversity surrounded, and isolated, by vast seas of harsh, hot desert. In these sky islands can be found flora and fauna that exist in few other places in North America. Subtropical birds and other animals use these mountains as the northern reaches of their ranges, so it's not uncommon to find quetzal-like birds and even jungle-loving jaguars flitting and stalking around the misty creeksides of these forested ranges.

The central and north-central region of Arizona is also very mountainous, though the ranges here are somewhat smaller and older than those in the south. Around Prescott the Bradshaws and the Sierra Prieta reach to about 9,000 feet and are covered in pine. They were once, and perhaps still are, strewn with the precious minerals that became the impetus for one of the state's first mining booms. Throughout the state there are several other ranges and many detached, lonely peaks, many of them high and timbered and others mid-sized and rocky, covered in cactus and creosote and old mining tunnels.

If you pay attention to your elevation—and the "wrinkled" nature of the state assures that you are changing elevation all the time—you can generally predict what the weather will be like and which plants and animals you are likely to see; of course, it's not all strictly delineated, and the various life zones often bleed into one another. Between 4,500 and about 7,000 feet you're in the **Upper Sonoran zone,** characterized by scrub oak, piñon pine, juniper, manzanita, and sagebrush grasslands; this zone is often called the chaparral. The midlands of the state, at around 6,000 feet and higher, are marked by the **transition zone,** a scrubby land of short dry bushes stretching into the ponderosa pines. Above 8,500 feet or so thick stands of evergreen conifers and white aspen are common. Above 9,500 feet or so, a height reached in Arizona primarily by climbing up towering mountains, the **subalpine zone** has tough Engelmann spruce and bristlecone pine, and above that it's all barren rocks and tundra.

GEOGRAPHY AND GEOLOGY

When dinosaurs roamed the earth this desert was a swampy and wet place. Over the eons different portions of Arizona were covered by shallow seas that flowed in, flourished, and then dried up or retreated. Eventually the Arizona you see took shape—mountains rose, volcanoes burst and created new land, and plates slid apart and crashed into each other, creating upland plateaus and digging deep canyons with the erosional help of rivers, wind, and aridity.

The **Colorado Plateau** dominates the northern portion of the state, covering about two-fifths of its area; its nearly 200-mile southern edge, the **Mogollon Rim,** borders the scrub-and-pine belt of the transition zone. Below that is the **basin and range province** of the desert country, stretching from the western to the eastern border and south to Mexico. The elevations in the basin and range swing from sea level to about 4,000 feet above it, though several large mountain ranges dot the lowlands and rise beyond 9,000 feet. In the uplands of the plateaus, deep canyons plunge into the layers of ancient rock. The bottom of the Grand Canyon, which is cut into the Colorado Plateau, is a low, hot desert. The highest points in the plateau country reach above 12,000 feet and are dominated by tundra and bare cold boulders.

It is the contrast between the plateau and the basin and range provinces that make Arizona such a rare landscape. Both have their origins deep in geologic time. The plateau country began to form in its current shape around 600 million years ago, when the continent was relatively flat and layer after layer of limestone, sandstone, siltstone, and shale were deposited by tropical seas moving in and then receding, leaving behind dunes and stream deposits and eroding the older layers for some 300 million years. Then the dune deposits started to harden and petrify, creating the strange swirling rock-dune sandstone one sees all over the plateau region. Volcanic eruptions around the plateau added to the great piling of sediment, while rivers and lakes and inland seas flushed in and then dried up or receded. But the plateau itself, while it was eroded and cut and sculpted and formed, remained relatively stable in contrast to the other lands around it, which changed mightily. About 70 million years ago the land all around the southwest began to rise, pushing the plateau from about sea level to more than 10,000 feet above it. Great mountains were thrust up out of the ground all around the region, and the earth stretched with underground tension to create the basin and range province to the west and south of the plateau. According to the U.S. Geological Survey, about 20 million years ago a "great tension developed in the [earth's] crust . . . and the basin and range province broke into a multitude of down-dropped valleys and elongated mountains" similar to what we see today in Arizona's desertlands. But the Colorado Plateau remained stable and eventually rose nearly a mile higher than the basin and range. The Colorado River fell through the plateau and cut deep into the rock, carving the Grand Canyon—a process that started less than six million years ago.

A visit to Grand Canyon reveals much of the story of the continent's geologic formation. The top layers of rock, through which the Colorado first cut, called the Kaibab Formation, are around 270 million years old, while the gneiss and schist of the inner canyon are about 1.8 billion years old. Many geologists believe that the lower 2,000 feet or so of the canyon was cut and eroded just in the last 750,000 years—the blink of a geologist's eye. The canyon was formed by the great cosmic need of all water to return to the sea from whence it came: Water falls—that's its sole mission in life—and huge torrents of water carrying loads of dry, rocky sediment fall hard and fast and cut deep into the rocks of an uplifted plateau. As the cuts get deeper, the land around it gives way and falls apart, thus creating the deep, wide and wonderful hole in the plateau that has made Arizona famous.

The Rivers

The state's rivers, though many of them are dry for much of the year these days, have made human culture possible in Arizona. The **Gila River,** nearly dead today, was the main east–west waterway, stretching from the mountains of New Mexico all the way to the lower Colorado along the western border. The banks of the Gila's tributaries, the **Verde,** the **San Pedro,** the **Salt,** and the **Santa Cruz,** saw the rise of several complex and creative cultures over the centuries, including the Hohokam, the Saldo, the Sinagua, and the Mogollon. The state's main river, the **Colorado,** drains the vast Colorado Plateau and stretches from Wyoming all the way to Mexico. Much of the river through Arizona, about half of its total length, has historically been difficult to access because it flows deep within intricately carved canyons. Tributaries of the Colorado, like the Little Colorado in the northeastern portion of the state and the Bill Williams River in the central-west, have also been important to human settlement in Arizona. The Little Colorado provided a reasonable water supply for the Ancestral Puebloan cultures that settled on the high plains and, much later, was the source of life for Mormon pioneers in the 19th century.

© TIM HULL

The Verde River in North-Central Arizona supports a lush riparian habitat, teeming with life.

Most of the state's rivers are no longer wild, having been dammed and controlled, a process that started, on a major scale, in the late 19th and early 20th centuries with the era of reclamation. Because wild desert rivers like the Gila, Salt, and Colorado were subject to intense flooding and severe drought, it was difficult for European settlers to rely on their quirky flows for agriculture. The federal government was also eager to harness the rivers' power to create hydroelectricity and to build vast reservoirs of water that could be sent to the growing agricultural and urban areas of Arizona, California, and elsewhere. Beginning at the turn of the century with the building of Roosevelt Dam on the Salt, which helped make Phoenix and the Valley of the Sun first an agricultural boomtown and then an urban megalopolis, the era of reclamation saw most of the state's rivers dammed, ending with the damming of the Colorado River at Glen Canyon in the mid-20th century. Earlier, the biggest dam of them all, Hoover, was constructed in Black Canyon on the Colorado

at the Arizona-Nevada border, creating the world's largest man-made lake, **Lake Mead,** and making the agricultural blunder called the Imperial Valley, in California, possible. The damming of any river changes that river irrevocably; the damming of the Colorado at Glen Canyon altered the stretch of the West's greatest river that created the Grand Canyon so much that it is unrecognizable from its previous form. Even the color of the river is different. The Colorado River, the red river, used to flow muddy and warm through the canyon, hence its name, because it was full of the sediment that helped cut the great gorge. Since the dam was built, most of that sediment is deposited behind the dam in the reservoir known as Lake Powell, and the river flows cool and green through the inner gorge. This has led to a complete change in the river's downstream ecosystem, as the ancient cycles of flood and drought have changed to a predicable, constant flow, thus changing the very character of the river and making it difficult for native species to survive.

The dry ponderosa pine forest above Prescott is scanned for wildfires from this mountain-top lookout station.

CLIMATE

Contrary to popular belief, many regions of Arizona experience four seasons. Even on the desert, while summers are long and hot below 5,000 feet or so, the sky island mountain ranges experience little pockets of seasonally based weather.

Spring is the best time to be on Arizona's lowland deserts. From late February until May temperatures typically hang around the high 70s and 80s from the lower Colorado River region across the desert belt to the New Mexico border.

The highland summer is warm—even hot—during the day and cool at night, ranging from the mid- to high 80s to the low 60s at night. In late summer the smell of wet pine needles precedes each late-afternoon, "monsoon" rainstorm, and a mist rises when the cold raindrops hit the warm rocks.

While it also rains during the late summer on the deserts, during the beloved "monsoon" season, the storms only serve to make an already unbearable heat humid as well. Summers in the desert are intensely hot and listless. The daytime highs range from the high 90s to 110°F or even 120°F at their worst, while at night the lows rarely fall below the 80s. In Tucson and Phoenix it is not uncommon to experience several months straight of 100°F or higher temperatures with little or no rainfall.

The monsoon season, which, to be strictly correct, should be called simply the summer rainy season, occurs when shifting winds from the south encourage late-afternoon downpours, often attended by thunder and lighting, nearly everyday from July into September. During this time of year the dry washes and riverbeds throughout the state are subject to flash flooding, as torrents of rain flow through the channels from the uplands to the desert. Never stop or park in a dry wash during this time of year—it could become a raging river rather quickly, even if the sun is shining overhead. Monsoon storms are highly localized—so much so that it is sometimes raining in the backyard and not in the front yard. Hiking up a canyon during this time of year can be dangerous and sometimes deadly; you never know if it's raining in the mountains above you, and that water could show up anytime, falling off the mountain and rushing through the canyon and taking hikers with it. Also, washes fill up quickly during the rainy season and often trap drivers trying to cross them, necessitating rescues that are expensive and dangerous for first responders. Never venture into a flooded wash, no matter how shallow it appears. Unless you visit Arizona during the two months or so of the summer rainy season, or during the couple months in winter when it may be snowing in the highlands and raining intermittently on the deserts, you're not likely to experience anything but sunshine.

In the highlands during spring you'll encounter cool days and cold nights, and it has even been known to snow across the pine belt in April or later. Depending on the length and strength of the winter, there will typically be snow in the north-central high country in February and even into March

Fall (Oct.–Dec. or Jan.) comes on cold and barren in the highlands, and the ground crunches with fallen leaves. The "second spring" begins on the desert. The weather gets perfect again, from the high 60s to the 80s, with cool, light-jacket nights. This is the time of year when the snowbirds arrive from Wisconsin and Illinois to set up camp until it starts to get hot. After December, the winter rains come to the desert and it starts to snow in the high country, and for a very brief couple of weeks everybody in the state is cold and housebound.

Winter temperatures can fall below freezing in the highlands and regularly reach lows of 20°F or below and highs in the 40s and 50s. On the deserts during this time, highs fall to the low 60s and even into the 50s, and lows regularly fall below 30°F. Only a few places in the state receive significant snowfall—Flagstaff, the Kaibab Plateau, and the White Mountains. In these places the snow can be deep enough to close roads and halt normal life.

ENVIRONMENTAL ISSUES

With its delicate and finely balanced biomes and some of the most dramatic and exotic scenery on earth, Arizona has over the generations been a haven, a laboratory, and a rallying point for environmentalists and ecologists. One of the biggest threats to the state's extremely varied ecosystems is simple growth; much of the desert has been paved over and crowded with homes, while the upland forests host droves of overbuilt homes just waiting for a wildfire to burn them to their foundations. It may seem strange that a land so naturally inhospitable to human occupation is, year after year, listed as one of the top two or three fastest-growing states in the nation. There are no signs that this trend is going to let up any time soon. The constant influx of people has led over the years to environmental problems far beyond the mere pavement of desert and clearing of forests. Growth and the state's founding impetus to glean profit from the land have led to the overpumping of groundwater and the damming and taming of most of the state's rivers. This has altered the green riverways so completely that many species of native fish are now as good as gone,

a reminder from Smokey

© ELIZABETH JANG

and nonnative plants line the mostly dry riverbeds, crowding out native riverine flora like cottonwoods and willows.

Climate change, scientists say, is likely to increase the state's environmental woes, and, coupled with an ongoing drought that has been, more or less, eating away at the state for more than a decade, may lead to shortages on the Colorado River, water from which the vast majority of urban Arizonans depend. Some scientists have recently predicted that Lake Mead may dry up by 2025, while others believe the current human culture in Arizona may, one day in the future, suffer the same collapse as did the Anasazi, the Hohokam, and other complex societies who have tried to make a go of it here, leaving behind the ambitious ruins of their rise and fall but not much else.

There are numerous organizations fighting to save Arizona and its rare natural beauty from destruction and overuse, and over the last few decades the state, many local governments, and especially the diverse citizenry have taken a more proactive approach to conservation. Visiting Tucson's midtown neighborhoods gives the visitor the best evidence of this, where one can see an increasing number of homes with solar panels on their roofs and corrugated rainwater tanks rising from behind their fences. The federal government, which controls many of the state's most famous environmental treasures, has over the last several years set aside more and more of the remaining open and wild lands as wilderness areas and national monuments. However, in recent years the high price of copper and the rising cost of energy have led to renewed explorations and plans to dig strip mines on public lands, a reality that has again started familiar debates over resource conservation that have been raging for decades. Groups like the Nature Conservancy and the Tucson-based Sky Island Alliance and Center for Biological Diversity are using a variety of methods, including simple capitalism, science-based advocacy, and the federal courts,

This sign in Sedona reminds you to please stay on the trail.

to make sure that large swaths of Arizona remain open and wild.

Visitors to Arizona can help keep the state beautiful and clean by adhering to a few simple, common-sense rules. First of all, as always, pack out what you pack in. Always stay on the trails, don't feed wild animals, and never, ever take any vehicle off the road or the trail, including a bike. If you're an off-highway vehicle (OHV) enthusiast, stick to the set-aside off-road areas in the national forests (which can be identified through the U.S. Forest Service's Arizona websites or at the local offices). Also, if you're visiting any of the state's many national forests during the summer, there are likely to be campfire and smoking restrictions enforced throughout the state due to high temperatures and ongoing drought. Make sure you are familiar with these restrictions and that you follow them to the letter. Nearly all of the state's huge, catastrophic wildfires in recent years have been caused by humans.

Flora and Fauna

FLORA

The state's flora is, like the land itself, extremely diverse, ranging from weird desert rarities to tall, thick evergreens.

Trees and Bushes

The official Arizona state tree is the palo verde, a green-skinned desert-dweller that can grow up to 25 feet high. The tree proliferates throughout the Lower Sonoran zone and is often a close neighbor to the saguaro, the baby buds of which use the palo verde's cover to hide and grow. Other common desert trees are the ubiquitous mesquite, which has often been used for firewood and building, and its beans have nourished people and animals alike. Both the mesquite and the palo verde bloom yellow in the spring.

Ironwood trees, drought-resistant evergreens, grow along slopes and washes in the

There are many species of agave growing in Arizona, and some reach the mammoth proportions of this one.

desert. Bushy plants crowd the desert as well: creosote is everywhere, as is stickery, **catclaw,** and **rabbitbrush,** all of which bloom yellow. Adding a little red to the bloom-time is the **ocotillo,** which is everywhere in the desert and resembles a sprouting group of pipe-cleaners. Throughout the desert and into the chaparral of the transition zones you'll see several sword-cluster species of **agave,** an important plant to the human population in that it can be turned into mescal and tequila. The *agave parryi,* or **century plant,** blooms only once with a tall stalk of yellow flowers.

In the scrublands and chaparral and higher you'll see scrub oak, piñon pine, juniper, manzanita, and other brushy trees. In the high country, above 6,000 feet or so, you'll see ponderosa pine mainly. Higher still, in the mountain forests near the North Rim of the Grand Canyon, in the White Mountains and elsewhere, fir, spruce, and aspen forests dominate. Along many waterways you'll see big cottonwoods and willows and sycamores.

Cacti

The most famous of Arizona's cacti, the **saguaro,** looks like it does because it is perfect: every form has a function. Its green skin allows for photosynthesis, normally the job of leaves on less individualistic plants. Its spongy flesh and ribbed contours encourage water-storage; the saguaro can collect and store up to 200 gallons of water from a single rainfall, which can get it through the year. Its telltale needles protect it from the incessant gnawing of hungry desert creatures. Its splashy white blossoms (seen in April, May, and June—the blossoms are Arizona's official state flower) and its juicy red fruits (eaten for eons by the desert's native inhabitants) assure the rising of another generation. The best place to commune with these perfectly adapted desert plants is Saguaro National Park near Tucson.

You'll see various species of cactus throughout the Lower and into the Upper Sonoran

© TIM HULL

Saguaros live for up to 175 years; this is how they die.

zones. Most cactus are easily recognizable if you know their names: **organ pipe, barrel, beaver tail, claret cup,** and **hedgehog** cactus generally look like their sobriquets suggest, albeit spiky and standoffish versions. The famous **prickly pear** cactus can be identified by its red fruit-blooms, which are turned into jellies and even maragarita mix.

Wildflowers

In the early spring, especially after a rainy winter, the desert bajadas, the sloping flatland that stretches out from the desert mountain ranges, and valleys bloom with color as dormant wildflowers burst back to life. Various shades of photogenic whites, yellows, blues, reds, and purples contrast with the uniform rich green of the well-watered springtime desert to create a truly beautiful but ephemeral scenery. Some of the most common bloomers are the light-purple **Arizona lupine,** the deep yellow **Mexican gold poppy,** the dark pink **Parry's penstemon (or Parry's beardtongue),** and the virginal white **desert lily.** In summer the

northland meadows and grasslands bloom with wild color as well. The best, most accessible places to see wildflowers in the spring are Picacho Peak State Park between Phoenix and Tucson and the Superstition Mountains east of Phoenix. You'll also see the desert in bloom in places like Saguaro National Park near Tucson and throughout the Santa Cruz Valley south of Tucson.

FAUNA
Mammals

Arizona's official state mammal is the **ringtail**, a relative of the raccoon often called a ringtailed cat or a miner's cat because of its rodent-eating proclivities. Its huge, bushy, white-and-black-ringed tail is its identifying feature, but it's not likely you'll see one unless you're nocturnal. The **mountain lion** or cougar is found, and hunted, throughout the state; smaller **bobcats** are often seen lounging near water features in Sonoran Desert backyards, and scrawny **coyotes** can be spotted quickly crossing highways throughout the state. In the

The collared peccary, a common desertland animal, is also called the javelina.

The blue heron is a common sight from the banks of the Verde River.

western deserts a few **bighorn sheep** still cling to the dry rocky cliffs.

A few different species of **jackrabbit** can be found all over, and **white-tailed deer** and **mule deer** live from the bottom of the Grand Canyon to the mountain heights and most places in between. **Pronghorn** live on the high grasslands in herds. The **collared peccary** or javelina (which resembles a wild pig but is actually related to the rodent family) is everywhere in the desert and the transition zone, so much so that they are generally considered pests. The **black bear** lives in the mountains throughout the state, and various species of **bats** come out in the Arizona night, responsible for pollinating and continuing the state's signature cactus forests.

Birds

The small, flitting **cactus wren,** which lives among the spiky plants, is the Arizona state bird, while the tall **roadrunner** may be its most recognizable. The **red-tailed hawk** proliferates in the desert sky, hunting rodents. The **California condor** has been reintroduced into the wild around Grand Canyon country. Though not a native to the state, the jagged canyon country was deemed a perfect place to acclimate the threatened, prehistoric-looking bird into the wild.

Water birds, including the elegant **great blue heron,** hang around the state's riparian areas, and **wild turkeys** are somewhat common in oak and pine woodlands. One of the most common birds in the desert is the **Gambels quail,** which can often be seen crossing streets followed by a ragged line of tiny offspring. The **turkey vulture** is constantly soaring slowly in the ever-blue dryland sky. Various owl species are common in the woodlands and the deserts, and the **gila** and the **acorn woodpecker** are always tapping away at some tree or woodland home.

Southern Arizona is a mecca for bird enthusiasts, who stalk the region's Sky Islands mountain range looking for rare subtropical birds like the **elegant trogan,** a green, red, white, and black bird related to the jungle-loving quetzal.

Fish

The **apache trout,** a gold-and-black native Arizona species, is the official state fish. Because of changes to the ecosystem and other factors, 28 of the state's 31 native fish are threatened, endangered, or as good as extinct. Still, in the mountain streams and lakes popular with anglers, you'll find rainbow and brown trout, bass, and others. In the lowland lakes there's bass, crappie, sunfish, catfish, and trout.

Reptiles

The desert is known as the home of the rattlesnake, seen more and more these days as the suburban attack on the desert continues. A few species of rattlesnakes are found in Arizona. The **western diamondback,** which has lent its name to the state's world-champion professional baseball team, lives in the desert and the mountains and has deadly venom. Its skin is gray with brown, diamond-shaped splotches along the back and a series of black-and-white bands just above its rattle. As with

nearly all animals, the Diamondback will leave you alone if you afford it the same courtesy. The light-brown **western rattlesnake** lives throughout the state, and the **Arizona ridge-nosed rattlesnake** lives in the woodlands of southeastern Arizona, a reddish-brown or gray hunter of rodents and lizards.

Several different species of **lizard** can be seen all over the lowlands, doing push-ups on hot rocks. The desert's most recognizable residents, these tiny leftover dinosaurs come in many shapes and sizes. One of the biggest is the fat and venomous **gila monster,** with is beady skin and languid looks. The monster can be seen sunning itself sometimes in and around Tucson. The only venomous lizard in the United States should be given a wide berth if encountered.

The slow and wise **desert tortoise** hides out from the desert sun in its burrow, and if it makes it past its soft-shell youth—when it's a favorite of predatory birds—it can live up to a hundred years or more. Frogs and toads in Arizona include the **Arizona tree frog,** a

A snake slithers along the banks of the Verde River.

© TIM HULL

lime-green forest resident, and the **western spadefoot toad,** which lives in the desert in a burrow, a blotchy greenish brown with grey tints.

Insects and Arachnids

The **bark scorpion** is the crabby, pinching demon of the desert underworld; its venom is dangerous if it finds its way to the blood. The **grand western cicada** makes a racket in the woodlands on summer evenings. The hirsute **desert tarantula** looks much meaner than it is, cruising about in the early morning and early evening. You're bound to encounter gnats and mosquitoes and other tiny pests in desert riparian areas and around upland lakes.

History

PREHISTORIC CULTURES

Small bands of ice-age migrants were probably moving through North America as many as 20,000 years ago or more, but the pioneer Southwesterners are still widely considered to be the Clovis people (named for their spear points, first found in Clovis, New Mexico), who hunted big game in what is now Arizona about 10,000 to 16,000 years before the common era. Climate change and the overexploitation of the mammoths and great ground sloths of the Pleistocene ended this epoch by about 8,000 B.C. From then until pottery-making cultures began to rise around the time of Jesus, the Archaic-era hunter-gatherers made a long, successful go of it here, moving between the forested highlands and the deserts seasonally to hunt and gather wild foods. By the late Archaic period these bands were living in semi-permanent camps in pit houses and were growing corn likely introduced by migrants from Mesoamerica.

The first millennium A.D. saw the rise of several sophisticated and mostly sedentary cultures in Arizona, the most successful of which were the **Anasazi** on the Colorado Plateau, the **Mogollon** in eastern Arizona and New Mexico, and the **Hohokam** in the river valleys of the Sonoran Desert. These cultures would rise and fall in stages, with rises generally coinciding with wet times and falls subsequent to droughts. By A.D. 700 or so the Anasazi were building above-ground, rock-and-mud, urban-like villages that would become known as pueblos, from the Spanish for town or city. The Anasazi culture would briefly rise to become something of an empire in the plateau country, with New Mexico's Chaco Canyon as its ruling capital.

On the low deserts, the Hohokam constructed a network of irrigation canals in the river valleys around what are now Phoenix and Tucson, and lived in complex, hierarchal agricultural societies that built adobe great houses and ceremonial ball courts. Around A.D. 1150 many of the dramatic cliff dwellings began to appear throughout the Southwest. These cultures had mostly run their course by A.D. 1450 due to a variety of factors—ecological, climatic, and social. For generations the monuments and ruins they left behind have fascinated scientists and tourists alike.

Sometime in the 1400s or before, the Athapaskan culture migrated south to the area from the far north in Canada; these tribes would later become those known as the **Apache** and the **Navajo.** These tribes were not related to any of the cultures living in the region at the time they arrived. The Apache eventually moved to Southeastern Arizona, where they would have a epochal battle for supremacy with the U.S. Army in the late 19th century, while the Navajo stayed in the Colorado Plateau area and learned about dry-land farming from their puebloan neighbors, while also spending a good amount of time raiding those same neighbors. They would eventually be nearly killed off by the U.S. Army under the direction of Kit Carson. After a long and brutal internment outside of their harsh but beloved Four Corners lands, the Navajo signed a treaty with the U.S. in 1868 that allowed them to return to the

© TIM HULL

a close-up view of Betatakin, the village ruins located in the Navajo National Monument

plateau country, where they remain today and have grown to become North America's largest tribe. The Hopi, who live on a small reservation on three mesas in the middle of Navajoland, are the descendants of the Anasazi who lived in the region's dramatic cliff dwellings and pueblos. They were never forced off the land that they consider to be their homeland—the same harsh and seemingly inhospitable mesas they still live on today—but they were subject, as were the Navajo and Apache, to periodic attempts by the federal government to "Americanize" them by sending their children to government-run schools off the reservation, forcing them into a cash and labor economy very different from their subsistent lifestyle, and converting them to Christianity. A large number of Navajo today are Christians and there are churches throughout the reservation. Many Hopi have held on to their native religious beliefs and seem to live in a separate, more ancient time.

THE EUROPEANS ARRIVE

The impenetrable northern reaches of the Spanish Empire in Mexico were essentially unexplored by Europeans when **Alvar Nunez**

Cabeza De Vaca found himself shipwrecked and lost in the grasslands and deserts of what is now the Southwestern United States and Northern Mexico in the 1520s. And though he and his companions—one of them, Estevan, was a Moorish slave or indentured servant— probably never made it to Arizona proper, the tales they told of their adventures when they finally returned to civilization inspired subsequent discoveries in the great north. In 1539 Fray Marcos de Niza and Estevan trekked north to discover the Seven Cities of Cibola, rumors of which Estevan and Cabeza de Vaca had heard during their ordeal. Estevan scouted ahead and was killed by the Native Americans, who lived not in golden cities but in regular old mesa-top pueblos not too different from those that still exist on the Hopi reservation in Arizona and in the Rio Grande Valley of New Mexico. Nevertheless, de Niza's report suggested that the golden cities may indeed be a reality, and that was enough to inspire an ambitious expedition in 1540 led by **Francisco Vasquez de Coronado** in search of the reported riches. Coronado found none, but his expedition moved through what is now eastern Arizona. In the 1690s **Father Eusebio Francisco Kino** began his journeys into Southern Arizona and Sonora, bringing cattle to the region for the first time and establishing several long-lasting missions, including San Xavier del Bac near Tucson, to this day still celebrating mass in its dark, cool interior. By the 1750s the Spanish crown had established a presidio or fort at Tubac, which was moved to the Tucson valley in 1775. Southern Arizona comprised the northern reaches of the Spanish New-World empire, though it was sparsely populated and a violent, dangerous place to live. Spanish cattle ranchers and other hardy settlers fought Apaches and others for the right to live in the region, but for decades the north would remain too isolated and too dangerous to grow much. The Mexicans won their independence from Spain in 1821 and so took over administration of the vast northlands. The wilderness was exploited somewhat for its resources, used for cattle ranching and placer mining by tough Mexican explorers, but mostly it was too far from the center of power and was too dangerous to be of much worth to the new nation.

In the later 1820s trappers, hunters, and mountain men like James Ohio Pattie, Antoine Leroux, and Pauline Weaver became some of the first Anglo-Americans to venture through Arizona, in search of beaver pelts. Such men would in turn guide the **Army of the West** and the Mormon Battalion through the state in 1846 and 1847 during the Mexican War, which was fought primarily in Mexico. After the war ended in 1848, much of what is now the Southwest became U.S. property, and in 1850 a huge area that included Arizona and New Mexico became the New Mexico Territory. In 1854 the land between the Gila River and the Mexican border—Southern Arizona, basically—was added to the territory through the **Gadsden Purchase.**

In 1849 and for several years afterward, thousands of Americans passed through Arizona headed for gold and glory in California. Those hard-rock, hard-luck miners would return east to the state a few years later in search of the gold and silver most of them had failed to find

on the coast. Several boundary, land, railroad, and scientific surveys of Arizona and the West during the 1850s brought this far corner of the continent greater attention and interest from the East.

TERRITORIAL YEARS

It was the increasing mining activity in the state that, among other factors, led President Lincoln to establish the Arizona Territory in 1863, disconnecting it from the huge conglomerate of land called New Mexico. The capital was established at Prescott, in the state's mineral-laden midlands, and the East's economic exploitation of the land, albeit on a much smaller scale than it would become, commenced. During the Civil War Tucson was a confederate hotbed for a time before being occupied by the U.S. Army. After the Civil War ended, immigration and exploration of the Southwest picked up considerably. Still, when **John Wesley Powell** completed the first river-run through the Grand Canyon in 1869, the population of the territory was less than 10,000 persons.

Pioneer cemeteries, like this one in the abandoned mining town of Helvetia, dot the desert.

© TIM HULL

Settlers trickled in over the coming years, spurred here to find treasure, to cure their tuberculosis, for adventure, science, and cheap land made available by the federal Homestead and Desert Land Acts. Despite this, the territory remained a wild and dangerous place for most. The Apache, Navajo, and other tribes didn't feel they should have to give up the land they had conquered to white settlers, many of whom were looking to get rich quick exploiting the land and then leave. From 1871 until **Geronimo's** final surrender in 1886, the U.S. Army fought a brutal war with the Apache and other tribes. The Apache were eventually defeated at a high cost to both parties, and the majority of the tribe was sent to Oklahoma, where they became prisoners of war for many years. They struggled to hold to their traditional ways and remain a strong culture, but privation and the machinations of a government that did not understand them took their toll. Eventually the Apaches were allowed to return to Arizona to reservations that include parts of their traditional homelands, and today they operate successful casinos and resorts.

Mining has long been one of the state's primary economic engines.

With the end of the Apache wars the territory moved one step closer to large-scale settlement and development. In the 1880s the railroad arrived and transformed the region, bringing in more people and materials than ever before. By 1889 the Phoenix area had already begun to dominate the territory, and with the construction of Roosevelt Dam on the Salt River in 1911, the Valley's agricultural boom was just on the horizon. In 1912, Arizona entered the union as the 49th state.

STATEHOOD AND BEYOND

The first half of the 20th century in Arizona was dominated by the era of reclamation. The federal government used taxpayer money to develop the state's water resources, damming rivers for irrigation, water storage, and hydroelectric power, creating a huge agricultural industry in the process. Phelps Dodge and other mining giants ripped huge holes in the lands to extract low-grade copper, while Anglo owners and managers on the whole treated the Mexican and Native American miners, and those who worked in the agricultural industry as seasonal laborers—without whom Arizona agriculture would not have been possible—poorly, even criminally on many occasions.

At the same time, more residents and visitors began to realize that there was more to the fantastic Arizona landscape than profit and loss, and this era saw the rise of national parks and monuments, national forests, and state-level protection of important lands. Beginning around the 1920s, boosters in Phoenix and Tucson and elsewhere began to see the economic benefits of attracting tourists to the sunny state, and by 1950 or so tourism had replaced the extractive industries in importance. During the two World Wars the federal government set up training bases and military installations in the state that led to a growth spurt, and the advent of swamp coolers and air conditioners stimulated a population boom in Arizona that has yet to really let up.

Economy and Government

ECONOMY

Arizona's economy for much of the past was ruled by the boom-and-bust realities of the extractive and agricultural industries. Worldwide prices, the fickleness of the market, and the constant threat of a destructive act of nature made economic life here before World War II a wild ride. Booms in the cattle industry in the 1890s and cotton before and during World War I created large industries in the state virtually overnight. The overgrazing of an arid-land open range and monocultural agriculture took their individual tolls, and both of these members of the state's well-known "five C" economy actually influenced life here on a major scale for a relatively short time. The other of the Five C's (sometimes four)—copper, cotton, cattle, citrus, and climate—have fared better than cotton and cattle, both of which are now very minor elements of the state's economy. Copper mining, the state's claim to fame in economic circles

for several generations, was nearly moribund until mid-decade, when worldwide prices hit record levels (thanks, in large part, to a global building boom centered in China, and the ubiquity of copper in consumer electronic products and other modern necessities). Previously mothballed pits have opened again, and start-up firms from outside the state are searching the desert for new pit sites. This may be just a blip on the overall economic radar screen, however. The extractive and agricultural industries are no longer the primary economic engines of Arizona and the West and haven't been for some time. According to a recent report by the Tucson-based Sonoran Institute, fewer than 5 percent of the West's counties have more than 20 percent of employment in traditional extractive industries, and agriculture and ranching made up just 4 percent of total employment in the west as of 2000.

A boom in single-family housing and urban

The Valley of the Sun and Central Arizona, seen here near Coolidge, were once a prolific agricultural empire.

© TIM HULL

Arizona is still one the nation's top producers of copper ore.

and suburban development has enraptured the state for several decades, though as of this writing that boom has predictably gone bust. Still, despite its boom-and-bust ways the state has often been somewhat impervious to national economic slowdowns, primarily because of its always-steady growth. Growth fuels itself, and an economy that is growing is always perceived to be healthy. Between 2000 and 2006, Arizona's population grew by about 20 percent. The deep truth of the Arizona economy, and one that holds for the entire West, is that the service industry (much of it tourism-related), with its low wages and transient workers, is the hottest-running economic engine here and has been for many years. All over the West, non-labor income like investments, disability, and retirement payments come in a close second to the service industry as a top economic driver.

The median household income in Arizona is about $44,000 with 2.6 people per household. Some 15 percent of Arizonans live below the poverty line.

GOVERNMENT

Arizona's government has had a contrary relationship with the federal establishment since before statehood. The state's entrance into the union was delayed for some time because the legislature, backed by a majority of the public, refused to give up a section of its constitution that allowed for the popular recall of judges. Today the bickering between the two continues over public land issues and border control. The truth is that the federal government made Arizona and it controls a good portion of the land in the state still. With history as an example, it's easy to see that had the federal government not protected huge portions of the state as national forests, monuments, parks, and wilderness areas, outside (mostly Eastern) economic interests would have used that land for their own profit, as they have the majority of Arizona's natural resources since long before statehood.

The state's government for most of its history has been interested, like nearly everybody else, in developing and taking from the land, and the various land-hungry interests who at one time or another were in favor—be they mining, agricultural, ranching, or military—have dictated policy. This is not as true today as it has been in the past, however.

While Arizona is known today as a staunchly "red" state, that has not always been the

© TIM HULL

The Arizona Capitol Building in downtown Phoenix is now a museum and visitor center.

case and it likely won't be for much longer. Southern-style Democrats ruled the state for a few generations until **Barry Goldwater** and the conservative revolution found success here and on the national stage in the 1960s. Since then the state has been a Republican stronghold, and a conservative one at that. There are a few "blue" enclaves, notably Tucson and the Navajo Nation. However, the state's demographics seem to be changing, and the voter rolls are swelling not with Republicans and Democrats, but with Independents. Republican **John McCain,** one of Arizona's longtime senators who is often lauded for his independent bent, is as of this writing the presumptive GOP nominee in the 2008 presidential race.

People

Most Arizona residents are émigrés to the state, and most have lived here a relatively short amount of time. The majority of the state's 6.1 million residents live in Pima and Maricopa Counties, in and around the two large urban areas of Phoenix and Tucson. About a million persons live in Pima County and some 3.7 million live in Maricopa. About 13 percent of Arizonans are over 65, but 26 percent are under 18. The former statistic is expected to rise significantly as more and more baby boomers retire and move to the sunbelt, just as their parents did in the 1960s and 1970s. On par with nationwide averages, about 81 percent of Arizonans are high school graduates, and 24 percent have at least a bachelor's degree. A full 68 percent of Arizonans own their homes.

While the majority of Arizonans are still in most corners of the West referred to as Anglos, and the state was largely founded and developed by Anglos—much more so than was its neighbor New Mexico—people of Hispanic or Latino origin have a significant influence on the economy and culture here, especially in Southern Arizona and in both large urban areas. According to the U.S. Census Bureau, 29 percent of Arizonans are of Hispanic or Latino origin, compared to 15 percent nationwide.

The influence of Latino culture, especially that of Mexico, can be seen throughout the state. Much of the finest art, music, and food to be found in Arizona has its origins in Mexico, to which the entire land area of the state used to belong, not too long ago.

Native Americans make up about 5 percent of the population; the largest tribe, the Navajo Nation, has some 298,000 members. Other tribes include the O'odham people, formerly the Papago. The **Tohono O'odham** live on a large reservation southwest of Tucson and operate casinos near the city. In the Phoenix area, the **Akimel O'odham,** or the Gila River Indian Community, live on a reservation and operate casinos as well. Other tribes in the state include the Hopi, the Yavapai near Prescott, the Apache, and the Colorado River tribes of Western Arizona.

Unlike many of the other Native American nations on the continent, Arizona's tribes are still living today on what they consider their ancestral homelands, albeit smaller portions of that homeland set aside by the federal government under the reservation system. And while poverty is generally the rule on the reservations, Arizona's Native Americans have made important contributions to the artistic, cultural, political, and economic life of the state. The finest artists to come out of Arizona are Native American, and many are known the world over for their arts and crafts based on traditional designs and patterns but adapted and evolved to speak to a contemporary world.

Most of the state's Native American tribes have compacts allowing them to operate casinos, and those casinos are popular and profitable; still, many Arizona Native Americans live below the poverty line even though access to education, health care, and jobs has increased somewhat over the years.

RELIGION

Religious life in Arizona is diverse and complex. **Catholicism** is popular among Latino and Hispanic residents and with many Anglos as well, while the **Church of Jesus Christ of Latter-day Saints,** or the Mormons, has been established in some rural areas of the state since the 19th century.

A 2008 Pew Forum survey found that 25 percent of Arizonans identified as Catholics, and 23 percent identified as Evangelical Protestants. Mainline Protestants make up about 15 percent of the religious population, and LDS adherents are about 4 percent. A surprising 22 percent see themselves as "unaffiliated."

LANGUAGE

The majority of Arizonans speak English, though some 26 percent of residents speak a language other than English at home (likely Spanish), according to the U.S. Census Bureau. From time to time over the years there have been calls for and votes on making English the official language of the state, usually attending some new round of anger and fear over illegal immigration, which, owing more than

© KATHIE CURLEY

Beauty, symbolism, and superb craftsmanship are frequently found in Navajo arts and crafts.

© TIM HULL

The Virgin of Guadalupe, shown here at San Xavier del Bac, is an enduring and ubiquitous symbol to borderland Catholics.

anything else to Arizona's proximity to Mexico, is an ever-present political issue. The reality is that Spanish is used throughout the state and especially in the urban areas. You'll see and hear it everywhere. You may also hear several Native American languages as you travel around the state, including the intricate Hopi language and the Navajo tongue, which was used by the famous code talkers of World War II—one of the only "codes" never to be broken.

THE ARTS

Most of the prominent non–Native American artists and writers associated with Arizona were émigrés. **Edward Abbey,** author of the *Monkey Wrench Gang* and many other books continues, nearly two decades after his death, to influence writing and environmental politics in the state. A friend of Abbey's, Doug Peacock (Hayduke from Abbey's novel) has written an

excellent war memoir, *Walking it Off,* and several books about grizzly bears. Another Abbey friend, Tucsonan **Charles Bowden,** has a national reputation as a nonfiction writer and has produced some of the best books ever about the disaffection and dark ironies of sunbelt culture. **Leslie Marmon Silko** wrote the closest thing we yet have to an Arizona epic; her *Almanac of the Dead* examines the ancient and contemporary Southwest and the confluence of the two. The prolific **Zane Grey,** one of the progenitors of the Western genre, spent a lot of time in Arizona's Rim Country and based many of his books in the state.

The German painter **Max Ernst** came to Arizona in 1946, settling in Sedona and painting the state's surrealistic landscapes in the manner it deserved. His work is on display at the **Phoenix Art Museum.** There are hundreds of painters and sculptors living and working in Arizona today. Many of them congregate in Sedona, Tucson, Tubac, Bisbee, Jerome, and elsewhere. Each of these towns and cities has many galleries dedicated to individual artists, styles, and groups. The famed **Cowboy Artists of America** group was founded in Sedona in 1965, and the aesthetic traditions of the group are still highly visible in the state's galleries and museums.

Arizona has produced a few pop stars, most notably **Linda Ronstadt,** whose family has deep roots in Tucson. **Alice Cooper** grew up in the Valley of the Sun and still resides there, operating a popular downtown rock-and-jock-themed restaurant and bar. The Tempe music scene had a minor worldwide reputation in the 1990s thanks to bands like the **Gin Blossoms** and the **Refreshments.** Singer **Stevie Nicks** is from the Phoenix area, as is **Wayne Newton.**

Thanks to its desert scenery and always-clear skies, Arizona has had a vibrant movie-making scene on and off since the silent era. Classic films like *Arizona, Stagecoach,* and *Oklahoma* have been filmed in the state, along with *The Planet of the Apes, The Three Amigos,* and hundreds of others. The fortunes of Arizona's film industry tend to rise and fall with the popularity of the Western.

ARIZONA'S NATIVE AMERICAN ARTS AND CRAFTS

There are hundreds of Native American artists living in Arizona. The majority are Hopi and Navajo, and they live on reservations in the far northeastern corner of the state. Many Indian artists sell their work at markets and fairs held throughout the year in Phoenix, Tucson, Flagstaff, and elsewhere. Silverwork, carvings, pottery, rugs, and paintings of the Hopi, Navajo, and others have been highly desired since territorial days.

Because it's made by Native Americans, many people approach this art with a lot of preconceived notions; especially prevalent are notions about authenticity and tradition. Some people expect every Indian artist and artisan to be adhering to some ancient set of guidelines set down before real time began, a method that washes each squash-blossom necklace and kachina doll carving with some undeniable spiritual patina. Like most artistic movements, however, the provenance of the Southwestern Indian Arts and Crafts tradition is far more complex.

Think of these artists as working within similar confines as did painters and sculptors of the Western European tradition before and during the Renaissance. Such artists were bound more often than not to paint and sculpt imagery from the Bible or Greek and Roman Mythology, and they could count on their public immediately recognizing the scenes and characters they depicted. However, within this rather narrow tradition, there existed astonishing variety.

Consider, as an example, the story of how silverwork was introduced to the Navajo. In the 1850s, Navajo ironworker Atsidi Sani (Old Smith) added silver to the old Navajo tradition of making jewelry out of shell and stone. The Hopi and Zuni later learned from the Navajo. The oral tradition says the Southwest's Indians were taught metal work in general by the Europeans; Atisidi Sani is said to have learned silversmithing from a smith called Nakai Tsosi or "Thin Mexican." More and more Navajo learned the art during the tribe's tragic imprisonment at Fort Sumner at Bosque Redondo, and the Navajo are said to have taught their Pueblo neighbors, mostly the Hopi and the Zuni, to work silver.

The silver in the early days and for a long time after mostly came from Mexican and U.S. coins. Reservation traders like John Lorenzo Hubbell, at Ganado, paid the Navajo to teach it to each other, then sold the products to tourists. Some of the best silversmiths gave up raising livestock and farming and were able to become full-time artisans, a pattern that still plays out today.

It was during the golden age of Southwestern tourism that the authenticity of Indian jewelry became an issue. The artists were, of course, encouraged to create work specifically for tourists, who flocked to the reservations and pueblos on the Fred Harvey Indian Detours. Writer and trader Mark Bahti writes that these pieces were often lightweight, with "horses, tipis, arrows, thunderbirds . . . designed to fit the tourist notion of what Indian jewelry was *supposed* to look like." But, as Bahti points out, what was Indian jewelry actually "supposed" to look like? Nobody could really say, and they still can't. By the 1920s, manufactured copies were being made outside the Southwest and then shipped in to be sold as authentic, spurring the artists to join together in co-ops and guilds, many of which of are still in operation and are still training new artists.

The 1970s brought about a boom in the market for Pueblo and Navajo jewelry, and today there is a really diffuse sense of what is traditional and what is innovative. Innovation – the artist responding not only to tradition but to the world around him or her – can be seen everywhere at Indian Markets throughout Arizona.

ESSENTIALS

Getting There and Around

BY AIR

If you're flying into Arizona, you'll likely find yourself at **Phoenix Sky Harbor International Airport** (3400 E. Sky Harbor Blvd., 602/273-3300, www.phoenix.gov/skyharborairport/). One of the Southwest's largest airports, Sky Harbor has three terminals served by more than 20 domestic and international airlines. The airport is just three miles east of downtown Phoenix and easy to find. There's a free shuttle system that will take you between terminals.

The only other serious choice is **Tucson International Airport** (520/573-8000, www.tucsonairport.org), which hosts 12 different airlines and offers daily flights to both coasts and other destinations. If you book a flight to Tucson it may be slightly more expensive than flying into Sky Harbor in Phoenix, and you probably won't get a direct flight; in many cases, you'll have to fly into Sky Harbor, switch planes, and then fly south to Tucson—just a 1.5-hour drive on I-10. If you're renting a car anyway, it's probably a better idea to fly into Phoenix and then drive from there, unless you are just going to Tucson and Southern

© ELIZABETH JANG

Arizona, then a direct flight into TIA makes more sense.

Flagstaff, Prescott, Tusayan near the Grand Canyon, Yuma, and other towns have airports, though they are small and offer mostly regional routes. There are also several smaller regional airports around the Valley of the Sun, offering regional flights to Southwestern and west coast ports. If you're coming from the west coast or some other Southwestern city, you might look into regional flights to your Arizona destination; otherwise, Sky Harbor and then a rental car is your best bet no matter where you're headed in Arizona.

BY TRAIN

Amtrak's Southwest Chief Route, which mirrors the old Santa Fe Railway's Super Chief Route of the grand Fred Harvey days, stops twice daily (one eastbound, one westbound) at Flagstaff's classic **downtown depot** (1 E. Route 66, 800/872-7245), the former Santa Fe headquarters and also the town's visitors center (800/842-7293). The route crosses the country from Chicago to L.A., dipping into the Southwest through northern New Mexico and northern Arizona. There are long-term plans for a high-speed railway between Phoenix and Tucson, and possibly to other parts of the state, though likely such a useful project is a generation or more away from being realized. The Southwest, while built and populated largely by the railroads, continues to hold strong to the car culture, and that isn't going to change anytime soon.

BY CAR OR BUS

You need a personal vehicle to get around in Arizona. A significant part of the fun of a trip to the great Southwest is the road trip, and there's just too much scenery and too many spur-of-the-moment stops to go any other way. Ideally, for everyone involved, we'd all ride our bikes across the state. We'd

see everything up close and slow, the air would be clean and we'd all be in great shape and great friends. It's feasible to do such a thing, for there are innumerable back roads throughout the state that allow one to quit the Interstate slipstream; from time to time you'll see a weighted-down group of riders pulling trailers and looking dead-eyed along one of the two-lanes through the desert, but one suspects the elevational challenges in this hump-backed land would be too great for most us. It's a good idea to reserve a rental car before you travel.

If you'd like to carry your home along with you on the Arizona road, or you desire to re-live a favorite sitcom moment or two, look into renting an RV. All over the state these days you'll see rented RVs touring the monuments and landscapes of the west, packed with families and groups of friends. In Phoenix, check out **RV Rental Outlet** (2126 W. Main St., Mesa, 888/461-0023, 480/461-0023, or 480/461-0025, www.rvrentaloutlet.com).

Greyhound (www.greyhound.com) provides bus service between major towns, mostly along the Interstate routes. This isn't a very efficient way to travel around Arizona, but you could do it. Check out the website for schedules and station locations.

TOURS

If you're looking for the knowledgeable assistance of an expert, you can hire **Open Road Tours** (800/766-7117, www.openroadtours.com) to guide and shuttle you in comfort all over the state. Such tours are only recommended for those who like to be around a lot of other people and who enjoy groups. Arizona's tourist track is well established and easy to negotiate, and a tour guide is not necessary. Most of the best sights are controlled by the federal government, specifically the Parks Service, and rangers are always on hand to answer questions and give free, informative tours.

Accommodations

Arizona is known around the world for the high-luxury resort accommodations offered in Tucson, Phoenix, Scottsdale, Sedona, and elsewhere. The best of these spa resorts appear to require their own zip code and guidebook, and the rich and pampered people who frequent them can spend weeks in Arizona without venturing beyond the gates. The best of these all-inclusive, posh spa-resorts in Phoenix, Scottsdale, Tucson, and Sedona are listed in the chapters for those cities.

The state is also fortunate to have a number of historic hotels still in operation, though updated and remodeled; and there are also not a few boutique hotels and bed-and-breakfasts operating out of historic buildings which used to serve some important territorial function. In the old mining town of Jerome in

CLOTHING OPTIONAL ACCOMMODATIONS

There's something about the powerful Arizona sun, especially when it shines hard on the desert country, that makes one want to wear as few clothes as possible. While this usually isn't recommended, what with society's conventions and the danger of overexposure to the dastardly rays, those who enjoy the popular world of "naturism" will want to check out one of the clothing-optional resorts in the desert just north of Phoenix. **Shangri La Ranch** (44444 N. Shangri La Rd., New River, 623/465-5959, www.shangrilaranch.com, office hours 10 A.M.–5 P.M. daily, $32 per couple daily fee, $70-105 for a room, $10 per night camping, $15 for RV hookup) is a family-oriented nudist resort with rooms, camping, and an RV park. It offers numerous activities, a huge swimming pool, and a friendly staff. While there are no bathing suits allowed in the pool, the philosophy of Shangri La seems to be live and let live, so you can "ease into" the nudist lifestyle if you're not already a committed naturist. The setting is gorgeous, way out in the scrubby desert about 45 minutes north of Sky Harbor Airport off I-17 near New River. This is most definitely a family place, so they expect you to be respectful and adhere to the rules of conduct.

While not strictly a place for nudists, the **Essence of Tranquility Natural Hot Spring** (6047 S. Lebanon Loop, Safford, 928/428-9312 or 877/895-6810, www.geocities.com/essenceoftranquility), about two hours east of

Tucson on I-10, in the shadow of 10,000-foot-high Mount Graham, offers private, clothing-optional hot spring baths in which you can soak away all your stress and trouble. The baths are charmingly decorated and private; a bigger communal bath requires clothing. Though a bit on the rustic side, Essence of Tranquility is a wonderful place to visit if you love hot springs and want to meet like-minded soakers. If you want to stay the night or longer at the baths, you can camp ($15), which includes use of a communal kitchen and barbecue area and unlimited use of the tubs, or rent a tepee for $35 per night for two people, or $80 for up to eight people. Rustic but comfortable casitas are also available for $50-60 per night. You can also make a reservation for ear coning (an alternative-medicine method of cleaning and detoxifying the ears), shiatsu and Swedish massage, or a detoxifying sweat wrap. If you're just going for the day, expect to pay $10 per person for use of the baths. While most of the baths are clothing-optional, the owners don't allow any "open nudity." They also discourage bringing children along.

If you're headed out this way to visit the baths, you might also think about hiking in the sky island heights of Mount Graham, or fishing at nearby **Roper Lake State Park** (101 E. Roper Lake Rd., 928/428-6760, www.pr.state.az.us/parks/parkhtml/roper.html), where there's also a natural hot spring bath (clothing required).

North-Central Arizona, the **Jerome Grand Hotel** used to be the once-thriving boom-town's hospital. Another old mining town, Bisbee, in Southern Arizona, has a B&B operating out of a former schoolhouse. Of course, the most distinctive accommodations in both towns are widely thought to be haunted. There are several elegant hotels from the 1920s and 1930s still operating, though with new-century comforts and conveniences, including the **Hassayampa Inn** in downtown Prescott, and **La Posada** in Winslow.

Bed-and-breakfast inns proliferate throughout Arizona, and nearly every region has several. Many of the best B&Bs can be contacted through the **Arizona Association of Bed and Breakfast Inns** (www.arizona-bed-breakfast.com).

If you're just looking for a place to flop between adventures, there is an abundance of chain hotels in every major city and town, and in small towns near national parks and monuments and off the Interstates.

Food

The eating-local food revolution has not missed Arizona; throughout the state you'll find numerous restaurants dedicated to using local and all-natural ingredients, harkening back to a simpler time when we knew a bit more about our food. In the old mining towns of Bisbee in Southern Arizona and Jerome in Northern Arizona you'll find a few high-style restaurants serving an eclectic blend of Southwestern and haute cuisine. In Scottsdale, Phoenix, and throughout the Valley of the Sun, your head will spin from all the options, most of them highly creative and dedicated to a fusion of the Native and the new. On the high grassland plains in Winslow, just south of the Navajo Nation, you'll find one of the best restaurants in the Southwest, **The Turquoise Room,** inside the refurbished and beautiful **La Posada** hotel, a restaurant that reaches back to the past of the Fred Harvey Company, when elegant accommodations and fine dining on locally grown and prepared food were the norm, even in the outback—which Winslow in many ways still is today. On the very edge of the Grand Canyon you'll find surprisingly creative and delicious cuisine at the beautiful **El Tovar** restaurant in Grand Canyon Village. Head to either the Navajo or Hopi reservation nearby and you can sample the native cuisine, centered mainly around mutton and corn and a kind of Mexican-Native American amalgam called the Navajo (or Hopi) taco—a delicious hunk of fry bread piled high with meat and beans.

MEXICAN FOOD

Because so many Arizona residents are from somewhere else, you'll find all the world cuisines well represented in even the most seemingly out-of-the-way places; however, one style reigns supreme: Mexican food. The cuisine of Mexico is very popular throughout the United States these days, and travelers to Arizona and the border region are likely to have at least a passing knowledge of the favorites. However, in Southern Arizona, the Valley of the Sun, and most of the other parts of the state you'll experience a higher quality and more authentic dining experience than you can find at the big national chains. Tucson and the Nogales (especially if you cross the "the line" and try one of the restaurants in the tourist section of Nogales, Sonora, Mexico) are the best places in the state to eat Mexican food. In Tucson you'll fine dozens of restaurants featuring a variety of regional Mexican foods, but the most prevalent is the style of Northern Mexico, "El Norte"—after all, it wasn't that long ago that this region was not the extreme south of the United States, but rather the extreme north of Mexico.

A ranching frontier, Northern Mexico—specifically the states of Sonora and Chihuahua—have a cuisine based on beef, beans, cheese, and chilies—the comfort food of Mexico. You are more likely to find flour tortillas in Northern Mexico than in the central and southern regions, as the desert and semi-desert land is harder on corn than on wheat. A popular ranchland delicacy is machaca, also called carne seca—dried, shredded beef that is available at nearly every restaurant as a filling for burritos and tacos or on its own. Many Tucson restaurants are famous for their carne asada, or grilled meat, thin strips of beef spiced and grilled and then stuffed in tacos or burritos or served on its own with rice and beans. Another popular northern dish is menudo, available at many Tucson and Phoenix-area taco stands and restaurants. It's a kind of soup made with tripe and hominy and cow's foot and is said to cure hangovers—it is often offered only on the weekends.

Throughout the southern portion of the state it's also easy to find excellent Mexican seafood. Tucson is only four or five hours from the Sea of Cortez, and many locals have vacation homes along the desert coast. Places serving fish tacos, shrimp cocktail, and other seafood delights abound. There are also a few restaurants in the state that serve a more complex, gourmet version of Mexican cuisine. At these places, listed in the Tucson and Phoenix restaurant sections, you'll be able to sample the intricate moles and chicken and pork dishes of central and southern Mexico.

Tips for Travelers

In many ways Arizona was saved by tourists. If travelers didn't love the state's scenery and history so much, the Grand Canyon may have long ago been strip-mined and the last of the desert paved over. Instead, the natural wonders have been to a large degree saved forever, and a vibrant and busy tourism industry has grown up here. Because of this, it's easy to be a tourist in Arizona; herein you'll find a few tips to make it even easier.

INTERNATIONAL TRAVELERS

The U.S. government's **Visa Waiver Program** allows tourists from 27 different countries to visit without a visa for up to 90 days. To check if your country is on the list go to http://travel .state.gov/index.html. Even with a waiver, you still need to bring your passport and present it at the port of entry.

The many national parks and monuments in Arizona are well equipped for international tourists. They all offer guides and other literature in a variety of major languages and are used to working with international travelers. Arizona and the Southwest in general are very popular destinations for European and Japanese travelers especially, and in the summer, no matter where you're from, you could very well meet one of your compatriots on the South Rim or at Monument Valley.

ACCESS FOR TRAVELERS WITH DISABILITIES

Many of the best sights in Arizona are accessible to disabled travelers in one way or another. The Grand Canyon and most of the other major federal parks have accessible trails and viewpoints. For advice and links to other helpful Internet resources, go to www .disabledtravelers.com, which is based in Arizona and is full of accessible travel information, though it's not specific to the state. The **National Accessible Travelers Database** may also be helpful. For questions specific to Arizona, you may want to contact the state Department of Administration's **Office for Americans with Disabilities** (100 N. 15th Ave., Suite 361, Phoenix, 602/542-6276, 800/358-3617, or TTY: 602/542-6686, www .azada.gov).

TRAVELING WITH CHILDREN

A family trip around Arizona is necessarily a road trip. Is there such a thing as an entirely kid-friendly road trip? At any rate, Arizona is an ideal place for an active, outdoor vacation involving the whole family. Most of the major sights, especially the national parks and monuments, cater to families and offer a host of fun and educational programs for kids. Phoenix and Tucson both have excellent zoos, both of them kid-centric. Rangers at all the parks and monuments are usually eager to explain and illuminate the sights for kids, and the **Junior Rangers** program, offered at most of the parks, is a fun and educational way to get your kids engaged with nature—and it even includes a photo-ready swearing-in ceremony. Kids under 16 are admitted free to federal parks, monuments, and recreation areas.

SENIOR TRAVELERS

The best thing those 62 years old or older can do before visiting Arizona is to purchase an **America the Beautiful–National Parks and Federal Recreational Lands Senior Pass**. This golden ticket will get you and up to three adults into every national park and monument for the rest of your life. It costs just $10, paid one time in person at any federal park. In Arizona, where most of the best attractions and sights are under federal control, this adds up to big savings and should encourage all families to bring along Grandma and Grandpa wherever they go.

The popular **Elderhostel** (11 Avenue de Lafayette Boston, MA 02111, 800/454-5768, www.elderhostel.org) organization offers several programs in Arizona; go to www.elder hostel.org/programs/state.asp?whatState=AZ for an up-to-date list.

GAY AND LESBIAN TRAVELERS

Arizona is no more or no less gay-friendly than most other states. The gay community is strong and diverse in both Phoenix and Tucson, the state's two major cities. There aren't really gay districts, as such, though in Phoenix the **Melrose District,** on 7th Avenue between Camelback and Indian School Roads, is sometimes considered one.

The **Greater Phoenix Gay & Lesbian Chamber of Commerce** (P.O. Box 2097, Phoenix, AZ 85001, 602/266-5055, www .gpglcc.org) has lists of the state's gay and gay-friendly accommodations. The Valley's *Echo Magazine* (www.echomag.com, 602/266-0550) is an excellent source of news and culture for the gay community, as is *'N Touch News Magazine* (www.ntouchaz .com). Lesbians should check out the **Women's Community Connection** (http://connection .www9.50megs.com/).

In Tucson, *The Tucson Observer* (520/622-7176, www.tucsonobserver.com) has news about the local gay community, and **Wingspan** (425 E. 7th St., 520/624-1779, www.wingspan.org) is the Old Pueblo's GLBT community center.

Health and Safety

THE ARIZONA SUN

Whether you're hiking deep into Grand Canyon or walking sun-splattered paths through a saguaro forest or simply strolling through the Phoenix Zoo, you must be aware that the incessant sun, the driving reason for most visits to Arizonaland, can quickly become a dangerous threat to your health. To eliminate this threat, thus allowing you to bask only in the sun's friendly attributes, practice moderation and prevention. Rather than worship, the sun requires timidity: Stay in the shadows, covered from head to toe. If you're not willing to do this, as most aren't, then at least wear a hat with a wide brim, use high-SPF sunscreen, cover your neck, and, preferably, wear long sleeves. This applies not only to back-country desert adventurers and hikers; mere sightseekers, especially those with fresh-faced children in tow, are just as susceptible to sun- and heat-related health issues—more so, in fact: the less fit you are, the higher the danger.

The least of what the sun can do to you is not to be taken lightly. A **sunburn,** which comes on quicker than you'd think, can lead to skin cancer, and that can lead to death. If you get a sunburn there's little you can do, save try to make yourself more comfortable. Stay out of the sun, of course, and try to keep cool and hydrated. There are dozens of over-the-counter balms available, but simple aloe works as well as anything. A popular home remedy is to gently dab the burned areas with vinegar. If the burn starts to blister, reaching the dreaded third-degree stage, skin cancer becomes a very real threat. Again, the best way to avoid sunburn is to stay out of the sun; barring that, cover up and follow common sense. Those with fair skin and children should be even more cautious.

Hikers, shoppers, sightseers, golfers, and anybody else exerting themselves under high-heat conditions should watch out for **dehydration.** When your body becomes dangerously depleted of fluids, you'll notice first that you are not urinating regularly and your saliva has dried up. You may become irritable and confused; your skin may turn gray and your pulse may race. Children especially can become dehydrated quickly. The best way to avoid dehydration is to limit your exertion during the hottest part of the day and to drink a lot of water. If you feel the symptoms of dehydration coming on, get to a cool, comfortable place and take in fluids, and rest.

Hikers should take along a few packets of electrolyte powder, similar to Gatorade and the like, and a separate water bottle to mix it in—these can be life-savers. If you exert yourself in the heat and sun and fail to replace the fluids flowing out, your body can become depleted of electrolytes and fluids. Such is the path to **heat exhaustion,** a dangerous condition that can turn fatal if not treated. You begin to feel nauseated, dizzy, and weak, and your muscles cramp. Again, if you experience any of these symptoms, get to a cool comfortable place quickly and drink water and something with sodium and potassium in it, like an electrolyte drink.

Dehydration and heat exhaustion, while dangerous and unpleasant, pale when compared to **heat stroke,** sometimes called sun stroke or heat hyperpyrexia, a severe, dangerous health threat that is frequently fatal or, if not fatal, often changes a victim's future health significantly and irrevocably. Heat stroke occurs when the body's temperature-regulating capacity fails; this can be caused by either relatively short exposure to extremely high heat—like, say, a short, strenuous run on a 120°F July afternoon in Yuma—or prolonged exposure to relatively high temperatures, as in, a 15-mile hike in 90°F heat. And that's only if you're in good shape. It would take far less to cause heat stroke in most of us. The first and most important sign of heat stroke is a lack of sweating. If you stop sweating in a situation where you *should* be sweating, take notice. Sweating is your body's way of regulating its temperature, so it stands to reason that if you stop sweating, there may be something wrong with your body. Your heart rate will speed up noticeably and your skin will become dry; you'll get a headache and become confused. At its worst, heat stroke leads to unconsciousness, convulsions, and death. Once you notice you're not sweating, you must get help immediately: get to an emergency room as soon as possible.

ALTITUDE SICKNESS

The mountains in Arizona reach up to 12,000 feet rarely, and more frequently up to 10,000 feet. Though most visitors won't be going that high, you should be aware that a few of the state's mountain towns sit between 5,000 and 8,000 feet above sea level. Lowlanders in relatively good shape may get headaches, a little dizziness and shortness of breath while walking around Flagstaff or other of the state's mountain towns, but very few will experience serious **altitude sickness**—the result of not getting enough oxygen, and therefore not enough blood flow to the brain. Still, take it easy in the higher elevations if you begin to feel tired and out-of-breath, dizzy or euphoric. If you have heart or lung problems you need to be more aware in the higher elevations; the best thing to do is to get a prescription for oxygen from your doctor and carry it with you if you plan on spending a lot of time in the mountains.

HIKING SAFETY

Most hiking safety is based on common sense: take enough water, wear a hat and good shoes, take along something to eat, don't go alone, and make sure somebody knows where you're going and when you're planning on being back. In the desert, such common sense takes on added meaning. It's best to avoid taking long, strenuous hikes in the desert between May and September. Unless you're a masochist or a tough guy or girl without mercy, you probably won't enjoy it and it can get very dangerous very fast. If you do go out in the summer, however, don't go out during the hottest part of the day—stick to early morning or evening, though even at these times the heat can be brutal.

Besides the usual hiking gear that every hiker should have—water, food, a hat, shoes, etc.— Arizona hikers should carry a **tourniquet** with them; if you happen to get bitten by a rattlesnake or a scorpion—not a very likely occurrence at all—you'll want to tie the tourniquet around the area to slow the blood flow, and the venom, until you can get to a hospital and the antivenin. The best way to avoid a snakebite is to avoid snakes. They are not going to bother you unless you bother them or surprise them. Keep an eye on the ground while you're hiking; if a snake, rattler or otherwise, is in your general vicinity, leave the area. Cover your ankles and keep your hands and feet out of dark holes, and don't put your hands on a rock without looking at it first.

OTHER CONCERNS

West Nile virus and the **Hanta virus** are the long-shot threats to your health in Arizona, and both can be avoided by taking precautions. Use insect repellent to ward off the former and simply stay away from rodents to avoid the latter.

Threats from humans come in all the usual forms. Lock your vehicle wherever you go, even in the most remote locations. Don't pick up hitchhikers, anywhere.

Information and Services

Your **cell phone** will work in most parts of Arizona, though there are large swaths of the Navajo and Hopi reservations where cell service is spotty at best, and mostly nonexistent. Cell phones don't usually work in the backcountry, but it's worth taking it along just in case.

You'll find high-speed, wireless **Internet** service throughout the state at the majority of hotels and motels, and in cafés and libraries everywhere. Even the remote reservation lands are wired in.

AREA CODES AND TIME ZONES

Arizona has five area codes. For eastern Maricopa county, including Tempe, Mesa, and most of Scottsdale, dial 480; for Phoenix proper dial 602; for western Maricopa county, dial 623; for all of Southern Arizona, including Tucson, dial 520; and for all of Northern Arizona, including Prescott, Flagstaff, Jerome, the Grand Canyon, and the West Coast (including Yuma and Lake Havasu City) dial 928.

Arizona is in the Mountain Time Zone (MST) and is one of the few places in the country that does not switch over to daylight saving time from the second Sunday in March to the first Sunday in November. The Navajo Nation in northeastern Arizona does switch to daylight saving time, adding even a time change to complete the foreign-country feel of that region.

TUCSON'S COMMUNITY RADIO: KXCI 91.3 FM

Hidden away in an old brick house in Tucson's Armory Park Historic District is one of the best radio stations in the West.

Since the early 1980s **KXCI Community Radio** (220 S. 4th Ave., 520/622-5924 request line, 520/623-1000 office line, www.kxci.org) has been broadcasting an outrageously eclectic mixture of music, news and cultural programming that has contributed greatly to making Tucson a place where people slightly left of center feel welcome and comfortable. This full-time job is done by a staff of mostly volunteer, nonprofessional DJs, many of whom learn the ropes in a DJ class offered annually by the station.

Most weekdays the majority of daytime air is taken up by the "Music Mix," a brew of new and old alternative rock, roots, country, Latino, jazz, electronica, world music and classic pop that's so unpredictable you shouldn't be surprised to hear Willie Nelson followed by the White Stripes followed by a new tune from your favorite Afghani hip-hop artist.

Most nights there's a line-up of genre-specific shows. Mondays feature a "locals only" broadcast that showcases the best of Tucson's fertile music scene, while on Tuesdays country-western, alternative country, and Americana rule. Wednesday is Latino night, and on Saturday you'll hear bluegrass in the morning and in the afternoon Kidd Squidd's Mystery Jukebox, during which the Kidd, who has an unmatched knowledge of music in all its forms, plays a few hours' worth centered around a creative theme.

Because KXCI is supported by grants and donations from listeners, there are no commercials and nobody is beholden to an absentee corporation dictating playlists. This can make for near daily discoveries of music that you didn't know was out there. Tune in to KXCI at 91.3 on the FM dial, or at www.kxci.org.

MAPS AND TOURIST INFORMATION

The **Arizona Office of Tourism** (1110 W. Washington St., Suite 155, Phoenix, AZ, 602/364-3700 or 866/275-5816, www.arizonaguide.com) will send you a free print or electronic version of the official state guide, and its website is full of information and lists of accommodations, events, and restaurants throughout the state. If you're planning to spend a lot of time in the state's national forests, you can get maps and information beforehand from the **National Forest Service, Southwestern Region** (333 Broadway SE, Albuquerque, NM 87102, 505/842-3292 www.fs.fed.us/r3/), or from the websites for the individual forests, listed in the chapters in which they appear. The **Arizona BLM State Office** (One North Central Ave., Suite 800, Phoenix, AZ 85004-4427 or 602/417-9200, www.blm.gov/az/st/en.html) also has a lot of information on the state's wildlands, and the **Arizona State Parks Department** (1300 W. Washington, Phoenix, AZ 85007, 602/542-4174, www.pr.state.az.us) has information on all the parks managed by the state. Passes and reservations for state and federal parks can be obtained and made online or at the parks themselves.

RESOURCES

Suggested Reading

HISTORY

Armstrong, William Patrick. *Fred Harvey: Creator of Western Hospitality*. Bellmont, AZ: Canyonlands Publications, 2000. A slim introduction to Harvey and his accomplishments. Available at many Grand Canyon bookstores, it puts a positive spin on the "Civilizer of the West" and the marketing of the Southwestern Style.

Bandelier, Fanny, trans. *The Journey of Alvar Nunez Cabeza de Vaca*. Chicago: Rio Grand Press, 1964. This strange first-person account marks the true beginnings of American Literature. The conquistador spent years of privation with various northern-Mexico Indian tribes after being shipwrecked near Florida in the late 1520s. He became a slave, a shaman, and a trader before finally finding his way back to civilization and inspiring the later "discovery" of the Southwest by the Spanish.

Corel, Edwin. *The Gila: River of the Southwest*. New York: Holt, Rinehart and Winston, 1951. Using Arizona's once-mighty east–west riverway as his hub, Corel jumps off in many directions, exploring human history and culture under the influence of the Gila, which, along with its major tributaries—the Salt, the Santa Cruz, the San Pedro, and the Verde—was been the main pumping artery of Arizona civilization for centuries.

Hall, Sharlot M. (Crampton, C. Gregory, ed.). *Sharlot Hall on the Arizona Strip: A Diary of a Journey Through Northern Arizona in 1911*. Flagstaff, Northland Press, 1975. Hall, a semi-famous regional writer of the frontier and early statehood, took an arduous trip to the isolated Arizona Strip and lived to write about it. The editor's notes provide a short but thorough introduction to the human history of the region.

Jones, Billy M. *Health-Seekers in the Southwest 1817–1900*. Norman: University of Oklahoma Press, 1967. A scholarly but readable study of health migration in the 19th century. It turns out, according to Jones, that the Wild West was really a "health frontier" full of reluctant settlers who ventured West to cure TB and other ailments.

Limerick, Patricia Nelson. *The Legacy of Conquest: The Unbroken Past of the American West*. New York and London: W.W. Norton & Company, 1987. An unromantic reconsideration of the history of the Western frontier. Limerick finds that it was a distinctly American hunger for resources, profit, and real estate that built and ruled the West, not the six-gun and its stoic, free-shooting hero.

Luckingham, Bradford. *The Urban Southwest*. El Paso: Texas Western Press, 1982. A study of the rise of four major Southwestern cities, including Phoenix and Tucson.

Martin, Douglas D. *An Arizona Chronology: The Territorial Years, 1846–1912*. Tucson: University of Arizona Press, 1962.

Martin, Douglas D. (Patricia, Paylore, ed.) *An Arizona Chronology: Statehood 1913–1936*. Tucson: University of Arizona Press, 1966. A retired newspaperman, Douglas spent years searching through old Arizona newspapers, gathering the major headlines from 1846 to 1936. The series provides a general and surprisingly entertaining understanding of the march of Arizona history.

Powell, Lawrence Clark. *Arizona: A History*. Albuquerque: University of New Mexico Press, 1990. A more recent edition of the book first published in 1976, Powell's history is not a definitive blow-by-blow but rather a series of essays on various chapters in Arizona's history and culture. A much-admired Southwestern writer, librarian, and scholar, Powell lived in Tucson for many years. His *Southwest: Three Definitions* (Benson: Singing Winds Bookshop, 1990) is an excellent trilogy of essays on the landscape and culture of the Southwest.

Sheridan, Thomas. *Arizona: A History*. Tucson: University of Arizona Press, 1995. A very well-written and informative general history.

Smith, Dean. *The Great Arizona Almanac: Facts About Arizona*. Portland, OR: WestWinds Press, 2000. Former newspaperman Smith compiled this almanac, with entries on Arizona history, travel, current events, famous residents, mileage charts, zip codes, and area codes. It's in dire need of a new edition but is still very useful and interesting.

Sonnichsen, C. L. *Tucson: The Life and Times of an American City*. Norman: University of Okalahoma Press, 1982. A thorough telling of the Old Pueblo's long history from its founding in 1776 as a presidio up to the early 1980s.

Waters, Frank. *The Colorado*. New York: Holt, Rinehart and Winston, 1951. The great Western writer known for his novel *The Man Who Killed The Deer*, Waters was also a master of nonfiction. Though he penned this book

about the Colorado River and all that it influences in the 1940s, in a Southwest unrecognizable from what it is today, the greater part of his story still seems true—a classic of that "sense of place" all writers seek.

NATIVE AMERICANS, ANTHROPOLOGY, AND ARCHAEOLOGY

Dentdale, Jennifer Nez. *Reclaiming Diné History: The Legacies of Navajo Chief Manuelito and Juanita*. Tucson: University of Arizona Press, 2007. A compelling account of the Navajo Nation written by the first Navajo woman to earn a Ph.D. in history. Dentdale gives the oral history of her people just as much, if not more credence than she does the mostly white-written accounts that claim to be official and complete. This method reveals, among other things, that women played a much larger role in traditional Navajo society than "colonial" records credit.

Hall, Edward T. *West of the Thirties: Discoveries Among the Navajo and Hopi*. New York: Doubleday, 1994. The great anthropologist tells stories about his work with the Navajo and Hopi during the Great Depression, evoking a time when the remote Indian Country was practically inaccessible.

Houk, Rose. *Sinagua*. Tucson: Western National Parks Association, 1992. Pick up this short volume at any of the national parks or monuments you're sure to visit in Arizona; it's a concise introduction to the Sinagua and their land, part of a series sold throughout the state.

Kosik, Fran. *Native Roads: The Complete Motoring Guide to the Navajo and Hopi Nations*. Tucson: Rio Nuevo, 2005. Kosik knows the reservation lands well and includes a lot of fascinating historical tidbits; recommended to anyone wishing to go deeper than most into Indian Country.

Lamb, Susan. *A Guide to Navajo Rugs.* Tucson: Western National Parks Association, 1992.

Lamb, Susan. *A Guide to Pueblo Pottery.* Tucson: Southwest Parks and Monuments Association, 1996. These handy guides, available at park and monument book shops and most of the gift shops and tourist attractions in Indian Country, explain the basics of rug and pottery identification—just enough to hook you in and whet your appetite for collecting the arts and crafts of the Navajos and Pueblos.

Waters, Frank. *Book of the Hopi.* New York: Penguin, 1963. Though this history of the Hopi and retelling of their myths and legends sometimes gets a cold shoulder from scholars, Waters' book has a narrative thrust that makes the Hopi story seem immediate and meaningful not just to the Hopi and a few anthropologists, but to all of us.

Wright, Barton. *The Complete Guide to Collecting Kachina Dolls.* Flagstaff: Northland Press, 1977. A classic guide to the Katsinam spirits and what they mean.

GRAND CANYON

Ghiglieri, Michael P. and Thomas M. Myers. *Over the Edge: Death in Grand Canyon.* Flagstaff: Puma Press, 2001. A popular collection of macabre stories about tumblers and jumpers, drowners, and killers in the Grand Canyon. One of the few books of its kind that is updated quite regularly.

Grattan, Virgina L. *Mary Colter: Builder Upon Red Earth.* Grand Canyon: The Grand Canyon Association, 1992. A very readable account of architect Mary Jane Colter's life and career. Colter seems to be little known outside the Southwest, though she deserves a wider reputation for her fanciful Grand Canyon creations and the rustic Arts-and-Crafts elegance of her Harvey Houses.

Hughes, Donald. *In the House of Stone and Light.* Grand Canyon Natural History Asso-

ciation, 1978. A relatively short, well-written account of the human history of the Grand Canyon, concentrating mainly on the Anglo development of the South Rim and the evolution of Grand Canyon National Park.

Powell, John Wesley. *The Exploration of the Colorado River and Its Canyons.* New York: Dover, 1961. A reprint of Powell's 1895 classic *Canyons of the Colorado,* this firsthand account of two journeys through the canyon on the Colorado River is essential reading (and it is surprisingly readable) for anyone interested in the continuing story of the confluence of man and Grand Canyon.

Schullery, Paul. *The Grand Canyon: Early Impressions.* Boulder, CO: Colorado Associated University Press, 1981. Includes essays by John Muir and others, showing that writers and other visitors have struggled mightily to describe and comprehend the canyon since people have been visiting it.

THE ENVIRONMENT AND NATURAL HISTORY

Carter, Jack L. et al. *Common Southwestern Native Plants: An Identification Guide.* Silver City, NM: Mimbres Press, 2003. A thorough but easy-to-use guide to plants you're likely to see in Arizona; includes common species of the deserts, the forested mountains, and the plateau country.

Grubbs, Bruce. *Desert Sense: Camping, Hiking & Biking in Hot, Dry Climates.* Seattle, WA: The Mountaineers Books, 2004. If you're going to be hiking or riding a bike in the desert, especially if you're doing it in the summer, consider picking up this or a similar book to familiarize yourself with desert survival beyond the basics of bring water and wear a hat.

Kavanagh, James, ed. *The Nature of Arizona.* Blaine, Wash: Waterford Press, 1996. A useful all-in-one guide specific to the state; most guides attempt to lump everything together under "Southwest." Lists and provides illustrations of the state's flora and fauna, including mammals, snakes, fish, birds, and spiders.

Logan, Michael F. *The Lessening Stream: An Environmental History of the Santa Cruz River.* Tucson: University of Arizona Press, 2002. A professor paints an attractive and elegiac portrait of what the river used to be like and explains why it isn't like that anymore.

Olin, George. *50 Common Mammals of the Southwest.* Tucson: Western National Parks Association, 2000. An introduction to Arizona's mammals, slim with attractive illustrations; part of a series available throughout the state.

Quinn, Meg. *Wildflowers of the Southwest.* Tucson: Rio Nuevo, 2000. If you're going to be hiking in the desert in spring pick up this guide to the many wildflowers that bloom throughout the state.

HIKING

Tessmer, Martin. *50 Hikes in Arizona.* Woodstock, VT: The Countryman Press, 2004. An excellent guide to the best hiking trails in the state, with detailed descriptions of each trail and precise directions to the trail heads. Includes all regions of the state.

Thybony, Scott. *Grand Canyon South Kaibab Trail Guide.* Grand Canyon Association, 2006. Pick up these small, inexpensive guides to the major Grand Canyon trails at most canyon-area bookstores. They contain a lot of information for being so small, and several color photos show you what's ahead. Each guide also includes an interesting history of the trail.

Grand Canyon Bright Angel Trail Guide. Grand Canyon Association, 2004.

Grand Canyon Hermit Trail Guide. Grand Canyon Association, 2005.

Grand Canyon North Kaibab Trail Guide. Grand Canyon Association, 2005.

Warren, Scott, S. *100 Classic Hikes in Arizona.* Seattle, WA: The Mountaineers Press, 2000. Has 50 more hikes than *50 Hikes in Arizona.* For those looking not only for the best, most popular hikes but also the less-known and little-used.

LITERATURE

Abbey, Edward. *The Monkey Wrench Gang.* New York: Harper Collins, 2000. Abbey's best-known novel, first published in 1975, is a crazy comic western with radical environmentalists as its heroic gang of outlaws.

Abbey, Edward. *One Life At a Time, Please.* New York: Henry Holt and Company, 1987. Abbey was the Southwest's resident poet-provocateur, a major influence on a few generations of western writers and environmentalists. It has yet to be decided if he was writing literature disguised as polemics or the other way around, but he is an essential voice in the long project to justify the ways of the west to the rest of the country. This volume of essays from the late 1970s and the 1980s includes his thoughts on Lake Powell.

Bowden, Charles. *Blue Desert.* Tucson: University of Arizona Press, 1986.

Bowden, Charles. *Frog Mountain Blues.* Tucson: University of Arizona, 1987. Bowden's voice is overwhelming once you get into it. His essays, reportage, and nature writing chronicle the darker side of the sunbelt.

Internet Resources

TOURISM SITES

Arizona Office of Tourism
www.arizonaguide.com

The official site for the state's Office of Tourism has basic information on the state's regions and lists various possible itineraries.

Discover Navajo
www.discovernavajo.com

The official site of the Navajo Nation's tourism group has basic information about visiting the nation—where to stay, what to do, and what not to do. It has a large number of links to tour companies.

Grand Canyon National Park
www.nps.gov/grca

The Grand Canyon's official website has basic information on the park; go here for information about backcountry permits. For reservations and information on the park's accommodations, go to **Xanterra South Rim's** site at www.grandcanyonlodges.com.

Flagstaff Convention and Visitors Bureau
www.flagstaffarizona.org

This site has general information on visiting Flagstaff, the northland, and the Grand Canyon along with helpful listings.

Greater Phoenix Convention & Visitors Bureau
www.visitphoenix.com

The official site for Phoenix and the Valley of the Sun has a pretty comprehensive list of restaurants and hotels in the valley.

Metropolitan Tucson Convention and Visitors Bureau
www.visittucson.org

This is Tucson and Southern Arizona's official tourism site.

Sedona Chamber of Commerce
www.visitsedona.com

The official site for Sedona tourism has general information on Sedona, Oak Creek Canyon, Red Rock Country, and the Verde Valley.

NEWS AND CULTURE

Arizona Daily Star
www.azstarnet.com

Tucson's morning daily is free on this site, with news and information on all of Southern Arizona.

Arizona Republic
www.azcentral.com

The state's largest newspaper is free online every day, and the site has a robust Arizona travel guide and a useful dining and entertainment section.

Phoenix New Times
www.phoenixnewtimes.com

This site is the best place to go for entertainment and cultural listings and alternative news and commentary about life in the Valley of the Sun.

Tucson Weekly
www.tucsonweekly.com

Southern Arizona's best source of alternative news, political blogs, and cultural and entertainment news and listings.

Index

A

Abbey, Edward: 115, 252, 272, 303, 317
Abyss, The: 223
accommodations: 307-308; see also specific place
Aerospace Maintenance and Regeneration Center (AMARC): 94
affordable travel: 17
agriculture: 287, 295, 298, 299
Airport Mesa: 173
air travel: general discussion 305-306; Flagstaff 145, 306; Grand Canyon 230, 306; Phoenix (Sky Harbor International Airport) 14, 21, 73-74, 305; Tucson 18, 106, 305; Yuma 283, 306
Ajo: 113
Algodones Dunes: 281-282
Allen, Rex: 128
Allen Street/National Historic District: 124-125
All Soul's Procession: 98
Alpina: 181
altitude sickness: 311-312
Amado: 114
AMARC (Aerospace Maintenance and Regeneration Center): 94
Ambos Nogales: 115-116
Amerind Foundation: 129
"A" Mountain: 99-100
Amtrak: 306
Anasazi: 20, 27, 190-192, 195-196, 204, 224, 295, 296
Andy Devine Days Parade & Community Fair: 264
Angel's Window: 232-233
animal life: 285, 292-295, 316-317
Annual Cowboy Poets Gathering: 154
Antelope Canyon Navajo Tribal Park: 251
Antelope House Ruin: 196
Apache: general discussion 295, 296, 297, 298, 302; Cochise Stronghold 18, 19, 129; Cochise Trail 119, 120, 128, 129; Fort Verde Historic Park 164; Fort Whipple Museum 152; Mogollon Rim 178; Salt River Canyon 70
Apache Lake: 68
Apache-Sitgreaves National Forests: 178
Apache Trail (Route 88): 66-70
Apple Annie's Orchard: 128-129
arachnids: 295
arboretum: 70
archaeology/archaeological sites: general discussion 20, 27, 295; Amerind Foundation 129; Arizona State Museum 88; Arizona State University Museum of Anthropology 39; Besh-Ba-Gowah Archaeological Park 69; Canyon de Chelly National Monument 20, 195-196; Casa Grande Ruins National Monument 18, 20, 64, 70-71; Catalina State Park 93; El Presidio Historic District 82; Grand Canyon 213, 223-224; Homolovi Ruins State Park 204; Honanki 175; Montezuma Castle National Monument 15, 20, 164-165; Montezuma Well 166; Navajo National Monument 20, 190-192; Palatki 175; Petrified Forest National Park 201; petroglyphs 39-40, 88, 166, 201, 246; Pueblo Grande Museum and Archaeological Park 20, 36; reading suggestions 315-316; San Pedro Riparian National Conservation Area 122; Tonto National Monument 20, 68-69; trip planning 20; Tucson Museum of Art and Historic Block 84; Tusayan Museum and Ruin 223-224; Tuzigoot National Monument 163; Walnut Canyon National Monument 20, 146, 147, 148-149; Wupatki National Monument 20, 145-148
architecture: Arcosanti 72; Arizona Biltmore 17, 52, 65; Arizona Temple 41; Chapel of the Holy Cross 169; Desert View Watchtower 224; Fox Theatre 95; Frank Lloyd Wright 14, 17, 52, 57-58, 65; Hoover Dam 259; La Posada 202-203; Mary Jane Colter 201, 202-203, 215, 218-219, 221, 223, 224, 239, 316; north Tucson 89; Painted Desert Inn Museum 201; Pima County Courthouse 82-83; reading suggestions 316; Santa Cruz County Courthouse 115; San Xavier del Bac 94-95; Taliesin West 14, 17, 57-58, 65; see also historic houses and districts
Arcosanti: 72
area codes: 312
Arivaca: 111-112
Arivaca Cienega: 111-112
Arizona Biltmore: 17, 52, 65
Arizona Capitol Museum: 35
Arizona Cardinals: 45
Arizona Center: 49
Arizona Diamondbacks: 44, 100
Arizona Doll and Toy Museum: 33
Arizona Fine Art Expo: 61
Arizona Folklore Preserve: 121

Arizona Historical Society Museum (downtown Tucson): 84
Arizona Historical Society Museum (University of Arizona): 88
Arizona Historical Society Sosa-Carrillo-Fremont House Museum: 83
Arizona Historical Society's Pioneer Museum: 139
Arizona Hot Springs: 260
Arizona Inn, The: 16, 19, 101
Arizona International Film Festival: 97
Arizona Museum of Natural History: 40-41
Arizona Opera (Tucson): 97
Arizona Opera Company (Phoenix): 46
Arizona Science Center: 33
Arizona-Sonora Desert Museum: 16, 18, 19, 85-86
Arizona State Fair: 48-49
Arizona State Museum: 88
Arizona State University: 39-40; accommodations 51; food 55-56; nightlife 48; orientation 31; sights 39-40, 65; sports teams 45-46
Arizona State University Art Museum: 39
Arizona State University Museum of Anthropology: 39
Arizona State University Sun Devils: 45-46
Arizona Strip: 241-253; map 206-207; reading suggestions 314; trip planning 11, 242-243
Arizona Temple Visitor's Center: 41
Arizona Theatre Company: 97
Army of the West: 297
art galleries/exhibits: general discussion 303; Carefree 58; Chloride 268-269; Desert Botanical Garden 38; Flagstaff 139; Greer 180; Hopi House 218, 219, 228; Jerome 161, 162; Kingman 264; Mesa 40; Phoenix (downtown) 14, 17, 34-35, 303; Prescott 153-154; Scottsdale 57, 61; Sedona 170, 171; Tempe 38-39; trip planning 10, 14, 17; Tubac 112; Tucson 84, 88-89, 90, 97; Wickenburg 71; Yuma 280; see also Native American art and culture
Asarco Mineral Discovery Center: 108-109
Ashurst Lake: 142
Aspen Forest Overlook: 191
asteroid craters: 204
astronomy: see observatories
ASU: see Arizona State University
Asylum, The: 14, 162
Atascosa Lookout Trail: 115
automobile travel: see car travel

B

Bacavi: 200
Bajada Loop: 88
Baldy Saddle: 110
Barrett-Jackson Antique Auto Auction: 61
Barrio Historico District: 83
Barrio Libre: 83
Barrio Viejo: 83
baseball: 44, 45, 46, 48, 97, 100
Bashford House: 152
basin and range province: 285-286
basketball: 44, 100
Bear Canyon: 92
Bear Canyon Lake: 178
Bear Canyon Trail: 92
Beaver Creek Recreation Area: 166
Beaver Dam Wilderness Area: 244
Beaver Street Brewery: 15, 144
Bell Rock: 173
Bell Rock Loops: 174
Benson: 123
Besh-Ba-Gowah Archaeological Park: 69
Betatakin: 20, 190, 191-192
Big Lake Recreation Area: 181
Big Nose Kate's Saloon: 125
biking: Flagstaff 141; Grand Canyon 226; Greer 180, 181; Indian Bend Wash Greenbelt 59; Lake Mead National Recreation Area 260; McDowell Mountain Regional Park 59; Papago Park 43; Plateau Lakes 142, 143; Prescott National Forest 155-157; reading suggestions 316; Red Rock Country 173, 174; Reid Park 99; Saguaro National Park 88; South Mountain Park and Preserve 42; Tempe Town Lake 38; Tucson Mountain Park 100
Bill Williams River National Wildlife Refuge: 273
Biosphere 2: 93
Bird Cage Theatre: 125
birds/bird-watching: general discussion 285, 293; Arizona-Sonora Desert Museum 86; Bill Williams River National Wildlife Refuge 273; Buenos Aires Wildlife Refuge 111, 112; Cibola National Wildlife Refuge 273; Crescent Moon Ranch 158; Dead Horse Ranch State Park 164; Grand Canyon 226; Grand Canyon Railroad 231; Hassayampa River Preserve 71; Imperial National Wildlife Refuge 272, 282; Madera Canyon 18, 19, 109-110, 111; Mormon Lake 142; Patagonia-Sonoita Creek Preserve 118; Prescott National Forest 157; Ramsey Canyon

Preserve 19, 121; San Pedro Riparian National Conservation Area 122; trip planning 13, 18, 19; Verde Canyon Railway 163
Bisbee: 18, 19, 24, 126-127
Bisbee Mining and Historical Museum: 126
Black Canyon: 261, 262, 287
Black Canyon Lake: 178
Black Mesa: 11, 197
Black Mountains: 267
Blessing of the Vine Festival: 119
boating: Apache Lake 68; Bullhead City 269; Canyon Lake 67; Glen Canyon National Recreation Area 251, 253; Goldwater Lake 156; Grand Canyon 236, 238-239, 240, 249; Imperial National Wildlife Refuge 282; Lake Havasu City 270, 271-272, 273, 274; Lake Mead National Recreation Area 258, 260, 261, 262; Lynx Lake Recreation Area 156; Martinez Lake 282; Parker 275-276; Patagonia Lake State Park 117; Pena Blanca Lake 115; Plateau Lakes 142, 143; Roosevelt Lake 68; Tempe Beach Park 38; Verde River Scenic Area 167
Bob Parks' Horse Fountain: 57
Bog Spring-Kent Spring Loop: 110
Bonito Lava Flow: 148
Boothill Graveyard: 124
border crossings: 13, 18, 115-116, 194, 242, 243, 244, 269
Boulder Beach: 261
Boulder Islands: 261
Bowden, Charles: 303, 317
Bowl of Fire: 260
Boyce-Thompson Arboretum State Park: 70
Boyton Canyon Trail: 173
Branigar/Chase Discovery Center: 139
breweries: 15, 48, 56, 140, 144, 154, 159, 274
Bridge in the Redwall, The: 234
Bright Angel Lodge: 16, 21, 218, 227
Bright Angel Point: 232
Bright Angel Trail: 22, 23, 218, 222, 224-225, 236-237, 317
Brighty: 232
Buckskin Mountain State Park: 275
budget travel: 17
Buenos Aires Wildlife Refuge: 111-112
Bullhead City: 269
bushes: 291
bus travel: 306; see also specific place
Butterfly Lodge Museum: 180
Butterfly Magic: 90

C

Cabeza De Vaca, Alvar Nunez: 296, 314
Cabeza Prieta National Wildlife Refuge: 272
cabin rentals: 158; see also specific place
cacti: general discussion 291-292; Night-blooming Cereus 90; Organ Pipe Cactus National Monument 113; Saguaro National Park 16, 18, 19, 86-88; Tucson Mountain Park 100; see also specific place
Cactus Forest Drive: 88
Calexico: 123
Camelback Mountain: 41
Camel Head & Snoopy Rock: 173
Cameron: 188, 209
Cameron Trading Post: 188
camping: see specific place
Canada Goose Drive: 273
canoeing and kayaking: Bill Williams River National Wildlife Refuge 273; Glen Canyon National Recreation Area 253; Goldwater Lake 156; Grand Canyon 239; Imperial National Wildlife Refuge 282; Lake Havasu City 274; Lake Mead National Recreation Area 262; Prescott 156; Tempe Beach Park 38; Verde River Scenic Area 167
Canyon de Chelly National Monument: 15, 20, 195-196
Canyon Lake: 67
canyons: Antelope Canyon Navajo Tribal Park 251; Bear Canyon 92; Black Canyon 261, 262, 287; Canyon de Chelly National Monument 15, 20, 195-196; Echo Canyon Recreation Area 41-42; Fish Creek Canyon 68; Glen Canyon National Recreation Area 251, 253; hiking safety 288-289; Little Colorado Gorge 209; Madera Canyon 18, 109-111; Marble Canyon 249-250; Oak Creek Canyon 15, 175; Palm Canyon 272; Ramsey Canyon 19, 121; Red Rock Country 173; Sabino Canyon 92-93; Salt River Canyon 70; Sycamore Canyon Wilderness Area 166-167; Topock Gorge 273; Tsegi Canyon 20, 190-192; Tumacacori Highlands 115; Verde Canyon Railway 163; Vermillion Cliffs National Monument 247-248; Virgin River Gorge 243-244; Walnut Canyon National Monument 15, 20, 146, 147, 148-149; White Rock Canyon 260; see also Grand Canyon
Canyon View Information Plaza: 221
Canyon View Trail: 191
Cape Royal Drive: 232-233
Carefree: 14, 52, 58-59

Carefree Fine Art & Wine Festival: 58
Carl Hayden Visitor Center: 252
car travel: 306; trip planning 13, 14-16, 18; *see also* car culture; scenic drives
Casa Grande Ruins National Monument: 18, 20, 64, 70-71
casinos: 97, 166, 180, 243, 269, 275, 276, 282, 283, 302
Catalina State Park: 93
Cathedral Rock: 173
Catholicism: 302, 303
Catlin Court Historic District: 49
Cattail Cove State Park: 271-272
Cave Creek: 14, 58-59
caves: 18, 19, 122-123, 241
Cedar Ridge: 225
Celebración de la Gente: 140
Celebration of Fine Art: 61
Celebrity Theatre: 46
cell phones: 312
Center for Creative Photography: 89
Center for High Altitude Training: 139
Century House Museum: 280
Chapel of the Holy Cross: 169
Chase Field: 44
Chi Hoo Tso Indian Market: 197
children's activities: general discussion 309-310, 311; Arizona Doll and Toy Museum 33; Arizona Historical Society Museum 88; Arizona Mills 49; Arizona Science Center 33; Besh-Ba-Gowah Archaeological Park 69; Enchanted Island Amusement Park 37; Garden for Children 90; Goldfield 67; Grand Canyon 22; Grand Canyon Railroad 231; Heard Museum 35; Phoenix Zoo 37; Reid Park Zoo 89; Splash Playground 38
Chimney Rock: 173
Chinese Cultural Center: 36, 37
Chinle: 15, 194-195
Chiricahua National Monument: 18, 21, 77, 129-130
Chiricahua Regional Museum: 128
Chloride: 268-269
Christmas celebrations: 150, 154
Christopher Creek: 177
churches/missions/chapels: Arizona Temple Visitor's Center 41; Chapel of the Holy Cross 169; First Christian Church 65; LDS temple (St. George, Utah) 244; Mission San Jose de Tumacacori 18, 112; San Cayetano de Calabazas 112; San Xavier Del Bac 18, 21, 94-95, 97; shrines 83, 117; St. Augustine Cathedral 83

Cibola National Wildlife Refuge: 273
cinemas: Flagstaff 140; Grand Canyon 211; IMAX theaters 33, 211; Phoenix 33, 47; Tucson 95, 96-97; Willcox 128; Yuma 280
civil war reenactments: 71, 97
Clarksdale: 162-163
Clear Creek Loop: 237-238
Cliff Dwellers: 248
climate: 12, 13, 17, 288-289; *see also specific place*
clothing: 13
clothing-optional accommodations: 307
Clovis people: 122, 295
Cochise Stronghold: 18, 19, 129
Cochise Trail: 119-130
Coconino Center for the Arts: 139
Coconino National Forest: 141, 158
Coconino Overlook: 234
Coffee Pot Restaurant: 15, 172
Coffee Pot Rock: 173
colleges: *see universities*
Colorado City-Hillsdale: 244, 250
Colorado Plateau: 146, 285, 286
Colorado River: general discussion 286, 287, 290; Grand Canyon 22, 236, 238-239, 249; Hualapai Indian Reservation 240; Lee's Ferry 248-249; Lower Colorado River 11, 254-283, 288; reading suggestions 315, 316
Colorado River Indian Reservation: 275
Colorado River Indian tribes: 275, 302
Colorado River Indian Tribes Museum and Library: 275
Colter, Mary Jane: 201, 202-203, 215, 218-219, 221, 223, 224, 239, 316
Cooper, Alice: 303
Copper Square: 31
Coronado, Francisco Vasquez de: 121-122, 296-297
Coronado National Memorial: 18, 19, 24, 121-122
Coronado Trail: 181
Cortez Street: 154-155
Cottonwood: 163-164
Courthouse Plaza: 150, 152
Cowboy Artists of America: 35, 153, 303
Cowboy Hall of Fame: 128
Coyote Buttes Permit Area: 247-248
Cricket Pavilion: 46
cross-country skiing: *see skiing*
Crystal Palace Saloon: 125
cuisine: 308-309; *see also specific place*
culinary festivals: 61, 98
customs/immigration: 116, 309

D

dams: general discussion 252, 272, 287; Glen Canyon Dam 251, 252, 287; Hoover Dam 258-259; Parker Dam 275; Roosevelt Dam 28, 67, 68, 287
David Yetman Trail: 100
daylight saving time: 183, 312
Dead Horse Ranch State Park: 164
Deer Valley Rock Art Center: 39-40
DeGrazia Gallery in the Sun: 90
dehydration: 311
Delgadillo's Snow Cap Drive-In: 267
demographics: 301-302
Desert Botanical Garden: 37-38
Desert Caballeros Western Museum: 71
deserts: 113, 284, 285-286, 288, 289; see also specific place
Desert View Drive: 223
Desert View Watchtower: 224
Devine, Andy: 264, 265
Día de los Muertos: 140
Dia de San Juan: 97-98
Dillinger, John: 84, 100-101
Diné: see Navajo
Dinner Bell, The: 14, 159
dinosaurs: 33, 41, 189-190
disabled travelers: 309
disc golf: 142
Dive Park: 261
Dodge Theatre: 46
Douglas: 21, 127-128
Downtown Phoenix Partnership, The: 31-32
driving: see car travel
Dude Fire: 177, 178
Dutchman's Trail: 66

E

Eager-Springerville: 181
East Fork Trail: 181
East Valley (Phoenix): 37-41; accommodations 51; food 55-56; nightlife 48; orientation 31; recreation 38, 43; shopping 49, 50; trip planning 14; see also Arizona State University
Echo Canyon Recreation Area: 41-42
economy: 187, 299-300, 302
Ed Schieffelin Territorial Days: 125
El Charro Café: 19, 105
El Encanto: 14, 59
Elgin: 18, 116-117, 118-119
El Presidio Historic District: 82
El Presidio Inn Bed & Breakfast: 101

El Presidio Park: 83
El Tiradito Shrine: 83
El Tovar: 16, 21, 218, 226-227, 308
emergency services: see medical services
Encanto-Palmcroft Historic District: 36-37
Encanto Park: 36-37
Enchanted Island Amusement Park: 37
environmental issues: 27, 252, 272, 287, 289-290, 317
Ernst, Max: 303
Ethnobotanical Garden: 90
Explore Navajo Interactive Museum: 189

F

Falling Water: 58
Family Arts Festival: 97
fauna: 285, 292-295, 316-317
festivals and events: Phoenix 48-49; Scottsdale 58, 61; Tucson 97-98; see also specific place
Fiesta Bowl: 48
film festivals: 97, 140, 170
film productions: 86, 170, 193, 194, 265, 281, 303
films: see cinemas
fire lookouts: 115, 157, 158
fires: 91, 177, 178, 290
First Christian Church: 65
First Mesa: 199
Fish Creek Canyon 68
fish/fishing: general discussion 294; Apache Lake 68; Big Lake Recreation Area 181; Crescent Moon Ranch 158; Dead Horse Ranch State Park 164; Fools Hollow Lake Recreation Area 179; Glen Canyon National Recreation Area 251, 253; Granite Basin Recreation Area 156; Horsethief Basin Lake 158; Lake Havasu City 270, 271, 272, 274; Lake Mead National Recreation Area 258, 261, 262; Lee's Ferry 249; Lynx Lake Recreation Area 156; Martinez Lake 282; Papago Park 43; Parker 275; Patagonia Lake State Park 117; Pena Blanca Lake 115; Plateau Lakes 142, 143; Rim Lakes Recreation Area 178; Roosevelt Lake 68; Roper Lake State Park 307; tournaments 273-274
Flagstaff: 131-145; climate 134-135, 289; geography 285; Grand Canyon, driving to 229, 230; Internet resources 318; transportation 137, 145, 306; trip planning 10-11, 15, 134-135; vicinity 145-149
Flagstaff Mountain Film Festival: 140

Flagstaff Nordic Center: 142
flora: 10, 284, 285, 291-292, 316-317
food: 308-309; see also specific place
food festivals: 61, 98
Fools Hollow Lake Recreation Area: 179
football: 45, 46, 48
foreign travelers: 309
forest fires: 91, 177, 178, 290
forests, petrified: 15, 200-202
Fort Huachuca: 120
Fort Verde Historic Park: 164
Fort Whipple Museum: 152-153
fossils: 33, 41, 122, 189-190
Fossil Springs: 165
Fountain, The: 59
Fountain Park: 59
Four Corners Monument: 194
Fourth Avenue District: 19, 84-85, 99
Fox Theatre: 95
Fredonia: 246
Friends of the San Pedro River: 122
Frog Mountain: 91
fruit orchards: 128-129

G

Gadsden Hotel: 21, 127-128
Gadsden Purchase: 81, 107, 297
gambling: see casinos
Ganado: 196
Garden Gallery: 90
gardens: see parks and gardens
Gates Pass: 100
Gates Pass Trail: 100
gay and lesbian travelers: 310
gem and mineral shows/swap-meets: 97, 276
geography/geology: 285-287
Geronimo: 119, 298
Gila River: 286, 287, 314
Gila River Indian Community: 302
Gin Blossoms: 303
Glen Canyon Dam: 251, 252, 287
Glen Canyon National Recreation Area: 251, 253
Glendale: see West Valley (Phoenix)
Globe: 69
Goldfield: 67
gold panning: 67, 156
Goldwater, Barry: 301
Goldwater Lake: 156
golf: Green Valley 109; Phoenix 43, 52; safety
    311; Scottsdale 52, 59-60; Tempe 43; trip
    planning 10, 17; Tubac 114; Tucson 100, 102
gondola rides: 270
Goulding's Lodge: 194

government: 300-301
Grady Gammage Memorial Auditorium: 65
Grand Canyon: 212-241; airport 230, 306; food
    227-228, 239, 308; gateway towns 209-212,
    229-230; geology 286; Grand Canyon-
    Parashant National Monument 245-246;
    hiking safety 226; Internet resources 318;
    maps 206-207, 216-217; permits: 235, 236,
    239-240; reading suggestions 219, 316,
    317; tours 231; trip planning 11, 13, 16, 21-23,
    213-215
Grand Canyon Base Camp #1: 211
Grand Canyon Caverns: 241
Grand Canyon Lodge: 232, 233
Grand Canyon-Parashant National Monument:
    245-246
Grand Canyon Railroad: 21, 215, 230-231
Grand Canyon Railroad Hotel: 23, 231
Grand Canyon-The Hidden Secrets: 211
Grand Canyon Village: 16, 21, 215-218, 308
Grand Canyon Visitors Center: 22, 211
Grand Canyon West: 240-241
Grandview Point: 223
Granite Basin Recreation Area: 156
Granite Dells: 156
Granite Mountain: 156, 157
Green Valley: 107-109
Greer: 180-181
Grey, Zane: 24, 177, 303
Groom Creek Loop Trail: 157

H

Hackberry General Store: 267
Hall, Sharlot: 152, 314
Hannigans Meadow: 181
Hano: 199
Hanta virus: 312
Harvey, Fred: 201, 202-203, 215, 218, 239, 314
Hassayampa Inn: 158, 308
Hassayampa River Preserve: 71
Havasu National Wildlife Refuge: 273, 274
Havasupai Indian Reservation: 240
health/safety: 226, 227, 288-289, 310-312
health seekers: 102, 314
Heard Museum: 14, 17, 34-35
Heard Museum Guild Indian Fair & Market: 48
Heard Museum North: 35
Heard Museum Spanish Market: 49
Heard Museum West: 35
heat, coping with: 310-311
heat exhaustion/stroke: 311
helicopter tours: 231, 241
Heritage Square: 32-33

Hermit Road: 221-223
Hermit's Rest: 221, 222, 223
Hermit Trail: 226, 317
high-altitude training center: 139
High Desert: 200-204
Highway 93: 268-269
hiking: Arizona-Sonora Desert Museum 85-86;
   Buenos Aires Wildlife Refuge 111-112; Canyon
   de Chelly National Monument 15, 20, 195,
   196; Catalina State Park 93; Chiricahua
   National Monument 129-130; Cibola National
   Wildlife Refuge 273; Cochise Stronghold
   129; Coronado National Memorial 19, 122;
   Crescent Moon Ranch 158; Dead Horse
   Ranch State Park 164; Fossil Springs 165;
   Glen Canyon National Recreation Area
   251; Grand Canyon (Inner Canyon) 22-23,
   235-238, 239; Grand Canyon (North Rim)
   232, 233-234; Grand Canyon (South Rim)
   22, 222, 223, 224-226; Grand Canyon-
   Parashant National Monument 246;
   Grand Canyon West 241; Greer 180-181;
   Hassayampa River Preserve 71; Horsethief
   Basin Lake 158; Huachuca Mountains
   121; Hualapai Mountain Park 264; Juan
   Bautista de Anza National Historic Trail
   113; Kaibab Plateau 246-247; Kofa National
   Wildlife Refuge 272; Lake Mead National
   Recreation Area 260; Lee's Ferry 248;
   Lost Dutchman State Park 66; Madera
   Canyon 18, 110, 111; Meteor Crater 204;
   Mingus Mountain Recreation Area 160;
   Mount Graham 307; Navajo National
   Monument 191-192; Oak Creek Canyon 175;
   Patagonia Lake State Park 117; Patagonia-
   Sonoita Creek Preserve 117-118; Phoenix
   41-42, 43; Picacho Peak State Park 18, 71;
   Pinetop-Lakeside 179; Pipe Spring National
   Monument 245; Plateau Lakes 142, 143;
   Prescott National Forest 155-157; Rainbow
   Bridge National Monument 253; Ramsey
   Canyon 19, 121; reading suggestions 316,
   317; Red Rock Country 173, 174, 175; Rim
   Lakes Recreation Area 178; Sabino Canyon
   92; safety 226, 227, 288-289, 311; Saguaro
   National Park 88; San Francisco Peaks 141;
   San Pedro Riparian National Conservation
   Area 122; Santa Catalina Mountains 91, 92;
   Scottsdale 59; Sentinel Peak 100; Sunset
   Crater Volcano National Monument 148;
   Superstition Mountains 65-66; Sycamore
   Canyon Wilderness Area 166-167; Tonto
   National Monument 68-69; Tonto Natural
   Bridge State Park 177-178; trip planning
   13; Tucson Mountain Park 100; Tumacacori
   Highlands 115; Verde Hot Springs 165;
   Vermillion Cliffs National Monument
   247-248; Virgin River Gorge 244; vortex
   tours 174; Walnut Canyon National
   Monument 149; White Mountain Trail System
   179; Wupatki National Monument 148
Hispanic population: 301-302
Historic Cameron Trading Post and Lodge: 209
Historic Elks Opera House: 154
historic hotels: general discussion 307-308;
   Arizona Biltmore 17, 52, 65; Bisbee 19, 127;
   Douglas 127-128; Flagstaff 15, 143; Grand
   Canyon (North Rim) 232, 233; Grand
   Canyon (South Rim) 218, 226-227; Greer 181;
   Jerome 162; Kingman 265; La Posada 15,
   202-203, 308; Nogales, Arizona 115; Phoenix
   (downtown) 50, 51; Prescott 158-159, 308;
   Tombstone 126; Tucson 100-101, 103; Yuma
   283
historic houses and districts: Allen Street/
   National Historic District 124-125; Arizona
   Historical Society Sosa-Carrillo-Fremont
   House Museum 83; Barrio Historico District
   83; Bashford House 152; Butterfly Lodge
   Museum 180; Catlin Court Historic District
   49; Century House Museum 280; El Presidio
   Historic District 82; Encanto-Palmcroft
   Historic District 36-37; Flagstaff 137; House
   Rock Valley 248; Hubbell Home 196; Jerome
   State Historic Park 161-162; Kingman 264;
   Kolb Studio 219; La Casa Cordova 84; Lonely
   Dell Ranch Historic Site 248; Morley Avenue
   115; Old Town Cottonwood 163-164; Pipe
   Spring National Monument 24, 244, 245;
   Prescott 149-150, 152, 153; Riordan Mansion
   State Historic Park 24, 137-138; Rosson
   House 32-33; Sedona Heritage Museum
   169-170; Stevens House 33; Taliesin West
   14, 17, 57-58, 65; Teeter House 33; Tucson
   Museum of Art and Historic Block 84;
   Willcox 19, 128; Williams 209; Yuma 280-281;
   Zane Grey Cabin 24, 177; see also Old West
Historic Route 66 Fun Run: 264
Historic Route 66 Museum: 264
historic trading posts: 190, 196, 209
history: 295-298, 314-315
hockey: 45
Hogs 'n Heat Barbecue and Nut Fry: 72
Hohokam: Arizona Museum of Natural History
   41; Besh-Ba-Gowah Archaeological Park
   69; Casa Grande Ruins National Monument

18, 20, 64, 70-71; Catalina State Park 93; Deer Valley Rock Art Center 39-40; El Presidio Historic District 82; history 26, 27, 28, 79, 295; Pueblo Grande Museum and Archaeological Park 20, 36; trip planning 20
Holbrook: 15, 200
Homolovi Ruins State Park: 204
Honanki: 175
Hoover Dam: 258-259
Hoover Dam Tour: 259
Hoover Dam Visitor Center: 259
Hopi: general discussion 27, 295, 296, 297, 302, 303, 304; Canyon de Chelly National Monument 195-196; Desert View Watchtower 224; Grand Canyon 218, 219, 228; Heard Museum 34, 35; Homolovi Ruins State Park 204; Hopi Festival of Arts and Culture 140; Hopi Mesas 197-200; Museum of Northern Arizona 139; Navajo National Monument 190-192; Painted Desert Inn Museum 201; reading suggestions 315, 316; San Francisco Peaks 141; Sedona 171; Smoki Museum 153; Southwest Indian Art Fair and Market 97; Tuba City 188; Williams 210; Wupatki National Monument 20, 147
Hopi Cultural Center: 199
Hopi House: 218, 219, 228
Hopiland: 197-200; cuisine 308; etiquette 199; maps 184-185, 198; transportation 183, 185; trip planning 11, 182-183
Hopi Mesas: 197-200
Hopi Point: 222
horseback riding: Flagstaff 143; Grand Canyon West 241; Greer 180; Nogales, Arizona 115; Phoenix 42-43; Prescott 157; Scottsdale 59; Tucson 100
horse shows: 61
Horsethief Basin Lake: 158
hospitals: see medical services
Hotel Congress: 16, 19, 100-101
Hotevilla: 200
hot springs: 165, 260, 307
houseboating: 251, 253, 258, 261, 262
House Rock Valley: 248
Huachuca Mountains: 19, 121, 285
Hualapai Indian Reservation: 240-241, 267
Hualapai Mountain Park: 264
Hualapai Trailhead: 264
Hubbell Trading Post National Historic Site: 196
Humphrey's Peak Trail: 141
Hunter Trail: 71

I

IMAX theaters: 33, 211
Imperial Dunes: 281-282
Imperial Dunes Recreation Area: 281-282
Imperial National Wildlife Refuge: 272-273, 282
Indian Bend Wash Greenbelt: 59
Indian Gardens: 23, 218, 225
indigenous peoples: see archaeology/archaeological sites; Native American art and culture; specific tribe
information and services: 312-313; see also specific place
Inner Canyon (Grand Canyon): 22-23, 235-240
inner tubing: 43-44
Inscription House: 191
insects: 295, 312
international travelers: 309
International Wildlife Museum: 85
Internet resources: 318
Internet service: 312
Island Trail: 149
itineraries, suggested: 14-23

J

jeep tours: 67, 175
Jeffs, Warren: 250
Jerome: 14, 24, 160-162, 308
Jerome Grand Hotel: 14, 162, 308
Jerome Historical Society Museum: 161
Jerome State Historic Park: 161-162
Jet Skiing: 271, 273, 275
Jobing.com Arena: 45
John Wesley Powell Museum and Visitor Information Center: 251
Jordan Historical Park: 169-170
Josephine Saddle: 110
Joshua Tree Forest Parkway: 268
Juan Bautista de Anza National Historic Trail: 113
Junior Rangers program: 22, 310

K

Kachina Trail: 141
Kaibab Plateau: 11, 246-247
Kartchner Caverns: 18, 19, 122-123
kayaking: see canoeing and kayaking
Kayenta: 16, 192-193
Keet Seel: 20, 190-191, 192
Ken Patrick Trail: 233
Kingman: 262-266

Kitt Peak National Observatory: 113
Knoll Lake: 178
Kofa National Wildlife Refuge: 272
Kohls Ranch: 177
Kolb Studio: 219
Kris Eggle Visitor Center: 113
Kykotsmovi: 200

L

La Casa Cordova: 84
La Fiesta de Los Vaqueros: 97
Lake Havasu: 269-274
Lake Havasu City: 269-274
Lake Havasu Marine Associations Annual Boat
    Show: 273
Lake Havasu State Park: 271
Lake Mead: 258, 259-260, 287, 290
Lake Mead National Recreation Area: 258-262
Lake Mohave: 258, 262
Lake Powell: 11, 250-253, 287
land: 284-290
languages: 302-303
La Posada: 15, 202-203, 308
Latino cuisine: 308-309
Latino population: 301-302
Latter-day Saints (LDS): general discussion
    250, 302; Arizona Strip 241, 242, 244-245,
    248, 250, 251; Mesa: 37, 41; Tuba City
    188-189; Tucson 83; White Mountains
    177, 181
Laughlin, Nevada: 269
Laughlin River Run: 269
lava fields: 141, 145-148
Lava Flow Trail: 148
Lavender Pit Mine: 126
LDS: see Latter-day Saints (LDS)
Ledge Ruin: 196
Lee's Ferry: 248-249
Le Fevre Overlook: 247
lesbian and gay travelers: 310
life zones: 284-285, 291-292
Lipan Point: 223
literature, suggested: 317
Little Colorado Gorge: 209
Locomotive Park: 264
Lodge on the Desert: 19, 101
London Bridge: 270-271
Lonely Dell Ranch Historic Site: 248
Lookout Studio: 219
Lost Dutchman Mine: 66
Lost Dutchman State Park: 66

Lowell, Percival: 138
Lowell Observatory: 138
Lower and Upper Lake Mary: 142
Lower Ruin trail: 69
Lute's Casino: 283
Lynx Lake Recreation Area: 156

M

Madera Canyon: 18, 109-111
Main Street Plaza (Yuma): 280-281
mammals: 292-293, 317
maps: 313
Marble Canyon: 249-250
Maricopa Point: 222
Mark Hahn Memorial Havasu 300 APBA
    National Team Endurance Race: 273
Marshall Lake: 142
Martinez Lake: 282
Massai Point: 129
Mather Point: 221
Maytag Zoo: 37
McCain, John: 301
McDowell Mountain Regional Park: 59
media: 318; see also specific place
medical services: Hopiland 200; Phoenix 73;
    Tucson 107
Melrose District: 49, 310
Mesa: accommodations 51; bookstore 50; map
    40; orientation 31; sights 37-38, 40-41
Mesa Arts Center: 40
Mesa Contemporary Arts: 40
Mesquite, Nevada: 242, 243
Meteor Crater: 204
Mexican food: 308-309
Mexico-U.S. border: 18, 115-116
Mile-and-a-Half Resthouse: 225
Mile High Grill & Spirits: 14, 162
Miller Peak Wilderness Area: 121
Mingus Mountain: 160
Mingus Mountain Recreation Area: 160
Mi Nidito: 16, 19, 105
mining industry: 298, 299, 300
mining towns and attractions: Ajo 113; Arizona
    Historical Society Museum 88; Asarco
    Mineral Discovery Center 108-109; Bisbee
    19, 24, 126-127; Chiricahua Regional Museum
    128; Chloride 268-269; Clarksdale 162-163;
    Douglas 127-128; Globe 69; Goldfield 67;
    Grand Canyon 222; Jerome 24, 160-162;
    Kayenta 192; Lost Dutchman Mine 66;
    Oatman 268; Prescott 149-160; Superior 69;

Superstition Mountain Museum 66; Tombstone 18, 24, 123-126; Tubac 18, 21, 112-115; Wickenburg 71-72
missile site tours: 109
Mission San Jose de Tumacacori: 18, 112
Mogollon Indians: 295
Mogollon Rim: 10, 178, 285
Mohave Museum of History and Arts: 264
Mohave Point: 222-223
monsoon season: 288-289
Montezuma Castle National Monument: 15, 20, 164-165
Montezuma Well: 165-166
Monument Valley Navajo Tribal Park: 16, 193-194
Moran Point: 223
Morley Avenue: 115
Mormon Lake: 142-143
Mormons: see Latter-day Saints (LDS)
motorcycle enthusiasts: 58, 67, 69, 160, 203, 241, 267, 269, 281
Mountain Artist Guild Spring Festival: 154
Mountain Artists Summer Festival: 154
Mountain Empire: 18, 21, 116-119
mountains: 285, 286, 288-289
Mount Elden Trail System: 141
Mount Graham: 307
Mount Hopkins Fred Lawrence Whipple Observatory: 111
Mount Humphrey: 141, 285
Mount Lemmon: 91, 98
Mount Wrightson: 19, 110
movie productions: 86, 170, 193, 194, 265, 281, 303
movie theaters: see cinemas
Mt. Baldy: 181
mule rides: 234, 238
Murray Springs Clovis Site and Trail: 122
museums: Amerind Foundation 129; Arizona Capitol Museum 35; Arizona Doll and Toy Museum 33; Arizona Historical Society Museum (downtown Tucson) 84; Arizona Historical Society Museum (University of Arizona) 88; Arizona Museum of Natural History 40-41; Arizona Science Center 33; Arizona-Sonora Desert Museum 16, 18, 19, 85-86; Arizona State Museum 88; Arizona State University Art Museum 39; Arizona State University Museum of Anthropology 39; Asarco Mineral Discovery Center 108-109; Grand Canyon 218, 219, 221, 223-224; Heard Museum 14, 17, 34-35; International Wildlife Museum 85; Mesa Contemporary Arts 40; Museum of Northern Arizona 15, 138-139; Phoenix Art Museum 14, 17, 35, 303; Phoenix Museum of History 34; Pima Air and Space Museum 93-94; Pueblo Grande Museum and Archaeological Park 20, 36; Scottsdale Museum of Contemporary Art 57; Superstition Mountain Museum 66; Titan Missile Museum 109; Tucson Museum of Art 84; University of Arizona Museum of Art 88-89; see also historic houses and districts; specific place
music festivals: 97, 154, 170
music scene: 303; see also specific place

N
Nampaweap: 246
Nampeyo: 199, 218
NASCAR Checker Auto Parts 500: 49
NASCAR Subway Fresh Fit 500: 48
National Accessible Travelers Database: 309
National Geographic Grand Canyon Visitors Center: 22, 211
National Historic Landmarks: 109, 124, 138, 158, 196, 218-219, 226-227
national parks/monuments: Bill Williams River National Wildlife Refuge 273; Cabeza Prieta National Wildlife Refuge 272; Canyon de Chelly National Monument 15, 20, 195-196; Casa Grande Ruins National Monument 18, 20, 64, 70-71; Chiricahua National Monument 18, 21, 77, 129-130; Cibola National Wildlife Refuge 273; Coronado National Forest contacts 106; Coronado National Memorial 18, 19, 24, 121-122; Glen Canyon National Recreation Area 251, 253; Grand Canyon-Parashant National Monument 245-246; Havasu National Wildlife Refuge 273, 274; Imperial National Wildlife Refuge 272-273, 282; Junior Rangers program 310; Kofa National Wildlife Refuge 272; maps and information 313; Montezuma Castle National Monument 15, 20, 164-165; Navajo National Monument 20, 190-192; Organ Pipe Cactus National Monument 113; Petrified Forest National Park 15, 200-202; Pipe Spring National Monument 24, 244-245; Prescott National Forest 155-157; Rainbow Bridge National Monument 253; Saguaro National Park 16, 18, 19, 86-88; San Pedro Riparian National

Conservation Area 122; senior passes 310; Sunset Crater Volcano National Monument 15, 145-148; Tonto National Monument 20, 68-69; Tumacacori National Historic Park 112; Tuzigoot National Monument 163; Vermillion Cliffs National Monument 247-248; Walnut Canyon National Monument 15, 20, 146, 147, 148-149; Wupatki National Monument 15, 20, 145-148; Zion National Park 244

National Register of Historic Places: 83, 100-101, 149, 158-159, 164, 209

National Trail: 42

Native American art and culture: general discussion 295-296, 297, 298, 302, 303, 304, 308; All Indian Rodeo and Fair 113; Arizona Museum of Natural History 41; Arizona-Sonora Desert Museum 86; Arizona State Museum 88; Cameron 209; Chiricahua Regional Museum 128; Colorado River Indian Tribes Museum and Library 275; Grand Canyon 218, 227, 228; Heard Museum 34-35; Heard Museum Guild Indian Fair & Market 48; Mohave Museum of History and Arts 264; Morning Star Traders 99; Museum of Northern Arizona 138-139; Museum of Northern Arizona Heritage Program 140; Navajo Bridge 250; Phippen Museum of Western Art, The 153; Pueblo Grande Museum Indian Market 49; reading suggestions 315-316; San Xavier Plaza 94; Sedona 170, 171; Smoki Museum 153; Southwest Indian Art Fair and Market 97; Tohono Chul Park 90; Tumacacori National Historic Park 112; Tusayan 211; Wa:k Powwow 97; Williams 210; see also archaeology/archaeological sites; specific tribe

nature preserves and wilderness areas: Arizona-Sonora Desert Museum 85-86; Beaver Dam Wilderness Area 244; Hassayampa River Preserve 71; McDowell Mountain Regional Park 59; Miller Peak Wilderness Area 121; Paiute Wilderness Area 244; Paria Canyon-Vermillion Cliffs Wilderness Area 247; Patagonia-Sonoita Creek Preserve 21, 117-118; Pusch Ridge Wilderness Area 92; Ramsey Canyon Preserve 19, 121; South Mountain Park and Preserve 42-43; Superstition Wilderness Area 65-66; Swansea Wilderness Area 275; Sycamore Canyon Wilderness Area 166-167; Tohono Chul Park 90; Tucson Mountain Park 100; Tumacacori Highlands 115; wildlife refuges 111-112, 272-273, 274, 282; see also national parks/monuments; state parks/monuments

Nature Trail (Madera Canyon): 110

naturism: 276, 307

NAU (Northern Arizona University): 139

Navajo: general discussion 187, 295-296, 298, 302, 303, 304; Arizona Strip 242, 245; Cameron 209; code talkers 193, 303; Explore Navajo Interactive Museum 189; Flagstaff 140; Grand Canyon 218; Heard Museum 35; Hubbell Trading Post National Historic Site 196; Monument Valley Navajo Tribal Park 16, 193-194; Navajo National Monument 20, 190-192; Page 251; Rainbow Bridge National Monument 253; reading suggestions 315-316; Smoki Museum 153; Southwest Indian Art Fair and Market 97; Tuba City 190; Williams 210; Window Rock 196-197

Navajo Bridge: 249-250

Navajo County Historical Society museum: 200

Navajo Nation: 186-197; cuisine 308; etiquette 187-188; Internet resources 318; map 184-185; transportation 183, 185; trip planning 11, 15-16, 20, 182-183

Navajo National Monument: 20, 190-192

Navajo Nation Council Chambers: 197

Navajo Nation Fair: 197

New Horizons' Pro-Am Bass Tournament: 274

news: 318; see also specific place

Newton, Wayne: 303

Nicks, Stevie: 303

Night-blooming Cereus: 90

Nightfall: 98

nightlife: see specific place

Nogales, Arizona: 18, 115-116

Nogales, Mexico: 18, 116

Northern Arizona Book Festival: 140

Northern Arizona University (NAU): 139

North Kaibab Trail: 234, 236-237, 238, 317

North Rim (Grand Canyon): 214, 231-235

Northshore Road: 260

Northshore Summit Trail: 260

North Thumb Butte Trails: 157

North Valley (Phoenix): 57-64; accommodations 14, 52, 59, 62; itineraries 14; orientation 31; shopping 50, 61; sights 35, 39-40, 57-58, 65

nudity: 276, 307

Nutrioso: 181

O

Oak Creek Canyon: 15, 175
Oatman: 268
Oatman Hotel: 268
Oaxaca Restaurant: 14, 172
observatories: 111, 113, 138
Office for Americans with Disabilities: 309
OK Corral and Historama: 124, 125
Oktoberfest on Mt. Lemmon: 98
Old Baldy Trail: 110
Old City Hall (Nogales, Arizona): 115
Old Oraibi: 199-200
Old Town Cottonwood: 163-164
Old Town Jubilee: 282
Old Tucson Studios: 86, 98
Old West: Hualapai Indian Reservation 240;
    Old Tucson Studios 86; reading suggestions
    314-315; trip planning 10, 24; Yuma 24,
    277-281, 283; see also historic houses and
    districts; mining towns and attractions;
    railroad towns and attractions
O'Neill, Bucky: 152, 218
O'odham: 27, 87, 90, 97, 107, 113, 302
Ooh Aah Point: 225
opera: 46, 65, 97, 154
Oraibi: 199-200
Organ Pipe Cactus National Monument: 113

P

packing: 13
Page: 250-253
Painted Desert: 15, 188, 189, 201
Painted Desert Inn Museum: 201
Painted Desert Trail: 272-273
Paiutes: 190, 241, 242, 244-245
Paiute Wilderness Area: 244
Palace Restaurant and Saloon, The: 14, 159
Palatki: 175
Palisade Visitor Center: 91
Palm Canyon: 272
Papago: see O'odham
Papago Park: 30, 37-38, 43
Paria Canyon-Vermillion Cliffs Wilderness
    Area: 247
Parker: 275-276
Parker Dam: 275
Parker Strip: 275
parks and gardens: Arizona-Sonora Desert
    Museum 86; Boyce-Thompson Arboretum
    State Park 70; Chinese Cultural Center
    37; Desert Botanical Garden 37-38; El
    Presidio Park 83; Encanto Park 36-37;
    Ethnobotanical Garden 90; Garden for
    Children 90; Indian Bend Wash Greenbelt
    59; Jordan Historical Park 169-170;
    McDowell Mountain Regional Park 59;
    Papago Park 30, 37-38, 43; Reid Park 99;
    Rose Tree Inn Museum 125; Sentinel Peak
    100; Standin' on the Corner Park 203;
    Tempe Beach Park 38; Tohono Chul Park 90;
    Tucson Botanical Gardens 89-90; Window
    Rock Navajo Tribal Park 197; see also
    national parks/monuments; state parks/
    monuments
Patagonia: 18, 116-118
Patagonia Lake State Park: 117
Patagonia-Sonoita Creek Preserve: 21, 117-118
Payson: 177-179
Peach Springs: 240-241, 267
Peacock, Doug: 303
Peavine Trail: 156
pecan growing: 109
Pena Blanca Lake: 115
people: 301-303
Peralta Trail: 66
Percival Lowell's tomb: 138
Petrified Forest National Park: 15, 200-202
petroglyphs: 39-40, 88, 166, 201, 246
Phantom Ranch: 13, 22, 237-238, 239
Phippen Museum of Western Art, The: 153-154
Phippen Museum of Western Art Show & Sale:
    154
Phoenix (downtown and central): 31-37;
    accommodations 50-51; food 53-55;
    nightlife 48; shopping 49
Phoenix (greater): 25-56; general discussion
    287, 288; information and services 73;
    Internet resources 318; maps 4-5, 28-29, 32,
    38, 40; Sky Harbor International Airport 14,
    21, 73-74, 305; trip planning 10, 14, 21, 30-31;
    vicinity 64-72
Phoenix Art Museum: 14, 17, 35, 303
Phoenix Coyotes: 45
Phoenix Mountains: 41-42
Phoenix Museum of History: 34
Phoenix Suns: 44
Phoenix Symphony: 46
Phoenix Zoo: 37
Phoneline Trail: 92
photography etiquette: 188, 199
photography exhibits: 89
Picacho Peak State Park: 18, 71
Piestewa Peak Summit Trail: 41, 42
Pima Air and Space Museum: 93-94
Pima County Courthouse: 82-83
Pima Point: 223

Pimeria Alta Historical Society: 115
Pine: 177
Pine Country Restaurant: 23, 210
Pinetop-Lakeside: 179
Pipe Spring National Monument: 24, 244-245
planetariums: 33
Plank Road: 281, 282
planning your trip: 10-24; *see also specific place*
plants: 10, 284, 285, 291-292, 316-317
Plateau Lakes: 142-143
Plateau Point: 225
Plaza of Pioneers, The: 84
Point Imperial: 232
Polacca: 199
politics: 300-301
Ponsi Hall: 199
population: 301-302
poverty: 187, 302
Powell, John Wesley: 213, 222, 251, 297
Powell, Lawrence Clark: 123, 315
Powell Point: 222
Powerhouse Visitor Center: 264
Powerplant Tour: 259
Prescott: 10, 14, 149-160, 285, 306
Prescott, William Hickling: 153
Prescott Bluegrass Festival: 154
Prescott Frontier Days and the World's Oldest Rodeo: 154
Prescott National Forest: 155-157
Pueblo Grande Museum and Archaeological Park: 20, 36
Pueblo Grande Museum Indian Market: 49
Pusch Ridge Wilderness Area: 92

QR

Quartzsite: 276
radio station: 313
rafting: *see river-running*
railroad towns and attractions: Flagstaff 135, 137; Fred Harvey railroad hotels 202-203; Goldfield 67; Grand Canyon Railroad 21, 215, 230-231; Holbrook 200; Kingman 262, 264; Railroad Tunnel Trail 260; Verde Canyon Railway 163; Willcox 128; Winslow 202
railroad travel: general discussion 137; Flagstaff 137, 145, 306; Grand Canyon 21, 215, 230-231; Tucson 106
Rainbow Bridge National Monument: 253
rainy season: 288-289
Ramsey Canyon: 121
Ramsey Canyon Preserve: 19, 121
Reader's Oasis: 276

reading suggestions: 314-317
recreation areas: Beaver Creek Recreation Area 166; Big Lake Recreation Area 181; Echo Canyon Recreation Area 41-42; Fools Hollow Lake Recreation Area 179; Glen Canyon National Recreation Area 251, 253; Granite Basin Recreation Area 156; Imperial Dunes Recreation Area 281-282; Lake Mead National Recreation Area 258-262; Lynx Lake Recreation Area 156; Rim Lakes Recreation Area 178; Sabino Canyon Recreation Area 92; Virgin River Canyon Recreation Area 244
Red Hills Visitors Center: 87
Red Rock Country: 15, 172-175
Red Rock Pass: 173
Red Rocks Music Festival: 170
Red Rock State Park: 175
Refreshments (music band): 303
Reid Park: 99
Reid Park Zoo: 89
religion: 302
reptiles: 294-295
reservations: Grand Canyon 13, 235, 236, 239-240; trip planning 12; *see also specific place*
resorts: clothing-optional 307; Phoenix 52; Scottsdale 52, 62; trip planning 10, 17; Tubac 114; Tucson 102
restaurants: 308-309; *see also specific place*
Retablo of Ciudad Rodrigo: 89
Rex Allen Arizona Cowboy Museum: 128
Rex Allen Days: 128
Rialto, The: 95
Ribbon Falls: 238
Rim Country: 175-181
Rim Country Museum: 177
Rim Lakes Recreation Area: 178
Rim Road: 178
Rim Trail: 225
Rincon Mountains District: 88
Riordan Mansion State Historic Park: 24, 137-138
River Island Unit: 275
river-running: Grand Canyon 236, 238-239, 249; Hualapai Indian Reservation 240; Salt River 43-44; Verde River 167; *see also specific place*
rivers: 286-287, 314, 315, 316, 317
River Trail: 237
road travel: *see car travel*
Roaring Springs: 234
rock art: 39-40, 88, 166, 201, 246

rock formations: Antelope Canyon Navajo Tribal Park 251; Bowl of Fire 260; Chiricahua National Monument 77, 129-130; Grand Canyon Caverns 241; Granite Dells 156; Kartchner Caverns 18, 19, 122-123; Monument Valley Navajo Tribal Park 193-194; Papago Park 30, 37, 43; Petrified Forest National Park 15, 200-202; Picacho Peak State Park 71; Rainbow Bridge National Monument 253; Red Rock Country 172-175; Sunset Crater Volcano National Monument 15, 145-148; Tonto Natural Bridge State Park 177-178; Vermillion Cliffs National Monument 247-248; Window Rock 197; see also canyons
Rock Springs Café: 14, 23, 72
rodeos: 97, 113, 154
Rod's Steak House: 23, 210
Romero Canyon Trail: 93
Romero Ruin Interpretive Trail: 93
Ronstadt, Linda: 303
Room With A View: 158
Roosevelt Dam: 28, 67, 68, 287
Roosevelt Lake: 68
Roper Lake State Park: 307
Rose Tree Inn Museum: 125
Rosson House: 32-33
Round Valley: 181
Route 66: driving Historic Route 66 266-268; driving to Grand Canyon West 241; Flagstaff 137, 140; Holbrook 200; Kingman 262, 264, 265; Seligman 241, 267; Williams 209; Winslow 202, 203
Route 66 Days: 140
Route 88 (Apache Trail): 66-70
Royal Elizabeth Bed and Breakfast Inn, The: 101
RV touring: 306

S

Sabino Canyon: 92-93
Sabino Canyon Recreation Area: 92
Sabino Canyon Visitors Center and Bookstore: 92
safety/health: 226, 227, 288-289, 310-312
Saguaro National Park: 16, 18, 19, 86-88
Sahuarita: 107-109
Salado: 20, 68-69
Salt River: 70, 286, 287; tubing 43-44
Salt River Canyon: 70
Sam Hughes Inn: 101, 103
San Cayetano de Calabazas: 112
Sandal Trail: 191
sand dunes: 281-282

San Francisco Peaks: 10, 135, 137, 141-142, 285
Sanguinetti House Museum: 280
San Pedro Riparian National Conservation Area: 122
San Pedro River: 286
Santa Catalina Mountains: 90-92, 285
Santa Cruz County Courthouse: 115
Santa Cruz River: 286, 317
Santa Cruz Valley: 21, 107-119
Santa Maria Spring: 226
Santa Rita Mountains: 109-112, 285
San Xavier del Bac: 18, 21, 94-95; Wa:k Powwow 97
San Xavier Plaza: 94
scenic drives: Apache Trail (Route 88) 66-70; Canada Goose Drive 273; Canyon de Chelly National Monument 196; Carefree 14, 58; Cave Creek 14, 58; Chiricahua National Monument 129; Cibola National Wildlife Refuge 273; Coronado Trail 181; Flagstaff 135; Grand Canyon (North Rim) 232-233; Grand Canyon (South Rim) 221-223; Historic Route 66 266-268; Imperial National Wildlife Refuge 272; Mingus Mountain 160; Mogollon Rim 178; Northshore Road (Lake Mead) 260; Oak Creek Canyon 175; Parker Dam 275; Petrified Forest National Park 201; Red Rock Country 173, 175; Saguaro National Park 88; Santa Catalina Mountains 90-92; Scottsdale 58; trip planning 13, 14-16, 18; Tucson Mountain Park 100; U.S. Highway 93 268-269; Vermillion Cliffs Highway 242, 243-250; White Mountain Scenic Road 179; see also specific place
Schultz, Hart Merriam: 180
Schultz, James Willard: 180
scorpions: 295, 312
Scottsdale: 57-64; accommodations 14, 52, 62; food 62-63; Heard Museum North 35; orientation 31; trip planning 10, 14
Scottsdale Arabian Horse Show: 61
Scottsdale Arts Festival: 61
Scottsdale Center for the Performing Arts: 61
Scottsdale Culinary Festival: 61
Scottsdale Museum of Contemporary Art: 57
scuba diving: 258, 261
seasons: see climate
Second Mesa: 199, 200
Sedona: 167-175; accommodations 158, 171-172; food 159; Internet resources 318; trip planning 11, 14
Sedona Arts Festival: 170
Sedona Heritage Museum: 169-170

Sedona International Film Festival: 170
Sedona Jazz on the Rocks: 170
Sedona Plein Air Festival: 170
Seligman: 241, 267
Sells: 113
senior travelers: 310
Sentinel Peak: 99-100
Seven Falls: 92
Sharlot Hall Museum: 152
Shongopavi: 199, 200
shopping: *see specific place*
Show Low: 179
Shrine of the Ages: 229
shrines: 83, 117
Sichomovi: 199
Sierra Vista: 120-121
Signal Hill Picnic Area: 88
Silko, Leslie Marmon: 303
silverwork: 304
Sinagua: 20, 146-147, 148-149, 163, 164-165,
   166, 175, 315-316
Singing Wind Bookshop: 123
sinkholes: 165-166
Siphon Draw Trail: 66
Skeleton Point: 226
skiing: Flagstaff 141, 142; Grand Canyon 235;
   Greer 180, 181; Tucson 91
Sky Harbor International Airport: 14, 21, 73-74,
   305
Sky Island mountains: 10, 18-19, 21, 121, 288
sky islands: 285, 288
Skyride: 141-142
Skywalk: 241
Slide Rock State Park: 15, 175
Smoki Museum: 153
snakebites: 312
Snake Dance: 199
snakes: 294
Snoopy Rock: 173
snowboarding: 141
Snowbowl: 141-142
snowmobiling: 142
snowshoeing: 142, 180-181, 235
Sonoita: 116-119
Sonoran Desert: general discussion 27, 75,
   284; Arizona-Sonora Desert Museum 16, 18,
   19, 85-86; Cabeza Prieta National Wildlife
   Refuge 272; Imperial National Wildlife
   Refuge 272; Saguaro National Park 16, 18,
   19, 86-88; Scottsdale 58, 59; Superstition
   Mountains 65-66; Tucson 79; *see also
   specific place*

Sosa-Carrillo-Fremont House Museum: 83
Southern Pacific Depot: 128
South Kaibab Trail: 22, 23, 225-226, 236-237
South Mountain Park and Preserve: 42-43
South Rim (Grand Canyon): 212, 214, 215-231;
   Internet resources 318; trip planning 21-22
South Rim Drive: 196
Southwest Indian Art Fair and Market: 97
Spanish conquest: 24, 296-297, 314
Spanish language: 303
Spider Rock Overlook: 196
spiders: 295
Splash Playground: 38
sports teams: Phoenix 44-46, 48; Tucson 100;
   see also specific sport
sports training, high-altitude: 139
Spring Training: 45, 48, 97, 100
Squaw Peak: 41
Standin' on the Corner Park: 203
stargazing: 111, 113, 138
statehood: 298
state parks/monuments: Boyce-Thompson
   Arboretum State Park 70; Buckskin
   Mountain State Park 275; Catalina State
   Park 93; Cattail Cove State Park 271-272;
   Dead Horse Ranch State Park 164; Homolovi
   Ruins State Park 204; information and maps
   313; Jerome State Historic Park 161-162;
   Lake Havasu State Park 271; Lost Dutchman
   State Park 66; Patagonia Lake State Park
   117; Picacho Peak State Park 18, 71; Red
   Rock State Park 175; Riordan Mansion
   State Historic Park 24, 137-138; Roper Lake
   State Park 307; Slide Rock State Park 15,
   175; Tombstone Courthouse State Historic
   Park 125; Tonto Natural Bridge State Park
   177-178; Tubac Presidio State Historic Park
   24, 112; Yuma Quartermaster Depot State
   Historic Park 279-280; Yuma Territorial
   Prison State Historic Park 24, 278-279
St. Augustine Cathedral: 83
Steele Visitor Center: 138
Sterling Pass to Vultee Arch: 173
Stevens House: 33
St. George, Utah: 242, 243, 244
Strawberry Shimmer: 177
subalpine zones: 284-285
Submarine Rock: 173
Summerhaven: 91
Summit Trail (Echo Canyon Recreation Area):
   41-42
sun, coping with: 310-311

Sun Devils: 45-46
Sunset Crater Volcano National Monument: 15, 145-148
Sunset Vista Trail: 71
Supai Tunnel: 234
Superior: 69
Superstition Mountain Museum: 66
Superstition Mountains: 65-66
Superstition Wilderness Area: 65-66
Super Trail: 110
Surprise: 35
Swansea Wilderness Area: 275
swimming: Beaver Creek Recreation Area 166; Catalina State Park 93; Lake Havasu City 270, 272; Lake Mead National Recreation Area 258, 261, 262; Patagonia Lake State Park 117; Tempe 38; Verde Valley 165
Sycamore Canyon Trail: 115
Sycamore Canyon Wilderness Area: 166-167

T

Taliesin West: 14, 17, 57-58, 65
Teeter House: 33
Telles Grotto Shrine: 117
Tempe: accommodations 51; food 55-56; map 38; nightlife 48; orientation 31; recreation 38, 43; shopping 49; sights 37-39, 65; trip planning 14; see also Arizona State University
Tempe Beach Park: 38
Tempe Center for the Arts: 38-39
temperature: see climate
Tempe Town Lake: 38-39
Temple of Music and Art: 95
Tewa Indians: 199, 218
theaters: Phoenix 46-47; Ramsey Canyon 121; Scottsdale 61; Tempe 38-39; Tucson 95, 97; see also cinemas
Third Mesa: 199-200
35th Parallel: 262, 264
Three-Mile Resthouse: 225
Thumb Butte: 157
Thumb Butte Loop Road: 157
Thumb Butte Picnic Area: 157
Thunderbird Lodge: 15, 195
time zones: 183, 312
Titan Missile Museum: 109
Tohono Chul Park: 90
Tohono O'odham: see O'odham
Tombstone: 18, 24, 123-126
Tombstone Courthouse State Historic Park: 125
Tombstone Epitaph Museum: 124-125
Tombstone Rose Tree Festival: 125
Tombstone Western Heritage Museum: 125
Tonto National Monument: 20, 68-69
Tonto Natural Bridge State Park: 177-178
Topock Gorge: 273
Toroweap Point: 246
Tortilla Flat: 67
tour guides: 306; see also specific place
tourism: 298, 300, 304
tourist information: 313, 318
tourist season: 12, 17
trading posts, historic: 190, 196, 209
trail rides: see horseback riding; mule rides
Trailview Overlook: 222
train travel: see railroad travel
Transept Trail: 233
transition zones: 284-285, 291-292
transportation: 305-306; see also specific place
travel tips: 309-310
Treasure Loop Trail: 66
trees: 291
trip planning: 10-24; see also specific place
Truxton: 267
Tsegi Canyon: 20, 190-192
Tsunami on the Square: 154
Tubac: 18, 21, 112-115
Tubac Festival of the Arts: 112
Tuba City: 188-190
Tubac Presidio State Historic Park: 24, 112
Tucson: 75-107; climate 76, 79, 81, 288; cuisine 308-309; driving from Phoenix 70-72; environmentalism 290; geography 285; Internet resources 318; radio station 313; reading suggestions 315; transportation 106, 305; trip planning 10, 18, 19, 21, 76
Tucson Botanical Gardens: 89-90
Tucson City Parks and Recreation: 99
Tucson Convention Center: 83
Tucson Culinary Festival: 98
Tucson Folk Festival: 97
Tucson Gem & Mineral Show: 97
Tucson Mountain Park: 100
Tucson Mountains District: 87-88
Tucson Museum of Art and Historic Block: 84
Tucson Symphony: 97
Tumacacori: 18, 21, 112, 115
Tumacacori Highlands: 115
Tumacacori National Historic Park: 112
Turquoise Room: 15, 203-204
Tusayan: 211-212, 306
Tusayan Bike Trails: 226
Tusayan Museum and Ruin: 223-224

Tuweap: 246
Tuzigoot National Monument: 163

U

Uncle Jim Trail: 233
universities: Northern Arizona University 139;
  University of Arizona 88-89, 100; *see also*
  Arizona State University
University of Arizona Museum of Art: 88-89
University of Phoenix Stadium: 45, 48
Upper Ruin trail: 69
Upper Sonoran zones: 284-285, 291-292
U.S. Airways Center: 44
U.S. Angler's Choice Fishing Tournament:
  273-274
U.S. Army Intelligence Museum: 120
U.S. Highway 93: 268-269

V

Valentine: 267
Valley of the Sun: *see* Phoenix (greater);
  Scottsdale
Valley View Overlook Trail: 88
V-Bar-V Ranch Petroglyph Site: 166
Verde Canyon Railway: 163
Verde Hot Springs: 165
Verde River: 164, 167, 286, 287
Verde River Greenway: 164
Verde River Scenic Area: 167
Verde Valley: 15, 160-167
Verkamp's Curios: 229
Vermillion Cliffs Highway: 242, 243-250
Vermillion Cliffs National Monument: 247-248
Village of Oak Creek: 171
Virginia G. Piper Theater: 61
Virgin River Canyon Recreation Area: 244
Virgin River Gorge: 243-244
Visa Waiver Program: 309
VNS Book Sale: 48
vortexes: 169, 173, 174

W

Wahweap Marina: 253
Wa:k Powwow: 97
Waldron Trail Junction: 226
Walnut Canyon National Monument: 15, 20,
  146, 147, 148-149
Walpi: 199
waterfalls: 92, 173, 238, 240
waterskiing: Apache Lake 68; Canyon Lake
  67; Glen Canyon National Recreation Area
  251, 253; Lake Mead National Recreation
Area 262; Patagonia Lake State Park 117;
  Roosevelt Lake 68
Watson Lake: 156
weather: *see* climate
websites: 318
Wesley Bolin Memorial Plaza: 35
Western Navajo Fair: 190
West Fork of Oak Creek Trail: 173
West Nile virus: 312
West Valley (Phoenix): accommodations 51-52;
  food 56; Heard Museum West 35; nightlife
  48; orientation 31; shopping 49
Whiskey Row: 14, 154
White House Overlook: 196
White House Ruin: 15, 20, 195, 196
White Mountains: 11, 175-181, 285
White Mountain Scenic Road: 179
White Mountain Trail System: 179, 181
White Rock Canyon: 260
Why: 113
Wickenburg: 71-72
Widforss Trail: 233
wilderness areas: *see* nature preserves and
  wilderness areas
wildflowers: general discussion 292; Arizona-
  Sonora Desert Museum 86; Cabeza Prieta
  National Wildlife Refuge 272; Greer 180;
  Oatman 268; Organ Pipe Cactus National
  Monument 113; Picacho Peak State Park 71;
  reading suggestions 317; trip planning 11, 12;
  Tucson 79
wildlife/wildlife-watching: general discussion
  285, 292-295; Arizona-Sonora Desert
  Museum 85-86; Buenos Aires Wildlife
  Refuge 111-112; Cabeza Prieta National
  Wildlife Refuge 272; Grand Canyon (North
  Rim) 232; Grand Canyon (South Rim) 226;
  Grand Canyon Railroad 231; Havasu National
  Wildlife Refuge 273, 274; Imperial National
  Wildlife Refuge 272-273, 282; International
  Wildlife Museum 85; Kofa National Wildlife
  Refuge 272; Martinez Lake 282; Mormon
  Lake 142; Patagonia-Sonoita Creek Preserve
  118; reading suggestions 316-317; San Pedro
  Riparian National Conservation Area 122;
  Tohono Chul Park 90; trip planning 13;
  wildlife refuges 111-112, 272-273, 274, 282;
  see also birds/bird-watching
Willcox: 19, 128
Willcox Commercial Store: 128
Willcox Rex Allen Theater: 128
Williams: 23, 209-211, 229-230
Willow Beach: 262

Window Rock: 196–197
Window Rock Navajo Tribal Park: 197
Windsor Beach: 271
Windsor Castle: 245
windsurfing: 142
wine festivals/wineries: 58, 118–119
Winslow: 15, 202–204
Winterhaven: 19, 91
Wisdom's Café: 18, 114
"Wishing Shrine": 83
Woodchute Trail: 160
Wright, Frank Lloyd: 14, 17, 52, 57–58, 65
Wupatki National Monument: 15, 20, 145–148
Wupatki Pueblo Trail: 148
Wyatt Earp Days: 125

XYZ

Yaki Point: 223
Yavapai Indians: 302

Yavapai Observation Station: 221
Yavapai Point: 221
Yuma: 277–283; airport 283, 306; vicinity 272–273
Yuma Crossing Days Festival: 282
Yuma Downtown Art Center: 280
Yuma Quartermaster Depot State Historic Park: 279–280
Yuma River Daze: 282
Yuma Territorial Prison State Historic Park: 24, 278–279
Yuma Theatre: 280–281
Zane Grey Cabin: 24, 177
Zion National Park: 244
zoos: 37, 89
Zuni: 97, 140, 190, 304
Zuni Festival of Arts and Culture: 140

Map Index

Arizona: 2-3
Cochise Trail, The: 120
Flagstaff: 136
Flagstaff and North-Central Arizona: 132-133
Grand Canyon and The Arizona Strip, The: 206-207
Grand Canyon Village: 216-217
Hopi Reservation: 198
Lower Colorado River, The: 256-257
Kingman: 263
Mesa, Downtown: 40
Navajo and Hopi Country: 184-185
Phoenix, Downtown: 32

Phoenix, Greater: 4-5
Prescott: 151
Route 66, Driving Historic: 266
Tempe: 38
Tucson: 80
Tucson and Southern Arizona: 76-77
Rim Country and The White Mountains: 176
Santa Cruz Valley and The Mountain Empire: 108
Sedona: 168
Valley of the Sun, The: 28-29
Yuma: 278

Photo Credits

page 6: Highway 89A through the House Rock Valley is one of many lonely stretches through the Arizona Strip. © Tim Hull

page 7: This dancing nude is one several installed in front of the Herberger Theater in downtown Phoenix; John Henry Waddell, "Dance", 1969-1974. © Tim Hull; Arizona flag © Elizabeth Jang; Singing Wind donkey © Tim Hull

page 8: bell in Tlaquepaque Plaza, Sedona © Elizabeth Jang; There are many species of agave growing in Arizona, and some reach the mammoth proportions of this one. © Tim Hull

page 9: Butterflies are everywhere in the desert. © Tim Hull; The Mormon outpost at Pipe Springs on the Arizona Strip was the first telegraph station in Arizona. © Tim Hull

page 10: Phoenix seen through the feature known as Hole-in-the-Rock at Papago Park. © Tim Hull

page 11: horses at Pipe Springs National Monument © Tim Hull; Mexican Goldpoppy lines a trail at Picacho Peak State Park, between Tucson and Phoenix. © Tim Hull

page 12: Mules still do much of the heavy lifting in and out of the Grand Canyon. © Tim Hull; A tough pine clings to the edge of the Mogollon Rim in North-Central Arizona. © Tim Hull

page 13: A red sandstone butte is cast half in shadow along the road leading to Lee's Ferry on the Colorado River. © Tim Hull; a forgotten political mural on an Oatman building © Tim Hull

page 14: Cacti's spines are used to discourage hurtful munching. © Tim Hull

page 15: Chapel of the Holy Cross in Sedona © Margaret L. Jackson / mljackson@esedona.net; The ancient and the brand new at Petrified Forest National Monument. © Tim Hull; the multi-colored and stained high walls of Canyon de Chelly, above the White House Ruin © Tim Hull; Mary Colter's masterpiece, La Posada Hotel in Winslow. © Tim Hull

page 16: It often snows in the winter at the canyon's South Rim. © Tim Hull

page 17: Built-in furniture is one of architect Frank Lloyd Wright's signature quirks, seen here in a room at Wright's winter quarters in Scottsdale, Taliesin West. © Tim Hull

page 18: During the summer rainy season, usually small Madera Creek becomes a torrent as it falls through Madera Canyon in the Santa Rita Mountains. © Tim Hull

page 19: The closest you are likely to get to an elusive mountain lion is at the Arizona-Sonora Desert Museum. © Tim Hull

page 20: The Sinagua, not Montezuma and the Aztecs, built this limestone cliffhouse in the Verde Valley of North-Central Arizona. © Tim Hull

page 21: Lichen-covered hoodoos stand together at Chiricahua National Monument near Willcox in southeastern Arizona. © Tim Hull; Hopi House, a gift shop and arts museum, was built with native materials. © Elizabeth Jang

page 22: The remote Kaibab Plateau on the Grand Canyon's North Rim is often cloaked in winter snow. © Tim Hull

page 23: An early-morning mule train crosses a bridge over the Colorado River in Grand Canyon's Inner Gorge. © Tim Hull; Rod's Steak House, where even the menus are shaped like steers © Elizabeth Jang

page 24: Route 66 cowboy in Williams, the "Gateway to the Grand Canyon" © Elizabeth Jang

Acknowledgments

This book is dedicated to my parents, Roger and Kathy Hull. I would like to thank them for always supporting me and for bringing me to Arizona and then keeping me here all these years. Thanks to my friends Ryan and Regina Lord and Jason and Jen Shaw for their encouragement and advice. Thanks to Janis Barrett, Grace, Claire, Sam and Benjamin "Red Dog" Barrett for coming along on a few trips and making the research fun. Thanks also to Tom Hull for hiking with me and being my brother, and to Graham Harrington and Jenni Tobias for their support and friendship. Thanks to Nick Prevenas for finding the announcement that led to this assignment, and thanks to all the other folks at the Green Valley News for putting up with me all those years. A special thanks to Jim Lamb for advice on the border section and for his friendship and mentoring. Thanks to Steve Sanderson for use of his wonderful library. Thanks to Michelle Cadden, Kevin McLain, Kevin Anglin, Elizabeth Jang, and everybody else at Avalon Travel. Lastly, thanks to Katie Sanderson, for everything.

www.moon.com

For helpful advice on planning a trip, visit www.moon.com for the **TRAVEL PLANNER** and get access to useful travel strategies and valuable information about great places to visit. When you travel with Moon, expect an experience that is uncommon and truly unique.

HANDBOOKS | METRO | OUTDOORS | LIVING ABROAD

MAP SYMBOLS

▬▬ Expressway	**[** Highlight	✗ Airfield	⚑ Golf Course
▬▬ Primary Road	○ City/Town	✈ Airport	**P** Parking Area
▬▬ Secondary Road	◉ State Capital	▲ Mountain	▲ Archaeological Site
▭▭ Unpaved Road	⊛ National Capital	✛ Unique Natural Feature	▮ Church
------ Trail	★ Point of Interest		▮ Gas Station
·········· Ferry	• Accommodation	⚐ Waterfall	Glacier
━╍━╍ Railroad	▼ Restaurant/Bar	▲ Park	Mangrove
▬▬ Pedestrian Walkway	■ Other Location	▣ Trailhead	Reef
⊔⊔⊔⊔ Stairs	Λ Campground	✗ Skiing Area	Swamp

CONVERSION TABLES

$°C = (°F - 32) / 1.8$
$°F = (°C \times 1.8) + 32$
1 inch = 2.54 centimeters (cm)
1 foot = 0.304 meters (m)
1 yard = 0.914 meters
1 mile = 1.6093 kilometers (km)
1 km = 0.6214 miles
1 fathom = 1.8288 m
1 chain = 20.1168 m
1 furlong = 201.168 m
1 acre = 0.4047 hectares
1 sq km = 100 hectares
1 sq mile = 2.59 square km
1 ounce = 28.35 grams
1 pound = 0.4536 kilograms
1 short ton = 0.90718 metric ton
1 short ton = 2,000 pounds
1 long ton = 1.016 metric tons
1 long ton = 2,240 pounds
1 metric ton = 1,000 kilograms
1 quart = 0.94635 liters
1 US gallon = 3.7854 liters
1 Imperial gallon = 4.5459 liters
1 nautical mile = 1.852 km

MOON ARIZONA
Avalon Travel
a member of the Perseus Books Group
1700 Fourth Street
Berkeley, CA 94710, USA
www.moon.com

Editors: Kevin McLain, Michelle Cadden
Series Manager: Kathryn Ettinger
Copy Editor: Valerie Sellers Blanton
Graphics Coordinator: Elizabeth Jang
Production Coordinator: Elizabeth Jang
Cover Designer: Elizabeth Jang
Map Editor: Kevin Anglin
Director of Cartography: Mike Morgenfeld
Cartographers: Chris Markiewicz, Brice Ticen,
    Kat Bennett, Suzanne Service
Indexer: Jean Mooney

ISBN-10: 1-59880-147-3
ISBN-13: 978-1-59880-147-7
ISSN: 1538-120X

Printing History
1st Edition – 1986
10th Edition – November 2008
5 4 3 2 1

Publisher's Note: Bill Weir wrote the first nine
editions of *Moon Handbooks Arizona*.

KEEPING CURRENT

If you have a favorite gem you'd like to see included in the next edition, or see anything
that needs updating, clarification, or correction, please drop us a line. Send your
comments via email to feedback@moon.   or use the address above.